Lecture Notes in Computer Science 1737

Edited by G. Goos, J. Hartmanis and J. van Leeuwen

T0223308

Springer

Berlin
Heidelberg
New York
Barcelona
Hong Kong
London
Milan
Paris
Singapore
Tokyo

Peggy Agouris   Anthony Stefanidis (Eds.)

Integrated Spatial Databases

Digital Images and GIS

International Workshop ISD'99
Portland, ME, USA, June 14-16, 1999
Selected Papers

 Springer

Series Editors

Gerhard Goos, Karlsruhe University, Germany
Juris Hartmanis, Cornell University, NY, USA
Jan van Leeuwen, Utrecht University, The Netherlands

Volume Editors

Peggy Agouris
Anthony Stefanidis
University of Maine
Department of Spatial Information Science and Engineering
National Center for Geographic Information and Analysis
5711 Bordman Hall, Room 348, Orono, ME 04469-5711, USA
E-mail: {peggy,tony}@spatial.maine.edu

Cataloging-in-Publication data applied for

Die Deutsche Bibliothek - CIP-Einheitsaufnahme

Integrated spatial databases : GIS and digital images ; selected papers /
International Workshops ISD '99, Portland, ME, USA, June 14 - 16, 1999. Peggy
Agouris ; Anthony Stefanidis (ed.). - Berlin ; Heidelberg ; New York ;
Barcelona ; Hong Kong ; London ; Milan ; Paris ; Singapore ; Tokyo : Springer,
1999
  (Lecture notes in computer science ; Vol. 1737)
  ISBN 3-540-66931-0

CR Subject Classification (1998): I.4, H.2, H.3, I.5, I.2

ISSN 0302-9743
ISBN 3-540-66931-0 Springer-Verlag Berlin Heidelberg New York

© Springer-Verlag Berlin Heidelberg 1999
Printed in Germany

Typesetting: Camera-ready by author
SPIN: 10749923   06/3142 – 5 4 3 2 1 0   Printed on acid-free paper

Preface

This volume contains the papers presented at the workshop on "Integrated Spatial Databases: Digital Images and GIS" (ISD'99) held in Portland, Maine, on June 14-16, 1999. Its scope was to address the integration of digital images and GIS, and the many research issues related to this challenge.

The *need* for this integration is dictated by modern decision-making processes, which are becoming increasingly aware of the spatial nature of data, and by the expanding demand for up-to-date, easily accessible spatial information for everyone. As a result, this need brings forward several issues that have to be addressed by the relevant scientific communities. The necessity of ensuring the spatial and temporal validity of spatial databases, of improving and expanding geospatial analysis capabilities, and of addressing the integration of huge volumes of multiple versions and types of spatial information are but a few of these issues.

The *potential* for integration on the other hand has recently become much more apparent and feasible. In addition to the obvious compatibility of digital imagery and GIS, this potential is supported by concurrent rapid advancements in a variety of fields, especially digital image analysis, geographic information science, and database research. Accordingly, this workshop intended to provide a needed forum for bringing together experts from these overlapping but not always interacting scientific communities.

The 18 papers included in this volume resulted from nearly 40 original submissions, went through a double refereeing process. Extended paper proposals were initially reviewed to select workshop presentations, and full papers were subsequently reviewed for publication in this volume.

The papers in this volume could be grouped in a variety of ways. The classification in four areas selected here was meant to reflect the cyclical nature of the integration process itself: applications bring forward needs for theoretical developments, which in turn enable novel applications, which subsequently impose new needs and demand further extensions in the supporting theoretical concepts and foundations. Therefore, we decided to follow a rather unorthodox path in organizing the contents of this volume. Contrary to tradition, we begin with application-relevant sections and algorithms, and conclude with theoretical models. Of course, this separation is primarily organizational rather than contextual, and at times might appear artificial, as theoretical issues are addressed in application-oriented papers, and vice versa.

We greatly appreciate the work of the many people who made this happen. The National Science Foundation and the National Center for Geographic Information and Analysis provided valuable support, financial and otherwise. The program committee and additional external reviewers helped steer the meeting and mold these proceedings. Blane Shaw, Peter Doucette, and the other members of the organizing committee did an excellent job in taking care of the endless organizational details that accompany such an event and the publication of this volume. Last but not least, we would like to express our appreciation to the authors and participants of ISD'99, who made the meeting a memorable one, and these proceedings a valuable contribution to the relevant literature.

October 1999   Peggy Agouris and Anthony Stefanidis

Acknowledgments

This workshop was partially supported by the National Science Foundation (NSF), Directorate for Computer and Information Sciences and Engineering, Division of Information and Intelligent Systems (IIS), through CAREER grant number 9702233, and by the National Center for Geographic Information and Analysis (NCGIA).

Workshop Organization

Workshop Chair:
Peggy Agouris, University of Maine

Program Committee Chair:
Anthony Stefanidis, University of Maine

Program Committee:
Kate Beard, University of Maine
Panos Chrysanthis, University of Pittsburgh
Max Egenhofer, University of Maine
Wolfgang Foerstner, University of Bonn, Germany
Andrew Frank, Technical University of Vienna, Austria
Dieter Fritsch, University of Stuttgart, Germany
Mike Goodchild, University of California - Santa Barbara
Armin Gruen, Swiss Federal Institute of Technology, Switzerland
Thanasis Hadzilacos, Computer Technology Institute, Greece
Marinos Kavouras, National Technical University of Athens, Greece
David Mark, State University of New York at Buffalo
Dave McKeown, Carnegie Mellon University
Martien Molenaar, ITC, The Netherlands
Dimitris Papadias, University of Science and Technology, Hong Kong, China
Hanan Samet, University of Maryland - College Park
Tapani Sarjakoski, Finnish Geodetic Institute, Finland
Timos Sellis, National Technical University of Athens, Greece
Shashi Shekhar, University of Minnesota
Nektaria Tryfona, Aalborg University, Denmark
Vassilis Tsotras, University of California - Riverside
Marc van Kreveld, Utrecht University, The Netherlands

Local Arrangements:
Blane Shaw, University of Maine

Organizing Committee
Chair: Peter Doucette, University of Maine

Sotiris Gyftakis, University of Maine
Giorgos Mountrakis, University of Maine
Panos Partsinevelos; University of Maine

Table of Contents

Object Extraction from Raster Imagery

View Alignment of Aerial and Terrestrial Imagery in Urban Environments

Christopher Jaynes

Dept. of Computer Science
University of Kentucky
jaynes@cs.uky.edu

Abstract. We introduce an algorithm that fuses information from aerial and terrestrial views for the automatic reconstruction of high-resolution building models within built-up areas. Calibrated aerial photography is commercially available for wide areas of coverage and has been shown to be a useful source of information about the location of buildings at the site, their 2D footprint [8,10], and their rooftop shape [1,6,9]. In contrast, terrestrial imagery is usually uncalibrated, not available commercially for most urban areas, and difficult to acquire. These ground-level images do, however, provide close-range, high-resolution views not normally available in aerial data. Our approach uses the pose information typically associated with aerial surveillance imagery to acquire an initial three-dimensional model of the buildings at the site. Uncontrolled, terrestrial imagery is then aligned to the model using a symbolic model matching and pose a refinement technique. Once aligned, ground-level views can be used to enhance the site model in a number of ways. High-resolution façade textures can be mapped onto the model geometry using the recovered pose information and standard texture mapping algorithms. The same algorithms allow explicit segmentation of building facades from terrestrial views as regions of pixels that project to vertical structures in the model. Context sensitive processing can be applied to these façade regions for the symbolic extraction of surface structures such as windows, doors, and pillars.

1 Introduction

This paper addresses the problem of the automatic reconstruction of large-scale urban environments from multiple viewpoints. In particular, we are concerned with the fusion of high-altitude aerial photography with terrestrial imagery in order to provide a more complete model than can be recovered from either source independently. Aerial images are commercially available for wide-areas of coverage, are acquired using calibrated cameras, and usually accompanied by accurate, georeferenced camera pose information. Uncontrolled aerial photography can usually be calibrated through user-assisted standard photogrammetric techniques. In contrast, ground-level photography is not available on demand and must be collected for specific urban regions when it is required. Collection of a set of terrestrial views that provide significant coverage of an urban site can be a costly process and, other than approaches that make use of sophisticated telemetry hardware and calibrated sensors

P.Agouris and A.Stefanidis (Eds.): ISD'99, LNCS1737, pp. 3-19, 1999
© Springer-Verlag Berlin Heidelberg 1999

[5], ground-level data is not accompanied by photogrammetrically accurate camera pose information.

Models extracted from aerial images provide sufficient constraints to register the uncontrolled ground-based views to a common reference frame. Aligned terrestrial images can provide high-resolution information to the modeling process that facilitates model refinement, more accurate site visualization, and context-sensitive extraction of doors, windows, and other building façade structure.

These observations are the primary impetus for the view-alignment approach to urban reconstruction. Using the accurate pose information associated with aerial surveillance of the urban site, an initial three-dimensional model is acquired. Ground level views provide information not seen in any aerial view and are automatically aligned using a model-fitting procedure that minimizes the distance between image line features and the projected model edges.

We assume that overlapping, controlled aerial images are available for the site under consideration. In addition, high-resolution, ground level photographs are collected at several different locations within the site and contain at least one building façade. Figure 1 shows typical aerial and terrestrial views of a built-up area. We do not impose specific viewing constraints on the terrestrial images thus allowing an untrained user with a digital camera to collect data for integration into the model. We are interested in scenarios in which terrestrial images are collected via a head or vehicle-mounted camera moving through an urban area, whose intrinsic parameters are known. We do not assume that data is collected in any particular manner as the sensor may be moving through the site in pursuit of potentially different goals. In a similar scenario, sensors may be distributed throughout the site, mounted at specific locations, but have not been calibrated using traditional techniques. Under these conditions, no rigid assumptions about the position and orientation of the sensor can be justifiably made.

The algorithm makes use of a digital elevation map, computed from overlapping, controlled, aerial images to acquire an initial three-dimensional site model [4,9,13]. Terrestrial images, taken throughout the site, are then aligned to the model using initial pose estimates derived from an accompanying GPS sensor and digital compass. Terrestrial images are processed in order to extract significant lines that may represent building façade boundaries and surface structure. Error in the initial pose estimate for each images is minimized by an iterative refinement technique that reduces the difference between model lines and the set of significant lines extracted from the terrestrial view.

The approach is discussed in detail in the following two sections. Results of the algorithm are presented for two different datasets and several conclusions are drawn from an analysis of the approach that suggest new directions for the research.

Fig. 1. Typical aerial image (left) and uncontrolled ground-level view (right). Aerial images provide significant information about the location and footprint shape of buildings, while ground-level imagery contains high-resolution unique views of the site.

2   Initial Model Acquisition and Aerial Image Processing

In order to avoid the use of sophisticated telemetry hardware and controlled ground-level images, we assume the presence of a three-dimensional model which can then be used to automatically calibrate ground-level views.   The initial model is acquired using previously developed techniques for the automatic reconstruction of buildings from aerial images [4,9].   Controlled aerial imagery is often commercially available and, in the case of uncalibrated aerial survey data, aircraft positional sensors typically provide sufficient constraints for accurate user-assisted photogrammetric calibration.

Researchers have made use of calibrated aerial sensors to develop several automated [1,4,7,8,9] and semi-automated [5,12] reconstruction systems.   The acquisition of urban environmental models has a long and sophisticated research history (for survey see [14]) and recent approaches, that incorporate high-resolution digital elevation maps have been shown capable of accurate reconstruction of a wide variety of building types [1,4,6,9,11].   Although the automatic reconstruction of buildings from aerial images is not the focus of the work presented here, it plays a critical role in our approach.   This section briefly describes our approach to the acquisition of an initial model using a set of calibrated aerial images.   For a more detailed description of the algorithm see [9].

Initially, a set of overlapping, controlled aerial images are used to compute a high-resolution digital elevation map using standard photo-correlation techniques [13]. Figure 2 shows an aerial image of a built-up area and the corresponding digital elevation map used as input to the reconstruction phase of the system.

The reconstruction algorithm segments the DEM into regions likely to contain buildings by detecting rooftop boundaries as closed polygons in the registered optical image [10] or segmenting the DEM directly through a recursive application of the surface recognition and fitting procedure [9]. Segmented regions are then processed by a model-indexing phase that recognizes the DEM as one of several potential rooftop models.

 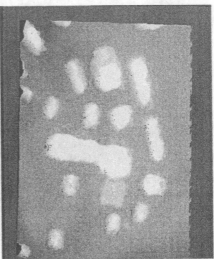

Fig. 2. Downlooking view of built-up area (left) and corresponding digital elevation map (right) Initial model acquisition requires calibrated aerial images and a digital elevation map (DEM)[1].

The model-indexing algorithm estimates the surface orientation of small surface patches fit to the DEM and constructs an orientation histogram derived from the estimated surface normals at each patch. This orientation histogram is then correlated with orientation histograms associated with a set of pre-defined common rooftop shapes. These orientation histograms, sometimes called the Extended Gaussian Image, are normalized so that they are both scale and translation invariant. The set of stored surface shapes that most closely match the orientation histogram of the surface under consideration are fit to the DEM using a least-squared model refinement technique. The model surface and shape parameters that converge to the lowest fit error are inserted into the site model

Because the DEM is a set pointwise of elevation estimates, surface normal information must be derived to extract an appropriate Gaussian image representation. The set of points within the region under consideration are triangulated into a surface mesh using the well-known Delanuy algorithm. The triangulated surface is a set of triangular surface patches, from the original pointset. The Delunay tessellation maximizes the smallest angle per triangular patch, minimizes the maximum circumscribing circle, and minimizes the maximum enclosing circle for each triangle. Figure 3c shows a triangulated surface computed from a DEM (Figure 3b) for a peaked roof building.

---

[1] Digital Elevation Map computed using the Terrest system courtesy H. Schultz and the Computer Vision Laboratory at the University of Massachusetts.

The local orientation of the elevation data is estimated by computation of the outward surface normal. The surface normal is computed as the cross product of the direction vectors defined by two points in the surface patch and the patch mass center. Because it is assumed that the normal of the plane representing the footprint of the rooftop is aligned with the gravity vector, the surface normal pointing in the positive Z direction is used to determine the cell on the Gaussian sphere that will receive a "vote" for a particular orientation. To avoid sensitivity problems with the method in which orientation space is discretized, votes are smoothed over the sphere via a Gaussian function. For the results shown here, the orientation histogram contains 240 buckets, reflecting a tessellation based on the semiregular icosahedron. Figure 3 shows a peak roof building, the computed digital elevation map, and the corresponding orientation histogram used for shape recognition.

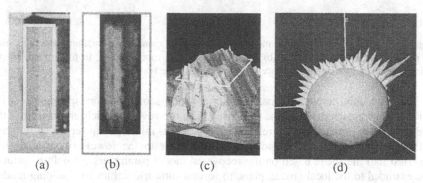

(a)   (b)   (c)   (d)

Fig. 3. (a) Peak-roof building in aerial image and detected rooftop boundary polygon. (b) Digital elevation map extracted from registered optical image and detected polygon. (c) Surface mesh fit to DEM. (d) Orientation histogram constructed from surface mesh, correlated with histograms in a surface database provides the basis for building recognition.

Each histogram extracted from the DEM is correlated with the set of precomputed histograms representing common rooftop shapes. Each surface in a predefined database may represents several models that are discrete parameterizations of the rooftop surface. For example, the peaked-roof surface is represented in the database by many models at different pitch angles (10-degree increments for the results shown here). Figure 4a shows several different rooftop shapes and their corresponding orientation histograms used for the recognition of rooftop class.

Conceptually, the image histogram (the histogram constructed from the DEM) is compared with the model histogram by first aligning the two spherical histograms via a rotation, and computing a weighted correlation score. This is done many times, for small relative rotations about the Z-axis between the two histograms. Indexing, then, selects the best surface model, and an initial set of parameters to be used for a final model fit.

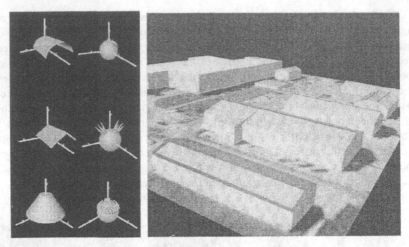

Fig. 4. (a) Several different shape models and their corresponding orientation histograms used to recognize building rooftops. (b) Reconstructed peak-roof building, in foreground, model using the model indexing and surface fitting algorithm (see text).

The algorithm outputs the maximum correlation score and corresponding relative orientation for each model in the database. The top several models are then fit to the DEM using the model and the relative orientation as initial parameters in an iterative refinement procedure. The model that converges to the lowest fit error is then inserted into the scene based on the recovered model parameters. Rooftop surfaces are extruded to the local ground plane to form a complete volumetric building model. Figure 4b shows the recovered model, using the example data in Figure 3.

3   Automatic View Alignment

The role of the view alignment phase is to register terrestrial images, taken at various locations throughout the site, with a common site-model reference frame. We are interested in developing algorithms that impose the least number of constraints on the ground-level sensors, do not employ expensive specialized hardware, and do not require the interaction of a sophisticated user during the data collection phase. Terrestrial images are taken at somewhat arbitrary positions and orientations within the model using a camera with known intrinsic characteristics. Typically, terrestrial images contain at least one building façade that is then matched against the buildings present within the site model.

The initial pose of each terrestrial image is estimated through the use of a GPS device and a digital compass. Typically, measurements produced by a commercial GPS device include 3-5 meter errors with systems that employ differential error reduction contain less than ½ meter horizontal and vertical error. Ground-level images are collected and stored in an imagery database along with their corresponding pose estimates. The terrestrial image database, prior to final view alignment, can be visualized geometrically as part of the site model to which the images belong.

Positional estimates for each camera location are inserted into the model as a sphere at a location derived from the GPS estimate with a radius based on the expected error in the GPS sensor. This measure includes the increase in error that occurs when satellites are occluded due to vertical structures in the urban environment. Figure 5 shows the visualized viewing spheres based on three terrestrial images collected at the Ft. Benning site (see Results Section).

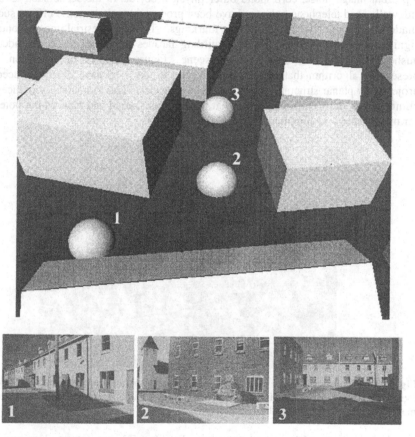

Fig. 5. Viewing positions of three cameras visualized as part of the site model (top) and their corresponding images (below). Location of each viewing sphere is based on a GPS estimate and sphere radii represents estimated error in viewing location.

Once data has been collected on the ground, the view-alignment procedure proceeds in three steps. First, each ground-level image is processed to extract a set of lines likely to correspond to building facades in the image. These salient line segments are then matched to the three-dimensional model by adjusting the initial viewing position of the image to bring model and image lines into close alignment. Finally, the aligned views projected into the model to increase model resolution and completeness. The following sections discuss each stage of the alignment algorithm in further detail.

3.1 Extracting Salient Lines

Straight-line segments in terrestrial views provide important information about the location of cultural features in the scene. The view-alignment algorithm assumes that extracted image lines will match building structures present in the site model such as corners, rooftop boundaries, and façade edges. However, extracted line segments may represent image noise, correspond other physical objects in the scene such as trees, sidewalks, and telephone poles, or have been produced by photometric effects such as shadows or unmodelled façade surface markings. Typical terrestrial images contain a significant number of shadows and building facades are likely to be occluded by bushes, trees, and other objects in the scene. Figure 6 depicts this situation. We present an algorithm that extracts line segments likely to have been produced by projectively planar structures such as building facades. This dramatically reduces the number of model-to-image matches that must be considered and reduces the potential for mismatches and alignment error.

Fig. 6. Typical terrestrial image. Building façades are a primary feature in ground-level images located in dense urban areas. However, shadows, surface markings, and significant occlusions make direct façade detection a difficult problem.

Images are processed by a line detection algorithm [3] that extracts line segments based on an analysis of the local image gradient and iteratively groups them into longer lines based on colinearity and proximity constraints. The algorithm has been shown to be capable of extracting long line segments across small image gaps and performs particularly well in the detection of long line segments commonly found in built-up areas [4.]. Figure 7 shows the set of line segments extracted from the image in Figure 6.

Fig. 7. Line segments extracted from terrestrial view.

Salient lines are detected from the image segments by first grouping lines into collinear bundles and then filtering these bundles using a vanishing point analysis technique. A straight line is fit through the grouped segments to generate a single straight line representing the underlying line bundle. The approach has been shown to work well in reducing the number of image lines not associated with projective planar structure such as building facades [12]. The new line, referred to as a line *pencil* is weighted by an overlap percentage measured as the projected length of contributing line segments versus the total length of the line pencil in the image. Line pencils whose weight does not exceed a threshold are removed. For the results shown here, line pencils that had less than 15 percent of their length accounted for by image lines were removed.

By selecting lines that significantly contribute to collinear structure, a set of line pencils, more likely to correspond to human-made features are discovered. However, straight-line features such as shadows that are not part of the planar surface structure of the building façade are likely to cause misalignment during the model-matching phase of the algorithm. Line pencils are further filtered based on the observation that the approximately planar structure of the building façade will give rise to line pencils that share a common vanishing point in the image. We assume that, due to building boundaries and other façade features such as windows and doors, there will be several line pencils that will share a common vanishing point.

Vanishing points are computed by intersecting all pairs of line pencils. Next, these points are clustered based on their proximity into a set of image points. Clusters are computed by partitioning the infinite image plane into predefined regions. The size of each region is based on image variance and increases linearly with the distance from the image center. This linear increase in size accounts for the linear increase in positional error of the intersection with respect to the distance from the underlying image segments. All intersections fall into a vanishing point cluster based on these predefined regions. Vanishing point clusters who have less than three line pencils as members are eliminated on the basis that they are not consistent with an approximately planar structure in the image. Figure 8 shows the line pencils that have been filtered on the basis of collinear support and vanishing point consistency. Note that the strong edge produced by the shadow across the building façade was eliminated through vanishing point analysis.

Fig. 8. Set of salient line pencils used to align terrestrial view with the initial model.

Only 23 pencils remain of the more than 800 image line segments that were detected in the terrestrial image. Five of the remaining lines are actual building edges and will be present in the corresponding site model. Matching edges in the model to salient line pencils increases robustness and reduces the complexity required to align terrestrial images with the site.

3.2 Model-Matching

Using the initial pose parameters as an estimate, the six extrinsic parameters of the camera's position and orientation are solved for using a least-median squared technique that minimizes the error between salient image lines and projected model lines.   A global fit-error measure determines the set of extrinsic parameters that minimizes the distance, in the camera frame, between model lines and image line pencils.

Error between a particular model line L_i and the set of line pencils in the image is measured as the projected distance of each model line endpoint L_{i0} , L_{i1} to the plane formed by the image line pencil and the optic center. The projection of L into the image is performed using the current viewing transform that is derived form the known camera intrinsic parameters and the estimated values for the rotation matrix **R** and translation T that aligns the camera with the site reference frame. Error in the current extrinsic parameters is measured as the median of the sum of the errors in each model line. Note that model lines that do not fall in the image based on the current **R** and T (for example, lines that are hidden by the model or project outside of the image) are not included in the error measure. In particular:

$$E(\mathbf{R},T) = median\left[\sum_{i=0}^{n}\sum_{j=0}^{1}(\lambda_i(\vec{N}_i \cdot (\mathbf{R}L_{ij} + T)))^2\right] \qquad (1)$$

where $\vec{N}_i$ is the vector normal to the plane formed by the image center and the line pencil M_I . Lambda is a nonlinear weighting that attenuates the contribution of error from line pencils that are far apart in the image space by computing the average distance from a line pencil to the projected model line endpoints. Lambda is assists in the stability of the nonlinear refinement procedure by assuming corresponding lines should appear close in the image based on the accuracy of the initial viewing estimate and is given by:

$$\lambda_i = c \cdot e^{\frac{\sqrt{(M_0 - L_{i0})^2} + \sqrt{(M_1 - L_{i1})^2}}{2}} \qquad (2)$$

where c is a normalizing constant. Figure 9 illustrates how error is measured for a single model line versus a single line pencil.

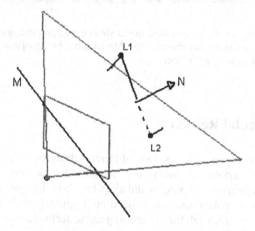

Fig. 9. Error for a single model line L is measured by the perpendicular distance of each of its endpoints to the plane formed by the line pencil M and the image center.

Our method for the measurement of alignment error is similar to that of [2] except, using constraints derived from the domain, we match model lines against the more stable line pencil features. In addition, we make use of a nonlinear attenuation of error based on image distance in order to reduce instabilities that arise from line pencils that are not present in the model, and hence far from any corresponding lines.

An iterative gradient descent technique, often called the downhill simplex method, solves for **R** and T that minimize equation 1. The recovered position and orientation of the sensor, combined with the known intrinsic parameters allow for the complete alignment of each terrestrial image with the site reference frame and the controlled aerial images.

Figure 10a shows the model, as seen from the initial estimated viewing parameters that corresponds to the building in Figure 6. Using the line pencils shown in Figure 8 the model-matching algorithm converges on a final set of extrinsic parameters that minimize the distance between model-lines and the image pencils. Figure 10b shows the model, projected into the terrestrial view, using the recovered viewing transform.

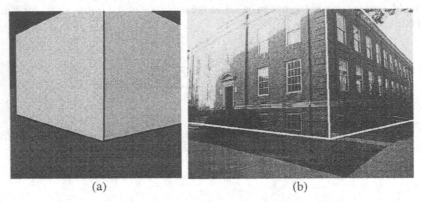

(a)   (b)

Fig. 10. (a) Building model, as seen from initial viewing position and orientation, derived from GPS and digital compass measurements. (b) Model lines, backprojected into terrestrial view using the recovered viewing parameters.

4   Experimental Results

The approach is applied to two different datasets. The first experiment demonstrates the system's ability to automatically acquire site models from controlled, overlapping aerial images and align terrestrial images taken at the site. The second experiment makes use of a hand-built ground truth model in order to demonstrate the accuracy of the image alignment technique in the presence of an accurate model. Results for both scenarios are demonstrated and discussed in the following subsections.

4.1 View Alignment to Reconstructed Site Model

Using the aerial image and digital elevation map depicted in Figure 5, an initial model of the urban area was reconstructed by segmenting rooftops in the optical image and selecting an appropriate surface model for each building using the techniques described in this paper. A final model was recovered by fitting the indexed surface models to the DEM and extruding rooftop models to the recovered ground-plane. The reconstructed site model is shown in Figure 11.

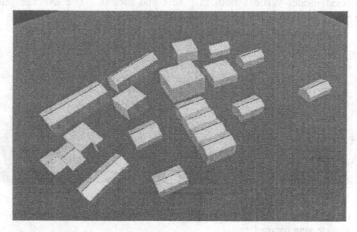

Fig. 11. Model of the urban site recovered from the aerial image and DEM depicted in Figure 2.

(a)   (b)

Fig. 12. (a) Ground-level image from viewing position 3 (see Figure 5). (b) Computed line segments.

Ground-level views were aligned to the model by extracting salient line pencils and matching to reconstructed model. Figure 12a shows the ground-level view from viewing location 3 (see Figure 5). Figure 12b shows the initial set of line segments extracted from the image that were then grouped into salient line bundles (Figure 12a).

After line filtering only 12 line pencils remained for matching against the reconstructed model. Notice that lines segments corresponding to shadows and other features not present in the reconstructed model have been removed, drastically reducing the complexity of the alignment phase.

The model-fitting algorithm was run using the extracted line pencils and the set of model lines visible from the initial viewing position. The refinement algorithm converged after 1123 iterations over the six-dimensional search space of extrinsic parameters. The change in position and orientation of camera 3 after view alignment are given respectively by: $\Delta T=[1.201, 3.42, -0.21]$, ($\delta\omega =0.001$, $\delta\phi = 0.013$, $\delta\kappa = -0.188$). Error in the aligned views, both in the reconstructed model and the recovered pose, can be measured between building corners in the image and corresponding backprojected model vertices both in pixels and meters. The average inter-vertex error for viewing position 3 was 6.3 pixels of 0.68 meters.

(a)   (b)

Fig. 13. (a) Salient line pencils. (b) Model lines, backprojected into ground-level view using the recovered viewing parameters.

Using the aligned terrestrial image, high-resolution information can be directly incorporated into the three-dimensional model for subsequent visualization and context-based extraction of building façade structure such as windows and doors. Each image pixel is projected into the model along a viewing ray based on the recovered transform. If it intersects a vertical surface then it is texture-mapped onto the three dimensional model. Figure 14 shows the partially texture-mapped model after image 3 has been aligned with the common site reference frame.

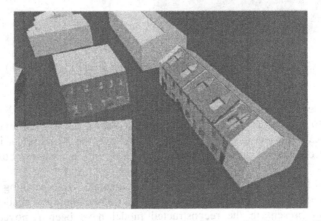

Fig. 14. High-resolution texture information reprojected into the model after view alignment, as seen from a novel viewing position.

4.2 Alignment to Ground Truth Model

In order to test the accuracy of the alignment approach, a ground-truth model for a building complex was constructed by hand from available map and survey data. Once the initial model was acquired, a single, ground level photograph was taken of the complex using a digital camera with known intrinsic parameters and is shown in figure 15a. The position and orientation of the camera relative to the model was computed in order to compare the alignment approach presented here with a known set of viewing parameters. Several points were selected in the image whose corresponding positions in the world were known. Using standard calibration techniques, the six baseline extrinsic parameters of the camera were recovered.

The initial position and orientation of the camera were estimated at the time the image was captured using a GPS sensor and digital compass. The baseline model, as seen from the estimated viewing parameters, is shown in figure 15b.

(a)   (b)

Fig. 15. (a) Ground-level view for the office building scene. (b) Baseline model, as seen from the initial viewing parameters.

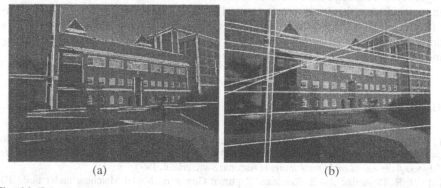

(a)   (b)

Fig. 16. Extracted line segments. (b) Salient lines pencils after line grouping and vanishing point analysis.

The line extraction algorithm was run to produce a set of 189 line segments. Line segments were then grouped into collinear line bundles and filtered based on

vanishing point analysis (see "Extracting Salient Lines") to produce 12 salient line pencils that were matched against the baseline model. Figure 16 shows the initial line segments and final set of line pencils used for matching.
The model-matching algorithm was then run to convergence to recover the final viewing parameters. The baseline model, as seen from the derived viewing location and orientation is shown in Figure 17a. The model lines, backprojected into the ground-level view, are shown in figure 17b.

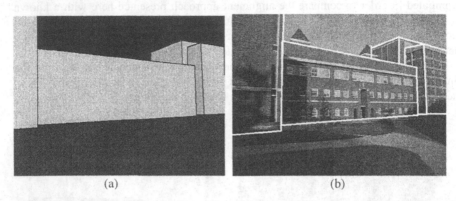

(a)   (b)

Fig. 17.   (a) Baseline model as seen from recovered viewing position. (b) Baseline model edges backprojected into ground-level view using the recovered viewing parameters for subjective evaluation of accuracy.

As a preliminary study of algorithm accuracy, the recovered viewing parameters were compared to the camera position and orientation computed by-hand. The mean error in position was less than one-half meter (0.47m) while mean orientation error was less than one-degree (0.32^0). However, even small rotational errors can lead to large world space error under certain viewing conditions. As an example of this see Figure17b. Although the recovered transform had a mean orientation error of less than one degree, this leads to an error of 1.2 pixels measured at the top vertex of the office tower on the right which corresponds to an error of 1.3 meters in the world. We are exploring techniques that will account for these errors by automatically selecting more appropriate ground level views to incorporate into the model.

Bibliography

[1]   E. Baltsavias, S. Mason, and D. Stallman. "Use of DTM/DSMs and Orthoimages to support Building Extraction." " *International Workshop on Automatic Extraction of Man-Made Objects from Aerial and Space Images*, Ascona, Switzerland, 1995.
[2]   J. R. Beveridge and E. Riseman. "Optimal Geometric Model Matching under Full 3D Perspective." *CVGIP: Image Understanding* 61(3):351-364, 1995.
[3]   M. Boldt, R. Weiss, and E. Riseman "Token-Based Extraction of Straight Lines" *IEEE Trans. On Systems, Man, and Cybernetics.*
[4]   R. Collins, C. Jaynes, Y. Cheng, X. Wang, F. Stolle, E. Riseman, and A. Hanson. "The Ascender System: Automated Site Modeling from Multiple Aerial Images" *Computer Vision and Image Understanding* 72(2)., pp 143-162. 1998.

[5]   S. Coorg, N. Master, and S. Teller. "Acquisition of a Large Pose-Mosaic Dataset", *International Conference on Computer Vision and Pattern Recognition*, pp. 872-878. San Juan , Puerto Rico, 1997.

[6]   A. Fischer, T. Kolbe, and F. Lang "Integration of 2D and 3D Reasoning for Building Reconstruction Using a Generic Hierarchical Model", *Workshop on Semantic Modeling for the Acquisition of Topographic Information from Images and Maps*, Bonn, Germany, 1997.

[7]   J. Gifford and D. McKeown. "Automating the Construction of Large-Scale Virtual Worlds" *Proc. DARPA Image Understanding Workshop*, 1994.

[8]   A. Huertas and R. Nevatia. "Detecting Buildings in Aerial Images", *Computer Vision, Graphics, and Image Processing*, vol. 13, 1980.

[9] C. Jaynes, A. Hanson, E. Riseman, H. Schultz "Automatic Building Reconstruction from Optical and Range Images", *International Conference on Computer Vision and Pattern Recognition*, San Juan , Puerto Rico, 1997.

[10]   C. Jaynes, F. Stolle, and R. Collins "Task Driven Perceptual Organization for the Extraction of Rooftop Polygons", IEEE *Workshop on Applications of Computer Vision*, Sarasota, FL, Dec. 1994.

[11] N. Haala and M. Hahn. "Data Fusion for the detection and reconstruction of buildings" *International Workshop on Automatic Extraction of Man-Made Objects from Aerial and Space Images*, Ascona, Switzerland, 1995.

[12]   M. Partington and C. Jaynes. "Detection of Approximately Planar Structure from Vanishing Point Analysis", Technical Report. Department of Computer Science, Univerity of Kentucky, May, 1999.

[13] H. Schultz. "Retrieving Shape Information From Multiple Images of a Specular Surface" IEEE PAMI 16(2), 1994.

[14] J. Shufelt. "Performance Evaluation and Analysis of Monocular Building Extraction from Aerial Imagery", IEEE PAMI 21(4), 1999.

Automated Extraction of Linear Features from Aerial Imagery Using Kohonen Learning and GIS Data

Peter Doucette[1], Peggy Agouris[1], Mohamad Musavi[2], and Anthony Stefanidis[1]

[1] Department of Spatial Information Science & Engineering, University of Maine
Boardman Hall, Orono, Maine 04469
{doucette, peggy, tony}@spatial.maine.edu
[2] Department of Electrical and Computer Engineering, University of Maine
Barrows Hall, Orono, Maine 04469
musavi@eece.maine.edu

Abstract. An approach to semi-automated linear feature extraction from aerial imagery is introduced in which Kohonen's self-organizing map (SOM) algorithm is integrated with existing GIS data. The SOM belongs to a distinct class of neural networks which is characterized by competitive and unsupervised learning. Using radiometrically classified image pixels as input, appropriate SOM network topologies are modeled to extract underlying spatial structures contained in the input patterns. Coarse-resolution GIS vector data is used for network weight and topology initialization when extracting specific feature components. The Kohonen learning rule updates the synaptic weight vectors of winning neural units that represent 2-D vector shape vertices. Experiments with high-resolution hyperspectral imagery demonstrate a robust ability to extract centerline information when presented with coarse input.

1 Introduction and Motivation

Automation of the extraction of GIS features from remotely sensed imagery continues to generate a considerable amount of activity among researchers across several disciplines. A primary goal of Automated Feature Extraction (AFE) is to minimize the level of human effort required to vectorize information from raster images for GIS database population, which currently remains a labor intensive task. AFE algorithm prototypes continue to evolve to keep pace with increasing data variety, utility and availability. Despite substantial improvements in recent years, many of the proposed AFE techniques have yet to achieve adequate levels of practicality in support of GIS data capture on a large scale. The unresolved issues remain a formidable challenge, and the inherently ill-posed nature of the problem is well recognized in the literature. By necessity, methods usually require varying degrees of human interaction, i.e., are *semi*-automated, and typically address specific feature and/or input source types. Results indicate that sufficient levels of generalization and reliability must be attainable for any AFE algorithm to withstand realistic demands placed upon it relative to manual extraction [1]. At the same time, algorithmic complexity needs to remain sufficiently manageable to accommodate user interface realities.

P.Agouris and A.Stefanidis (Eds.): ISD'99, LNCS1737, pp. 20-33, 1999
© Springer-Verlag Berlin Heidelberg 1999

As next-generation remote sensing platforms deliver imagery with higher spatial and spectral resolutions, the demand for high-resolution GIS data for use at larger map scales increases. Feature extraction from an image has an associated measure of absolute accuracy that is ultimately determined by the scale at which the extraction is performed. Whereas, the spatial resolution of an image sets an upper limit on the scale at which features are resolvable. GIS data that are considered for use at scales appreciably larger than they were extracted at are of limited value in terms of accuracy. In addition, projection and datum transformations of GIS data can introduce nonlinear positioning discrepancies. Such "coarse-resolution" GIS data often serve as a valuable reference source for manual or automated re-extraction of existing database features with respect to higher resolution imagery.

1.1 Approach

This paper introduces a novel application of Kohonen's *self-organizing map* (SOM) algorithm [2] for semi-automated extraction of linear features. The SOM belongs to a class of artificial neural networks (ANN, or simply NN) founded upon concepts of Hebbian [3] and competitive learning. The use of certain NNs, including the SOM, for radiometric image classification has existed in remote sensing literature for several years. Evaluation studies have thus far been met with mixed reviews when comparing the efficiency of NNs versus traditional Bayesian methods for image classification. However, the use of the SOM in the proposed approach is not concerned with radiometric values of pixels per se. Rather, it is the 2-D spatial patterns of the classified pixels that are of main interest. A "low-cost" radiometric classification is favored in the interest of practicability, as inherent classification error is anticipated and tolerated. Fig. 1 illustrates the process in which classified image pixels from a low-cost classification, together with coarse-resolution GIS data, serve as the SOM input. The algorithm possesses properties that facilitate robust centerline extraction and vectorization concurrently. Certain operational similarities exist between SOMs and the active contour model of *snakes* [4], in which deformable curves locate linear features via an iterative solution. A fundamental difference between SOMs and snakes is that the former exemplifies a center-of-gravity approach, whereas the latter is edge-based. The strengths of the SOM that are of key interest in this application include its generalization ability when presented with noisy input, its relative nondependence on edge definition, its light computational load, and its simplicity of implementation.

Section 2 discusses the fundamental concepts behind the self-organizing map. Section 3 considers simulations with synthetic data to demonstrate basic SOM operating characteristics. Section 4 considers preliminary results with a HYDICE image and integration with existing coarse-resolution GIS vector data. Section 5 provides a summary, and considers future research directions.

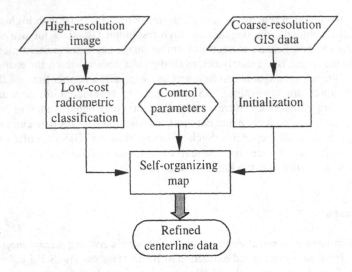

Fig. 1. Overview of extraction process

2   The Self-Organizing Map

Kohonen's SOM (a.k.a., *self-organizing feature map* (SOFM), and *kohonen network* (KN)) belongs to a specific class of neural networks that are characterized by unsupervised and competitive learning. Unsupervised learning has long been associated with clustering methods. As with any cluster seeking technique, sample data points are segregated into a predefined number of groups for which similar statistical characteristics are shared. The process iterates until a convergence criterion is satisfied. Where the SOM differs from a typical clustering method is in its use of a topological structure to spatially *order* cluster centers.

2.1 Network Architecture

A fundamental trait of the SOM is the topological structure of the network. Fig. 2 illustrates the general form of a two-dimensional SOM grid network. The m-dimensional input space, $\{\Re^m\}_i$ should not be confused with the d-dimensional network space, denoted $\{\Re^d\}_N$. Although d can take on any value, a network topology is typically one or two-dimensional since the objective of the SOM is to define a mapping from $\{\Re^m\}_i$ onto $\{\Re^d\}_N$, where $m \geq d$. If $d = 1$, only one row or column is considered. The input is an m-dimensional vector $\mathbf{X} = [x_1, x_2,..., x_m]^T \in \{\Re^m\}_i$, where each component of $\mathbf{X}$ is connected to every node, or *neuron* in the network. In the current application, a probability density function defined as $p(\mathbf{X})$ in $\{\Re^m\}_i$ consists of the spatial coordinates (x, y) of S classified image pixels, so $m = 2$.

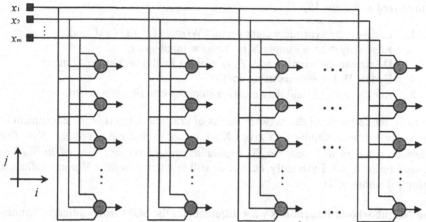

Fig. 2. Two-dimensional SOM network of nodes (neurons) in $\{\Re^2\}_N$

2.2 Kohonen Learning

Let a vector $\mathbf{X}$ with $m = 2$ represent image pixel coordinates for each SOM input as,

$$\mathbf{X} = [x, y]^T \in \{\Re^2\}_I. \qquad (1)$$

In fig. 2, each connection, or *synapse*, between a component of $\mathbf{X}$ and any single node (i, j) located in network space $\{\Re^2\}_N$, has an associated weight. The *contents* of each weight vector are defined in $\{\Re^2\}_I$, which has the same dimensionality of $\mathbf{X}$, or,

$$\mathbf{W}_{(i,j)} = \left[w_{(i,j),x}, w_{(i,j),y}\right]^T \in \{\Re^2\}_I. \qquad (2)$$

By initializing the contents of $\mathbf{W}$ in $\{\Re^2\}_I$ for each node, the goal of competitive learning is to reward the node (i, j) that optimally satisfies some similarity measure between a given $\mathbf{X}$ compared against all $\mathbf{W}_{(i,j)}$. Using the Euclidean norm as the similarity metric, the *winning* node is defined as,

$$winning\_node(i, j)^* = \arg \min_{(i,j)} \left\| \mathbf{X} - \mathbf{W}_{(i,j)} \right\|, \text{ for } i = 1, 2, ..., I; \ j = 1, 2, ..., J. \qquad (3)$$

where I and J are the total number of nodes per row and column respectively in fig. 2. $\mathbf{W}$s are then updated according to,

$$\mathbf{W}_{(i,j)}(n+1) = \mathbf{W}_{(i,j)}(n) + \eta(t) \cdot h_{(i,j)^*}(t) \cdot \left(\mathbf{X}(n) - \mathbf{W}_{(i,j)}(n)\right), \qquad (4)$$

where n represents an input sample from S total samples, $\eta(t)$ is a learning rate function defined as $0 < \eta(t) < 1$, and $h_{(i,j)^*}(t)$ is a neighborhood function defined as $0 < h_{(i,j)^*}(t) \leq 1$. t is measured in epochs, each of which represents a complete presentation of S input samples to the network. Multiple epochs are typically required for asymptotic convergence of the algorithm. The basic SOM algorithm can be summarized as follows [5]:

1. Initialize the synaptic weight vectors $\mathbf{W}(n=1)$ for all $(I \times J)$ nodes.
2. Randomly draw a sample $\mathbf{X}(n)$ from the input space.
3. Determine the winning node $(i, j)^*$ using a Euclidean similarity metric.
4. Update $\mathbf{W}$ for winners using eq. (4).
5. Return to step 2, and iterate until a stopping criterion is reached.

In effect, the response of the network that is of practical interest is the adjustment of nodes that are most similar to a given $\mathbf{X}(n)$, closer to that input vector. {*Note that reference made to a "node" in* $\mathfrak{R}_I$ *implies its weight vector,* $\mathbf{W}$, *and in* $\mathfrak{R}_N$, *its network index, (i, j)*}. Eventually, each node will gravitate toward a Voronoi influence region [6] within $p(\mathbf{X})$.

The Neighborhood Function is what differentiates the SOM from ordinary "winner-take-all" (WTA) competitive learning. The algorithm proceeds through two distinct phases: *ordering* and *convergence,* respectively. The progression of these phases is closely tied to an epoch dependent neighborhood function $h_{(i,j)^*}(t)$ centered on winning node $(i, j)^*$, and spanning a symmetrically lateral range r in $\{\mathfrak{R}^2\}_N$. The measure of r can take on a variety of forms as suggested in fig. 3(a). Accounting for r in the definition of the neighborhood function leads to $h_{(i,j)^*}(r(t))$, where $h_{(i,j)^*}(r(t)) = 1$ is fixed for the winner. During the ordering phase (small t), $r(t) >> 0$ to facilitate optimal spatial ordering of nodes in the input space. However, to achieve satisfactory convergence, $h_{(i,j)^*}(r(t)) \to 0$ as $t \to \infty$. This "shrinking" of the neighborhood function is accomplished algorithmically by $r(t) \to 0$ with $t \to \infty$. Nodes that fall within the extent of $r(t)$ are updated according to the shape of $h_{(i,j)^*}(r(t))$. Fig. 3(b) demonstrates a rectangular versus a Gaussian shaped $h(r)$. The effect of $h(r)$ is to define the "stiffness" of a deformable structure of nodes in the input space, which becomes more pliant as $t \to \infty$. For nodes falling outside $h_{(i,j)^*}(r(t))$, eq. (4) reduces to $\mathbf{W}(n+1) = \mathbf{W}(n)$, i.e., no change.

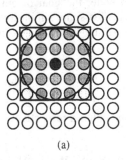

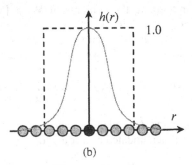

(a)   (b)

Fig. 3. (a) Euclidean (*circle*) and box (*square*) metrics for $r = 2$ in a 2-D lattice of nodes (*winning node is darkest*). (b) Neighborhood function for a given t (*dotted line is rectangular, and solid line is Gaussian*)

3 Simulations

Chain and *intersection* feature components are considered for extraction via the SOM algorithm. Chain components are composed of nodes with no more than two connections, for which a 1-D network topology is applied. Intersection components contain at least one node with three or more connections, for which a 2-D network topology is applied. Simple extraction simulations will demonstrate the application of the SOM on simulated linear feature components.

3.1 1-D Chain

Let an input space $\{\Re^2\}_I$ contain the (x, y) coordinates of a set of image pixels defined by probability density function $p(\mathbf{X})$. Assume that $p(\mathbf{X})$ represents a road feature component with no junctions, and a width > 1 pixel as shown in fig. 4. Recalling fig. 2, a 1-D network space topology $\{\Re^1\}_N$ is one row or column of nodes, which can be viewed simply as J nodes strung together in a chain. Fig. 4(a) demonstrates a configuration where $J = 10$ nodes are randomly initialized within the vicinity of the input feature. Although random initialization is not necessary (and in some cases undesirable), it serves mainly to demonstrate the ordering nature of the algorithm. The nodes are connected to one another with respect to their topological sequence in $\{\Re^1\}_N$. The extraction process is shown in figs. 4(b-d) for a rectangular neighborhood function defined as,

$$[\text{ordering phase}]: h(r) = \begin{cases} 1 & \text{if } r \leq 2 \\ 0 & \text{if } r > 2 \end{cases} ; \quad [\text{convergence phase}]: h(r) = \begin{cases} 1 & \text{if } r = 0 \\ 0 & \text{if } r > 0 \end{cases}, \quad (5)$$

and a simple stopping criterion,

$$\| \mathbf{K}(t+1) - \mathbf{K}(t) \| < Threshold, \quad \text{for } t = 1, 2, \dots \quad (6)$$

where,

$$\mathbf{K} = [\mathbf{W}_1, \mathbf{W}_2, \dots, \mathbf{W}_J]^T, \quad (7)$$

When $r = 2$, a winning node has four neighbors during the ordering phase, i.e., two on either side, except for nodes j_2, and j_9, which have three neighbors, and nodes j_1, and j_{10}, which have two. Nodes that occur at, or near the ends of the chain are subject to border effects [7] that pull them away from the ends of the feature, as is evident in fig. 4(c).

The task of ordering is to align nodes in $\{\Re^2\}_I$ according to their sequence in $\{\Re^2\}_N$, while concurrently mapping $p(\mathbf{X})$. The stiffness imposed on the deformable chain structure during ordering is the effect of updating neighbors along Euclidean directions toward the winning node. It is crucial that the initial neighborhood extent be set sufficiently large to ensure the excitation of each node during the process, thereby forcing global ordering. The alternative results in *dead* nodes, i.e., nodes that never become activated [8]. One can deduce from fig. 4(c) that feature shape (e.g., curvature), and total nodes J also have an impact on the manifestation of neighborhood effects. When ordering reaches a stable configuration, the convergence phase proceeds to shrink the neighborhood function such that only the winner is involved in updates as defined in eq. (5). The result is a relaxation of the stiffness level enforced on the neural chain.

In the absence of neighborhood constraints, the 10 chain nodes can be finely tuned to the centroids of their respective influence regions shown in fig. 4(d). Border effects also diminish during convergence. At the conclusion of a successful convergence, the chain nodes can be made to represent shape points of a vectorized centerline component that is topologically consistent in a GIS sense. In this manner, the process is tantamount to a vector skeletonization of $p(\mathbf{X})$.

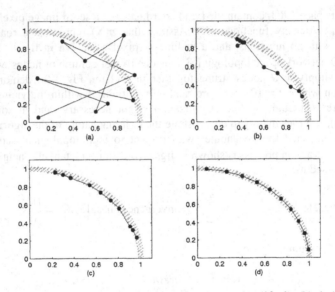

Fig 4. (a) feature input pixels (*gray*), and initial random nodes (*black*), (b) during ordering phase, (c) end of ordering/start of convergence, and (d) end of convergence phase

3.2 2-D Cross

Let an input space $\{\mathfrak{R}^2\}_I$ contain the (x, y) pixel coordinates of a 4-way intersection feature component as depicted in fig. 5. Referencing fig. 2, a 'cross' topology can be derived from $\{\mathfrak{R}^2\}_N$ by using a center row and column of nodes. Fig. 5(a) shows node initialization for a 5x5 cross topology of 9 nodes. Applying the same neighborhood function and stopping criterion as defined in eqs. (5-7), figs. 5(b-d) demonstrate the progression the extraction process. Since nodes are already ordered at initialization, the primary task of the ordering phase is to move nodes within the general vicinity of the input feature. Note that when the center node is the winner during ordering ($r \leq 2$), the entire cross structure is equally excited. The convergence phase then provides for fine adjustment, and reduction of border effects.

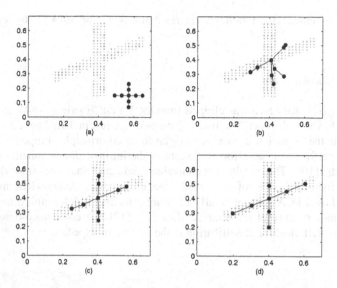

Fig 5. (a) intersection feature pixels (*gray*), and initial 5x5 cross of nodes (*black*), (b) during ordering, (c) end of ordering/start of convergence, and (d) end of convergence phase

In general, a limitation of this approach is the requirement that the mean of $p(\mathbf{X})$ for an intersection feature roughly correspond to its 'apparent' center, although no restriction is imposed on the angle of intersection. Sufficient symmetry must exist between $p(\mathbf{X})$ and network topology to ensure accurate placement of the center node. In lieu thereof, a proposed solution is to iteratively adjust and constrict a binary filter for $p(\mathbf{X})$ relative to the center node in $\{\Re^2\}_1$, until satisfactory alignment is achieved. This amounts to a neighborhood search of $p(\mathbf{X})$ in input space, which should not be confused with $h(r)$ for network space. To be effective, it is necessary that filter adjustments occur during the ordering phase. A sufficiently large initial network neighborhood is the key to generating adequate movement of the entire cross structure so that the filter center may be optimally positioned with respect to $E\{p(\mathbf{X})\}$.

4   Experiments with Hyperspectral Imagery

The SOM algorithm was tested with linear features from Hyperspectral Digital Imagery Collection Experiment (HYDICE) imagery. Acquisition was during July of 1996 over the U.S. Army's Yakima Training Center (YTC), located near Yakima, Washington. Imagery acquisition, post processing, and registration was conducted by Pacific Northwest National Laboratory (PNNL) as part of a multisensor feature extraction project [9] for the National Imagery and Mapping Agency (NIMA). The HYDICE aerial sensor is a push broom system that generates images with a spectral resolution of 210 bands spanning wavelengths of 0.4-2.5μm, with a nominal bandwidth of 10nm. Part of PNNL's post processing consisted of applying an optimized band reduction technique to the original 210 bands. The delivered HYDICE strip used in this study contains 44 bands with a spatial resolution of 1.0

meter, and a signed 16-bit radiometric resolution (-32,768 to +32,768 gray level range).

4.1 Image Classification

A 300x300-pixel study area was clipped from the HYDICE strip to serve as the base test image shown in fig. 6(a). The linear features of interest included paved roads, and the stream in the upper left corner. A covariance-based principle component analysis (PCA) was performed in an effort to determine the intrinsic dimensionality of the 44 image bands [10]. The resulting eigenvalues indicated that the first three PCs accounted for over 99% of the total image variance. Acknowledging that a correlation-based PCA can potentially be more effective at determining the optimal intrinsic dimensionality of multivariate data [11] [12], the covariance-based results were deemed sufficient for classification in the interest of expediency.

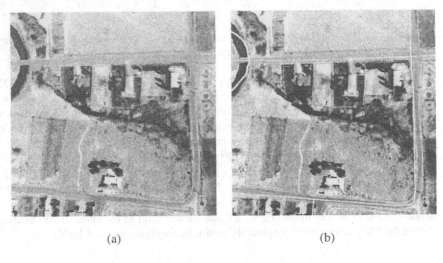

(a)   (b)

Fig. 6. (a) study area, and (b) superimposed with USGS 1:24,000-scale DLG vectors (*white*); (*stream is upper left, and the remaining vectors are paved road*)

Unsupervised classification using an ISODATA algorithm [13] was performed to facilitate the selection of training samples for supervised classification. The unsupervised strategy was to overestimate the number of classes in the scene, thereby making intra-class variance more detectable. Using manually selected training samples derived from the ISODATA results, several different parametric and non-parametric supervised classifiers were employed to classify the image. These ranged from a Bayesian maximum likelihood classifier (MLC), to several signal transfer NN based techniques including : error back-propagation [14], probabilistic neural network [15], and radial basis function [16]. A manually derived ground truth from the HYDICE image served as the basis for accuracy assessments. The different classifiers provided for several tradeoff options between accuracy, speed, and memory requirements. However, the objective of the classification was to provide optimized low cost results. To that end, the MLC tended to be favored for the particular image data and feature set.

A particularly relevant aspect of the radiometric classification is the type of error committed. From the perspective of SOM input $p(\mathbf{X})$, errors of commission are generally more problematic than errors of omission. As the SOM attempts to approximate $p(\mathbf{X})$, a certain amount of omitted information can be tolerated. However, as errors of commission increase, nodes are pulled away from their intended targets. Various methods can be employed to favor omission over commission errors, such as classification thresholding, and the use of morphological thinning techniques, post-classification.

4.2 Integration of GIS Data

Largely through years of manual collection efforts, GIS vector and raster data sets currently exists for much of the earth's surface at various resolutions, and referenced to various datums and projections. Current GIS trends indicate an increasing demand for finer resolution vector information world wide. In the present context, existing coarse-resolution GIS data implies coarseness with respect to more recently available high-resolution imagery. It also assumes nonlinear registration error associated with scale, datum or projection transformations. For example, fig. 6(b) shows 1:24,000-scale USGS Digital Line Graph (DLG) vectors that have been transformed from NAD27 to WGS84 for registration to the base image. Although nonlinear mis-alignment is visibly apparent, it is difficult to determine a true source of error since it is probably due to a combination of factors. Nonetheless, such coarse-resolution vectors may serve suitably as reference information for revised extraction in that they, 1) provide approximate locational information for algorithmic initialization, and 2) provide GIS topological information for enhanced automation. The former is one of the most effective means of speeding up convergence. The latter provides a blueprint for GIS component assembly. Existing GIS data may also be of use for automatic training sample derivation for supervised classification [17], although not performed in this study.

In the current application, GIS data integration begins with the decomposition of existing vector topology into Q individual components for a given image scene. In fig. 6(b), $Q = 7$ for the existing vector layer (which is more apparent in fig. 8). The objective is to identify a $p_q(\mathbf{X})$ for each component $q = 1, 2, ..., Q$. A node structure is initialized according to the shape points defining an 'old' vector component q. The number of nodes assigned to the new vector component to be extracted is dynamically adjusted according to a densification criterion. Overlapping search windows in $\{\Re^2\}_t$ centered on each node determine which image pixels are captured for SOM input. The search extents are initially set large enough to ensure sufficient capture of the target feature component. As $t \rightarrow \infty$, the node search windows constrict to reduce the influence from classification commission errors, or other nearby feature components. When all new vector components have been extracted, they are assembled with reference to the old GIS topology.

4.3 Extraction Results

Figs. 7 and 8 illustrates preliminary extraction results with a SOM application on selected image components using chain and cross networks. In all cases, a rectangular neighborhood function as defined in eq. (5) is used, with the exception of the cross topology during the convergence phase, which is defined as,

$$[\text{convergence phase}]: h(r) = \begin{cases} 1 & \text{if } r \leq 1 \\ 0 & \text{if } r > 1 \end{cases}. \tag{8}$$

Unlike the trivial cross simulation in section 3.2, a certain degree of stiffness in the node structure must be maintained during the convergence phase. The result is a more

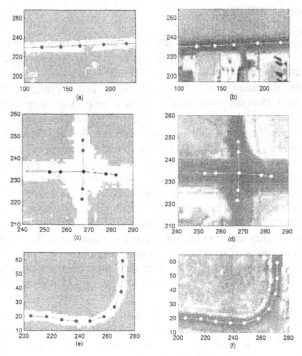

Fig. 7. Convergent SOM nodes superimposed on classified pixels of image components (a), (c) and (e); on original image, (b), (d) and (f)

stable fitting of the cross structure to $p_{(c)}(\mathbf{X})$. For instance, a cross with a convergent orientation of two connected "L"-shaped components is topologically inconsistent for GIS entry. The desired orientation assumes that of the network initialization, i.e., two intersecting line segments. The white pixels in figs. 7(a, c and e) are the result of a Bayesian radiometric classification of paved road. Note how moderate omission errors do not pose serious difficulties for centerline estimation (fig. 7(a)). Figs. 7(b, d and f) show the same results overlaying the original image. Fig. 8 shows a collection of seven extracted feature components prior to final assembly for the entire image.

Fig. 8. SOM nodes for extracted linear feature components in the image

Qualitative Performance Evaluation. Assuming the absence of gross blunders, assessment of absolute positional accuracy of the results is largely a subjective measure. Manual feature extraction is subject to individual human perception biases relative to the particular base image, which similarly come into play when assessing the accuracy of automated extraction. An ad hoc visual inspection of fig. 8 might estimate a horizontal accuracy for centerline node placement of roughly 1-2 meters relative to the base image. Although not performed, a statistical accuracy estimate would also be open to interpretation relative to a human derived ground truth.

Computational requirements are generally light, which is a distinctive feature of the SOM algorithm. In real-time mode, algorithmic extraction is generally faster than manual efforts. However, this comparison does not take into account the requirement for image classification to generate SOM input.

Problems for the SOM algorithm are created when two spatially adjacent feature class types are also inseparable spectrally, which is a common problem for low-level processing AFE methods. This causes nodes to be pulled away from feature centerlines during convergence. For instance, roads, driveways, parking lots, and rooftops (buildings) may represent distinct feature types for which asphalt or "blacktop" is a common compositional substance. To the extent that feature compositional similarity renders spectral separation ineffective, knowledge rule-based methods that exploit contextual and geometrical information are often employed [18].

As this paper is mainly concerned with exploring SOM techniques in support of relatively low-level AFE tasks, integration of such higher-level tasks is not considered at this stage.

5 Conclusions and Future Work

The presented application of Kohonen's SOM algorithm offers a novel alternative to semi-automated linear feature extraction from high-resolution aerial imagery. The SOM's generalization ability, coupled with its light computational needs demonstrates a potential for further development as a supplementary methodology in integrated applications. For instance, complementary aspects exist between 1-D SOM chains and ribbon snakes [19]. While both are deformable curve models, the former is center-of-gravity-based, whereas the latter is edge-based.

In evaluating supervised classifiers, compromises made among accuracy, computation speed, and memory usage is often the subject of debate in the literature. Regardless of methodology, the computing and human costs involved with rigorous supervised classification is often too high for many AFE applications. The presented approach suggests that moderate noise levels associated with low-cost image classifications may be tolerable for certain AFE tasks and methods. The supervised classification element of the approach portrays it as a kind of 'supervised SOM', and in this respect it is semi-automated. However, subsequent to image classification, the utilization of coarse-resolution GIS data holds the potential for nearly full automation. Future research is intended to extend SOM-based feature delineation to a wider variety of image spatial and spectral resolutions.

SOM parameters requiring judicious initialization and dynamic adjustment are, 1) the learning rate, 2) the neighborhood function, and 3) the number of nodes (I x J) composing the network topology, all of which are typically derived heuristically. *Fuzzy-kohonen* models that integrate fuzzy logic with Kohonen clustering have been suggested as an efficient method for automating Kohonen parameter adjustment [20], and are the subject of future research for this AFE application. In addition, *neuro-fuzzy* methods are being investigated for the integration of knowledge rules.

While this study focused on the extraction of linear features in only, the potential use of 2-D SOM topologies extended to region-based features is also the subject of further investigation. The anticipated approach operates in a manner similar to region growing, yet is not as sensitive noise.

Acknowledgements

This work was partially supported by the National Science Foundation through CAREER grant number IRI-9702233 and through grant number SBR-8810917.

References

1. Firestone, L., Rupert, S., Meuller, W.: Automated Feature Extraction: The Key to Future Productivity. Photogrammetric Engineering & Remote Sensing. Vol. 62, No. 6. (1996) 671-676
2. Kohonen, T.: Self-Organized Formation of Topologically Correct Feature Maps. Biological Cybernetics. Vol. 43. (1982) 59-69
3. Hebb, D.O.: The Organization of Behavior: A Neuropsychological Theory. Wiley, New York (1949)
4. Kass, M., Witkin, A., Terzopoulos, D.: Snakes: Active Contour Models, International Journal of Computer Vision, Vol. 1, No. 4. (1988) 321-331
5. Haykin, S.: Neural Networks. Upper Saddle River, New Jersey, Prentice Hall (1999)
6. Kohonen, T.: Self-Organizing Maps (2nd Ed.). Springer-Verlag Berlin Heidelberg (1997)
7. Kohonen, T.: Things You Haven't Heard about the Self-Organizing Map. Proceedings of the IEEE International Conference on Neural Networks, San Francisco. (1993) 1464-1480
8. Demuth, H., Beale, M.: Neural Network Toolbox User's Guide (Version 3.0). The MathWorks, Inc., Natick, MA (1998)
9. Steinmaus, K.L., Perry E.M., Foote H.P., Petrie, E.M., Wurstner S.K., Irwin D.E., Stephan A.J.: Hyperspectral Landcover Classification for the Yakima Training Center, Yakima, Washington. Pacific Northwest National Laboratory, Richland, Washington. PNNL-11871 (1998)
10. Langrebe, D.A.: Useful Information from Multispectral Image Data: Another Look. In: Swain, P.H., Davis, S.M.: Chapter 7 of: Remote Sensing: The Quantitative Approach. McGraw-Hill Int., New York (1978)
11. Eklundh, L., Singh, A.: A Comparative Analysis of Standardized and Unstandardized Principle Components Analysis in Remote Sensing. International Journal of Remote Sensing. Vol. 14, No. 7. (1993) 1359-1370
12. Jolliffe, I.: Principle Component Analysis. Springer-Verlag, New York (1986)
13. Tou, J.T., Gonzales, R.C.: Pattern Recognition Principles. Addison-Wesley, Reading, MA (1974)
14. Rummelhart D.E., McClelland J.L. (eds.): Parallel Distributed Processing: Explorations in the Microstructure of Cognition. Vol. 1. MIT Press, Cambridge, MA (1986)
15. Specht, D.F.: Probabilistic Neural Networks and the Polynomial Adaline as Complementary Techniques for Classification. IEEE Transactions on Neural Networks. Vol. 1, No. 1. (1990) 111-121
16. Poggio, T., Girosi, F.: Regularization Algorithms for Learning that are Equivalent to Multilayer Networks. Science, Vol. 247 (1990) 978-982
17. Walter, V., Fritsch, D.: Automatic Verification of GIS Data Using High Resolution Multispectral Data. In: International Archives of Photogrammetry and Remote Sensing (ISPRS). Vol. 32, Part 3/1. (1998) 485-489
18. Mckeown, D.A., Harvey, W.A., McDermott, J.: Rule-based Interpretation of Aerial Images. IEEE Transactions on Pattern and Machine Intelligence. Vol. PAMI-7, No. 5. (1985) 570-585
19. Neuenschwander, W., Fau, P., Szekely, G., Kubler, O.: From Ziplock Snakes to Velcro Surfaces. In: Gruen, A., Kuebler, O., Agouris, P. (eds.): Automated Extraction of Man-Made Objects from Aerial and Space Images. Birkhauser Verlag, Basel Boston Berlin (1995) 105-114
20. Tsao, E.C.-K., Bezdek, J.C., Pal, N.R. Fuzzy Kohonen Clustering Networks. Pattern Recognition. Vol. 27, No. 5. (1994) 757-764

Reconstruction of Building Models from Maps and Laser Altimeter Data

U. Stilla and K. Jurkiewicz

Research Institute of Optronics and Pattern Recognition (FGAN-FOM)
Eisenstockstr. 12, D-76275 Ettlingen, Germany
usti@fgan.de

Abstract. In this paper we describe a procedure for generating building models from large scale vector maps and laser altimeter data. First the vector map is analyzed to group the outlines of buildings and to obtain a hierarchical description of buildings or building complexes. The base area is used to mask the elevation data of single buildings and to derive a coarse 3D-description by prismatic models. Afterwards, details of the roof are analyzed. Based on the histogram of heights, flat roofs and sloped roofs are discriminated. For reconstructing flat roofs with superstructures, peaks are searched in the histogram and used to segment the height data. Compact segments are examined for a regular shape and approximated by additional prismatic objects. For reconstructing sloped roofs, the gradient field of the elevation data is calculated and a histogram of orientations is determined. Major orientations in the histogram are detected and used to segment the elevation image. For each segment containing homogeneous orientations and slopes, a spatial plane is fitted and a 3D-contour is constructed. In order to obtain a polygonal description, adjacent planes are intersected and common vertices are calculated.

1 Motivation

Three-dimensional city models find more and more interest in city and regional planning (Danahy, 1997). They are used for visualization (Gruen, 1998)(Gruber et al., 1997), e.g. to demonstrate the influence of a planned building to the surrounding townscape. Furthermore there is a great demand for such models in civil and military mission planning, disaster management (Kakumoto et al., 1997) and as basis for simulation e.g. in the fields of environmental engineering for microclimate investigations (Adrian & Fiedler, 1991) or telecommunications for transmitter placement (Kürner et al., 1993).

In industrial countries during the last years many maps have been stored digitally and additionally are available in vector form. Large scale topographical maps or cadastral maps show ground plans with no information on the height of buildings or shape of the roof. So far, information on height was derived from manual surveys or from stereo pairs of aerial images.

P.Agouris and A.Stefanidis (Eds.): ISD'99, LNCS1737, pp. 34-46, 1999

1.1 Laser Altimeter Data

Nowadays elevation data are commercially available from airborne laser scanners. Knowing the precise position and orientation of the airborne platform from differential Ground Positioning System (dGPS) and Inertial Navigation System (INS) measurements, the geographic position of the surface points in three spatial dimensions can be calculated to decimeter accuracy (Huising & Pereira, 1998). With current systems, points can be measured at approximately one point each 0.5 x 0.5 m^2 (Lohr, 1998). The sampled surface points distributed over a strip of 250-500m width allows the generation of a geocoded 2D array with elevation data in each cell (elevation image)(Fig. 1). Single flight strips are merged to a consistent digital surface model (DSM) of the whole survey area.

The run-time of a laser pulse reflected at the ground is used to calculate the distance between the sensor and a surface of the scene. If the laser beam illuminates a tree so multiple reflections at different ranges may occur. A certain percentage of the laser beam will be reflected by branches and leaves of the tree. Other parts will penetrate the foliage and will be finally reflected by the terrain surface. The reflected signal can be recorded and analyzed in *first pulse* or *last pulse* mode. While first pulse registration is the optimum choice when surveying the top of objects (e.g. canopy), last pulse registration should be chosen if the final elevation model should describe the ground surface. Fig. 1a shows a section of an image taken in first pulse mode in October. The foliage of the trees is visible. Fig. 1b was taken in last pulse mode in January. The branches and foliage are not visible and the building areas are smaller than in Fig 1a. In some areas no response could be received due to frost and ice. For the reconstruction of roofs we use the images of first pulse registration with a xy resolution of 1 m^2.

a   b

Fig. 1. Elevation data taken in (a) first pulse mode and (b) last pulse mode

1.2 Visualization

A simple way to visualize the elevation data is to assign a brightness value to the z-coordinate of each raster element. Combining this brightness with the z-coordinate in a 3D view leads to a plastic appearance of the raster data (Fig. 2). A more realistic appearance can be obtained by using an aerial image to texture the elevation data (Fig.

3). Nevertheless, the direct use of raster data has its limits for the purpose of a photorealistic animation or a geometric database of physical simulations or a query to an information system. First, the effort for storage and manipulation of data is high and second, an explicit description of the scene by objects, e.g. building models, is not available.

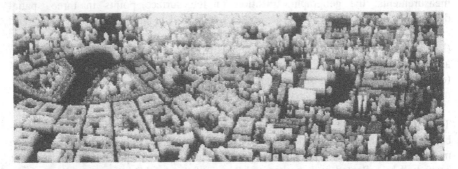

Fig. 2. 3D view of laser altimeter data (Karlsruhe, Germany)

Fig. 3. 3D view of laser altimeter data textured by an aerial image

1.3 Approaches for Automation

The manual construction and update of 3D building models is time consuming and expensive. That is why some authors propose approaches to automate the process of exploiting elevation data. In contrast to semi-automatic approaches (Gruen,

1998)(Guelch, 1997) we pursue approaches which allow a fully automatic reconstruction of buildings.

A detection of surface areas belonging to buildings is shown in Hug & Wehr (1997) by morphological filtering of laser images and examining local elevation histograms. The reflectivity obtained by processing the return signal energy is additionally used to separate segments of artificial objects from vegetation. Polygonal 3D-descriptions of buildings were not derived.

A polygonal description of a building is generated by the approach of Weidner & Förstner, (1995) using geometric constraints in form of parametric and prismatic models. The shape of buildings was limited to flat roofs or symmetric sloped gable roofs.

The reconstruction of more complex roof shapes can be found in (Haala and Brenner, 1997). A ground plan of a building is used to derive roof hypotheses. However, any roof construction based on this approach provides incorrect results if the roof structure inside the ground polygon does not follow the cues that can be obtained from the ground polygon (Haala and Brenner, 1997).

In our approach we also combine elevation data and map data to extract buildings - but the map data is not used to reconstruct the building roof.

2 Scene Analysis

The automatic generation of urban scene descriptions consists of a multistage process, using different information sources as maps, elevation data, aerial images. We describe structural relations of the object models by rules or so-called productions. The hierarchical organization of object concepts and productions can be depicted by a production net which - comparable to semantic networks - displays the part-of hierarchies of object concepts. Production nets are preferably implemented in a blackboard architecture in the environment system BPI (Blackboard-based Production System for Image Understanding, see Stilla, 1995).

In a first step we analyze the digital map by means of a production net in order to obtain a simple urban model consisting of prismatic objects.

3 Prismatic Objects

We use a large scale vector map which is organized in several layers, each of which contains a different class of objects (e.g. streets, buildings, etc.). Fig. 4a-c show a section of the scene, the large scale raster map (1:5000) and the layer *buildings* of the vector map. The topological properties connectivity, closedness, and containment of the non-ordered set of map-lines are tested by a production net of a generic model.

The aim of the analysis is to separate parts of buildings, to determine encapsulated areas and to group parts of buildings. The output of the analysis is a hierarchical description of the buildings or complexes of buildings (Stilla & Michaelsen, 1997).

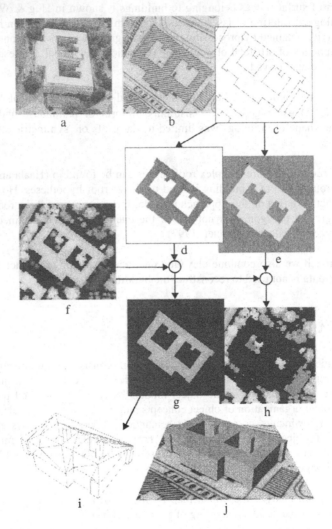

Fig. 4. Generation of prismatic objects from maps and elevation data

The result of the first step is used to mask the elevation data (Fig. 4f). In this way we obtain different elevation data for buildings (Fig. 4g) and non-buildings (surrounding)(Fig. 4h). Due to the fact that we use a buffer zone of some pixels (don't-care-area) along the polygon of the building contour, the negative building mask (Fig. 4e) is not the complement of the positive building mask (Fig. 4d).

For each building object of the map, a coarse 3D-description is constructed by a prismatic model. Depending on the task, the height of the covering plane can be calculated from the histogram using the (i) mean, (ii) median (for suppression of distortions), (iii) minimum (to get the height of the eaves) or (iv) maximum (to obtain the bounding box). This resulting wire-frame models is transformed into a surface model (Fig 4i,j) using an automatic triangulation.

Fig. 5. City model of prismatic objects (buildings)

4 Roof Reconstruction

Depending on the task a more detailed description of the buildings as such models shown in Fig. 5 is required. The roof has to be reconstructed from elevation data. Simple roof structures show characteristic histograms (Fig. 6).

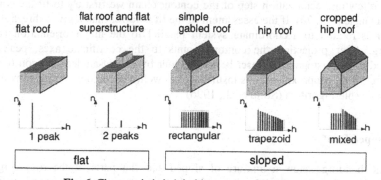

Fig. 6. Characteristic height histograms of simple roofs

Flat roofed buildings show a significant peak in the histogram (Fig. 6a). The high of the peak (peak area) is given by the base area. If a flat roofed building has a flat superstructure (e.g. penthouse, air conditioning or elevator equipment) the histogram shows an additional peak above the main peak (Fig. 6b). Simple gabled roofs show a rectangular histogram (Fig. 6c). Assuming the same base area, the width of the rectangle depends on the slope of the roof. A hip roof shows a trapezoidal histogram

(Fig. 6d). The length of the ridge determines the height of the right side of the histogram. A cropped hip roof shows a mixture of a rectangle and a trapezoid form (Fig. 6e). Since the ideal histogram forms are not present in real data, the discrimination of different sloped roofs by their histograms will generally not be possible.

4.1 Roof Hypotheses

Based on the histogram of heights flat roofs and sloped roofs are discriminated. If the distance between minimum and maximum height is smaller than a threshold, a flat roof is hypothesized (i). If the distance is large enough, the distribution is examined by the entropy relative to the elevation range. If this value is low, a flat roof with a flat superstructure is hypothesized (ii), otherwise sloped roof parts are assumed (iii).

4.2 Flat Roofs

In the case of (i) the position of the peak's maximum is searched and is assigned as the height value to the prismatic object. In the case of (ii) the minor peaks with a certain gap to the main peak are looked for (Fig. 7c). Between the peaks a minimum is searched and a threshold value is calculated. These thresholds are used to segment the elevation data (Fig. 7d-f). The segments are labeled and examined for compactness (circumference/area). Segments, which are too small or not compact, are not taken into consideration for further analysis (Fig. 7e). A compact segment of a size greater than a minimum area confirms the hypothesis (Fig. 7f) and the contour is accepted (Fig. 7g).

In the following vectorization step of the contour chain we first try to fit the contour by a rectangle (Fig. 7h). If the assessment of the fit is lower than a given threshold the contour is rotated to a coordinate system parallel to the major orientation of the building. After projecting the contour points to the coordinate axes, peaks are searched in the histogram to describe the contour by a right-angled polygon (e.g. L-structure). If this approximation is insufficient as well, the contour is approximated by a dynamic split algorithm (Stilla et al., 1996).

4.3 Sloped Roofs

Some buildings show a mixture of sloped and flat parts of the roof (Fig. 8). Additionally, there may occur parts of a building e.g., garage, terrace, balcony, canopy of the front door, etc. They are not assigned to the main roof, because there height is much lower.

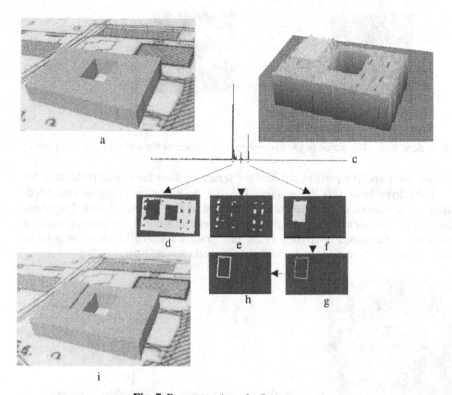

Fig. 7. Reconstruction of a flat superstructure

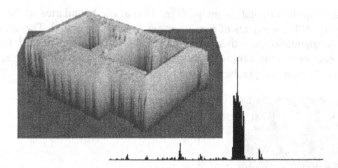

Fig. 8. 3D view of elevation data of a single building and the corresponding histogram

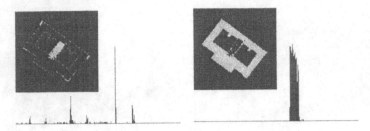

Fig. 9. Separation of elevation image into images of (a) lower or flat and (b) sloped roof parts

First the lower and flat parts of the roof are separated from the sloped parts. In order to test the hypothesis (iii) the gradient field of the elevation image is calculated. Different orientations of the gradient are displayed in Fig. 10a by different brightness values. From the orientation of the gradients possessing a minimum absolute value, a histogram is determined (Fig. 10b). In the histogram we search for peaks in order to determine major orientations and orientation intervals around them.

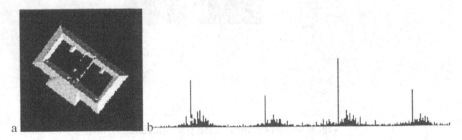

Fig. 10. Orientation of gradient. a) orientation image, b) histogram of orientations

By thresholding the orientation image (Fig. 10a) at the boundaries of the orientation intervals (Fig. 10b), segments of similar orientation are separated. The areas resulting from the segmentation are then morphologically dilated and eroded to fill small unknown enclosed areas, remove small regions, and separate components, which are connected only by a few pixels.

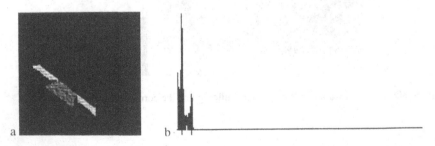

Fig. 11. Separated segment. a) absolute value of gradient, b) histogram

These segments of homogeneous oriented gradients may still contain areas of different slopes. For an obtained segment Fig. 11a shows the absolute values of gradients by corresponding brightness values. To separate such connected areas, the histogram of the slope is determined (Fig. 11b). If the distribution shows several significant peaks essentially differing in slope, then the segment is split into the corresponding areas. The result of the segmentation process is shown in Fig. 12.

Fig. 12. Segmented elevation image

Using segments of homogenous orientation and slope, spatial planes are calculated by a least square fit. Recalculating the z-coordinate for the contour points by the plane equation, we ensure a plain 3D contour chain (Fig. 13).

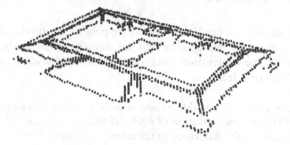

Fig. 13. 3D contour chains

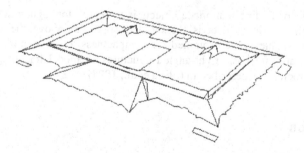

Fig. 14. 3D polygons of roof segments

A polygonal description is obtained by deleting points of the 3D contour chain (Fig. 14). Special attention is required at the neighboring edges of pairs of segments to receive a common line. Since edges of neighboring segments do not intersect in exactly one point, a common vertex has to be calculated. After this step, it may happen, that points of the bordering polygon do not exactly lie in a plane. In a following tessellation step the surface is split in further planar surfaces. The result of the reconstruction is shown in Fig. 15.

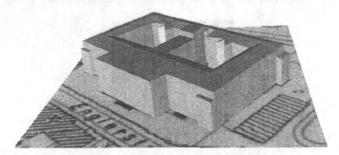

Fig. 15. Reconstructed sloped roof structure

5 Update of City Models

For updating the database of the 3D-city model we propose a procedure in two phases. In a verification phase the buildings which are already stored in the database are compared with the new elevation data by histogram characteristics. They are confirmed, modified or deleted.

In a classification phase new buildings are searched in the elevation data of non-buildings (Fig. 4h). The discrimination of artificial objects from natural objects can be done taking into account the difference in reflectance, elevation texture, local variance of surface gradients, vertical structure (elevation), and shape of the object surfaces (Hug and Wehr, 1997).

One possibility for finding man-made objects is to search for regular structures. For this purpose the elevation data is thresholded appr. 2m above the ground. The resulting binary segments are examined for compactness. In the contour of compact segments we search for basic right-angled structures. A model for composing basic right-angled structures is described in (Stilla et al., 1998).

6 Discussion

The proposed method can be applied to reconstruct complex roof shapes from maps and elevation data. The approach allows the recognition of additional structures (e.g. superstructures) which can not be derived from the building outlines shown in the map. It has been shown, that elevation histograms of laser altimeter data show characteristic features of roofs.

However, the reconstruction of small roof segments is not reliable. Those segments remain unconsidered or are reconstructed as prismatic objects. Additionally, difficulties occur when analyzing histograms of strongly sloped roof segments (high roof) oriented parallel to the grid. They show a set of peaks and look like a comb.

Using the segmentation approach, we have assumed, that roof parts have similar orientations and for the whole roof only a few orientations exists. If the histogram does not show a few major orientations, local relations have to be considered for reconstructing planar surfaces (Besl, 1988). Several segmentation algorithms which are based on region growing are described and compared in (Hoover et al., 1996).

Important for reconstruction is the evaluation of the results. For a quantitative evaluation, ground truths of a set of buildings and task-dependent assessment functions are necessary. Up to now only single objects are qualitatively evaluated. A comparison of the results with a measured CAD-Model is shown in Fig. 16.

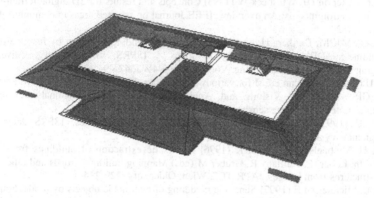

Fig. 16. Comparison of reconstructed segments and truth data (lines)

References

1. Adrian G, Fiedler F (1991) Simulation of unstationary wind and temperatur fields over complex terrain and comparison with observations. Beitr. Phys. Atmosph., 64, 27-48
2. Besl PJ (1988) Surfaces in range image understanding. New York: Springer
3. Danahy J (1997) A set of visualization data needs in urban environmental planning & design for photogrammetric data. In: Gruen et al. (eds) Automatic extraction of man-made objects from aerial and space images (II), 357-366, Basel: Birkhäuser
4. Gruber M, Kofler M, Leberl F (1997) Managing large 3D urban database contents supporting phototexture and levels of detail. In: Gruen et al. (eds) Automatic extraction of man-made objects from aerial and space images (II), 377-386, Basel: Birkhäuser
5. Gruen A (1998) TOBAGO - a semi-automated approach for the generation of 3-D building models. ISPRS Journal of photogrammetry & remote sensing, 53(2): 108-118

6. Guelch E (1997) Application of semi-automatic building acquisition. In: Gruen A et al. (eds.) Automatic extraction of man-made objects from aerial and space images (II), 129-138, Basel: Birkhäuser
7. Haala N, Brenner C (1997) Interpretation of urban surface models using 2D building information. In: Gruen A et al. (eds.) Automatic extraction of man-made objects from aerial and space images (II), 213-222, Basel: Birkhäuser
8. Hug C, Wehr A (1997) Detecting and identifying topographic objects in laser altimeter data. ISPRS, International archives of photogrammetry and remote sensing, Vol. 32, Part 3-4W2, 19-268.
9. Huising EJ, Gomes Pereira LM (1998) Errors and accuracy estimates of laser data acquired by various laser scanning systems for topographic applications. ISPRS Journal of photogrammetry and remote sensing, 53: 245-261
10. Hoover A, Jean-Baptiste, Jiang X, Flynn PJ, Bunke H, Goldof DB, Bowyer K, Eggert DW, Fitzgibbon A, Fisher RB (1996) An experimental comparison of range image segmentation algorithms. IEEE T-PAMI, 16(7):673-689
11. Kakumoto S, Hatayama M, Kameda H, Taniguchi T (1997) Development of disaster management spatial information system. Proc. GIS'97 Conf., 595-598
12. Kürner T, Cichon DJ, Wiesbeck W (1993) Concepts and results for 3D digital terrain-based wave propagation models: An overview. IEEE Journal on selected areas in communications, 11: 1002-1012
13. Lemmens MJPM, Deijkers H, Looman PAM (1997) Building detection by fusing airborne laser-altimeter DEMs and 2D digital maps. ISPRS, International archives of photogrammetry and remote sensing, Vol. 32, Part 3-4W2, 42-49
14. Lohr U (1998) Laserscan DEM for various applications. In: Fritsch D, Englich M, Sester M (eds) GIS - Between Visions and Applications. ISPRS, International archives of photogrammetry and remote sensing, Vol. 32, Part 4, 353-356
15. Stilla U (1995) Map-aided structural analysis of aerial images. ISPRS Journal of Photogrammetry and Remote Sensing, 50(4): 3-10
16. Stilla U, Michaelsen E, Lütjen K (1996) Automatic extraction of buildings from aerial images. In: Leberl F, Kalliany R, Gruber M (eds) Mapping buildings, roads and other man-made structures from images, IAPR-TC7. Wien: Oldenburg, 229-244
17. Stilla U, Michaelsen E (1997) Semantic modeling of man-made objects by production nets. In: Gruen A, Baltsavias EP, Henricsson O (eds) Automatic extraction of man-made objects from aerial and space images (II). Basel: Birkhäuser, 43-52
18. Stilla U, Michaelsen E, Jurkiewicz K (1998) Structural analysis of right-angled building contours. ISPRS, International archives of photogrammetry and remote sensing, Vol. 32, Part 3/1, 379-386
19. Shibasaki R (1998) Proceedings of UM3'98, International Workshop on Urban Multi-Media/3D Mapping., University of Tokyo, Institute of Industrial Science.
20. Weidner U, Förstner W (1995) Towards automatic building extraction from high-resolution digital elevation models. ISPRS Journal of photogrammetry and remote sensing, 50(4): 38-49

Comparison of the Potential of Different Sensors for an Automatic Approach for Change Detection in GIS Databases

Volker Walter

Institute for Photogrammetry (ifp), University of Stuttgart, Geschwister-Scholl-Straße 24,
D-70174 Stuttgart, Germany
Volker.Walter@ifp.uni-stuttgart.de

Abstract. This paper examines data from different sensors regarding their potential for an automatic change detection approach. After a brief discussion of the used approach, results are shown on examples of data from several sensors: scanned analogue aerial photos, an airborne digital line scanner (DPA camera system), the Indian satellite IRS-1C, the MOMS-2P camera and from a laser scanning system as an additional information source. The GIS data which have to be updated are from the German national topographic cartographic database (ATKIS) and were captured in the scale of 1 : 25,000.

1 Introduction

Geographic information systems (GIS) are dependent on accurate and up-to-date data sets. The manual revision of GIS data is very cost and time consuming. On the other hand more and more high resolution satellite systems are under development and will be operational soon - thus high resolution remote sensing data will also be available soon. With these new satellite systems it will be possible to capture large areas of the landscape in short time periods. However, a shortening of the updating cycles of GIS databases is only possible if the manual part of the updating process can be at least partly automated. A software package was developed to verify ATKIS data in an automatic way. ATKIS is the German topographic cartographic spatial database [1] and presently contains more than 60 different feature types for the whole area of Germany in the scale of 1:25,000 (beside this scale there are further levels of data aggregation in the scales 1:200,000 and 1:1,000,000 which were not used in this work). The software package was developed in such a way that data from different sensors can be used as a source and therefore it is possible to examine the potential of data from different sensors for the automatic change detection approach. Since not only satellite data but also data from airborne sensors were examined, the potential of future high resolution satellite systems can also be estimated.

P.Agouris and A.Stefanidis (Eds.): ISD'99, LNCS1737, pp. 47-64, 1999
© Springer-Verlag Berlin Heidelberg 1999

2   Automatic Change Detection of Remote Sensing Data

The approach for the change detection is fully automatic and can be subdivided mainly into two steps (see figure 1). In a first step the remote sensing data have to be classified pixel wise into different land use classes. This is done by a supervised maximum likelihood classification. The problem for an automatic approach here is the supervised part of the classification algorithm. Normally this part involves the work of a human operator and requires a lot of experience because the quality of the training areas is a crucial factor for the quality of the classification result. As the digitizing of the training areas is time intensive and new training areas have to be digitized for every new data set (because of atmospheric effects, different spectral diffusion depending on the sunlight, different spectral characteristics of vegetation depending on season or soil, etc.), a method is needed to derive the training areas in an automatic way. Having assumed that the number of wrongly captured GIS objects and the number of changes in the real world are substantially less than the number of all GIS objects of the data set, the training areas can be derived automatically from the already existing GIS data. The higher the quality of the training areas the better will be the result of the classification. Therefore, the object geometry is not used as stored in the GIS database - a preprocessing has to be performed first. A more detailed description of the computing of training areas can be found in [14] [15].

After the classification it must be decided which of the GIS objects do not match the remote sensing data. This can be objects where a change in the landscape has occurred or objects, that were not collected correctly. All GIS objects are subdivided into three classes. The first class contains all objects which could be detected with a high certainty in the remote sensing data, the second class contains all objects which are detected only partly and the third class contains all objects which could not be detected at all. The decision to which class an object belongs is made by measuring the percentage of pixels which are classified to the same object class as the object in the GIS database belongs to. Besides the percentage of correctly classified pixels, also the homogeneity of the classification result and the form are used for verification. A more detailed description of the verification of the classification results can be found in [14] [15].

3   Implementation

The approach is implemented in a software package based on UNIX and X-Windows. Figure 2 shows a selection of different windows of the program. The software was implemented in such a way that all parameters of the approach can be changed interactively by the user and stored as a project. Additionally a visualization component is available to explore the results interactively on the screen.

The software is designed in such a way that there exists no limitation regarding the resolution, the size or the channels of the images. This enables the examination of data from very different sources. In the following, results of the classification of images from different sensors are presented and examined for their potential for an automatic update of ATKIS data. Presently ATKIS contains more than 60 different object classes. It is clear that not all object classes can be distinguished alone by their spectral and textural characteristics without addition of further information sources. Therefore we divided all ATKIS objects into the five land use classes: *forest, settlements, agricultural areas, streets* and *water*.

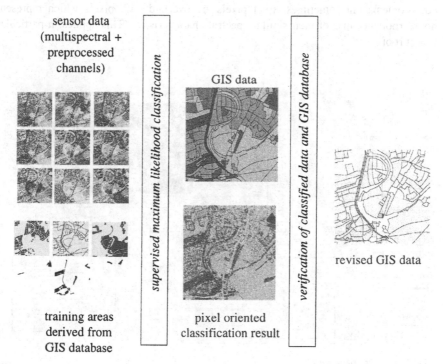

Fig. 1. Overview of the automatic approach for GIS change detection

4   Classification Results DPA

The Digital Photogrammetric Assembly (DPA) is an optical airborne imaging system for real time data collection. The ground pixel size depends on the flying height and is for example 0.60 m for multispectral data when flying 2300 m above ground. Besides the multispectral sensor, the DPA camera system offers also three panchromatic CCD line arrays for in-flight stereo imaging. For more details of the DPA camera see: [6].

The data of the test area have a ground pixel size of 0.75 m. This corresponds at an area of 2 km * 2 km to a pixel number of more than seven million pixels. Because the classification is a complex process, this leads to a high computing time as well as high memory requirements. However, experiences show that depending on the land use class high resolution must not necessarily improve the results of the classification. In order to find a compromise between quality of change detection and computer requirements the data were resampled to a pixel size of 2 m. Figure 3 shows the result of the classification of DPA data at an example. Forests are recognized being homogeneous and well detectable. Agricultural areas show sometimes inhomogeneities because of planting structures, but nevertheless they can be detected also very well. The land cover class which could be detected best is *water*. Larger streets are recognized without problems but sometimes street pixels are overlaid with pixels which represent house roofs because of their similar spectral characteristics. This applies in particular to flat roofs

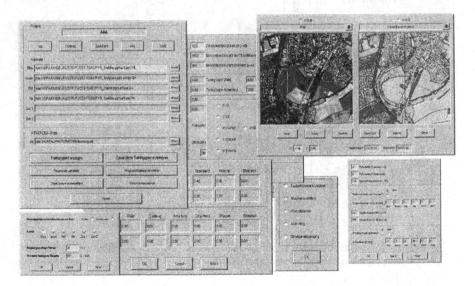

Fig. 2. Software package

The land use class *settlement* can not be recognized as homogeneous uniform areas, but it is subdivided into several classes. It can be seen that pixels are only recognized as settlement areas if they represent house roofs. The other pixels are classified as streets, forest and agricultural area depending on the "ground truth". The reason for this result is the high resolution of 2 m. More detailed results of the classification of DPA images can be found in section 9.

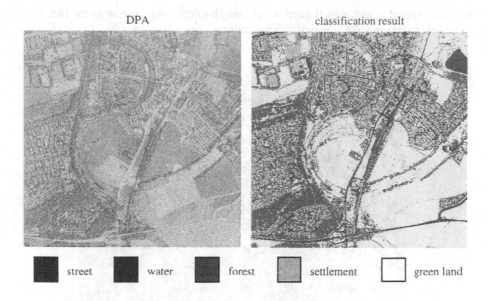

DPA   classification result

| street | water | forest | settlement | green land |

Fig. 3. Classification of DPA data

5   Classification Results IRS-1C

The Indian Remote Sensing Satellite IRS-1C carries a multispectral camera (LISS) with 25 m ground pixel size, a high resolution panchromatic sensor with 5.8 m ground pixel size and a wide field sensor for the optimized determination of vegetation indices with 188 m ground pixel size. The data used in this work are from the LISS camera. For more details of the IRS-1C satellite system see for example [12].

Figure 4 shows a classification result of IRS-1C data. The image is shown as a CIR image because IRS-1C does not capture data in the blue range. In order to improve the interpretation of the IRS-1C image, a DPA image of the same area is represented. Because of the low resolution, an interpretation of the data is very difficult for an operator. However, it can be seen in the classification result that at least some structures which have a size of only one pixel are classified correctly. But the further processing of the data is problematic because if an object is marked as uncertain it is very difficult for an operator to decide if there has been a change or not if he has only IRS-1C data as a decision base.

This problem can be seen even more clearly in figure 5. The test area consists completely of farmland with a small farm in the center of the figure. Although the IRS-1C-image shows a high spectral variance in the farmland, this is classified as a homogeneous area. The structure of the farm is also recognized very clearly. However, if the settlement object is marked as not found (since it contains only a small number of pixels classified as settlement) there is not enough information content in the IRS-1C to be able to interpret the situation correspondingly.

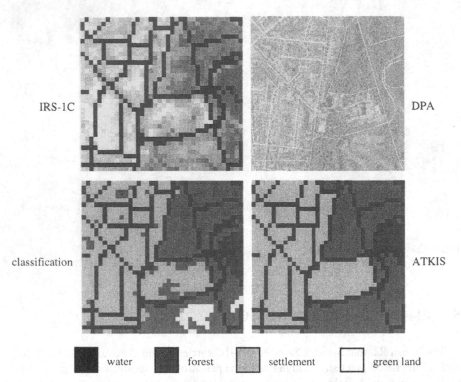

Fig. 4. Classification of IRS-1C data (example 1)

In summary it can be said, that IRS-1C data are only in a reduced manner suitable for the update of ATKIS data. Because of the low resolution only larger area objects can be recognized. An object must have a minimum size from 2 * 2 pixel so that it is classified certainly in the image. This corresponds to an extension of 50 m * 50 m. If objects have a high contrast to their neighboring objects and if the object border is close to the pixel boarder (no mixed pixels) smaller objects can still be recognized correctly. The biggest problem is the verification of the results. Because of the low geometric and radiometric resolution an interpretation of the classification result by a human operator is very difficult.

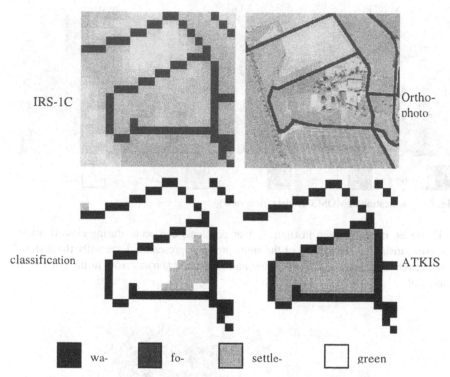

IRS-1C

Ortho-
photo

classification

ATKIS

wa-   fo-   settle-   green

Fig. 5. Classification of IRS-1C data (example 2)

6   Classification Results MOMS-2P

The Modular Optoelectronic Multispectral Scanner 2 (MOMS-2P) is docked to the Russian Space Station MIR. MOMS-2P combines a high resolution three-channel stereo module and a four-channel multispectral unit. The ground pixel size of the multispectral channels is 18 m. For more details of the MOMS-2P camera system see for example: [11].

Figure 6 shows an overview of the scene (mode C = green, red and near infrared channel plus high resolution nadir looking channel) that was used for the study. A pixel precise classification is also partially possible here. This can be seen especially at the river and at the border between farmland and forest in the lower left corner in the image.

MOMS-2P   ATKI   classificati-

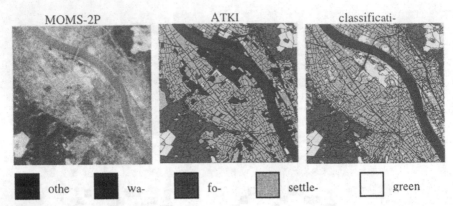

othe ■   ■ wa-   ■ fo-   ▨ settle-   □ green

Fig. 6. Classification of MOMS-2P data (overview)

However, it can be seen in figure 7 that problems can occur during classification. For comparison, an orthophoto of the same area is represented. Especially the distinction between the land use classes *forest* and *settlement* shows errors in the classification result.

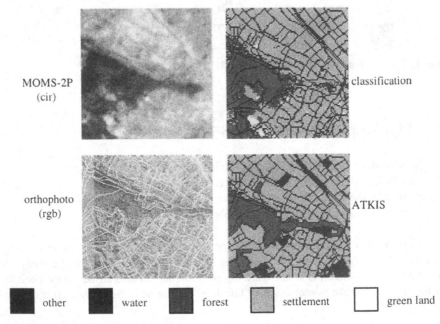

MOMS-2P (cir)   classification

orthophoto (rgb)   ATKIS

■ other   ■ water   ■ forest   ▨ settlement   □ green land

Fig. 7. Classification of MOMS-2P data

The bad classification result can be explained with the small contrast of the MOMS-2P image. Figure 8 shows a histogram comparison of the different channels of IRS-1C data (which was already represented further up) and the MOMS-2P data. It can be seen that all channels of the MOMS-2P image have gray value dynamics of far less than 100 different values. This is why the classification of the IRS-1C data lead to better results since images which are considerably more rich in contrast (in spite of lower technical specification of the camera concerning radiometric and geometrical solution) were available. The reason for the low contrast of the MOMS-2P image is presumably due to the weather conditions.

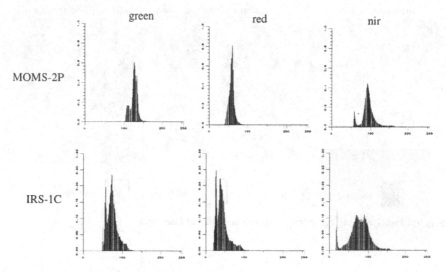

Fig. 8. Comparison of MOMS-2P and IRS-1C histogramms

7   Classification Results rgb Orthophotos and Laser Data

Because the software was developed in such a way that there exist no restrictions regarding the input data for the classification it is also possible to use laser data as an additional information channel. Figure 9 shows a classification result of a rgb ortho-photo (resampled to 2 m) without and with laser data as an additional channel. Espe-cially streets and building can be separated more precisely when using laser data.

The bad differentiation of streets and houses in the rgb classification results from the very similar spectral characteristics of these two classes. If, however, laser data are used as an additional channel, pixel that represent house roofs can be distinguished very well from pixel that represent streets because of their height above the ground.

The used part of the image represents an area where very good classification results can be achieved. However, problems arise in areas which are hidden by shadow. Figure 10 shows an example for this situation. Although laser data were used as an additional channel, the classification result is not very good. Especially pixel that represent streets have a completely different spectral characteristic in this example (streets are represented typically by very bright pixels) as in areas without shadow. In situations like this, street pixel are very often classified as forest because forests are represented typically by dark pixels.

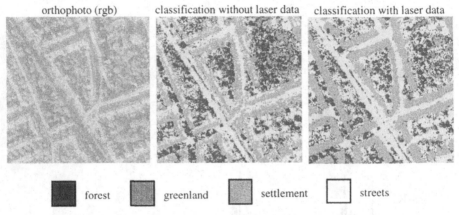

forest   greenland   settlement   streets

Fig. 9. Classification of rgb orthophoto with and without laser data

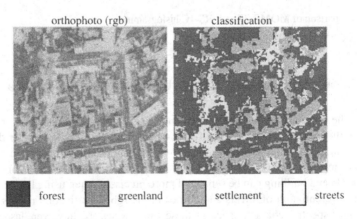

forest   greenland   settlement   streets

Fig. 10. Classification in shadow areas

In summary it can be stated that rgb data are not suitable to achieve homogenous good classification results. Even by adding of laser data no satisfying results can be achieved. A near infrared channel is necessary to classify pixels in shadow areas correctly.

8   Classification Results cir Orthophotos and Laser Data

A further test was the classification of cir images and laser data. The following examples were computed with a pixel size of 0.5 m to show the high potential of this combination of data. Figure 11 shows a classification result of a scanned cir orthophoto.

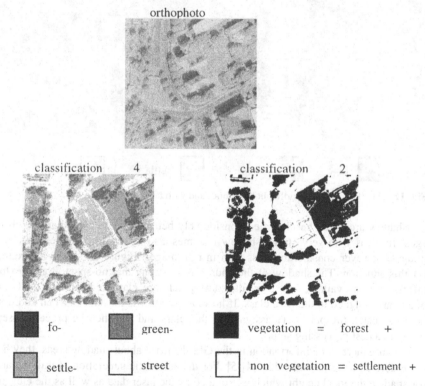

Fig. 11. Classification of a cir orthophoto

The results of the classification of the cir orthophoto can be compared with the results of the DPA data. The additional blue channel of the DPA sensor has barely new information in comparison with the cir channels of the orthophoto because it is strongly correlated with the green channel. It can be seen in the example that vegetated and non vegetated areas can be separated very well by the classification. More problems arise when differentiating streets and houses. These two classes have very similar spectral characteristics and therefore can be separated only very hard.

Figure 12 shows the classification result of the same part of the image with and without the use of laser data as an additional information channel. The laser data improve the classification result significantly because they have a complementary "behavior" as multispectral data. With laser data the classes *farmland* and *street* can be separated very good from the classes *forest* and *settlement* because of the different heights of the pixels above the ground whereas in multispectral data the classes *farmland* and *forest* can be separated very good from the classes *streets* and *settlement* because of the strongly different percentage of chlorophyll.

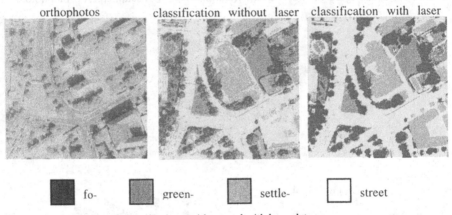

orthophotos   classification without laser   classification with laser

■ fo-   ■ green-   ■ settle-   □ street

Fig. 12. Classification of cir orthophoto without and with laser data

Shadow areas can be classified considerably better in cir images than in rgb images. In areas with very strong shadow it comes also to wrong classifications in cir images, however considerably less than in rgb images. Figure 13 shows an example for this situation. The shadow of the church is so strong that no spectral and textural information is available. As a result, some pixels are classified wrongly and some pixels are assigned to the zero class. If however shadow is introduced as an additional land use class, the pixels are assigned to this class and can then be processed separately in a post processing step.

Because there is no information in the GIS database about shadow areas, they have to be derived from the laser data [4][5]. For the automatic generation of training areas for shadow the local height which is provided by the laser data as well as the elevation and azimuth of the sun at the time of image acquisition is required. The elevation and azimuth of the sun can either be determined manually by an interactive measurement of the edge of a shadowed area in the image and the corresponding object height in the normalized laser data or derived automatically from the geographical latitude and longitude of the captured area and the time of image acquisition. Figure 14 shows the automatic processed training areas for the additional land use class shadow.

In order to avoid the *shadow* class in the final result the approach can be further refined by splitting each of this land use classes into one land use class for shadow areas and one land use class for non shadow areas. After the classification the shadow and non shadow pixels for each land use class are combined again to obtain one unique class for each type of land use. The final result of the classification algorithm for the whole test area is given in figure 15.

orthophotos   classification   without   classification   with

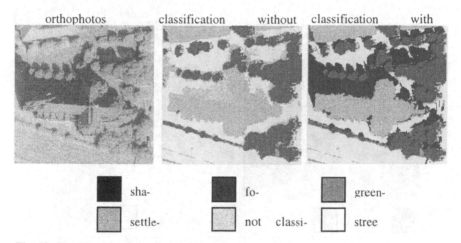

■ sha-   ■ fo-   ▨ green-

▨ settle-   ▨ not classi-   □ stree

Fig. 13. Classification with and without shadow as an additional class

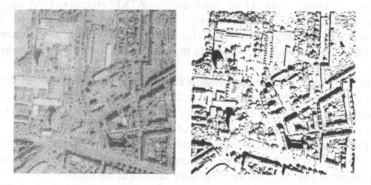

Fig. 14. Automatic detection of training areas for the additional land use class shadow

9   Verification of the Classification Results

All ATKIS area objects are subdivided into three different classes. The first class contains all objects which could be detected certainly in the DPA data, the second class contains all objects which are detected only partly and the third class contains all objects which could not be detected at all. The decision to which class an object belongs is made by measuring the percentage of pixels which are classified to the same object class as the object itself belongs to. Optionally the form and the homogeneity of the correctly classified pixels in the object are used. Very small or narrow objects are evaluated less strict than normal objects.

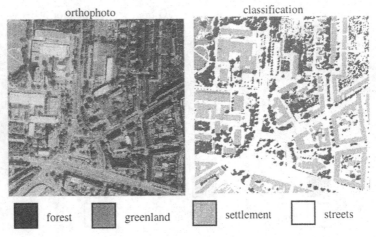

Fig. 15. Classification using 10 classes (5 for shadow areas and 5 for non shadow areas)

Figure 16 shows some results of the verification of ATKIS objects in DPA images. The DPA images are represented in the original resolution in the left column. The ATKIS geometry is superimposed in black. The classification result in a resolution of 2 m is represented in the middle column and the result of the verification in the right column.

Figure 16 a) shows two objects which were captured in ATKIS as greenland. In the DPA image it can be seen that meanwhile a settlement area was built up. The result of the verification is that these two objects cannot be found in the image because of the low number of pixels that were classified as greenland

Figure 16 b) shows a construction site where formerly a forest area and greenland was found. The changes in the landscape are so strong that nearly no pixel is classified as forest or farmland and therefore the objects are marked as not found.

Figure 16 c) shows an settlement objects which contains a big greenland area. The object is marked as partly found because at least the left part of the object was classified as settlement or streets.

Figure 16 d) shows two objects. It can be seen in the DPA image that a parking area is located in the greenland object. The pixels in the parking area are classified as streets or settlement. The majority of the pixels are classified as greenland but they are not distributed homogenous in the object. Therefore the object is marked as partly found. The neighboring smaller settlement objects consists almost completely of forest. This object cannot be found in the image and therefore it is marked as not found.

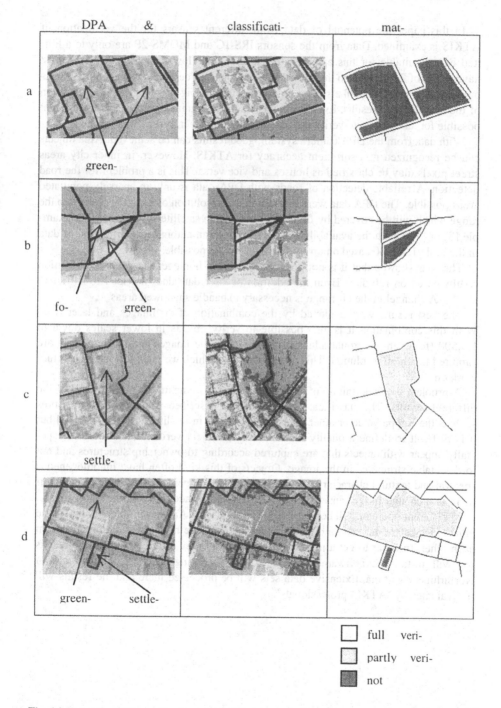

Fig. 16. Examples of the verification of ATKIS objects in DPA images

10 Summary

In this paper the potential of data from different sensors for the verification of ATKIS is examined. Data from the sensors IRS-1C and MOMS-2P are only to a limited extent suitable for this approach because of their low resolution. Objects must have a size of 2 * 2 pixel so that they can be recognized certainly in the figure. A recognition of line objects, like streets, is not possible. A big problem is the verification of the classification results. Even if objects can be recognized pixel precisely, it is not possible for an operator to verify the results without further information sources.

With data from the DPA camera system, good results can be achieved. Area objects can be recognized in a sufficient accuracy for ATKIS. However, in inner city areas street pixels may be classified as houses and vice versa. This is a problem for the road detection. A reliable detection of roads with DPA data is only in sparsely populated areas possible. The DPA data were resampled to a resolution of 2 m. This falls into the range which will be covered by future high resolution satellite systems (see for example [8] or [9]). With the availability of such systems an automated verification of data in the scale 1:25,000 based on up-to-date data will be possible.

The tests showed that it is not possible to achieve homogenous good classification results based on rgb data. Even the addition of laser data does not lead to sufficient results. A channel in the nir range is necessary to handle shadowed areas.

The best results were achieved by the combination of cir images and laser data. With this combination it is also possible to verify objects in lower scales down to 1:2,500 (for example ground plans of buildings) if the images and the laser data are captured in a high resolution. This is also the topic which we want to focus our future work on.

A problem is the definition of quality measures to compare the performance of the different sensors. The classification result can be described with statistical measures such as the Kappa value or other measures described in the literature [2] [10] [13] but it is difficult to define a quality measure for the object verification. Problems especially appear with objects that are captured according to ownership structures and not to detectable structures in the image. Objects of this kind often have inhomogeneous spectral and textural characteristics and even a human operator is not able to decide if there is a change in the landscape or not if he has no additional information source. Also different operator will come to different decisions. Another problem is that some object classes are defined ambiguously and therefore are not clearly delimitable from each other. In order to get a more practical oriented idea of the quality of the results we will install the software package at the Surveying Institute of the State of Northrhine-Westfalia. Extensive data sets will be processed there and the results will be evaluated by 'ATKIS professionals'.

Acknowledgments

This research is carried out by order of the Surveying Institute of the State of Northrhine-Westphalia, Germany. The project is supported by the German Aerospace Center (DLR – formerly DARA)

References

1. Arbeitsgemeinschaft der Vermessungsverwaltungen der Länder der Bundesrepublik Deutschland (AdV): Amtlich Topographisches-Kartographisches Informationssystem (ATKIS) Bonn (1988).
2. Congalton, R.: A Review of Assessing the Accuracy of Classifications of Remotely Sensed Data, Remote Sensing Environment 37, 35 – 46 (1991)
3. Haala, N., Stallmann, D., Staetter, C.: On the use of multispectral and stereo data from airborne scanning systems for DTM generation and landuse classification in: ISPRS Commission IV Symposium GIS – Between Visions and Applications, Vol. 32, Part 4, 203 – 209 (1998)
4. Haala, N., Walter, V.: Classification of urban environments using LIDAR and color aerial imagery in: Fusion of sensor data, knowledge sources and algorithms for extraction and classification of topographic objects, 3 - 4 June, Valladoid, Spain (1999)
5. Haala, N. Walter, V., Staetter, C.: Analysis of multispectral data from airborne pushbroom systems for DTM generation and landuse classification, in: Proceedings of the Fourth International Remote Sensing Conference and Exhibition / 21st Canadian Symposium on Remote Sensing, Ottawa (1999)
6. Hahn, M, Stallmann, D., Staetter, C.: The DPA-Sensor System for Topographic and Thematic Mapping, in: International Archives of Photogrammetry and Remote Sensing (ISPRS), Vol. XXXI, Part B2, 141 – 146, Vienna (1996)
7. Hahn, M., Staetter, C.: A scene labeling strategy for terrain feature extraction using multi-source data, in: International Archives of Photogrammetry and Remote Sensing (ISPRS), Vol. XXXI, Part B4, pp, 823 – 828, 1996, 435 – 441 (1998)
8. Jacobsen, K.: Status and Tendency of Sensors for Mapping, Proceedings of the International Symposium on Earth Observation System for sustainable Development, Bangladore, India, Vol. XXXII, Part I of International Archives of Photogrammetry and Remote Sensing (ISPRS), 183 – 190 (1998)
9. Kilston, S.: Capabilities of new Remote Sensing Satellites to support sustainable Development, Proceedings of the International Symposium on Earth Observation System for sustainable Development, Bangladore, India, Vol. XXXII, Part I of International Archives of Photogrammetry and Remote Sensing (ISPRS), 124 - 131 (1998)
10. Rosenfield, G, Fitzpatrick-Lins, K: A Coefficient of Agreement as a Measure of Thematic Classification Accuracy, Photogrammetric Engineering and Remote Sensing, Vol. 52, No. 2, 223-227 (1986)
11. Schiewe, J.: Cartographical Potential of MOMS-02/D2 Image Data in D. Fritsch and D. Hobbie (Eds.) Photogrammetric Week '95, Wichmann Verlag, 95 – 106 (1995)

12. Srivastava, P, et. al.: Cartographic Potential of IRS-1C Data Products, in: International Archives of Photogrammetry and Remote Sensing (ISPRS), Vol. XXX1, Part B4, 823 – 828, (1996)
13. Stehmann, V.: Selecting and Interpreting Measures of Thematic Classification Accuracy, Remote Sensing Environment 62, 77-89 (1997)
14. Walter, V.: Automatic classification of remote sensing data for GIS database revision, in International Archives of Photogrammetry and Remote Sensing (ISPRS), Vol. XXXII, Part 4, 641 – 648, (1998)
15. Walter, V., Fritsch, D.: Automatic verification of GIS data using high resolution multispectral data in: International Archives of Photogrammetry and Remote Sensing (ISPRS), Vol. XXXII, Part 3/1, 485 – 489 (1998)

Geospatial Analysis

Cost-Effective Determination of Biomass from Aerial Images[*]

H. Schultz[1], D. Slaymaker[2], C. Holmes[1], F. Stolle[1], A. Hanson[1], E. Riseman[1], M. Delaney[3], and M. Powell[3]

[1] Computer Science Department, University of Massachusetts, Amherst, MA 01003
{hschultz, cholmes, stolle, hanson, riseman}@cs.umass.edu

[2] Forestry and Wildlife Management Department,
University of Massachusetts, Amherst, MA 01003
dana@fnr.umass.edu

[3] Winrock International, 38 Winrock Drive, Morrilton, AR 72110-9370
{mdelaney, mpowell}@winrock.org

Abstract. This paper describes an ongoing collaborative research program between the Computer Science and the Forestry and Wildlife Management Departments at the University of Massachusetts to develop cost-effective methodologies for monitoring biomass and other environmental parameters over large areas. The data acquisition system consists of a differential GPS system, a 3-axis solid state inertial reference system, a small format (70mm) aerial survey camera, two video cameras, a laser profiling altimeter, and a PC based data recording system. Two aerial survey techniques for determining biomass are discussed. One primarily based on video and the other relying additionally on the 3D terrain models generated from the aerial photographs. In the first technique, transects are flown at 1,000 feet with dual-camera wide angle and zoom video, and a profiling laser operating at 238 Hz. The video coverage is used to identify individual tree species, and the laser profiler is used to estimate tree heights. The second procedure builds on this approach by taking sequences of 70mm photographs with an 80% overlap along a second higher altitude flight line at 4,000 feet. Detailed 3D terrain models are then generated from successive pairs of images. Several state-of-the-are computer vision algorithms are discussed, including the ITL system, which is an interactive ground cover classification system that allows an operator to quickly classify the large areas in a real-time, and Terrest, which is a highly robust 3D terrain modeling system. The work described in this paper is in a preliminary phase and all of the constituent technologies have not been fully integrated, we nevertheless demonstrated the value and feasibility of using computer vision techniques to solve environmental monitoring problems on a large scale.

[*] Sponsored by Grants from the National Science Foundation (EIA-9726401) and the National Fish and Wildlife Foundation (98-089)

P.Agouris and A.Stefanidis (Eds.): ISD'99, LNCS1737, pp. 67-76, 1999
© Springer-Verlag Berlin Heidelberg 1999

1   Introduction

The Computer Science (CS) and Forestry and Wildlife Management (FWM) Departments at the University of Massachusetts are engaged in a three-year NSF grant to develop cost-effective, automated techniques to monitor forests and other natural environments. Our long-term goal is to automate and improve environmental monitoring techniques currently employed by FWM through the use of a variety of computer vision techniques, including 3D terrain reconstruction, classification, and automatic video mosaicking techniques.

Biomass estimation is an important application domain for this work. The UN Convention on Climate Change held at Kyoto, Japan in 1997 established a framework for assigning economic value to carbon sequestered in biomass. The effective implementation of the treaty depends on developing cost-effective methods that accurately establish the biomass of tropical forests. Because of vast amount of forests that maybe affected by this treaty, current labor intensive in-situ methods that make extensive use of permanent plots for estimating biomass [1], [2] are not feasible.

To extend coverage and simplify data collection, a range of techniques are being evaluated that utilize the general approach of extrapolating information from small area point samples (e.g., permanent plots), to high-resolution transects observed from low-altitude aerial surveys, to low-resolution, large area analysis derived from satellite images. The focus of our current work is on studying the effectiveness of classifying vegetation using narrow strips of high-resolution video (0.1 m GSD), wide-angle video, laser altimeter profiles, and 3D terrain models generated from small format aerial photography (0.5 – 1.0 m GSD).

1.1 Historical Perspective

To fulfil the terms of the Kyoto treaty the U. S. Government asked for voluntary efforts on the part of American industries to comply with the goals set forth in Kyoto. As part of an effort to respond to this challenge, the American Electric Power (AEP), PacifiCorp and BP America in collaboration with The Nature Conservancy (TNC), Fundación Amigos de la Naturaleza (FAN), and the government of Bolivia, have established the Noel Kempff Mercado Climate Action Project. Approximately 630,000 hectares of forest have been withdrawn from logging or agricultural development and added to the Noel Kempff Mercado National Park in northeast Bolivia. To determine the standing forest biomass of this region, TNC contracted with the Winrock International Institute for Agricultural Development to develop a stratified sample of ground sites where individual trees could be measured over time. Staff from Winrock and the Noel Kempff Mercado Natural History Museum in Santa Cruz established 625 nested plot sites in five basic vegetation strata. Each site was divided into two concentric regions - an inner region with a 4-meter radius, and an outer region with a 14-meter radius. In the inner region all woody stems with a diameter at breast height (dbh) greater than 5 cm were measured; and in the outer region all stems with dbh greater than 20 cm were measured. These dbh values and tree counts were then extrapolated to a per hectare estimate of standing biomass for the region using standard allometric equations.

Setting up 625 plots in a tropical rainforest with few access roads was a major costly and time consuming undertaking. With the vast amounts of forest subject to carbon sequestering under the Global Warming Treaty, it became obvious that manual sampling techniques are not practical. To reduce the amount of labor and extend coverage, the Electric Power Research Institute (EPRI) contacted with the University of Massachusetts to develop low-cost, robust methodologies to measure biomass.

2   Approach to Computing Biomass

Our initial focus has been on evaluating two aerial survey techniques for determining biomass, one primarily based on video [10] and the other relying additionally on the 3D terrain models. For both setups a Trimble real-time differential GPS system was used to collect position information to approximately 1 meter in X,Y,Z, and a Watson Industries 3-axis solid state inertial reference system were used to collect orientation information to approximately 0.1 degrees in role and pitch and 0.5 degrees in azimuth. To enable temporal registration of the various data streams, time codes were added to the data during collection. A time code generator was used synchronize the video data, which was recorded on a VCR, and a time code stamp was added to all digital data during the recording process.

In the first technique, which we refer to as the 2D approach, transects are flown at 1,000 feet. The instrument package consisted of the GPS, inertial reference system, two down-looking video camera (one with a wide angle lens and one with a telephoto lens), and a profiling laser altimeter. Figure 1 shows an example of a video sequence, and Figure 2 shows an example of a geo-referenced laser altimeter profile. The wide-angle camera covered a swath approximately 320 meters wide, with 50 centimeter per pixel resolution. The other camera was set at 12X zoom, covering a 26 meter wide swath at 4 cm per pixel resolution, a sufficient scale to identify individual tree species.

The second sampling procedure builds on this approach by taking sequences of

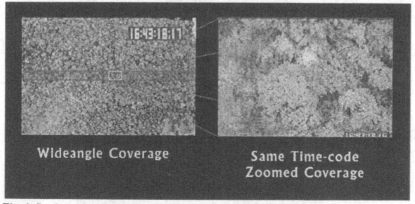

Fig. 1. Product of dual camera videography. Zoomed imagery tracks a swath down the center line of the wide angle coverage and can be matched by corresponding time codes.

photographs with an 80% overlap along a second higher altitude flight line at 4,000 feet. The images were taken with a 70mm Hasselblad MWX photogrammetric camera. Detailed 3D terrain models were then generated from successive pairs of images. An Intergraph SSK workstation was used to build the stereo model and the UMass Terrain Reconstruction System (Terrest) was used for image matching and differential rectification. The excessive overlap was necessary to maintain radiometric consistency between frames.

Techniques were tested by processing a preliminary data set collected in September 1998 over a mixed hardwood/conifer forest area at an AEP test site in Crooksville, Ohio. Thirty-one plot sites were established along two transects and a per hectare biomass estimated for each. Half of the plot measurement sets are presently being used to calibrate the resulting video strips and 3D terrain models. These results will then be tested against the remaining sites to determine the relative success of each approach. A more extensive test over much larger area is planned in Bolivia this spring, to be conducted in the Noel Kempff Mercado National Park expansion zone in Bolivia. That survey should provide more accurate estimates of biomass at a considerably lower cost.

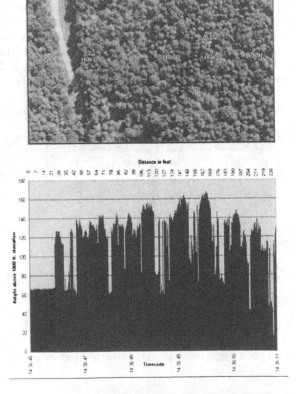

Fig. 2. An example of a laser altimeter profile registered to an aerial image.

3 Three-Dimensional Terrain Modeling Using Terrest

The ability to generate accurate, high-resolution digital elevation maps (DEM) is essential to our environmental monitoring strategy. On a low-resolution scale (5-30m) DEMs provide important topographic information, such as elevation, slope and drainage patterns. On a finer scale (1 m or less) DEMs can be used to count individual trees, and/or determine 3D textural qualities of the surface.

The UMass Terrest system was designed to automatically generate high-resolution 3D terrain models from aerial images when the viewing angles become oblique (incidence angles greater than 45 degrees), and/or when the camera separation becomes large (base-to-height ratio exceeds 1.5). The system incorporated several specific features that increase the accuracy, robustness, and utility of the system [7], [8]. Figure 3 shows an example of a terrain model generated from a pair of images.

Figure 4 shows a 768 × 768 pixel section of the DEM (generated from the green bands of two RGB images) and corresponding ortho-image taken from the center of the scene shown in Figure 3. To test the reliability of detecting trees in the 3D terrain model, two groups of four interpreters evaluated the DEM and ortho-image. The first group marked bumps in the DEM and looks for corresponding evidence of a tree in the ortho-image, while the second group identified trees in the ortho-image and looked for corresponding bumps in the DEM. Both groups found a reliability of at least 95%.

The Terrest system has recently been enhances to fuse information from multiple overlapping views (typically 3-6) [9]. When more than two images are available the system first produces separate DEMs from each ordered image pair. The system then fuses the individual DEMs using a robust method to produce an optimal terrain model consisting of a DEM, a geospatial uncertainty map, an ortho-image, and a set of 3D texture maps (see Terrain Classification below).

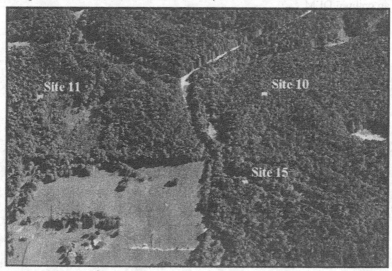

Fig. 3. A rendered view of the ortho-image draped over the DEM.

The technique relies on two key factors for generating robust 3D terrain models, (1) the ability to detect unreliable elevations estimates, and (2) the ability to fuse the reliable elevations into a single optimal terrain model. The technique is based on the concept of using self-consistency measures, first introduced by Leclerc et al., [4], [5] to identify unreliable points in a distribution. The focus of their work was to obtain a quality measure for point correspondences. Their algorithm obtained a probability distribution by counting the number of corresponding image points for each object point that is consistent with the viewing geometry within a specified error limit. We extended the self-consistency concept to the problem of detecting unreliable elements in a DEM, generated from stereoscopic image pairs.

The geospatial uncertainty, occluded surface patches, and false matches are inferred by analyzing asymmetries in the elevation and confidence level estimates produced by reversing the roles of the left and right images during the image matching phase. If Z_{AB} is the DEM generated with image A as the left and B as the right, and Z_{BA} is the DEM generated by reversing the roles of A and B, then anomalies in $Z_{AB} - Z_{BA}$ can be used to categorize DEM errors. Unreliable elevation estimates, characterized by large values in $Z_{AB} - Z_{BA}$, may result from surface discontinuities, non-Lambertian surface patches, such as water, and occlusions. For regions where Z_{AB} and Z_{BA} agree within a predetermined range, the geospatial uncertainty can be inferred directly from the variance of $(Z_{AB} - Z_{BA})$. Consequently, an elevation estimate is said to be self-consistent when $Z_{AB} - Z_{BA}$ is below a threshold. The self-consistency threshold is set as low-as possible to assure that all elevations arising from false image matches are rejected.

Figure 5 shows the results of a multi-image fusion. The processing started with 4 images, which resulted in 12 elevation estimates per pixel in the output grid. We then applied the self-consistency methodology and labeled each elevation estimate as reliable or unreliable. We then averaged all of the reliable estimates are each pixel to form an optimal DEM.

DEM   Ortho-image

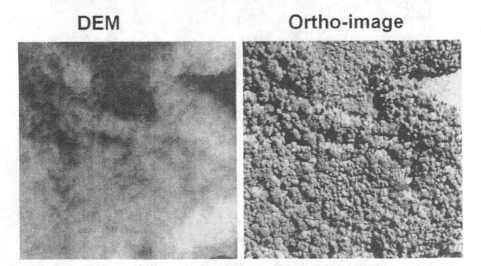

Fig. 4. The DEM and orhto-images used to test the reliability of detecting trees.

Rendered View | No. of consistent points

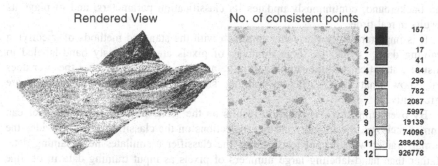

0	157
1	0
2	17
3	41
4	84
5	296
6	782
7	2087
8	5997
9	19139
10	74096
11	288430
12	926778

Fig. 5. A rendered view of the final 3D terrain model (left) and the number of self-consistent estimates used to compute each elevation.

4   3D World Texture Measures

We have recently shown that classification performance can be significantly improved by adding to the usual 2D image texture measures [3] a set of new 3D texture measures [13]. Our concept is that 3D textures are a function of recurring patterns caused by physical coarseness, roughness, and other characteristics of 3D surface structure, and that certain intermediate results generated during the process of generating a 3D terrain model are related to the 3D textures. We derived four 3D texture measures and used them in the ground cover classification problem. We found that 3D textures significantly improved the performance of a standard classification system. The experiments in [13] showed that including 3D texture features improved classification skill from 72.5% to 83.4%. We believe the implications of these findings for terrain feature extraction are far reaching.

The 3D texture features are derived during the image matching phase in the 3D reconstruction process. During image matching left-right pixel correspondences are determined to a fraction of a pixel width. As a result, the statistical properties of the pixel correspondences are sensitive to the microstructure of the surface (3D structure at length scales approximately equal to the ground sampling distance). The four 3D texture features are: (i) The confidence level assigned to each correspondence; (ii) the variability of confidence levels within a 17×17 window surrounding each correspondence; (iii) the deceleration length for each correspondence; and (iv) the variability of deceleration length within a 17×17 window surrounding each correspondence.

5   Terrain Classification Using ITL

Our classification system is based on the Interactive Teacher-Learner (ITL) paradigm [6], which employs a feedback mechanism between the operator (the Teacher) and a state-of-the-art real-time decision tree classifier (the Learner). The user receives feedback by interactively specifying training instances (using semi-automated graphical tools) and then seeing the effect that his/her actions had on the classifier.

An efficient state-of-the-art decision tree classification algorithm, which is running in the background, continuously updates its classification parameters, and displays its results in real-time.

It is important to contrast this approach with the standard methods of specifying training data. Typically, large numbers of pixels are laboriously hand-labeled to ensure a statistically valid sample. A large amount is selected because the user does not know what is a sufficient training size and which training instances are informative.

By overlaying the classification results on the scene in false color, the user can immediately see the impact that their selections on the classifier. This provides the human trainer with instant feedback as the classifier assimilates new training data. Rather than hand-labeling large numbers of pixels as input training data in off-line process, an operator trains the classifier by giving much more informed incremental training instances, e.g., correcting mistakes or defining new subclasses that are necessary for discrimination in the particular context. In this way natural user interaction leads to the judicious selection of a small amount of very important data in the training process.

Figure 6 shows a comparison between a scene classified using the ITL system and conventional batch processing, in which all the training data were selected in advance. The results of the comparison are shown in Table 1. The test was run using 17 features (12 standard 2D co-occurrence features, 4 3D texture features and the ortho-image). The percent correct were similar except that three orders of magnitude less training data were required with the ITL system.

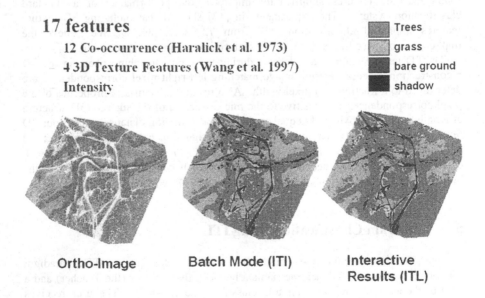

17 features
12 Co-occurrence (Haralick et al. 1973)
4 3D Texture Features (Wang et al. 1997)
Intensity

- Trees
- grass
- bare ground
- shadow

Ortho-Image   Batch Mode (ITI)   Interactive Results (ITL)

Fig 6. Comparison between ITL and batch mode processing.

	ITL	Batch
Mouse Clicks	30	
Training Examples	270	16916
% Correct	85.1	86.4
Tree Nodes	25	71

Table 1. ITL vs. batch processing evaluation.

To make the feedback mechanism between the teacher (user) and learner (computer) practical, the ITL system requires a classification system that efficiently updates as the users selects new training instances. The Incremental Tree Inducer (ITI) decision tree developed at UMass [11], [12] was selected for this purpose. In addition to being one of the most accurate implementation of a decision tree, ITI is capable of updating an existing decision tree without rebuilding the tree structure. Thus, when the operator selects new training instances, ITI updates the existing tree instead of rebuilding the decision tree. In addition, ITI uses only those features that contribute to the decision making process. As a result, there is no need to guarantee in advance that any particular feature will be useful because the decision tree methodology will only select those features that improve the discrimination between the user-defined training classes. Thus, there is no need to validate a priori the utility of features.

6   Conclusions

Although this work is in a preliminary phase and all of the constituent technologies have not been fully integrated, we have nevertheless demonstrated the value and feasibility of using state-of-the-art computer vision techniques (Terrest and ITL) to solve environmental monitoring problems on a large scale. In the near future we plan to integrate terrain modeling and classification so that some skilled in Forestry but not necessarily photogrammetry or computer science will be able efficiently extract reliable environmental information from video and aerial photography.

References

[1]   Brown, S., and A.J.R. Lugo: Biomass of tropical forests: a new stimate based on forest volumes. Science 223:1290-1293, 1984.

[2]   Brown, S., A.J.R. Gillespie, and A.E. Lugo: Biomass of tropical forests of south and southeast Asia. Canadian Journal of Forest Research 21:111-117. Crow T.R. 1978. Common regressions to estimate tree biomass in tropical stands. Forest Science 24:110-114, 1991.

[3]   Haralick, R., K. Shanmugam, and I. Dinstein: Textural Features for Image Classication," IEEE Trans.on Systems, Man, and Cybernetics, Vol. 3, No. 6, pp. 610-621, 1973.

[4]   Leclerc, Y.G., Q.T. Luong, and P. Fua: A Framework for Detecting Changes in Terrain, *IEEE Trans. Pattern Analysis and Machine Intelligence,* vol. 20, no. 11, pp. 1143-1160, November 1998.

[5]   Leclerc, Y,G., Q.T. Luong, et al.: Self-consistency: A novel approach to characterizing the accuracy and reliability of point correspondence algorithms, *DARPA Image Understanding Workshop,* Monterey, CA, 1998.

[6]   Piater, Justus H., Edward M. Riseman and Paul E. Utgoff: Interactively Training Pixel Classifiers. International Journal of Pattern Recognition and Artificial Intelligence 13(2), pp. 171-194, 1999.

[7]   Schultz, H.: Terrain Reconstruction from Oblique Views, Proc. DARPA Image Understanding Workshop, Monterey, CA, pp. 1001-1008, November 1994.

[8]   Schultz, H.: Terrain Reconstruction from Widely Separated Images, Proc. SPIE, Volume 2486, pp. 113-123, Orlando, FL, April 1995.

[9]   Schultz, H., Riseman, E., Stolle, F.: Error Detection and DEM Fusion Using Self-Consistency, Submitted to the 7th IEEE International Conference on Computer Vision, Kerkyra, Greece, September 1999.

[10] Slaymaker, D.M., K.M.L. Jones, C.R. Griffin and J.T. Finn: Mapping deciduous forests in Southern New England using aerial videography and hyperclustered multi-temporal Landsat TM imagery. Pages 87-101 in Gap Analysis: A Landscape Approach to Biodiversity Planning, J.M. Scott, T.H. Tear and F.W. Davis (eds). American Society of Photogrammetry and Remote Sensing, Bethesda, MD, USA, 1996.

[11] Utgoff, P. E.: An improved algorithm for incremental induction of decision trees, In Machine Learning: Proc. 11th Int. Conf, pp. 318-325, Morgan Kaufmann, 1994.

[12] Utgoff, P.E., N. C. Berkman, and J.A. Clouse: Decision tree induction based on efficient tree restructuring", Machine Learning 29(1), 5-44, 1997

[13] Wang, X., F. Stolle, H. Schultz, E. M. Riseman, and A. R. Hanson: Using three-dimensional features to improve terrain classification", In   Proc. Computer Vision and Pattern Recognition, pp. 915-920, 1997.

Spatial Pictogram Enhanced Conceptual Data Models and Their Translation to Logical Data Models

Shashi Shekhar[1], Ranga Raju Vatsavai[1,2], Sanjay Chawla[1], and Thomas E. Burk[2]

[1] Computer Science Department, University of Minnesota
EE/CS 4-192, 200 Union St. SE., Minneapolis, MN 55455
[shekhar|vatsavai|chawla]@cs.umn.edu
http://www.cs.umn.edu/research/shashi-group/
[2] Department of Forest Resources, University of Minnesota
115 Green Hall, St. Paul, MN 55108
tburk@forestry.umn.edu
http://terrasip.gis.umn.edu/

Abstract. The successful development of any geographic information system project needs the careful design and implementation of spatial databases via conceptual and logical data-modeling. This involves understanding the underlying spatial data model, spatial data types and operators, spatial query languages and spatial indexing techniques. Conventional entity-relationship diagrams have limitations for conceptual spatial data-modeling, since they get cluttered with numerous spatial relationships. In addition the logical data model gets cluttered with redundant tables representing materialization of the M:N spatial relationships. In this paper we present an extension to ER diagrams using pictograms for entities and as well as relationships. This approach effectively reduces the cluttering, as spatial relationships will become implicit. We have provided a complete grammar using "yacc" like syntax to translate the pictogram-extended ER diagram into a SQL3-level logical data model using OGIS-standard spatial data types.
Keywords: Spatial Databases, Pictograms, SQL3, OGIS, Entity-Relationship Diagrams, UML, Syntax Directed Translation.

1 Introduction

1.1 Spatial Databases

Spatial database [13], [20], [23], [24], management systems aim at the effective and efficient management of geographic data, which consists of images, points, lines, polygons, their topological relationships, and attribute data. In recent years, spatial databases have been applied to diverse application domains including forestry, agriculture, urban planning, geology, mining, water resource allocation, transportation, tourism, land use management, etc. With advancements in other areas like remote sensing, photogrammetry, GPS, etc., the data in

P. Agouris and A. Stefanidis (Eds.): ISD'99, LNCS 1737, pp. 77–104, 1999.

spatial databases is becoming diverse and there is a "growing need for conceptual data modeling".

A conceptual data model is a type of data abstraction that hides the details of data storage [21]. It uses logical concepts, which may be easier for most users to understand. Conceptual data modeling is usually carried out using graphical or visual tools. Users find that visual data-modeling approaches help them to understand and describe the contents of the database in an intuitive way. From the system perspective, visual approaches help to improve the processes of programming and system maintenance. Visual modeling tools allow users to model the data and their relationships in an intuitive way. Modeling is the key to the successful implementation of any project, and this is especially true for spatial data management projects, e.g. Geographical Information Systems(GIS).

Models of spatial information are usually grouped into two broad categories [7], *Field* and *Object* . We illustrate this dichotomy with the help of an example(see Figure 1). Imagine an idealized forest consisting of clusters of tree species. One area of the forest is populated by "Fir," another by "Oak," and yet another by "Pine". What is the best way of modeling the Forest and capturing its aggregate nature? Consider a function f which maps the underlying geographic space of the forest onto a set consisting of three values: {Fir, Oak, Pine }. Then f is a *field* whose varying spatial distribution captures the diversity of the Forest. The function f itself is like a "step" function: constant over the area where the trees are alike, and sharply jumping into a different value where the tree species changes. Now consider the places where function f changes values. In an idealized forest situation where the demarcation between the tree species is clearly defined, we should get the boundaries of polygons. Each polygon can be assigned a unique identifier and can be considered as a spatial entity having at least one non-spatial attribute associated with it, specifically the name of the tree species. So now we can conceptualize the Forest as a collection of polygons, each one corresponding to a different tree species. This is the *object* viewpoint. While the Forest example was amenable to both field and object models, there are situations where one choice is more popular. For instance, if we want to model the elevation of the earth's surface, then one often adopt the field model, while the object view seems more appropriate if one wants to track land-parcels for legal owner-ships and taxation purposes [7].

The most important problems in modeling spatial databases concern the geometry of the spatial objects, the geometric relationships between the objects, their representation at multi-resolutions, their geometric evolution over time, and their spatial integrity constraints.

1.2   Database Design and Entity-Relationship Model

Database Design: Database applications are modeled using a three-step design process [11]. In the first step, all of the available information related to the application is organized using a high level **conceptual data model**. At the conceptual level, the focus is on the datatypes of the application, their relationships and their constraints. The actual implementation details are left out

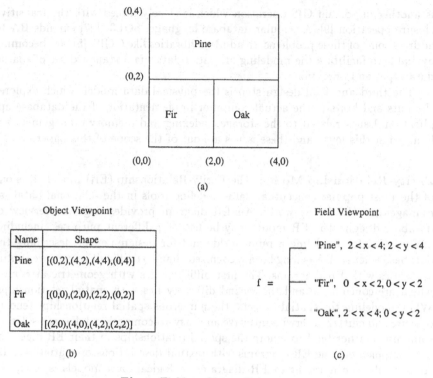

Fig. 1. Field vs Object dichotomy

at this step of the design process. Plain text combined with simple but consistent graphic notation is often used to express the conceptual data model. The Entity-Relationship(ER) model is one of the most prevalent of all conceptual design tools.

The second step, also called the logical data-modeling phase, is related to the actual implementation of the conceptual data model in a commercial DBMS. The data in a commercial database is organized using an implementation model. Examples of implementation models are **Hierarchical**, **Network** and **Relational**. The **Relational** model is the most widely implemented model in current commercial databases. In the Relational model, the datatypes, relationships and constraints are all modeled as **Relations**. Tightly coupled with the Relational model is the formal query language Relational Algebra(RA). RA consists of simple operations which allow access to the data that is organized in relations. The relational algebra is provably inadequate to express many important GIS operations. For example, the transitive closure operation cannot be expressed in relational algebra without making additional assumptions about the structure of the relation. The transitive closure operation is required to express recursive queries like "identify all fresh water sources (rivers) that can potentially be affected by a pollutant discharged into the ground water". Reclassification is another important GIS operation which is closely linked with the transitive closure operation [9]. A popular database language, SQL3 [27] extends RA to address some of these problems. In addition libraries like OGIS [5], are becoming available to facilitate the modeling of spatial data via a standard set of spatial data types and operations.

The third and final design step is the physical data model, which explores the nuts and bolts of the actual computer implementation of the database application. Issues related to the storage, indexing and memory management are handled at this level, and these issues are out of the scope of this paper.

Entity-Relationship Model: The Entity-Relationship (ER) model [4] is one of the most popular conceptual data-modeling tools in the relational database management (RDBMS) world. An ER diagram provides a good overview of database design. The ER model may be used for different purposes, including analysis–i.e, for modeling a mini-world– and for design–i.e, for describing the database schema. It has long been recognized that it is difficult to capture spatial semantics with ER diagrams. The first difficulty lies with geometric attributes which are continuous, and the second difficulty lies with spatial relationships. When modeling the spatial aspects, the numerous spatial relationships tend to obscure and clutter otherwise intuitive and easy-to-comprehend diagrams. Hence some users either tend to ignore the spatial relationships in their ER diagrams or to supplement the ER diagrams with textual descriptions of spatial aspects. As a result, the mapping of ER diagrams to logical data models is often not direct, and users have to perform manual edits.

1.3   Related Work and Our Contribution

Several researchers have proposed extensions [16], [25] to the existing modeling languages to support spatial data-modeling. The GERM model [26] provides a set of concepts as an add-on to the ER model for modeling GIS. Recently [1] proposed a Plug-in for Visual Languages and implemented a CASE tool, Perceptory, which supports spatial data-modeling. Perceptory is an extension of UML using the UML's stereotype construct. The stereo types are presented as pictograms to model the spatial data types. The pictograms can be inserted into the object-class boxes using simple graphical user interface provided by the Perceptory.

Whether using the ER or the OO approach, we must translate the design into tables in a RDBMS language, e.g. SQL3. Conventional databases do not support constructs for spatial data types. The present DBMS with object extensions made it possible to develop various GIS-related products on top of the extensions, for example ESRI's Spatial Database Engine [12], Paradise [10]. This approach has several advantages, the major one being that the GIS developer can take advantage of the functionality provided by these object relational databases and can build complex geographic analysis functions. Users also find that this approach allows them to more readily use their existing DBMS skills. There has been very little work done towards translating pictogram enhanced ER model to a RDBMS language.

In this paper, we present an approach to extending the ER diagrams with pictograms to facilitate the conceptual design of spatial databases in an intuitive and correct way. There are two novel aspects of pictograms in our work. First, we introduce relationship pictograms where as prior literature focuses on entity pictograms. Second, we provide a recursive grammar for pictograms to provide a formal syntax and facilitate automatic translation to OGIS spatial data types. The main contribution of this paper is a set of syntax-directed translation rules for converting a pictogram extended ER diagram into a logical data model. This translation will result in data definition language (DDL) constructs of SQL3. We show rules to generate spatial columns and datatypes from entity pictogram. We also provide rules to generate spatial integrity constraints from relationship pictograms. The translation procedure shows another major benefit of pictograms towards eliminating redundant tables, in logical data model for various many-to-many spatial relationships in the conceptual data model.

1.4 Scope and Outline

The role of the spatial database component is dependent on the type of database management system (DBMS) involved: relational, object-oriented or object-relational. Object-relational databases are increasingly becoming the choice for spatial database implementation, as they provide extension capabilities to the traditional databases. As a result, geometric data types can be efficiently implemented in ORDBMS. Here we focus on three aspects, namely conceptual data-modeling using pictogram extended ER diagrams, logical data-modeling by providing SQL3 DDL constructs, and the translation of pictogram-extended ER diagrams into logical data models using our grammar. The extension of ER diagrams with pictograms and rules to translate them into SQL3 constructs will help users design and implement spatial databases.

The remainder of this paper is organized into 5 sections. In section 2, we discuss the about conceptual data-modeling and the limitations of the ER model: we introduce the pictogram concept with its grammar and its use in conceptual data-modeling via ER diagrams. In section 3, we discuss logical data-modeling and OGIS and SQL3 support for spatial data types, and in section 4, we provide translation rules to map the pictogram extended ER diagram onto the logical data model. Finally, in section 5 we summarize the results.

2 Conceptual Data Modeling Using Spatial Pictogram Extension

2.1 The Entity-Relationship(ER) Model and Its Limitation

The ER model is one of the most popular high level conceptual data models. This model is graphical in nature, with boxes and arrows representing essential

data elements and their connections. The ER model integrates seamlessly with
the *Relational* data model, which in turn is one of the most prevalent logical
data model, the second step in the three-step design paradigm. The ER diagrams
have three principal components – entity sets, attributes and relationships. In
the ER model, the "miniworld" is partitioned into entities, which are characterized by attributes and interrelated via relationships. Entities are 'things' or 'objects' which have an independent physical or conceptual existence. Entities are
characterized by attributes. An attribute, or a set of attributes which uniquely
identifies instances of an entity, is called the key. Entities interact or connect
with each other through relationships. There are three kinds of relationships:
one-one – where each instance of one entity can only relate to one instance of
the other participating entity; many-one – potentially connects many instances of
one entity with one instance of the other entity participating in the relationship;
many-many – many instances of one entity can be related to many instances of
the other entity participating in the relationship.

We introduce an example, State-Park, which will be used throughout this
paper to illustrate the different concepts in spatial data-modeling. A State-Park
consists of **Forests**, which are a collection of **Forest-Stands** which correspond
to different species of trees. The State-Park is accessed by **Roads** and it has a
Manager. There are **Fire-Stations** which are directly responsible for monitoring fires in the State-Park. The state-park is dotted with **Facilities** like camping
groups and offices. Finally, there are **Rivers** which supply water to the different
facilities. The state-park database contains many spatial layers and images and
much attribute data. The layers considered in this example are forest, forest-
stand, road, river, facility, fire-station and fire-image. These layers will translate
into entities in the ER diagram. The properties of the entities will translate
into attributes; for example the river entity has attributes including its name,
length and geometry. The attributes of these layers are easily captured in the
ER diagram, as shown in the state-park example (see Figure 2). Note that the
conventional ER approach does not distinguish between spatial and non-spatial
attributes, and as a result geometry will be modeled as an attribute. Similarly,
the inherent spatial relationships associated with the spatial data need to be
explicitly modeled in the conventional ER approach. These limitations are summarized below.

Limitations of the ER Model: As the above discussion shows, the ER is
unable, at least intuitively, to capture some important semantics inherent in
spatial modeling. The ER model was originally designed with the implicit assumption of an object-based model. Therefore, a field model cannot be naturally
mapped using the ER model. For example, there is no notion of key attributes
and unique OID's in a field model. Although in traditional ER, the relationships
between entities are derived from the application under consideration, in spatial
modeling there are always inherent relationships between spatial objects. For
example, all of the topological relationships discussed above are valid instances
of relationships between two spatial entities. Then the question is, how can these

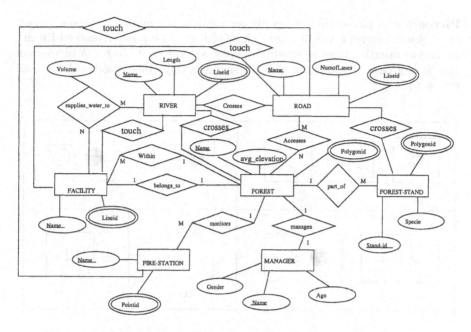

Fig. 2. An ER diagram for the State-Park example.

be incorporated into the ER model without cluttering the diagram? The type of entity used to model a spatial object depends on the scale of the "map". A city can be mapped as a point or a polygon, depending on the resolution of the map. The problem is, how should multiple representations of the same object be represented in a conceptual data model?

2.2   Pictograms for Spatial Conceptual Data-Modeling

Many extensions have been proposed to extend ER to make the conceptual modeling of spatial applications easier and more intuitive. The idea is to provide more constructs which capture the semantics of spatial applications and at the same time to keep the graphical representation simple. In this section we define pictograms with grammar and their use in conceptual data-modeling using the ER diagrams. The pictograms introduced in this section are not limited to extending ER diagrams, but they can also be used with the object-oriented modeling languages like UML [3], an emerging standard for data-modeling.

In rest of this section we show how pictograms can be used to capture concepts related to spatial geometry, spatial relationships and multiple spatial representations. We define the pictograms for both entities and the spatial relationships. The grammar is presented in graphical form. The grammar is similar to that of "yacc" [18] and the syntax is explained in the next section, along with translation rules.

Pictogram: A pictogram is generally represented as a miniature version (icon) of an object inserted inside of a box. These pictograms are used to extend ER diagrams by inserting them at appropriate places in the entity boxes. A pictogram can be of a basic shape, a user-defined shape, or any other possible shape (see fig. 4-A).

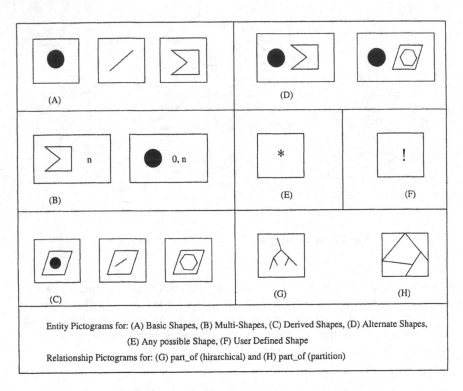

Entity Pictograms for: (A) Basic Shapes, (B) Multi-Shapes, (C) Derived Shapes, (D) Alternate Shapes, (E) Any possible Shape, (F) User Defined Shape

Relationship Pictograms for: (G) part_of (hirarchical) and (H) part_of (partition)

Fig. 3. Spatial pictogram examples

Shape: Shape is the basic graphical element of a pictogram, which represents the geometric types in the spatial data model. It can be a basic shape, a multi-shape, a derived shape, or an alternate shape. Most objects have simple(basic) shapes (see fig. 4-B).

Basic Shape: In a vector model the basic elements are point, line and polygon. In a forestry example, the user may want to represent a facility as a point (0-D), a river or road network as lines (1-D) and forest areas as polygons (2-D) (see fig. 4-D and 3-A).

Multi-Shape: To deal with objects which cannot be represented by the basic shapes, we have defined a set of aggregate shapes. Cardinality is used to quantify multi-shapes. For example, a river network is represented as "a line pictogram with its cardinality n". Similarly, features that cannot be depicted at a certain scale will have cardinality 0 (see fig. 3-B and 4-E).

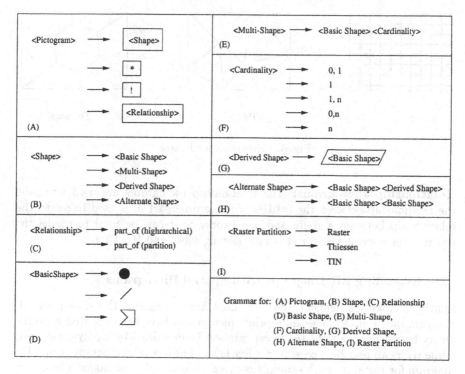

Fig. 4. Grammar for pictograms

Derived Shape: If the shape of an object is derived from the shapes of other objects, its pictogram is italicized. For example, we can derive a forest boundary (polygon) from its "forest type" boundaries (polygon), or a country boundary from the constituent state boundaries (see fig. 3-C and 4-G).

Alternate Shape: Alternate shapes can be used for the same object depending on certain conditions; for example, objects of size less than x units are represented as points while those greater than x units are represented as polygons. Alternate shapes are represented as a concatenation of possible pictograms. Similarly, multiple shapes are needed to represent objects at different scales; for example, at higher scales lakes may be represented as points, and at lower scales as polygons (see fig. 3-D and 4-H).

Any Possible Shape: A combination of shapes is represented by a wild card * symbol inside a box, implying that any geometry is possible (see fig. 3-E).

User-Defined Shape: Apart from the basic shapes of point, line and polygon, user-defined shapes are possible. User-defined shapes are represented by an exclamation symbol (!) inside a box (see fig. 3-F).

Raster Shape: The other basic spatial data type is the raster. Rasters represent a geographic image by a grid, where each cell of the grid contains information of a particular type. Examples are remote sensing images, digital elevation models, etc. (see fig. 5).

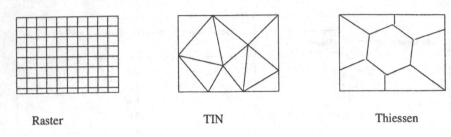

Raster   TIN   Thiessen

Fig. 5. Pictograms for Raster

Relationship Pictograms: The relationship pictograms are used to model the relationship between the entities. For example part_of is used to model the relationship between a route and a network, or it can be used to model the partition of a forest into forest stands (see fig. 3-G and H, 4-C).

2.3 Extending ER Diagrams with Spatial Pictograms

Spatial pictograms defined above are used here to extend the state-park ER diagram shown in 2). The appropriate pictograms have been inserted in to the entity boxes. For example, the forest can best be described by a polygonal layer, while river can best be represented a line layer. The spatial pictogram extend ER diagram for the state park example is given in figure 6. The major advantages of this approach are that, geometry is no more modeled as an attribute and relationships become implicit. The entity pictograms inserted into the entity boxes will be translated into spatial data types and spatial relationships will be translated into spatial integrity constraints. This translation process is defined in section 4.

3   Logical Data Model

In this section we describe OGIS model [5] for spatial data types along with SQL3 [27] for implementation of logical data model in a commercial database management system.

3.1   OGIS-Standard

As observed in the previous section, the spatial data is complex and the operations are different when compared to that of commercial databases. Recently the Open GIS Consortium [5] has standardized spatial feature geometry and spatial operations.

The OGIS specification defines a standard for *SQL* which supports the *storage* and query of spatial data. The spatial data that the specification supports is based on the *OGIS Geometry Object Model* and is shown in Figure 7. The non-instantiable class *Geometry* serves as the base class with subclasses for *Point,*

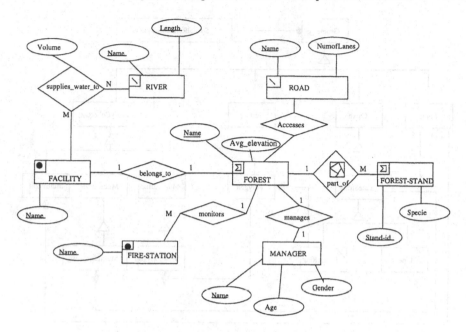

Fig. 6. ER diagram for **State-Park** with Pictograms

Curve(line) and *Surface(Polygon)*. There is also a parallel class of *Geometry Collection* which is designed to handle geometries corresponding to a collection of points, lines and polygons.

Conceptually, spatial entities are stored as tables with geometry valued columns. Instances of the entities are stored as rows in a table. Data types of spatial attributes are drawn from the *Geometry Model* while those of non-spatial attributes are from the standard SQL92 set. Implementation of a *Spatially-enabled* table called the feature table, are described for two target environments: *SQL92* and *SQL92 with Geometry Types*.

In the SQL92 environment, a geometry-valued column is implemented as a Foreign Key reference into a geometry table. A geometric value is stored using one or more rows in the geometry table. The geometry table may be implemented using either standard SQL numeric types or SQL binary types.

In the other implementation, *SQL92 with Geometry Types*, a geometry-valued column is implemented as a column whose SQL type is drawn from the set of Geometry Types. The standard SQL3 mechanism for extending the type system of an SQL database is through the definition of user-defined Abstract Data Types.

The SQL functions(methods) specified by the OGIS specification fall into three categories: 1) Basic functions on the Geometry data types, 2) Operators for testing topological relationships and 3) Functions that support spatial analysis. These functions are summarized in Table 1.

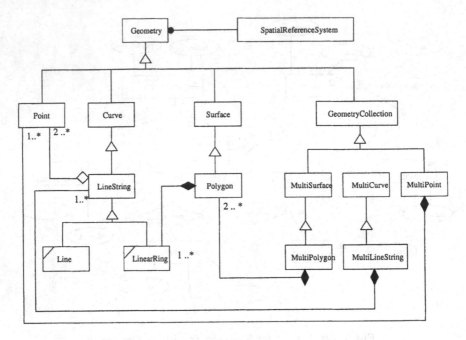

Fig. 7. OGIS Spatial Data Model [5] using UML notation

The OGIS-standard specifies the data types and the operations on these data types that are essential for spatial applications like GIS. For example, for the **Point** data type, an important operation is **distance**, which computes the distance between two points. The **length** operation is not a semantically correct operation on a **point** data type. This is similar to the argument that the **concatenation** operation makes more sense for a **character** data type than for, say, an **integer** type.

Though in a RDBMS the set of data types is fixed, in object-relational and object-oriented databases there is built in flexibility to expand the set of potential data types. While this flexibility is clearly an advantage, especially when dealing with non-traditional applications like GIS, the burden of constructing syntactically and semantically correct data types is now on the database-application developer. To share some of the burden, commercial database companies have introduced the notion of providing application-specific "packages" which provide a seamless interface to the database user. For example, Oracle has a *Spatial Data Cartridge* package [6] for GIS-related applications.

SQL3, the yet-to-be-approved draft for object-relational DBMS allows the user to define new data types within the overall framework of a relational database. We will not define the whole SQL3 standard but highlight two major extensions which will help understand what follows.

Basic Functions	SpatialReference()	Returns the Reference System of the geometry
	Envelope()	The minimum bounding rectangle of the geometry
	Export()	Convert the geometry into a different representation.
	IsEmpty()	Tests if the geometry is a empty set or not.
	IsSimple()	Returns True if the geometry is simple(no self-intersection)
	Boundary()	Returns the boundary of the geometry
Topological/ Set Operators	Equal	Tests if the geometries are spatially equal
	Disjoint	Tests if neither interiors nor boundaries intersect.
	Intersect	Tests if the geometries intersect
	Touch	Tests if the boundaries intersects and interior doesnot.
	Cross	Tests if the geometries cross each other.
	Within	Tests if the given geomtry is within another given geometry
	Contains	Tests if the given geometry contains another given geometry
	Overlap	Tests if the interiors intersect.
Spatial Analysis	Distance	Returns the shortest distance between two geometries
	Buffer	Returns a geometry that represents all points whose distance from the given is less than or equal to the specified distance
	ConvexHull	Returns the convex hull of the geometry
	Intersection	Returns the intersection of two geometries
	Union	Returns the union of two geometries
	Difference	Returns the difference of two geometries
	SymDiff	Returns the symmetric difference of two geometries

Table 1. Representative functions specified by OGIS

3.2   Creating User-Defined Data Types in SQL3

Abstract Data Type(ADT): A data type which can be defined using a CREATE TYPE statement. Like Classes in object-oriented technology, an ADT consists of attributes and member functions to access the values of the attributes. Member functions can potentially modify the value of the attributes in the data type and thus can also change the database state. An ADT can appear as a column type in a relational schema. To access the value that the ADT encapsulates, a member function specified in the CREATE TYPE must be used. For example, the following script creates a Point type, with the Distance as member function:

```
CREATE TYPE Point  (
     x         NUMBER
     y         NUMBER
     FUNCTION Distance(: u Point, : v Point) RETURNS NUMBER
  );
```

The colon before u and v signifies that these are local variables.

Row Type: Row types can be used to define a type of tuple. A row type specifies the schema of a relation. For example, the following statement creates a row type Point.

```
CREATE ROW TYPE PointType   (
        x          NUMBER
        y          NUMBER
);
```

We can now create a table which instantiates the row type. For example:

```
CREATE TABLE Pointtable of TYPE PointType.
```

SQL3 examples for line and polygon features:

```
CREATE TYPE LineType AS OBJECT   (
        startPnt   PointType;
        endPnt     PointType;
);

CREATE TYPE Points AS VARARRAY() OF PointType;


CREATE TYPE PolygonType AS OBJECT   (
        BoundaryPoints     Points;
);
```

This section illustrated the type-definition facility of SQL3. The example data types of PointType, LineType and PolygonType are to illustrate the SQL3 syntax and by no means capture the corresponding spatial data types in OGIS. It is assumed that a library of SQL3 data types implementing OGIS spatial data types will be available in the rest of this paper. Several vendors are working on providing this functionality.

4   Translation Rules

This section describes translation rules to map the pictogram extended entity-relationship diagrams onto a logical data model.

4.1   Syntax Directed Translation

We have used "yacc" [18] like syntax to describe the grammar and the translation rules. Words in angular brackets, e.g. ⟨pictogram⟩ denote non-terminating elements of the language. For example, the ⟨pictogram⟩ will be either translated into ⟨shape⟩ OR * OR ! inside a box. The general convention of representing OR in grammar is with a vertical bar (|), but for readability we have used an arrow (→) with each element participating in the OR condition. Now the ⟨shape⟩

will translate into ⟨*basicshape*⟩ OR ⟨*multi − shape*⟩ OR ⟨*derivedshape*⟩ OR ⟨*alternateshape*⟩. These translations continue till we reach a terminating element; for example, ⟨*basicshape*⟩ will finally be translated into either point, line or polygon shapes.

In translating a pictogram-extended ER diagram, we have used the same syntax rules. The strings in double quotes, e.g. "PointType" are literal constants and will not be translated further. The strings which are not in double quotes, e.g. BasicShape.dataType, on the right-hand side of the equality expression will be further translated till they reach literal constant elements, for example "Point-Type" or "LineType" etc. As defined earlier, a pictogram is either a specific shape OR any possible shape (*) OR a user-defined shape (!). So a pictogram data type is either a shape data type OR a user-defined data type OR a geometry data type. In the case of a user-defined data type, the translation will result in a terminating data type defined by the user. A non-terminating data type like a shape data type will get further translated, as described above, into terminating data types like "LineType" OR "PolygonType".

Cardinality quantifies the number of objects, so it indicates the presence or absence of the objects. So the cardinality will result in integrity constraints (IC). A 0,1 OR 0,n will mean that we have either 0 or many objects, allowing the absence of the object, which will translate into "NULL" allowed. A cardinality of 1 OR n OR 1, n will mean that we have at least one object, so the integrity constraint will become "NOT NULL". If no cardinality is specified with the pictogram, it is assumed to be as 1, so the default IC is "NOT NULL". The grammar and translation rules are summarized in the figure 8.

4.2 Translating Entity Pictograms to Data Types

Entity pictograms inserted inside the entity boxes will be translated into appropriate data types in SQL3. These data types are Point, Line and Polygon, and then can be created by the user as described in section 3. This translation will be done automatically by the translator using the syntax-directed translation. This translation is given here for the alternate shape pictogram.

Example
The alternate shape pictogram is used to show the condition or scale-based representation of spatial data. For example, at higher scales lakes may be represented as points and at lower scales as polygons. This can be modeled with the spatial pictogram shown in figure 9.

In the ER diagram this pictogram will be inserted into the lakes entity box. When the ER diagram is mapped onto the logical data model, the spatial pictogram inside the river entity box is translated into spatial data types using the grammar and translation rules. The derivation of alternate shape pictogram is shown in the figure 10.

The execution trace of a translation of the alternate pictogram into an SQL3 data type is shown below.

```
BasicShape1.dataType    = Point.                        {Rule No = 8}
BasicShape2.dataType    = Polygon.                      {Rule No = 10}
AlternateShape.dataType = union(Point, Polygon).       {Rule No = 16}
Shape.dataType          = AlternateShape.dataType.     {Rule No = 7}
                        = union(Point, Polygon).       {Rule No = 16}
Pictogram.dataType      = Shape.dataType.              {Rule No = 1}
                        = AlternateShape.dataType.     {Rule No = 7}
                        = union(Point, Polygon).       {Rule No = 16}
```

The pictogram data type is derived from rule 1 as a shape data type. Since the river entity box contains an alternate shape, from rule 7 we get an alternate shape data type as a union of point and polygon. The closest data type in the OGIS model for this union is "Geometry". We may change this to create the union type to have more precise semantics.

4.3   Translating Relationship Pictograms

Relationships among geographic entities(objects) are actually conditions on the objects' positions and are called spatial relationships [16]. Topological relationships are special cases of spatial relationships, and a formal database model for expressing topological relationships at the conceptual and logical levels can be found in [15]. Relationship pictograms will translate into spatial integrity constraints of the database. SQL provides a variety of techniques for expressing integrity constraints as part of database schema called "active" elements. Active elements will be created once and stored in the database, and they will be executed at appropriate times. To express spatial integrity constraints, we consider "assertions" which are interrelational constraints. Assertions are tested every time a modification to the relevant relation or relations is made. For example, the following assertion will enforce the constraint that "forest stands should be geometrically disjoint".

```
CREATE ASSERTION icDisjoint
BEFORE
        UPDATE OF geometry ON forest,
        UPDATE OF geometry ON forest_stand,
        INSERT ON forest,
        INSERT ON forest_stand,
        DELETE ON forest.
```

```
        DELETE ON forest_stand,
CHECK
        (NOT EXISTS
            (SELECT *
            FROM forest_stand fs1, forest_stand fs2
            WHERE fs1.stand_id <> fs2.stand_id
            AND fs1.geometry.overlap(fs2.geometry)
            )
        );
```

A specific example set of spatial integrity constraints implied from relationship pictograms is presented in section 4.5.

4.4 Translation of Entities and Relationships to Tables

If it were not for the spatial attributes, the ER model can be mapped seamlessly and intuitively onto the Relational model. There are five basic steps [11].

1. Map each entity onto a separate relation. The attributes of the entity are mapped onto the attributes of the relation. Similarly, the key of the entity is the primary key of of the relation. The relational schema is shown in Figure 11.

2. For relationships whose cardinality is 1 : 1, we place the key attribute of any one of the entities as a foreign key in the other relation. For example, the relation **Manager** may have a foreign key attribute corresponding to the primary key, the *Name*, of the **Forest** (see fig. 11).

3. If the cardinality of the relationship is $M : 1$, then place the primary key of $1 - side$ relation as a foreign key in the relation of $M - side$. For example, the relation **Fire-Station** has a foreign key which is the primary key of the relation **Forest**.

4. Relationships with cardinality $M : N$ have to be handled in a distinct manner. Each $M : N$ relationship is mapped onto a *new* relation. The name of the relation is the name of the relationship, and the primary key of the relationship consists of the pair of primary keys of the participating entities. If the relationship has any attributes, then they become attributes of the new relation. **supplies_water_to** is an example of an $M : N$ relationship between the entities **Facility** and **River**. The river name and the city name constitute the primary key, and the attribute *Volume* becomes an attribute in the new table. The standard translation for $M : N$ spatial relationships will result into numerous tables like crosses(road, forest_stand), touch(road, facility) etc. Note that many of these tables are redundant if standardized spatial data-types and operations (e.g. OGIS) are used in logical data model (e.g. SQL3).

5. For a multi-valued attribute, a new relation is created which has two columns: one corresponding to the multi-valued attribute and the other to the key of

the entity which owns the multi-valued attribute. Together, the multi-valued attribute and the key of the entity constitute the primary key of the new relation. For example, the **Forest-Stand** entity has a multi-valued attribute *Polygonid* which is an identification number(integer) for the geometric location of the city. *Pointid* is a multi-valued attribute since it is possible that a forest-stand spans two disjoint locations: for example, if a road cuts through a forest stand. We therefore have the relation **FSTAND-GEOM**. Similarly, we have relations **FOREST-GEOM, RIVER-GEOM, ROAD-GEOM ,FACILITY-GEOM** and **FSTATION-GEOM**. Note that some of these tables are not needed in a logical data model supporting standard spatial data types (e.g. OGIS).

4.5   Translation Example

In this section we show how the individual components described in sections refsec:ldm and refsec:rules fit together to translate the piece of ER diagram as shown in figure 12 (taken from fig. 6).

As described in section 4.4, the FOREST and FOREST-STAND entities will be translated into the following two tables in the database using the classical translation [11] of entity-relationship diagrams to tables.

CREATE TABLE Forest(
       name VARCHAR2(30) CONSTRAINT PK_forest PRIMARY KEY,
       avg_elevation NUMBER,
       geometry PolygonType
);

CREATE TABLE Forest_stand(
       stand_id NUMBER CONSTRAINT PK_foreststand PRIMARY KEY,
       species VARCHAR2(30),
       geometry PolygonType),
       partOf VARCHAR2(30) CONSTRAINT FK_partOf
             REFERENCES forest(name)
);

The spatial relationship pictogram part_of will be translated into spatial integrity constraints. The spatial-partitioning pictogram on "part_of (forest F, forest_stand fs)" relationship in figure 12 may be represented in terms of three simpler constraints listed below:

1. a forest_stand fs which is a "part_of" forest F, should be geometrically inside F.
2. two forest_stands should not geometrically overlap and
3. the geometric union of all forest stands in forest should cover the geometry of the forest.

The constraint that "any forest stand should be geometrically-within its forest" will be translated into the following SQL3 assertion.

CREATE ASSERTION icWithin
BEFORE
      UPDATE OF geometry ON forest,
      UPDATE OF geometry ON forest_stand,
      INSERT ON forest,
      INSERT ON forest_stand,
      DELETE ON forest,
      DELETE ON forest_stand,
CHECK
      (NOT EXISTS
            (SELECT *
            FROM forest f, forest_stand fs
            WHERE fs.partOf = f.name
            AND NOT fs.geometry.within(f.geometry)
)
      );

Forest stand polygons in the forest_stand layer are geometrically disjoint, and this will be translated into the following spatial integrity constraint.

CREATE ASSERTION icDisjoint
BEFORE
      UPDATE OF geometry ON forest,
      UPDATE OF geometry ON forest_stand,
      INSERT ON forest,
      INSERT ON forest_stand,
      DELETE ON forest,
      DELETE ON forest_stand,
CHECK
      (NOT EXISTS
            (SELECT *
            FROM forest_stand fs1, forest_stand fs2
            WHERE fs1.stand_id <> fs2.stand_id
            AND fs1.geometry.overlap(fs2.geometry)
)
      );

Finally to enforce that "the geometric union of all forest stands in a forest should cover the entire forest" we can define the following assertion in SQL3.

CREATE ASSERTION icUnion
BEFORE

```
            UPDATE OF geometry ON forest,
            UPDATE OF geometry ON forest_stand,
            INSERT ON forest,
            INSERT ON forest_stand,
            DELETE ON forest,
            DELETE ON forest_stand,
CHECK
            (NOT EXISTS
                    (SELECT f.name, f.Geometry,
                            GEOMETRIC_UNION (fs.Geometry) as P
                    FROM forest f, forest_stand fs
                    WHERE fs.partOf = f.name
                    GROUP BY f.name
                    HAVING NOT P.contains( f.geometry )
                    )
            );
```

A non-standard geometric aggregate function is assumed to compute the geometric union of adjacent polygons. This function takes a set of adjacent polygons (for e.g. forest_stands) and yields a single polygon (e.g. forest) representing the union (outer boundaries) of the constituent polygons. OGIS standard provides a binary operator, "union", where as GEOMETRIC_UNION is an n-ry operator. One can think of n-ry GEOMETRIC_UNION as a generalization of binary "union" in the same manner "sum" function in SQL generalizes binary "+" operator.

5   Conclusion and Future Work

A pictogram-extended ER model is presented as a conceptual data-modeling tool for spatial databases. There are two novel aspects of pictograms in our work. First, we have introduced relationship pictograms. Second, we have provided a recursive grammar for pictograms to provide a formal syntax and facilitate automatic translation to OGIS spatial data types. The main contribution of this paper is a set of syntax-directed translation rules for converting a pictogram extended ER diagram into a logical data model. This translation will result in DDL constructs of SQL3. We show rules to generate spatial columns and datatypes from entity pictogram. We have also provided rules to generate spatial integrity constraints from relationship pictograms. The translation procedure shows another major benefit of pictograms towards eliminating redundant tables, in logical data model for various many-to-many spatial relationships in the conceptual data model. The grammar and translation rules provided allow efficient database management and maintenance. The proposed model is applied to an actual example of a state-park database. This approach seems to be quite promising to the spatial database designer.

Spatial pictogram extension for conceptual data-modeling is not limited to ER diagrams. The same approach can be used to extend object diagrams using UML. In appendix A, we briefly present the extension for UML. Our future work will be to extend and develop a case tool for the visual-data modeling of spatial databases.

Acknowledgments

This research has supported through cooperative agreement with NASA (NCC 5-316) and by the University of Minnesota Agriculture Experiment Station project MIN-42-044. This work is also sponsored in part by the Army High Performance Computing Research Center under the auspices of the Department of the Army, Army Research Laboratory cooperative agreement number DAAH04-95-2-0003/contract number DAAH04-95-C-0008, the content of which does not necessarily reflect the position or the policy of the government, and no official endorsement should be inferred. This work was also supported, in part, by the National Science Foundation under Grant N0. 9631539.

We would like to thank Shrikanth Shankar for his help with SQL3 examples, and Xuan Liu, Chang-tien Lu at the Spatial Database Research Group for their useful comments. The comments of Christiane McCarthy have greatly improved the readability of this paper. Finally the comments of anonymous reviewers have greatly improved the technical accuracy of this paper.

References

1. Yavan Bedard. Visual modeling of spatial databases: Towards spatial pvl and uml. *GeoInformatica*, June, 1999.
2. G. Booch. *Object Oriented Analysis and Design*. Benjamin Cummins, 1992.
3. G. Booch, J. Rumbaugh, and I. Jacobson. *The Unified Modeling Language User Guide*. Object Technology Series, Addison-Wesley, 1999.
4. P.P.S. Chen. The entity-relationship model – towards a unified view of data. *ACM Trans. Database Systems*, 1(1):9–36, 1976.
5. Open GIS Consortium. Opengis simple features specification for sql,. URL: http://www.opengis.org/public/abstract.html, 1998.
6. Oracle Corporation. Oracle spatial. URL: http://www.oracle.com/database/options/spatial/index.html, 1999.
7. Helen Couclelis. People manipulate objects (but cultivate fields): Beyond the raster-vector debate in gis. In *Theories and Methods of Spatio-Temporal Reasoning in Geographic Space*, volume 639. Springer-Verlag, LNCS, 1992.
8. O. Cunther and W. Riekert. The design of godot: An object-oriented greographical information system. *IEEE Data Engineering Bulletin*, 16(3), 1993.
9. Vassilis Delis, Thanasis Hadzilacos, and Nectaria Tryfona. An introduction to layer algebra. In *Advances in GIS Research: Proceedings of the sixth International Symposium on Spatial Data Handling*. Taylor and Francis, 1994.
10. D.J.Dewitt, N.Karba, J.Luo, and J.M.Patel. Client server paradise. In *In Proceedings of the 20th Int. Conference on Very Large Databases*, 1994.

11. R. Elmasiri and S.B. Navathe. *Fundamentals of Database Systems.* Benjamin/Cummins, 1994.
12. ESRI. Spatial database engine. http://www.esri.com/base/products/sde/sde.htm.
13. R.H. Guting. An introduction to spatial database systems. *VLDB J., Special issue on Spatial Database Systems,* 3(4):357–399, 1993.
14. R.H. Guting. Graphdb: Modeling and querying graphs in databases. In *In Proceedings of the Int. Conference on Very Large Databases,* 1994.
15. Thanasis Hadzilacos and Nactaria Tryfona. A model for expressing topological integrity constraints in geographic databases. In *Theories and Methods of Spatio-Temporal Reasoning in Geographic Space,* volume 639. Springer-Verlag, LNCS, 1992.
16. Thanasis Hadzilacos and Nactaria Tryfona. An extended entity-relationship model for geographic applications. *ACM SIGMOD Record,* 26(3), 1997.
17. J.R. Herring. Tigris: A data model for an object-oriented geographic information system. *Computers and Geosciences,* 18(4):443–, 1992.
18. Levine John R, Tony Mason, and Doug Brown. *Lex and Yacc.* O'Reilly And Associates, 1992.
19. G. Kosters, B. Pagel, and H.W. Six. Object-oriented requirements engineering for gis applications. In *In Proceedings of the ACM Intl. Conference on Geographical Information Systems,* 1995.
20. N.Adam and A. Gangopadhyay. *Database issues in Geographical Information Systems.* Kluwer Academics, 1997.
21. S.B. Navathe. Evolution of data modeling for databases. *Commun. ACM,* 9(35):112–123, 1992.
22. J. Rumbaugh, W. Blaha, and Premerlani. *Object Oriented Modeling and Design.* Prentice Hall, 1991.
23. S. Shekhar, S. Chawla, S. Ravada, A. Fetterer, X. Liu, and C. t. Lu. Spatial databases–accomplishments and research needs. *IEEE Trans. Knowledge and Data Eng.,,* 11(1), 1999.
24. S.Shekhar and S. Chawla. Spatial databases: Concepts, implementaton and trends. Prentice Hall, 2000 (Expected).
25. S.Shekhar, M.Coyle, D.-R. Liu, B.Goyal, and S.Sarkar. Data models in geographic information systems. *Commun. ACM,* 40(4):103–111, 1997.
26. N. Tryfona and T. Hadzilacos. Geographic applications development: Models and tools for the conceptual level. In *In Proceedings of the ACM Intl. Conference on Geographical Information Systems,* 1995.
27. Jeffrey D. Ullman and Jennifer Widom. *A First Course in Database Systems.* Prentice Hall, 1997.
28. M.F. Worboys. Object-oriented approaches to geo-referenced information. *Intl. Journal of Geographical Information Systems,* 8(4), 1994.
29. M.F. Worboys, H.M. Hearnshaw, and D. Maguire. Object-oriented data modelling for spatial databases. *Intl. Journal of Geographical Information Systems,* 4:369–383, 1990.

A   Unified Modeling Language with Pictograms

Several researchers [17], and [29], have defined and developed data models for GIS based on object-oriented technology, which provides an attractive alternative environment and lends itself to modeling the semantics and processes of the real-world in a more integrated manner than the relational model. There are several object-oriented analysis and design approaches, with the most commonly used methodologies developed by [22], [2], etc. Recent efforts by industry and researchers have resulted in a Unified Modeling Language [3]. The UML is fast becoming a standard conceptual data modeling language for object-oriented or object-relational database management systems (OODBMS/ORDBMS).

GraphDB [14], GODOT [8], Worboy [28], OGIS [5], and GeoOOA [19] are some attempts to model GIS using the object-based approach. Worboy and GODOT propose extensive class hierarchies to model the geometry and topology of spatial objects. GraphDB supports the explicit modeling and querying of graphs.

Unified Modeling Language(UML) [3] is an emerging standard for conceptual data-modeling, in object-oriented domain. It is a comprehensive language to model structural schema and dynamic behavior at conceptual level. As far as database design is concerned we are only interested in modeling the static structure of the system. In some ways the UML is quite similar to the ER model we introduced earlier. Instead of ER diagrams, we now have class diagrams. Figure 13 is the equivalent UML representation of the State-Park example shown in Figure 2.

We now briefly describe the UML notations with reference to the **State-Park** example:

Class is the encapsulation of all objects which share common properties in the context of the application. It is the equivalent of the `entity` in the ER model. For example `Facility` is an example of a class which, at least abstractly, captures functioning units within the State-Park like restrooms, campsites and tourist-offices. We have extended the class diagrams with pictograms as in the case of the ER diagrams. This way it is clear that instances of the class `Facility` are spatial objects. More specifically, their spatial geometry is represented as points. This way all the spatial properties, relationships and operations that are valid for point objects are applicable to the class `Facility`.

Attributes characterize the objects of the class. Unlike in ER notation, there is no notion of a key attribute in UML. This is because in OO systems, all objects have a system-generated unique identification. This lack of explicit uniqueness does have profound ramifications when a UML diagram is mapped onto a relational or object-relational schema. Attributes also have a scope or visibility associated with them. The scope regulates access to the attribute from within or outside of the class. This in turn is essential to control the degree of modularity of the database design. There are three levels of scope, and each has a special symbol:

1. + *Public*: This allows the attribute to be accessed and manipulated from any class.
2. - *Private*: Only the class that owns the attribute is allowed to access the attribute.

3. # *Protected*: Classes that are derived("subtyped") from a Parent class have access to the attribute. We have chosen to make all the attributes in the **State-Park** example *Protected*.

Methods are functions and are part of the class definition. They are responsible for modifying the behavior or "state" of the class. The "state" of the class is embodied in the current values of the attributes. In object-oriented design, attributes should only be accessed through methods. In the **Facility** class, the *Name* attribute of the class is accessed through the method *GetName()*.

Relationships relate one class to the other or to itself. This is similar to the concept of relationship in the ER model. For database modeling, UML has two important categories of relationships: generalization and association:

Aggregation is a specific construct in UML to capture the part-whole relationship. For example, the class **Forest-Stand** is engaged in a part-whole relationship with the class **Forest**. Sometimes a class can be part of more than one class. To distinguish the two cases, the former is called *Strong* aggregation and the latter *Weak*.

Generalization is best described in the context of the spatial hierarchy shown in Figure 7. For example, the class **Geometry** is a generalization of its *subclasses* **Point**, **Line** and **Polygon**.

Associations show how objects of different classes are related. Like relationships in the ER model, associations can be *binary* if they connect two classes, or *ternary* if they connect three classes. The *supplies-water-to* is an example of an association between the classes **Facility** and **River**. Notice that there is a class **Supplies-water-to** connected to the *supplies-water-to* association via a dotted line. This is because the association itself has an attribute *volume*.

Comparison between ER and UML: The above discussion highlights the similarities between the ER and UML, for conceptual data modeling using pictogram extensions. These similarities are summarized here.

ER Diagrams	UML
Entity Set	Class
Attribute	Attribute
Inheritance	Inheritance
Aggregation	Aggregation

However there are subtle differences between these two approaches which are summerized below.

- it is difficult to add relationship pictograms to UML.
- there is no notion of methods in ERD.
- translation of UML into Object Oriented constructs/Java classes is easier.

Grammar	Rule	R. No	Semantic actions in 'C'-like syntax
<Pictogram>	→ Shape	1	{Pictogram.dataType = Shape.dataType;} {Pictogram.IC = "Shape.IC";}
	→ |!|	2	{Pictogram.dataType = "User Defined";}
	→ |*|	3	{Pictogram.dataType = "GeometricType";}
<Shape>	→ <Basic Shape>	4	{Shape.dataType = BasicShape.dataType;}
	→ <Multi-Shape>	5	{Shape.dataType = MultiShape.dataType;} {Shape.IC = "MultiShape.IC";}
	→ <Derived-Shape>	6	{Shape.dataType = DerivedShape.dataType;}
	<Alternate Shape>	7	{Shape.dataType = AlternateShape.dataType;}
<Basic Shape>	→ ●	8	{BasicShape.dataType = "PointType";}
	→ /	9	{BasicShape.dataType = "LineType";}
	→ ⬡	10	{BasicShape.dataType = "PolygonType";}
<Multi-Shape>	→ <Basic Shape> <Cardinality>	11	{MultiShape.dataType = BasicShape.dataType;} {MultiShape.IC = Cardinality.IC;}
<Cardinality>	→ 0,1 | 0,n	12	{Cardinality.IC = "NULL is O.K.";}
	1 | n | 1,n	13	{Cardinality.IC = "NOT NULL ";}
<Derived > Shape>	→ /<Basic Shape>/	14	{DerivedShape.dataType = BasicShape.dataType;}
<Alternate Shape>	→ <Basic Shape> <Derived Shape>	15	{AlternateShape.dataType = BasicShape.dataType;
	→ <Basic Shape> <Basic Shape>	16	{AlternateShape.dataType = "union" BasicShape.DataType + BasicShape.DataType;}
<Raster Partition>	→ Raster	17	{RasterShape.dataType = Raster.dataType;}
	→ Thiessen	18	{RasterShape.dataType = Thiessen.dataType;}
	→ TIN	19	{RasterShape.dataType = TIN.dataType;}
<RelationShip>	→ part_of(partition)	20	{RelationShip.IC = <a set of 3 integrity constraints describing set partition>;}
	→ part_of(highrarchical)	21	{RelationShip.IC = <a set of 3 integrity constraints describing highrarchical nature>}

Fig. 8. Translation Rules: Pictogram → Spatial data types (note: IC stands for integrity constraint)

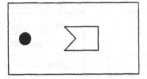

Fig. 9. An example of Alternate Shape from the state-park example

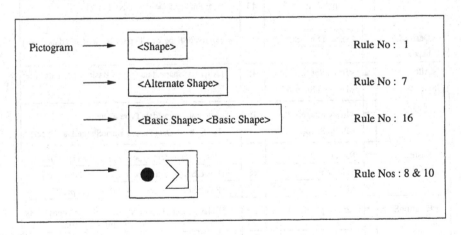

Fig. 10. The Derivation of Alternate Shape from grammar rules (Rule numbers refer to figure 8)

FOREST-STAND

Stand-id	Specie	Forest-name
(Integer)	(varchar)	(varchar)

RIVER

Name	Length
(varchar)	(Real)

ROAD

Name	NumofLanes
(varchar)	(Integer)

FACILITY

Name	Forest-name
(varchar)	(varchar)

FOREST

Name
(varchar)

FIRE-STATION

Name	ForName
(varchar)	(varchar)

SUPPLIES-WATER-TO

FacName	RivName	Volume
(varchar)	(varchar)	(Real)

MANAGER

Name	Age	Gender	For-name
(varchar)	(Integer)	(varchar)	(varchar)

FSTAND-GEOM

Stand-id	Polygonid
(Integer)	(Integer)

RIVER-GEOM

Name	Lineid
(Integer)	(Integer)

ROAD-GEOM

Rname	Lineid
(varchar)	(Integer)

FACILITY-GEOM

Name	Pointid
(varchar)	(Integer)

FOREST-GEOM

Name	Polygonid
(varchar)	(Integer)

....

ROAD-ACCESS-FOREST

RoadName	ForName
(varchar)	(varchar)

ROAD-TOUCHES-FACILITY

RoadName	FacilityName
(varchar)	(varchar)

RIVER-CROSSES-FOREST

RiverName	ForName
(varchar)	(varchar)

....

Fig. 11. Representative Tables: Relational Schema for the State-Park example

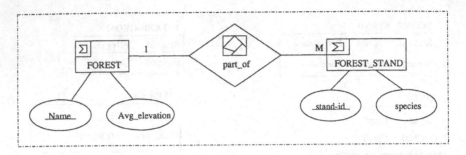

Fig. 12. Piece of Shape-Park ER Diagram with pictograms

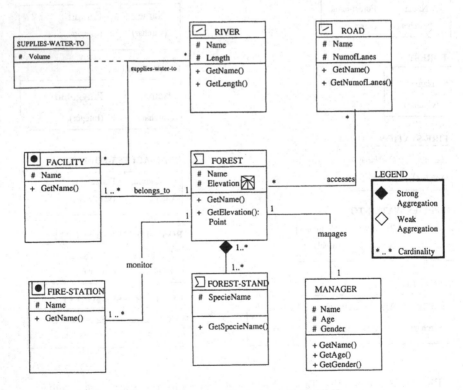

Fig. 13. The State-Park example in UML

Change Detection by Classification of a Multi-temporal Image

Ben Gorte

International Institute for Aerial Survey and Earth Sciences (ITC)
Enschede, The Netherlands
ben@itc.nl

Abstract. Keeping track of changes in our environment is an important application of remote sensing. To express those changes in terms or thematic classes can be done by comparing classifications of different dates, which, however, has the disadvantage that classification errors and uncertainties are accumulated. Moreover, spectral properties of classes in a dynamic environment may be different from those in a stable situation. This paper elaborates on the statistical classification of multi-temporal data sets, using a set of thematic classes that includes class-transitions. To handle the increased complexity of the classification, refined probability estimates are presented, which pertain to image regions rather than to the entire image. The required subdivision of the area could be defined by ancillary data in a geographic information system, but can also be obtained by multi-temporal image segmentation. A case study is presented where land-cover is monitored over an 11-years period in an area in Brazil with drastic deforestation.

1 Introduction

Various types of land cover govern much of the spectral reflection of the surface of the earth, which is measured by sensors on various remote platforms, such as multi-spectral and thermal scanners or push-broom arrays.

Reflections measured by satellite sensors depend on the local characteristics of the earth surface. In order to extract information from the image data, we must find out this relationship.

Classification is the transformation of continuous reflection measurements from remote sensing images into discrete objects, belonging to different thematic classes that correspond to land covers, such as wheat fields or conifer forests.

The subject of this paper is multi-temporal classification: we want to express changes in the terrain in terms of transitions of thematic classes, and derive this information from satellite imagery. The motivation is twofold:

- Dynamic environments are (from various perspectives) more interesting than static ones
- Satellite data are very suitable to observe changes, because up-to-date imagery is regularly available,

P. Agouris and A. Stefanidis (Eds.): ISD'99, LNCS 1737, pp. 105–121, 1999.
© Springer-Verlag Berlin Heidelberg 1999

In most parts of the world, land cover is highly dynamic. Apart from effects of seasonal rainfall, temperature and possible cyclicity of rainfall and droughts, man has influenced the vegetation by converting natural vegetation into agricultural lands where different crop rotations are practiced. Other dynamic aspects are the variable grazing pressure of range lands, forest fires, destruction of flood plain vegetation by floods, and so on. Whereas in static environments other data collection methods, such as aerial photography and ground surveying may offer higher thematic and spatial accuracy than satellite remote sensing, the frequent over-passes of the earth observation satellites allow one to monitor dynamic environments.

To monitor dynamics of the earth surface is of great importance for policy making. Planning is especially relevant and often urgent when the environment changes. Conversely, execution of policy causes changes in the environment, and monitoring those changes gives feed-back. To support this, up-to-data information extracted from satellite remote sensing data is highly valuable.

Raw satellite data consists of measurements of electro-magnetic radiation, emitted or reflected by the earth surface.

Before imagery is useful for policy makers information has to be extracted, which can take either a quantitative or qualitative form. Examples of quantitative or *ordinal* information from remote sensing data are in the family of *vegetation indices*, such as the Normalized Difference Vegetation Index (NDVI) [Clevers, 1988]. They indicate the amount of vegetation at any location in the area under consideration. Qualitative or *nominal* information is obtained from image data by *classification*, such as Maximum Likelihood (ML), which assigns a *class label* to each location in an area, from a set of (for example) land-use classes.

Change Detection

The above subdivision in reflection data, ordinal information and nominal information suggests change detection approaches on three different levels, on the basis of multi-temporal imagery, *i.e.* by comparison of:

1. reflection data, for example by differencing or rationing [Jensen, 1986]
2. quantitative information, such as vegetation indices [Lyon *et al*, 1998]
3. qualitative information (classifications) [Lillesand and Kieffer, 1994]

Looking at information extraction from the perspective of automatic vs. manual methods, it should be noticed that the three approaches are automatic at the *pixel* level. Usually, a subsequent *interpretation* step is required to explain the observed differences in terms of thematic changes at an *object* level.

In this paper, the focus will be on classification. The described method, however, does *not* rely on a straightforward comparison of independently created classifications, but integrates the classification and change detection in a single *multi-temporal classification*.

The idea is described in literature [Lillesand and Kieffer, 1994], [Jensen, 1986], but commonly discarded because of dimensionality and complexity problems. This paper applies a number of advanced techniques (local probabilities, segmentation into spatio-temporal objects) to handle those problems.

2   Classification

Classification determines a class from a user-defined set of N thematic classes for each image pixel. The choice is made on the basis of reflection measurements stored in that pixel.

The relationship between reflection, recorded in satellite imagery, and thematic classes is not one-to-one. Within different objects of a single class, and even within a single object, different reflections may occur. Conversely, different thematic classes cannot always be distinguished in a satellite image because they show (almost) the same reflection. In such cases, deterministic methods are not sufficient. A probabilistic approach, however, may be able to describe the spectral variations within classes and to minimize the risk of erroneous class assignments.

Feature Vectors and the Feature Space. In one pixel, the values in the M features can be regarded as components of a M-dimensional vector, the *feature vector*. Such a vector can be plotted in an M-dimensional space, called *feature space*.

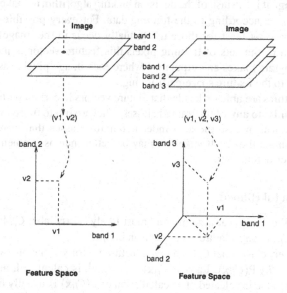

Fig. 1. Feature vectors in 2 and 3 dimensional feature spaces

Pixels with similar spectral characteristics, which are likely to belong to the same land cover class, are near to each other in the feature space, regardless how far they are from each other in the terrain and in the image. Pixels belonging to a certain class will hopefully form a so-called *cluster* in the feature space. Moreover, it is hoped that other pixels, belonging to other classes, fall outside this cluster, but in other clusters, belonging to those other classes.

The task of classification is to assign a class label to each feature vector, which means to subdivide the feature space into partitions that correspond to classes. This task can be achieved by *pattern recognition* [Ripley, 1996].

A classifier needs some knowledge about the relationship between classes and feature vectors Therefore, classification starts with a training phase, where the user trains the computer by telling for a limited number of pixels to what classes they belong **in this particular image**, followed by the decision phase, where the computer assigns a class label to all (other) image pixels, by looking for each pixel to which of the trained classes this pixel is most similar.

Training. During the training phase the user decides what classes to use. About each class some ground truth is needed, a number of places in the image area that are known to belong to that class. This knowledge must have been acquired beforehand, for instance as a result of fieldwork, or from an existing map, assuming that in some areas the class membership has not changed since the map was produced.

Decision Making. It is the task of the decision making algorithm to make a *partitioning* of the feature space, according to the training data. For every possible feature vector in the feature space (at least for those that actually occur in the image), the program decides to which of the sets of training pixels this feature vector is most similar. In addition, the program makes an output map where each image pixel is assigned a class label, according to the feature space partitioning.

Some algorithms are able to decide that feature vectors in certain parts of the feature space are not similar to any of the trained classes. They assign to those image pixels the class label *unknown*. In case the area indeed contains classes that were not included in the training phase, the result *unknown* may be better than assignment to one of the classes in the user-defined set.

2.1   Maximum Likelihood

Maximum likelihood aims at assigning a "most likely" class label C_i, from a set of N classes $C_1, \ldots, C_N$, to any feature vector $\mathbf{x}$ in an image.

The most likely class label C_i for a given feature vector $\mathbf{x}$ is the one with the highest *posterior probability* $P(C_i|\mathbf{x})$. Each $P(C_i|\mathbf{x})$, $i \in [1..N]$, is calculated, and the class C_i with the highest value is selected. The calculation of $P(C_i|\mathbf{x})$ is usually based on *Bayes formula*:

$$P(C_i|\mathbf{x}) = \frac{P(\mathbf{x}|C_i)\,P(C_i)}{P(\mathbf{x})}, \tag{1}$$

with

$P(\mathbf{x}|C_i)$: class probability density

In Bayes formula, $P(\mathbf{x}|C_i)$ is the probability that some feature vector $\mathbf{x}$ occurs in a given class C_i. It tells us what kind of $\mathbf{x}$s we can expect in a certain class C_i, and how often (relatively). It is the probability density of C_i, as a function of $\mathbf{x}$. Supervised classification algorithms derive this information during the stage.

$P(C_i)$: prior probability

$P(C_i)$ is called the prior probability of class C_i, the probability for any pixel that it belongs to C_i, irrespective of its feature vector. It can be estimated on the basis of prior knowledge about the terrain, as the (relative) area that is expected to be covered by C_i.

$P(\mathbf{x})$: (class-independent) feature probability density

For a certain $\mathbf{x}$, in order to find the class C_i with the maximum posterior probability $P(C_i|\mathbf{x})$ the various $P(C_i|\mathbf{x})$ must be only compared. Therefore, it is common to substitute $P(\mathbf{x})$ by a normalization factor

$$P(\mathbf{x}) = \sum_{j=1}^{N} P(\mathbf{x}|C_j)\, P(C_j) \tag{2}$$

2.2 Probability Density Estimators

Classification algorithms differ in the way they estimate class probability densities $P(\mathbf{x}|C_i)$.

Parametric. The most popular method is to assume that feature vectors within each class are drawn from a multi-variate normal distribution $N(\mu_i, \Sigma_i)$, where μ_i and Σ_i are the mean vector and the covariance matrix of class i, as estimated from the training samples. Then, the class probability densities are given by:

$$P(\mathbf{x}|C_i) = (2\pi)^{-M/2} |\Sigma_i|^{-\frac{1}{2}} e^{-\frac{1}{2}(\mathbf{y}^T \Sigma_i^{-1} \mathbf{y})}$$

with:

M : the number of features

Σ_i : the $M \times M$ variance-covariance matrix of class C_i, with elements σ^i_{jk}

$|\Sigma_i|$: the determinant of Σ_i

Σ_i^{-1} : the inverse of Σ_i

$\mathbf{y} = \mathbf{x}_p - \mu_i$ (μ_i is the class mean vector), as a column vector with M components

$\mathbf{y}^T$: the transposed of $\mathbf{y}$ (a row vector).

Gaussian maximum likelihood classifiers classify a pixel with feature vector $\mathbf{x}$ by calculating $P(\mathbf{x}|C_i)$ for each class, multiply the results by the respective class prior probabilities $P(C_i)$ and select the class where this product is largest. When this procedure is applied to all feature vectors in the feature space (rather than to all pixels in an image), a *feature space partitioning* is obtained (Fig. 2), which can be used as a lookup table to classify the image.

Since class probability densities are governed by distribution parameters, the classification is called *parametric*.

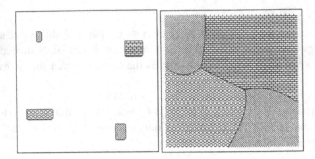

Fig. 2. Feature space with training samples (left) and the resulting feature space partitioning using Gaussian maximum likelihood (right)

Non-parametric. Non-parametric classifiers, such as k-Nearest Neighbor (k-NN) do not rely on any assumptions concerning the feature vector distribution within each class.

Instead, they consider a (small) subset of the training samples around the feature vector $\mathbf{x}_p$ to be classified, and assign the class label of to the majority of these samples.

The relationship between the k-Nearest Neighbor decision function and class probability density estimates can be explained intuitively. If many C_i pixels are found near to $\mathbf{x}_p$, apparently C_i has a high density in that part of the feature space. In addition, the total numbers of training samples should be considered. If the training set contains many more samples for C_i than for C_j, then also relatively many C_i samples, compared to C_j, will be found near to $\mathbf{x}_p$.

Let k_i ($i \in [1..N]$) be the number of C_i samples among the k nearest neighbors of $\mathbf{x}_p$. Therefore, $\sum k_i = k$. Two cases can be distinguished (Fig. 3):

Equal sampling: If equal numbers of samples were taken for each class, the values of k_i for $\mathbf{x}_p$ are proportional to the class probability densities $P(C_i|\mathbf{x}_p)$. The majority vote yields a non-parametric maximum class probability density classifier.

Proportional sampling: If the (expected) class proportions are reflected in the numbers of training samples per class, for example when sample locations were randomly chosen, the values of k_i are proportional to the enumerator $P(\mathbf{x}_p|C_i)\,P(C_i)$ of Bayes formula. With normalized $P(C_i|\mathbf{x}_p)$ ($i \in [1..N]$),

$$P(C_i|\mathbf{x}_p) = \frac{k_i}{k}$$

A non-parametric *maximum likelihood* decision is taken by the majority vote [Duda and Hart, 1973], [Mulder and Middelkoop, 1990].

3   Change Detection

A straightforward method to detect changes in terms of thematic classes is by *post-classification comparison* [Lillesand and Kieffer, 1994]. From two images of the same area, taken at different dates, two classifications are made independently using the same

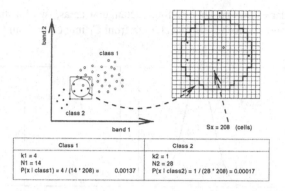

Class 1		Class 2	
k1 = 4		k2 = 1	
N1 = 14		N2 = 28	
P(x I class1) = 4 / (14 * 208) =	0.00137	P(x I class2) = 1 / (28 * 208) = 0.00017	

Fig. 3. k-Nearest Neighbor estimation of probability densities

set of N classes. Assuming that both classifications have the same geo-reference, a simple raster overlay will exactly indicate for each pixel to which class it belongs at both moments in time. This gives $N \times N$ possibilities, although only a subset of these will occur in a significant number of pixels.

The great disadvantage of this method is that the two classifications have errors and uncertainties. Therefore it is unsure whether a class label change in a certain pixel is caused by a change in the terrain or by a classification error. One may not assume that the errors in the classifications tend to be similar, such that most of them might go unnoticed during the comparison. Instead, errors in both classifications accumulate when detecting change [Jensen, 1986].

An alternative method, which will be elaborated here, is *classification of a multi-temporal data set*, in short *multi-temporal classification*. This involves combination of the two images, having M spectral bands each, into one multi-temporal data set with $M + M$ 'bands'. Of course, this requires a prior geometric correction of one image to the other, or of both images to the same geo-reference. A set of N' classes is defined, consisting of the original N classes $(C_1, \ldots, C_N)$, augmented with all relevant *change classes* $(C_1 \to C_2, \ldots, C_1 \to C_N, C_2 \to C_1, \ldots, C_N \to C_{N-1})$. The maximum number of classes in N' equals N^2, but during training it will probably appear that not all of these occur. Note, that training samples are needed for each class in the set. Therefore, the ground truth must contain sample areas for all kinds of changes.

To compare post-classification comparison with multi-temporal classification theoretically, let us consider a simplified case with single-band images taken at $t = t_0$ and $t = t_1$, and two classes C_1 and C_2, so $M = 1$ and $N = 2$. Assuming Gaussian distributions for the pixel values in each class, we find decision boundaries D_0 and D_1 to distinguish between the two classes at $t = t_0$ and $t = t_1$, respectively (Fig. 4, top). The class means for both classes and both times are also indicated.

If we create a 2-dimensional feature space from the two single-band images, by putting $t = t_0$ at the horizontal and $t = t_1$ at the vertical axis, then post-classification comparison is shown in Fig. 4 at the bottom-left. The feature space is partitioned by the decision boundaries D_0 and D_1 into four rectangular areas, two for the unchanged C_1 and C_2 pixels, and two for pixels that change from C_1 into C_2 or from C_2 into C_1.

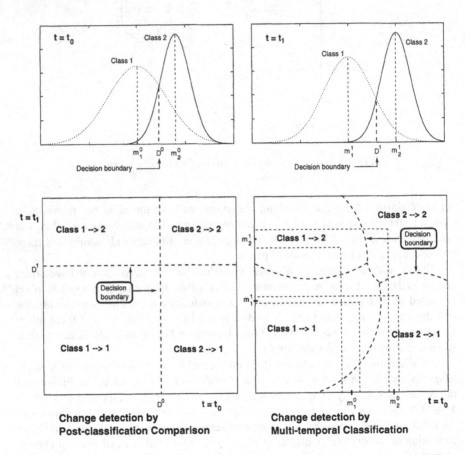

Fig. 4. Change detection using single-band images of two dates t_0 and t_1 with two classes. Top: independent classifications - Bottom: decision boundaries in combined spectral-temporal feature space.

The underlying assumption in post-classification comparison is that there is only one feature vector distribution in each class. The distribution is supposed to be the same for areas that are stable and those that are subject to change — either in the old or in the new image.

The justification for multi-temporal classification is that class distributions are *not* independent of the dynamic behavior of objects. This is especially clear in the 'new' image ($t = t_1$). Areas that recently changed to a new class (since $t = t_0$) look different from those that already belonged to that class since long ago. Objects usually need some time to develop. A new built-up area has a different reflection than an old one. Young forest looks different from old forest. On recently developed agricultural fields different crops are grown than on old fields.

But also in the 'old' image ($t = t_0$) spectral characteristics of objects that are going to change may differ from those that will remain the same. For example, only old forest is likely to be clear-cut, and agriculture on poor soils is more likely to change to grassland — of course, these dynamics highly depend on local circumstances.

Multi-temporal classification allows stable classes ($C_1 \rightarrow C_1, \ldots$), as well as change classes ($C_1 \rightarrow C_2, \ldots$) to have their own mean vectors and covariance matrices in the combined $M + M$-dimensional feature space, from which probability densities are derived. For each feature vector the class with maximum probability density can then be selected from the set of N^2 possible classes (Fig. 4, bottom right).

Drawbacks. Multi-temporal classification shows the following difficulties, for which solutions are sought in the remainder of the paper:

Efficiency A minor problem is posed by efficiency: Gaussian maximum likelihood classification requires two matrix – vector multiplications per pixel, and these take four times as long as the number of dimensions doubles (but only one classification has to be performed instead of two). The problem becomes more severe with k-NN classification, which is 'famous' for being slow: certain optimizations which make the algorithm much more feasible when dealing with three or four dimensional cannot be implemented for six or eight dimensions.

Training Post-classification comparison requires two times N sets of training samples, one for each class in both images. Multi-temporal classification needs additional samples for each kind of change that is expected to occur.

Complexity It is difficult to estimate the 'spectral' overlap of the increased number of classes in the combined spectral-temporal feature space, as well as the resulting classification error and uncertainty.

3.1 Probability Estimation Refinements

Classification relics on spectral separability of classes. When a pixel's feature vector falls in an overlapping area of two classes (for instance *grass* and *wheat*) in the feature space, this means that probably some pixels with this feature vector belong to *grass* and others, with the same feature vector, belong to *wheat*. The classifier will treat all of them in the same way and classify them as one class, either *grass* or *wheat*. Errors also occur with heterogeneous classes, such as *town*: a mixture of roads, roofs, trees, gardens, ponds etc. If these pixels are classified as *town*, then elsewhere some *forest* or *grass* pixels may be classified as *town* as well.

The problem of spectral overlap is going to be more severe in a multi-temporal classifications, because of the large number of classes. We want to improve the situation by refining the probability estimates.

Statistical classification methods do not always attempt to estimate various probabilities as accurately as possible. Perhaps it is assumed that the largest *a posteriori* probability occurs at the 'right' class also when the probabilities are estimated rather roughly.

- The probabilistics in Bayes' formula pertain to the entire image, while a decision is taken for each individual pixel. Having only one set of class *a priori* probabilities, the class assigned to a pixel depends on the situation in the entire image and is, therefore, influenced by areas that are far away from the pixel under consideration and have no relation with it.
- The assumption that reflections can be modeled as Normal distributions may be unrealistic for certain land-use classes, such as *built-up* and *agricultural* areas, which may consist of several land covers with different spectral signatures in different (unknown) proportions. Also signatures of land-cover classes are influenced by soil type, soil moisture, sun incidence angle (on slopes) etc. and may be inadequately modeled by Gaussian densities.

3.2 Local Probabilities

Estimates of the various probabilities can be refined by making them local, *i.e.* pertaining to parts of the area, instead of to the entire area [Strahler, 1980], [Middelkoop and Janssen, 1991]. It is necessary to subdivide the image into regions, such that different class mixing proportions occur in each region.

The subdivision can be made with additional (map) data, which may be stored, for example, in a geographic information system. The basic idea is that when deciding upon an class in a particular pixel, statistical data related to, for example, the soil type in that element are more relevant than statistics for the entire area.

A major objection against this approach is that such detailed statistics are generally not available.

Local Prior Probabilities. Methods exist to estimate class prior probabilities from measurement data [Duda and Hart, 1973], [Ripley, 1996].

In [Gorte and Stein, 1998] a method is presented to estimate class prior probabilities in an arbitrary segmentation of an image, on the basis on the distribution of reflections in each image segment. This method is based on the observation that posterior probabilities can be used to estimate class areas in an image region, by interpreting the class posterior probability at a pixel as the pixel's contribution to the total area of that class within the region [Duda and Hart, 1973]. For example, if 100 pixels in a region r have the same posterior probability value for class C_i, say $P(C_i|\mathbf{x}) = 0.7$, then their contribution to the total area A_i^r of class C_i in r equals 70 pixels.

Using all pixels p in the region, the area A_i^r, covered by class C_i in region r is the sum of the posterior probabilities $P(C_i|\mathbf{x}_p)$:

$$A_i^r = \sum_{p \in r} P(C_i|\mathbf{x}_p) \, , \tag{3}$$

where $\mathbf{x}_p$ is the feature vector of pixel p. Applying Bayes' formula gives:

$$A_i^r = \sum_{p \in r} \frac{P(\mathbf{x}_p|C_i) \, P^r(C_i)}{P(\mathbf{x}_p)} \, , \tag{4}$$

in which $P(\mathbf{x}_p)$ can be obtained by normalization, according to

$$P(\mathbf{x}_p) = \sum_{j=1}^{N} P(\mathbf{x}_p|C_j)\,P(C_j)\,, \tag{5}$$

where N is the number of classes.

The prior probability $P(C_i)$ for class C_i in region r can be estimated as the class area A_i^r divided by the total area A^r of r:

$$A_i^r = \sum_{p \in r} \frac{P(\mathbf{x}_p|C_i)\frac{A_i^r}{A^r}}{P(\mathbf{x}_p)}\,. \tag{6}$$

From this equation, A_i^r can be solved iteratively, given the class probability densities $P(\mathbf{x}|C_i)$, as estimated from representative training samples.

Given an additional data set, in which the mapping units are expected to correlate with class occurrence (soil, elevation, geomorphology, etc.), class prior probabilities can be obtained per mapping unit. These are more specific for a pixel in such a unit than the ones that are estimated by the user for the entire image area. This, in turn, will increase the reliability of the posterior probability estimates.

Local Probability Pensities. When applying Bayes' formula per region, it must be noted that also the probability densities $P(\mathbf{x}_p|C_i)$ are region dependent and cannot be modeled by a single class probability density function.

A modified non-parametric (k-Nearest Neighbor) was developed to estimate local class probability densities $P^r(\mathbf{x}_p|C_i)$, *i.e.* the probability that a class C_i pixel in region r has feature vector $\mathbf{x}_p$. The estimator needs to know the subset T_i^r of the class C_i training samples that was involved in the classification of r.

$P^r(\mathbf{x}_p|C_i)$ is estimated as being proportional to the number k_i of class C_i samples in a neighborhood with k samples around x, divided by N_i^r the number of elements in T_i^r.

A semi-parametric local probability density estimator can also be implemented. Here, the subsets T_i^r of the training data are selected non-parametrically as above, consisting of those samples that *would be* involved in a k-NN classification of a region. Subsequently, class mean vectors μ_i^r and covariance matrices Σ_i^r are based on those subsets and used to compute Gaussian class probability densities. Each region has its own covariance matrix, and determinants and inverse matrices have to be computed for all regions.

The improved estimates of prior probabilities and probability densities increase the reliability of the posterior probabilities and, therefore, enhance subsequent decision processes, such as maximum posterior probability class selection [Strahler, 1980]. Also the per-region class area estimates are more accurate than those obtained from standard Maximum Likelihood classifications.

A number of case studies has shown significant classification improvement using this method [Gorte, 1998], [Gorte and Stein, 1998] in mono-temporal cases. It is expected that also multi-temporal classification benefits from these refined probability estimates.

3.3 Segmentation

To be able to apply local class prior probabilities and probability densities, a meaningful subdivision of the image area is required. The previous section states that this subdivision can be derived from ancillary (GIS) data, which may concern, for example, soil, geology or elevation.

In the absence of such ancillary data it is possible to obtain the subdivision from the image itself, using *image segmentation*.

Whereas classification only deals with spectral image characteristics, image segmentation [Haralick and Shapiro, 1985], [Cross *et al*, 1988] takes spatial characteristics into account. The purpose of image segmentation is to subdivide an image into regions that are homogeneous according to certain criteria, such that these regions correspond to area objects in the terrain [Fu and Mui, 1981].

In a multi-temporal case the purpose of segmentation is to identify regions that are homogeneous with respect to *dynamics*. We want to group adjacent pixels that are subject to similar transitions through time into *spatio-temporal objects*.

In the case study, presented in Section 4, Thematic Mapper imagery of three dates was available. Only the first and last are used for multi-temporal classification, but all three are submitted to a multi-dimensional segmentation algorithm, as follows:

After geometric correction, normalized difference vegetation indices (NDVI) were calculated for all three years and combined to form a 3-dimensional feature space. This combination was submitted to a segmentation algorithm that is otherwise used for multi-spectral segmentation [Gorte, 1996]. The algorithm was designed to group adjacent pixels into regions that are homogeneous (within certain tolerances) with respect to feature-vectors in three bands — now it creates regions that are homogeneous with respect to NDVI-transitions: All pixels within a region have a similar 'NDVI-history'.

Generally, segmentation is a difficult subject [Pavlidis, 1986]. Although its purpose, to identify spatial (or even spatio-temporal) objects, is very appealing, it has to be admitted that this goal is seldom reached. We do not claim that the regions, identified by multi-temporal NDVI segmentation, coincide with meaningful objects in the terrain. Therefore, we are not going to assign a single class transition to each region. We do claim, however, that in each region a specific mixture of class transitions exists, and that estimation of the mixing proportions as prior probabilities significantly improves multi-temporal classification.

4 Case Study in the Pantanal Area, Brazil

The proposed method is illustrated using multi-temporal Landsat TM imagery of the Rio Verde do Mato Grosso area, located at the Eastern boundary of the Pantanal region, Mato Grosso do Sul, Brazil. During the last two decades important transformations in land cover took place mainly in the Planalto, where the native vegetation (shrubs and forest) was mostly replaced by intensive cultivation methods. The systematic deforestation involved denudation of soils and caused rapid erosion, with consequences for the flood regime in the whole Pantanal, where also an increased sedimentation rate was detected [Hernandez Filho *et al*, 1995]. The study area represents a good example where environmental dynamics linked to human activities have a strong impact on water management.

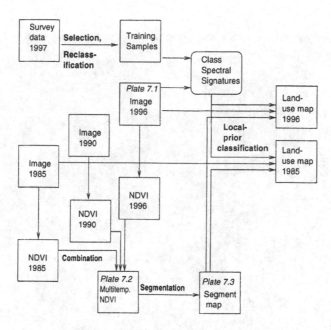

Fig. 5. Classification of 1985 and 1996 images with local prior probabilities according to segmentation of multi-temporal NDVI

The purpose of the case study is to assess the rather drastic land use changes in the Pantanal region since 1985. Available were three Landsat TM images of the Pantanal study area, from 1985, 1990 and 1996. A land-use survey from 1997 was available [Disperati *et al*, 1998] with classes according to level 3 of the CORINE legend (see also Chapter 20). From the survey map, training samples were selected in areas that were assumed to be the same in 1996 and 1997, allowing to establish spectral signatures for those classes using the 1996 image. Seven classes were selected, according to level 2 or the CORINE legend — in preliminary experiments, level 3 appeared too detailed for automatic classification of Thematic Mapper imagery. Two sets of samples were chosen, a training set and a test set.

Normalized difference vegetation index (NDVI) was computed for each year. The values clearly show the development of the amount of vegetation during the period 1985 – 1990 – 1996 and reflect land-use changes in the area.

The NDVI maps of the three years are combined and submitted to multi-dimensional image segmentation (Section 3.3). The result is displayed in a color composite (Fig 6), showing the NDVI of 1985 in blue, of 1990 in green and of 1996 in red. Red areas have little vegetation in 1985 and 1990, but vegetation increased between 1990 and 1996 — they are newly irrigated areas. White areas were densely vegetated all the time, whereas in blue and cyan areas vegetation has decreased, before or after 1990, respectively. The image shows quite some green areas. because 1990 was relatively wet.

Fig. 6. Multi-temporal segmentation of NDVI 1985 (blue), 1990 (green) and 1996 (red)

The result is a set of spatio-temporal regions. These are regions of adjacent pixels showing the similar vegetation development.

Iterative local prior probability estimation (section 3.2) was applied to the 1996 image, using one set of priors in each segment of the multi-temporal segmentation. This gives a 1996 land-use map. Comparison with the test set shows that an overall accuracy of 71% was reached using local prior probabilities, as compared to 61% with maximum likelihood classification using the same band combination. Maximum likelihood classification with six bands gives 67% accuracy [1]. Regarding this rather low accuracy, it should be noted that test set pixels were chosen at random from the survey data, without considering their spectral values.

Since the 1996 and 1985 images are of the same season, it was assumed that the spectral signatures derived for the 1996 image are also valid for the 1985 image. Under this assumption, also the 1985 land-use map could be made, despite the absence of ground truth for that year. Therefore, also a 1985 test set was not available.

---

[1] Iterative local prior estimation is developed for SPOT-XS with 3 bands.

To detect changes, a straightforward procedure is *post-classification comparison*, which involves overlaying the 1985 and 1996 land-use maps. The difficulty is that both classifications contain quite a large percentage of errors (which for 1985 is even unknown). Therefore, it is difficult to distinguish between real changes and those that are observed as a result of misclassification.

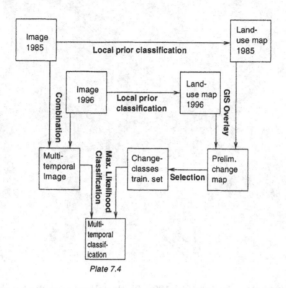

Plate 7.4

Fig. 7. Multi-temporal classification of combined 1985 - 1996 images with change classes

Alternatively, *classification of a multi-temporal data set* was applied (Figure 7). The 1985 and 1996 images were combined in a single 12 channel spectral-temporal data set. From the two land-use classifications pixels were selected having high *a posteriori* probabilities. Moreover, only those pixels were chosen that were surrounded by pixels of the same class, to reduce mixed-pixel effects at boundaries. The selected pixels are the most reliable ones in the two land-use maps. The resulting maps have eight different pixel values: 1 – 7 for the seven classes, plus 0 for *not selected*. Overlaying these two maps gives 64 combinations, 15 of which contain a 0 (zero) and are no longer considered. From the remaining 49 combinations 31 were selected: the seven *no change classes*, having the same class in both years, plus 24 *change classes*, belonging to one class in 1985 and to another in 1996. The remaining 18 combinations did not occur in significant amounts of pixels.

The resulting change map has very many pixels with value 0. The remaining pixels (with a change-class number between 1 and 31) were used as training set for a maximum likelihood classification of the combined – multi-temporal – image. The assumption is that the 31 classes are distinguishable in the 12-dimensional feature space. The result is shown in Figure 8, where the hatched areas indicate change: the narrow lines refer to 1985 and the wider ones to 1996.

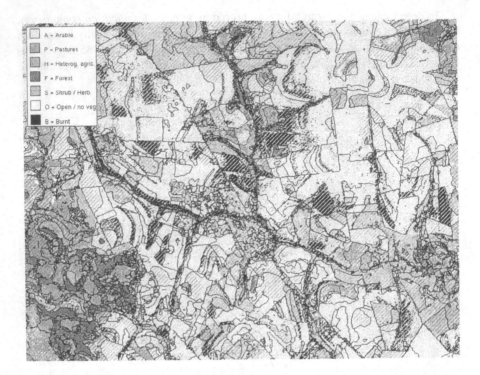

Fig. 8. Multi-temporal classification 1985-1996. Single-colored areas did not change. In hatched areas the narrow lines refer to 1985, the wide ones to 1996

5 Conclusions

The paper described multi-temporal classification as an alternative for post-classification comparison. The complexity resulting from the increased set of classes, which includes class-transitions, makes it necessary to use refined probability estimates, which pertain to image regions rather than to the entire image. Therefore, estimates for local prior probabilities and for local probability densities are proposed, which have proven to increase classification accuracy and reliability on earlier occasions. The required subdivision of the area could be defined by ancillary data in a geographic information system, but can also be obtained by multi-temporal image segmentation. As far as this can be judged at this stage of the Pantanal project, the results are promising. Further evaluation will take place in the near future.

Acknowledgments

The author would like to thank the Earth Sciences Department of the University of Siena, Italy, for providing the image data of the Pantanal area. The analysis of the data was carried out in cooperation with Riccardo Salvini, Ph.D. student in this Department.

References

[Clevers, 1988] J.G.P.W. Clevers, The application of a weigted infrared-red vegetation index for extimating leaf area index by correcting for soil moisture, *Remote Sens. Environ.* 29, pp. 25-37.

[Cross *et al*, 1988] A.M. Cross, D.C. Mason and S.J. Dury. Segmentation of remotely-sensed images by a split-and-merge process. *IJRS* 9(8), pp. 1329-1345.

[Disperati *et al*, 1998] Disperati L., G. Righini, M. Bocci, P.L. Pantozzi, A.P. Fiori, S. Kozciac and A.C. Paranhos Filho, *Land cover changes in the Rio Verdo de Mato Grasso region (Pantanal, Mato Grasso do Sul, Brasil) as detected through remote sensing and GIS analysis.* Technical report, Univ. of Siena (I).

[Duda and Hart, 1973] R.O. Duda and P.E. Hart, *Pattern classification and scene analysis.* John Wiley and Sons, New York, 465 pp. 1973.

[Fu and Mui, 1981] Fu and Mui, A survey on image segmentation, *Pattern Recognition*, 13:3-16, 1981.

[Gorte, 1996] B.G.H. Gorte. Multi-spectral quadtree based image segmentation. *IAPRS* vol. XXXI B3, Vienna, pp. 251-256.

[Gorte, 1998] B.G.H. Gorte (1998). *Probabilistic segmentation of remotely sensed images*, Ph.D. thesis, Wageningen Agric. Univ., the Netherlands.

[Gorte and Stein, 1998] B.G.H. Gorte and A. Stein (1998), Bayesian Classification and Class Area Estimation of Satellite Images using Stratification, *IEEE Trans. Geosci. Remote Sens.*, Vol. 36, No. 3, May 1998, pp. 803 – 812.

[Haralick and Shapiro, 1985] R.M. Haralick and L.G. Shapiro. Survey: Image segmentation techniques. *Computer, Vision, Graphics and Image Processing*, 29, 1985, pp 100-132.

[Hernandez Filho *et al*, 1995] Hernandez Filho P., Ponzoni F.J., Pereira M.N., Pott A., Pott V.J. and Silva M.P (1995) Mapeamento da vegetação e de uso da terra de parte a bacia do Alto Taquari (MS) considerando o procedimentode analise visual de imagens TM/LANDSAT e HRV/SPOT. In: *Encontro sobre sensoriamento remoto aplicado a estudos no Pantanal - Livro de Resumas.* Corumbà - MS, 9-12 de Outobro de 1995, 137-139.

[Jensen, 1986] J.R. Jensen, *Introductory digital image processing: a remote sensing perspective*, Prentice-Hall.

[Lillesand and Kieffer, 1994] T.M. Lillesand and R.W. Kiefer, *Remote sensing and image interpretation* - 3rd edition, Wiley, 745 pp.

[Lyon *et al*, 1998] J.G. Lyon, Ding Yuan, R.S. Lunetta and C.D. Elvidge, A change detection experiment using vegetation indices. *Photogrammetric Engineering & Remote Sensing*, Vol. 64, No. 2, February 1998, pp. 143–150.

[Middelkoop and Janssen, 1991] H. Middelkoop H. and L.L.F. Janssen. Implementation of temporal relationships in knowledge based classification or satellite images. *Photogrammetric Engineering & Remote Sensing*, Vol. 57, No. 7, pp. 937 – 945.

[Mulder and Middelkoop, 1990] N.J. Mulder and H. Middelkoop (1990). Parametric versus non-parametric maximum likelihood classification. *Proc. ISPRS Comm. III*, Wuhan.

[Pavlidis, 1986] T. Pavlidis, A critical survey of image analysis methods, *IAPR-8*, 1986, pp502-511.

[Ripley, 1996] B.D. Ripley. *Pattern recognition and neural networks*, Cambridge University Press.

[Strahler, 1980] A.H. Strahler. The use of prior probabilities in maximum likelihood classification of remotely sensed data. *Remote Sensing of Environment*, no. 10, pp. 135 – 163.

A Probabilistic Approach to Environmental Change Detection with Area-Class Map Data

Christopher B. Jones[1], J. Mark Ware[1], and David R. Miller[2]

[1] School of Computing, University of Glamorgan, Pontypridd, CF37 1DL, United Kingdom
{CBJones, JMWare}@glam.ac.uk
[2] Macaulay Land Use Research Institute, Aberdeen, United Kingdom
mi008@mluri.sari.ac.uk

Abstract. One of the primary methods of studying change in the natural and man-made environment is that of comparison of multi-date maps and images of the earth's surface. Such comparisons are subject to error from a variety of sources including uncertainty in surveyed location, registration of map overlays, classification of land cover, application of the classification system and variation in degree of generalisation. Existing geographical information systems may be criticised for a lack of adequate facilities for evaluating errors arising from automated change detection. This paper presents methods for change detection using polygon area-class maps in which the reliability of the result is assessed using Bayesian multivariate and univariate statistics. The method involves conflation of overlaid vector maps using a maximum likelihood approach to govern decisions on boundary matching, based on a variety of metrics of geometric and semantic similarity. The probabilities of change in the resulting map regions are then determined for each class of change based on training data and associated knowledge of prior probabilities of transitions between particular types of land cover.

1 Introduction

One of the major applications of geographically-referenced spatial data is that of monitoring change on the earth's surface. Change in natural and semi-natural environmental phenomena may reflect variation in climate, the dynamics of plant and animal communities and the influence of human activity in land and transport development, agriculture and the production of pollutants. Approaches to automated change detection based on existing spatial data sources differ according to the type of data that are used. A considerable volume of literature documents the application of satellite remote sensing, in which the evidence for change is based on comparison of either the radiometric pixel values and their combinations, such as in vegetation indices, or the classified pixels resulting from various methods of interpretation of the source data [1]. An alternative approach is based on the comparison of area-class polygon maps produced from interpretation of sources such as aerial photography and land surveys [2].

P. Agouris and A. Stefanidis (Eds.): ISD'99, LNCS 1737, pp. 122-136, 1999
© Springer-Verlag Berlin Heidelberg 1999

The results of change detection analyses based on comparisons of multi-date digital maps are subject to error from several sources. All methods may incur error in the surveyed location of spatial data elements and error in the locational registration of the respective datasets. In the case of classified data, errors arise due to variation in the definition of and the application of the classification systems and in the degree of generalisation. Comparison of radiometric data values, or their combinations or transformations, is also affected by factors such as variation in lighting conditions and in seasonal characteristics of vegetation and agriculture.

Studies of the reliability of change detection based on comparison of spatial datasets have been performed with regard to a range of methodologies, with the most extensive research being in the field of satellite remote sensing. Less effort has been expended on the development of automated change detection with area-class maps, whether derived from aerial photography, land survey, or indeed satellite image interpretation, yet they constitute a massive source of historical data on various aspects of the environment. Several studies have highlighted the problems of error in this context (e.g.[3], [4], [5], [6]). However there are many examples of automated change detection using either area-class maps or satellite imagery, in which reliability of the results is not reported (e.g. [7], [8], [9]), a situation which may be regarded as reflecting the lack of appropriate and readily implemented methods. Most geographical information systems do provide facilities that can be used to perform comparisons of polygon maps for purposes of change detection, but there is a shortage of effective tools for determining the nature of change. In particular it is difficult to evaluate the reliability of the results with regard to the sources of data on which they are based.

In this paper we address specifically the use of area-class polygon maps for automated change detection and present methods that are intended to assist in improving reliability while providing quantitative measures of the accuracy of the results. The approach adopted is based on the application of Bayesian statistical methods [10]. It is assumed that a variety of geometric and semantic measures associated with elements of the source data can be used, in combination with prior knowledge of the occurrence of transitions between different land-cover categories, to indicate that multi-date maps represent specific types of change. Training data, based on expert assertions of the presence and absence of change, are used to estimate the prior conditional density functions for each type of evidence. The training data used in this study relate to change in map boundaries and in land cover categories derived from aerial photographic surveys of Scotland. We present results of evaluating the method using expert-asserted ground truth data separate from that used in training.

In the remainder of the paper we start by reviewing existing methods of polygon map comparison and discuss the relevance of conflation methods in Section 2, before summarising the procedures employed here in Section 3. Section 4 describes the experimental results, and a conclusion is provided in Section 5.

2   Map Overlay Methods for Change Detection

Given a pair of polygon maps relating to different dates, a simple approach to determining differences between them, and hence potential regions of change, is to overlay the maps and analyse the resulting regions of intersection. Differences in classifications derived from the parent maps for a particular polygon indicate that the region may be categorised as representing change. If the source maps contain independently generated boundaries that are approximately coincident then sliver polygons can be expected to occur and the problem arises of distinguishing them from polygons that may represent genuine change [3]. Conventional GIS functionality allows the slivers to be removed if they are smaller than some areal threshold. However, the problem then arises of selecting an appropriate threshold value and in any event the result may be an arbitrary increase in the area of the adjacent polygon with which it is merged.

Chrisman and Lester [3] pointed out that sliver area by itself is not a reliable measure and proposed distinguishing between change and non-change slivers on the basis of their shape. This still does not distinguish the case where, though a sliver may be relatively small, it may include a separation between its opposite sides that exceeds a locational error distance threshold. Cherrill and McClean [4] suggested confining measurements of change to the internal zones of polygons that exclude a boundary error buffer, and they presented results of applying this method using a range of buffer sizes. The results reduced the incidence of what they considered to be erroneous change, though the technique leads to the exclusion from change analysis of what could be a significant proportion of the map area. It should be remarked however that Cherrill and McClean observed in their study that boundary location error was a much less important factor than that of area class differences due to disagreement between interpretations rather than to 'real world' change.

An alternative approach to resolving the problem of slivers in conventional GIS is to increase the size of a 'fuzzy tolerance' value that is used to control the merger of line vertices that belong to adjacent line features. A technique for performing this merger has been described by [11], but the method appears to merge vertices in a manner which, though distance-constrained, may result in an arbitrary location for the merged lines within the limits of the distance constraint. For maps containing boundaries with errors of different magnitudes, this could result in the degradation of better quality boundaries that may be moved in the course of the merge procedure. As suggested by Chrisman [12], when two boundary segments are considered to be equivalent, it may be preferable simply to delete the poorer quality line. A method of map overlay in which differing locational errors of the map components are taken into account has been described in [13] and [14]. A shortcoming of this and related techniques, such as [15] and [16], is that they adopt a very localised, largely point-based approach which fails to take account of higher level geometric and semantic characteristics of the parent linear features. This issue is addressed in the feature matching procedures developed in the work described here.

2.1   Map Conflation

The idea of overlaying a pair of maps, such that the better quality versions of equivalent parts of the maps are retained, is integral to the concept of map conflation (e.g. [17], [18]). An important part of conflation is the matching of equivalent features. When a lower quality representation is merged with a better quality equivalent, it is assumed that it brings with it other topologically linked features for which there may be no match between the maps. The result is a map in which the best quality elements of the sources are preserved while non-common elements are also retained in a topologically consistent manner.

As originally conceived, map conflation was intended to be applied to multiple representations of the same phenomena relating to a particular point in time. The concept is extended here to combine maps relating to different points in time. Thus where linear features or boundaries cannot be distinguished from each other, the resulting map should include the best known representation of the feature which may be the result of a merge process. Recent work on conflation [19] addresses the problems of data uncertainty with a rule-based approach using geometric and attribute matching procedures. Our approach is related, but differs in being concerned with change and in the explicit use of training data to analyse the statistical characteristics of change.

3   Probabilistic Change Detection Procedure

In the present study there are two types of event, concerning a pair of maps relating to different times, that can be evaluated probabilistically with Bayesian statistics. These are:
- sections of area boundaries being equivalent,
- land cover changing from one category to another.

The major functional stages in the procedure for change detection are as follows:
- training to determine the prior conditional probability distributions of evidence associated with the presence of boundary section equivalence and land-cover category change,
- overlay the two maps under consideration and identify paired sections of boundary that are indistinguishable at some probability level,
- merge matched line features, if a conflation is required,
- determine the probability that land-cover change has occurred for map regions in which the source land cover attributes differ.

3.1   Training

The training stage requires that an expert asserts the presence of each of the two types of event within training data that are representative of the context of change detection. Associated metrics of potentially relevant evidence are then analysed to estimate their conditional probability distribution. We now summarise metrics that have been considered in this study. It is important to stress however that the approach is generic and there are many potential items of evidence that might prove to be effective.

Evidence for Boundary Equivalence (Hypothesis H_1). Given an overlay of a pair of time-differing maps of the same area, an expert must identify nearby sections of boundary that represent the same (unchanged) boundary phenomenon on the ground. These pairs of asserted equivalent line portions are then analysed to evaluate the following metrics:

E1: Hausdorff distance between line sections a and b. This is a measure of the maximum lateral separation of *a* and *b*. If d_{ai} is the shortest distance from edge *i* of line *a* to its nearest neighbouring edge in *b* (taking account of all locations on each of the edges), and d_{bj} is the distance from edge *j* of line *b* to its nearest neighbour in *a*, then

$$E1 = \max(\max(d_{ai}), \max(d_{bj})).$$

E2: approximate average distance between line sections consisting of m *and* n *vertices, given by*

$$E2 = \frac{1}{m+n} \Sigma d_{ai} + \Sigma d_{bj}.$$

E3: difference in line length.

E4: difference in alternation (i.e. intersections with 'anchor line' connecting start and end).

E5: difference in trend orientation as determined by the 'anchor line'.

E6: difference between the pair of left-right attribute codes of each section of boundary. The difference between a pair of attribute codes can be measured as the weighted path length between the two codes within the hierarchical classification system to which they belong. If P is the set of edges e in the shortest path and each edge has a weight determined by a function W of the depth in the hierarchy of the node at the lower (most distant from the root) end of the edge, then combining the weighted left P_l and right P_r path distances

$$E6 = \Sigma W(e) + \Sigma W(e).$$

$$e \in P_l \qquad e \in P_r$$

Evidence for Change in Land Cover Type (Hypothesis H₂). The following items of evidence were considered in an effort to support the hypothesis of change in a single polygon for one type of land cover X to another type Y:

E7: (0 or 1) the attribute from map A is type X, while the attribute from map B is type Y.

E8: (0 or 1) there is a polygon of type Y adjacent to the polygon of type X in map A.

Conditional Probability Density Functions. For each of these items of evidence, the mean is determined and stored in the vector M and a covariance matrix C is constructed using the items of evidence (such as E1 to E6). Provided that the individual items of evidence are approximately normally distributed, or can be transformed to normality, the conditional probability density function [10] for a set of items of evidence E is represented by:

$$p(E|H) = \frac{1}{(2\pi)^{n/2} |C|^{1/2}} \exp[-\tfrac{1}{2}(E - M)^T C^{-1}(E - M)].$$

In the event of only a single item of evidence being used, then the conditional probability may be estimated directly from the training data.

3.2 Posterior Probabilities and Prior Probabilities

Given a set of items of evidence E it will then be possible to estimate the posterior probability of an event using the conditional probability density function with Bayes' rule:

$$p(H|E) = \frac{p(E|H)\, p(H)}{p(E)}$$

The prior probability p(E) can be derived in this case from the summation of the product $(p(E|H_i).p(H_i))$ for the hypothesis and its negation. The prior probability of a hypothesis p(H) should be based on expert knowledge that is relevant to the context. In the absence of such knowledge it may be approximated on the basis of the training data [20]. Thus $p(H_1)$ is estimated by the frequency with which an expert has asserted that a neighbouring line within a predetermined maximum tolerance distance of the source line is in fact equivalent to the source line. $p(H_2)$ may be found from analysis of land-cover transition matrices based on expert assertions of change between one land use type and another. An example of such a study that is relevant to the research described here is that of Hester *et al* [21]. In the case of types of transition for which no such prior knowledge is available it can be approximated from the training data by the proportion of the area of type X polygons that become type Y polygons, as verified by the expert assertions.

3.3   Locational Matching (Via Triangulation)

In order to identify candidate sections of pairs of lines that may prove to be regarded as indistinguishable, a search is performed to find for each edge of each line segment all edges of other line segments that are within a given tolerance distance, based on the locational accuracy of the relevant lines. The results of these searches are used to construct pairs of line sections that are mutually within the tolerance distance of each other, *i.e.* there is no part of one line that is further (when measured by shortest distance) than the tolerance distance from the other line section. Each section of a line segment is a sequence of component edges. However, because one part of an edge could be within tolerance and the other part out of tolerance, the source edges are split where such ambiguities arise. The spatial search for neighbouring edges is performed using a main-memory constrained Delaunay triangulation of the vertices of the linear features. Details of this type of procedure can be found in [22] and in [23].

For each line section there may then be several other line sections with which it might be regarded as equivalent. The posterior probabilities of equivalence with all candidates are estimated as summarised above. If a probability exceeds a specified threshold then the pair of line sections with the highest probability (maximum likelihood) is selected as equivalent.

3.4   Merging of Line Sections Deemed Equivalent for a Given Probability Level

Merging of equivalent line sections is carried out in a way that will give preference to one of the line sections if it is known to be of higher accuracy than the other line section. This could be the case if the source maps had been produced at different nominal scales or if the procedure for producing one of the maps was known to be more reliable than that for the other.

Assuming that two line sections a and b are to be merged, then the merged line section c is found by a weighted averaging of a and b where the weighting is governed by the relative accuracy of a and b. There are three steps in the merging process. First, vertices are added to a and b such that: (i) a and b have the same number of vertices; and (ii) vertices appear at proportionally equivalent distances along a and b. Each vertex in a now has a corresponding vertex in b. Next, c is found by calculating the weighted average of corresponding vertices in a and b (*i.e.* $v_c = W v_a + [1-W] v_b$, where $0 <= W <= 1$). If one line section is of a much higher accuracy than the other, the averaging procedure may be replaced by a procedure which simply selects the more accurate. As a result of the weighted averaging there will be sharp breaks between the merged and the adjacent unmerged line sections. The final step involves applying a local progressive weighting to provide a smooth transition (see Fig. 4 and Fig. 5). More details can be found in [24].

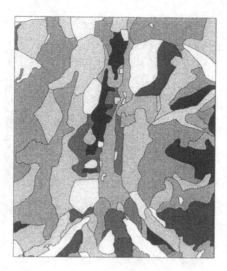

Fig. 1. 1946 test data

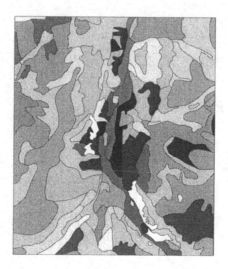

Fig. 2. 1988 test data

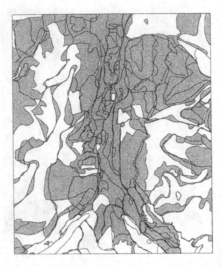

Fig. 3. 1946/1988 change map based only on feature attribute difference

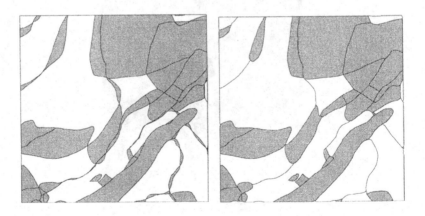

Fig. 4. Part of the 1946/1988 change map before (left) and after (right) boundary merging

3.5   Determine Change Probabilities for Each Region of the Map

The final stage of the change detection process is that of attaching posterior probabilities of land cover change to polygons resulting from the combination of the source maps. This stage may be performed on the conflated map or on the 'raw' intersection map.

Taking Account of Differences in Generalisation of Land Cover Classification. When comparing land cover maps in which the classification systems differ, or in which the nature of application of a classification system differs, care must be taken to identify differences in land cover category that are attributable only to differences in the degree of generalisation of the categories. Thus if one category is a generalisation of the other, then they cannot be treated as evidence of change. The semantic closeness metric for a single 'path' used in E6 may be appropriate to a consistently applied individual classification, but it provides a finite difference between a class and its immediate superclass. An alternative closeness measure E9 (based on that given in [25]), determines the number of non-common superclasses of a pair of categories, so that a parent-child relation gives a distance of zero. A third metric E10, which is potentially applicable to diverse classification schemes, determines the semantic distance based on the difference between the set of terms used to define a category [26]. Metrics E9 and E10 have been implemented as part of the current research project and enable candidate change polygons to be screened out of the result of the probabilistic change detection procedure.

Visualisation of the Results. Several methods have been used to present the results of the change detection procedures. At the simplest level the source maps and their intersected overlay can be displayed (Figs. 1-4). On a change map, those polygons that represent change with a confidence exceeding a specified probability may be highlighted. Alternatively the variation in confidence between different change polygons can be represented by a variable range of colour lightness and saturation (not illustrated here). A further refinement of the latter is to display the variable confidence, via lightness and saturation, of polygons that represent selected types of change. The degree of confidence with which area boundaries are merged can be illustrated by modifying the thickness of the corresponding boundary line symbol, as in Fig. 5.

4   Experimental Results

The functionality described in Section 3 has been implemented in the C programming language in combination with the Avenue scripting language of the ArcView GIS. The change detection functions can all be called from a modified version of the conventional ArcView user interface.

In order to evaluate the method, land cover maps and associated training data for 1946, and 1988 (Fig. 1 and Fig. 2) were obtained for the same 30km^2 region (at UK National Grid origin 282000E 790000N) in the Cairngorms from the Macaulay Land

Use Research Institute (MLURI). A requirement was that the maps be generated independently which was not initially the case. This resulted in a reinterpretation (by MLURI staff) of the selected 'squares' of the earlier map using the original aerial photography.

The newly generated maps were then overlaid in pairs and, for each boundary section on each map, a set of candidate equivalent boundaries was generated automatically. The expert mapper was asked to indicate which pairs of boundary sections were regarded as logically equivalent in the sense that they could not be distinguished from each other on the basis of location (though there could be an associated attribute change).

In addition the expert was asked to label those intersection polygons which corresponded to genuine ('real world') change in land cover, as well as those for which change was assumed to be unlikely. A distinction was made at this stage between changes involving human activity (such as plantation and felling) and those regarded as natural or semi-natural. The map data were then partitioned into training data and evaluative data and the parameters of the conditional probability density functions were estimated. The analyses referred to subsequently relate to comparison of the 1946 and 1988 maps.

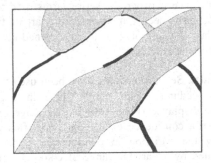

Fig. 5. Part of the 1946/1988 conflated change map. Line thickness relates to confidence in conflated lines (thicker lines represent lower confidence)

4.1   Boundary Merging

In a comparison of the 1946 and 1988 datasets, a buffering procedure was used to create a set of 294 candidate matching pairs of boundary segments. This set was divided into a training set of 150 with the remainder to be used as an evaluation dataset. In the training set, Kolmogorov-Smirnov tests for normality on the relevant items of evidence revealed that E3 was normally distributed. E1 and E2 required transformation to normality using the Box-Cox power transformation. E4 and E5 were found to be indistinguishable from random. However E5 was used at one level to filter out pairs of lines that exceeded 45 degree difference, as no such pairs were found to be equivalent in training. Preliminary observations indicate that E6 was not normally distributed and not a significant discriminator in this experiment. It may be envisaged however that it or a similar metric is likely to be of value in preventing merger of conceptually different types of boundary.

In the evaluation dataset, 64 out of 126 candidate matches were known to be matches on the basis of expert assertion. Of these, 55 were selected correctly as matches at the 50% confidence level, with 21 matches being identified incorrectly, giving 72% correct identifications. The remaining 9 expert asserted matches were recognised with a confidence level of less than 50%. At the 90% confidence level, 88% of identified matches were correct based on 30 correct matches (4 incorrect). The size of the samples at intermediate levels is too small to warrant reporting. However, the 90% confidence level results may be regarded as reasonable estimates of the reliability of the boundary matching results. These results were obtained when using the items of evidence E1, E2 and E3. It was found that lower success rates obtained when only using either E1, or E1 and E2.

Fig. 6. Unconflated (left) and conflated (right) maps showing change between heather types at the 56% confidence level. Boundaries in the right hand map have been merged at the 70% confidence level

4.2   Probability of Land Cover Change

A problem arose with determining conditional probability density functions for categorical change in that the large number of MLURI attribute codes (including mosaic codes) resulted in only a few specific transitions occurring sufficiently frequently to generate significant statistics. In order to generate more robust statistics, a subset consisting of the more frequent occurrences of the 49 MLURI codes was selected for experimental purposes. Theoretical considerations indicate that metric E8 would need to be used selectively for particular types of change. This item of evidence is that prior to change the change unit had a neighbour of the same type that it changed to. This is expected to be of most relevance to evaluation of change in natural and semi-natural vegetation. Preliminary results have not demonstrated that it is a very sensitive indicator and hence here we confine the probability analysis to the use of evidence E7 alone (i.e. that the feature attribute codes indicate a specific type of change). As is to be expected the results vary considerably according to the type of change.

In the case of change from heather to coniferous woodland, training indicated that following boundary matching all feature codes indicating change to coniferous woodland corresponded to all expert assertions of such change. As a consequence the posterior probability (confidence level) was found to be 100% and the evaluation data confirmed this level.

In contrast, for example, training indicated that feature codes showing change from one type of heather to another (Fig. 6) are prone to a high level of uncertainty, giving a posterior probability of 56%. In the corresponding evaluation data only 47% of polygons exhibiting change between heather types represented actual change. This discrepancy may reflect the relatively small sample sizes that were used. Thus of an initial 157 polygons indicating change between heather types, only 68 remained following boundary merging. These were split into a training set and an evaluation set, each of size 34.

5   Conclusions

This project has addressed the problem of evaluating and improving the reliability of automated environmental change detection using area-class polygon maps. Bayesian statistics have been applied to estimate the probability of equivalence of boundary segments and the probability of land-cover change within polygons resulting from overlaying the maps. The approach enables the possibility of merging boundary sections to create a conflated map representing the best quality geometric elements of the source maps. A variety of geometric and semantic evidence for change may be considered, and the methods lead to the possibility of improving the reliability of the results by increasing the amount of training data used to estimate conditional probability density functions. Preliminary results using training data from land cover maps of Scotland found a reasonably close match between the generated probability levels and those of expert assertions. It is anticipated that larger training datasets and refinement of the choice of metrics could improve the robustness of this approach.

There is clearly scope for further research to build on the results of this project. This includes evaluating alternative geometric and semantic difference metrics and investigating automatic adoption of appropriate metrics and constraints depending upon the source data types. There is also potential for developing more versatile, hybrid methods to combine conventional quantitative multivariate statistics with qualitative sources of evidence. Thus certain types of land cover change may be associated with particular spatial relationships with neighbouring features, or with physical characteristics of terrain and climate (introducing an analogy with contextual methods in remote sensing such as those of [27] and [28].

References

1. Singh A. (1989) 'Digital change detection techniques using remotely sensed data'. *International Journal of Remote Sensing* 10: 989-1003.
2. Kirby R.P. (1992) The 1987-1989 'Scottish national aerial photographic initiatives', *Photogrammetric Record* 14(80): 187-200.
3. Chrisman N.R. and M. Lester (1991) 'A diagnostic test for error in categorical maps'. *Proc Auto-Carto 10*, Baltimore, MD, ACSM/ASPRS, pp 330-348.
4. Cherrill A. and C. McClean (1995) 'An investigation of uncertainty in field habitat mapping and the implication for detecting land cover change'. *Landscape Ecology* 10(1): 5-21.
5. Aspinall R.J. and D.M. Pearson (1995) 'Desribing and managing uncertainty of categorical maps in GIS'. In Fisher P. (ed) *Innovations in GIS 2*, Taylor and Francis, pp 71-83.
6. Edwards G. and K.E. Lowell (1996) 'Modeling uncertainty in photointerpreted boundaries'. *Photogrammetric Engineering and Remote Sensing* 62(4): 377-391.
7. Schmidt M., H.E. Schreier and P.B. Shah (1995) 'A GIS evaluation of land use dynamics and forest soil fertility in a watershed in Nepal'. *International Journal of Geographical Information Systems* 9(3): 317-327.
8. Peccol E., A.C. Bird and T.R. Brewer (1996) 'GIS as a tool for assessing the influence of countryside designations and planning policies on landscape change'. *Journal of Environmental Management* 47: 355-367.
9. Green K., D. Kempka and L. Lackey (1994) 'Using remote sensing to detect and monitor land-cover and land-use change'. *Photogrammetric Engineering and Remote Sensing* 60(10): 1243-1251.
10. Johnson A.J. and D.W. Wichern (1998) *Applied Multivariate Statistical Analysis*. Prentice Hall.
11. Chrisman N.R., J.A Dougenik. and D. White (1992) 'Lessons for the design of polygon overlay processing from the Odyssey Whirlpool algorithm', *Proc. 5th Int. Symp. on Spatial Data Handling*, 2, International Geographical Union, pp 401-410.
12. Chrisman N.R. (1987) 'The accuracy of map overlays: a reassessment', *Landscape & Urban Planning* 14: 427-9.
13. Harvey F. 1994, 'Defining unmovable nodes/segments as part of vector overlay: The alignment problem', *Proceedings 6th Int. Symp. on Spatial Data Handling*, 1, International Geographical Union, pp 159-176.
14. Harvey F. and F. Vauglin (1996) 'Geometric match processing: applying multiple tolerances', *Proceedings 7th Int. Symp. on Spatial Data Handling*, 1, pp 4A.13-29.
15. Pullar D. (1991) 'Spatial overlay with inexact numerical data', *Proceedings AUTOCARTO 10*, ACSM-ASPRS, Falls Church, Va., pp 313-329.
16. Zhang G. and J. Tulip (1990) 'An algorithm for the avoidance of sliver polygons and clusters of points in spatial overlay, *Proceedings 4th Int. Symp. on Spatial Data Handling, 1*, International Geographical Union, pp 141-150.
17. Lupien A.E. and W.H. Moreland (1987) 'A general approach to map compilation', *AUTOCARTO 8*, ACSM-ASPRS, Falls Church, Va., pp 630-639.
18. Saalfield A. (1988) 'Conflation: automated map compilation'. *International Journal of Geographical Information Systems* 2(3): 217-228.
19. Cobb M.A., M.J. Chung H. Foley, F.E. Petry and K.B. Shaw (1998) 'A rule-based approach for the conflation of attributed vector data'. *GeoInformatica* 2(1): 7-35.

20. Sonka M., V.Hlavac and R. Boyle (1993) *Image Processing, Analysis and Machine Vision*. International Thomson Computer Press, London

21. Hester A.J., D.R. Miller and W. Towers (1996) 'Landscape-scale vegetation change in the Cairngorms, Scotland, 1946-1988: implications for land management'. *Biological Conservation* 77: 41-51.

22. Jones C.B. and J.M. Ware (1998) 'Proximity search with a triangulated spatial model'. *Computer Journal* 41(2): 71-83.

23. Jones C.B., J.M. Ware and C.D. Eynon (in press) 'Triangulated spatial models and neighbourhood search: an experimental comparison with quadtrees', *The Visual Computer*, accepted for publication.

24. Ware J.M. and C.B. Jones (1998), 'Matching and aligning features in overlayed coverages', *Proceedings of 6th International Symposium on Advances in Geographical Information Systems (ACM-GIS'98)*, pp 28-33.

25. Sintichakis M. and P. Constantopoulos (1997) 'A method for monolingual thesauri merging'. *Proceedings 20th Annual ACM SIGIR Conference on Research and Development in Information Retrieval*, Philadephia, USA, pp 129-138.

26. Tversky A. (1977) 'Features of similarity'. *Psychological Review* 84(4), 327-352.

27. Barr S. and M. Barnsley (1997) 'A region-based, graph-theoretic data model for the inference of second-order thematic information from remotely-sensed images'. *International Journal of Geographical Information Science* 11(6): 555-576.

28. Kontoes C., G.G. Wilkinson *et al* (1993). 'An experimental system for the integration of GIS data in knowledge-based image analysis for remote sensing of agriculture. *International Journal of Geographical Information Systems* 7(3): 247-262.

Formalisms and Modeling

Landscape Editing with Knowledge-Based Measure Deductions for Ecological Planning

Jörn Möltgen, Benno Schmidt, and Werner Kuhn

Institute for Geoinformatics, Westfälische Wilhelms-Universität Münster
Robert-Koch-Str. 26-28, D-48149 Münster, Germany
Phone: +49 251 83-31961, Fax: +49 251 83-39763
{moltgej, benno, kuhn}@ifgi.uni-muenster.de

Abstract. The approach presented suggests a new way of supporting planning processes. Planners from various disciplines can test and discuss planning scenarios at a workbench, where a virtual landscape is visualized in a 3-D real-time environment. With the defined paradigm of 'landscape editing', planners can model and manipulate virtual landscapes intuitively. They transform, add, move and delete by direct manipulation of geo-objects. With the help of such a human-computer interface, planners can specify planning scenarios visually and cooperatively. As soon as a planning scenario finds consensus, the system analyzes the modified model, detects the changes, and deduces measures to be carried out to achieve the specified objectives in the real world. To perform this last step, an interdisciplinary knowledge base has to be set up. Through the use of expert knowledge, planning processes become more transparent and understandable.

Motivation

The use of geographic information systems (GIS) and spatial decision support systems (SDSS) for monitoring tasks and ecological planning processes has become established in recent years. The coupling of GIS techniques and SDSS with 3-D visualization is the natural next step to support landscape planning with the creation, analysis and modification of virtual landscapes. For landscape planners, it is undisputed that a visual impression of the planned object is important, because they develop the object under the consideration of landscape aesthetics. *"In every natural setting these two elements – visual and spatial – combine to create a distinctive view. The landscape designer must have a firm grasp of the visual and spatial character of the setting before he can begin to develop it"* [12]. Moreover, 3-D visualization provides more insights to spatio-temporal or thematic relations than a text display or the traditional 2-D map [29, 31]. A 3-D approach is indispensable, especially for the task of designing a landscape model and the presentation of planning ideas. On the one hand, it helps the planners themselves to optimize their ideas. On the other hand, it enables planning laymen to assess planning drafts. Taking cognitive aspects into account, 3-D visualization facilitates the acquisition of 3-D information (e.g., terrain gradients or tree heights) and provides a better understanding of spatial relations affecting 3-D

P. Agouris and A. Stefanidis (Eds.): ISD'99, LNCS 1737, pp. 139-152, 1999
© Springer-Verlag Berlin Heidelberg 1999

objects (e.g., shadowing affects caused by trees). Furthermore, 3-D interaction mechanisms that are intuitively useable can be implemented.

The additional opportunity to derive or deduce measures for the restoration or maintenance of landscape elements is yet to be exploited. The traditional focus of SDSS aims at the composition of databases, spatial modeling, graphical display and analysis to support the decision-maker. Approaches should follow that integrate expert knowledge in these systems allowing the investigation of different scenarios before decision-making [22]. Knowledge-based SDSS (KBSDSS) represent the knowledge and the experience of experts for a special area of interest and combine *"the ability to simulate the heuristic reasoning of experts with an explanation facility for justifying their reasoning and conclusion"* [33]. It is well known that human beings with their vast experience are able to make better decisions than machines. However, for complex planning tasks, KBSDSSs are able to demonstrate interdisciplinary causes and effects.

Environmental planning is frequently a collaborative, multi-disciplinary activity. For a wide range of decision-makers, the goal is to reach a *"limited shared understanding of the current state of their geographical area, and threats to it, and the likely outcomes of various future actions..."* [28]. Hence, along with the prediction of landscape developments, there is a demand for tools that allow "computer-supported co-operative work" (CSCW). "Workbench"-like environments, in particular, [1, 30] used in the field of Virtual Reality (VR) technology offer big potential to meet this requirement, while providing ways to interact with 3-D landscapes. Consequently, the integration of table-based virtual environments and KBSDSSs is a very promising approach creating a new planning support paradigm.

The development of an interface which combines these abilities raises questions about input and output techniques and the user dialogue. This paper discusses possible answers. The fundamentals of such a visual, interactive knowledge-based system are presented as the landscape editing paradigm. The paper uses a case study in river ecology as a motivation and testbed for the ideas presented.

Note, that the system's functionality and the user interface will be defined from the ecological planner's point of view. Methods from the field of computer science will be used to specify the requirements formally and to provide means to implement the specified system.

VR Hardware Components

For a better understanding of the following ideas, we will explain how the suggested VR hardware works and describe the basic application facilities. Principally, the hardware provided by the SpatialViSC initiative of the University of Münster [25, 23] works similar to environments such as the "Responsive Workbench" (developed at the German National Research Center for Information Technology, GMD, and at Stanford University) or the "ImmersaDesk" (Pyramid Systems, Inc.). The system consists of a projection table which can be regarded as a large monitor (screen size 1,36 m x 1,02 m). Reflected by a huge mirror, the images generated by a powerful projector are projected on the bottom side of a semi-transparent pane. This pane can be aligned horizontally.

A graphics workstation generates stereoscopic image pairs, e.g. at a frequency of 50 Hz per eye. A 3-D rendering toolkit is used to calculate these image pairs. To make sure that the observer's left eye sees only the image calculated for the left eye's position, and the right eye sees the corresponding right-eye view, the user wears glasses consisting of closeable LCD shutters. Image generation and shutter release signals are synchronized using a synchronization signal from the workstation's graphics board. This way, the user gets the impression of 3-D objects floating above the table's projection pane (see figure 1; note that this is a manipulated photo).

To allow interaction, the user's head position and the position of a hand-held stylus are tracked. A video-based tracking system is used here [8]. Using two cameras situated on both sides of the projection table, the tracking system simultaneously tracks the real-space 3-D position of two infrared LEDs, one fixed on the shutter glasses, the other one at the tip of the stylus. This information is passed to the rendering software that calculates the corresponding images.

In this environment, immersion into the virtual world is limited to the sight pyramid defined by the observer position and the four table corners. 3-D editing operations will be performed intuitively using the stylus.

Since the users still perceive their real-world environment, the configuration offers large potential in the field of CSCW. It is hardly possible yet to render stereoscopic images for more than two tracked simultaneous observers (for n users, a refresh rate of $2 \cdot n \cdot 50$ Hz is required to obtain a flicker-free picture). However, observation of the technical evolution of hardware, allows one the forecast that stereoscopic visualization using projection tables and tracking facilities could serve as common basis for discussions for a group of planners very soon.

Task Analysis: Ideal Model of Interaction

This chapter describes a potential use case showing the task flow of an ecological planner using a KBSDSS linked to a 3-D landscape editor. An example from the field of flood plain planning has been chosen for the concrete planning task description. The planner has the objective to work out a concept for the redevelopment of the flood plain into a restored stage.

Our vision comprises the following operation steps. First, a 3-D model of a flood plain is displayed, which gives an impression of the current landscape state. It shows the following objects:

• river bed at a large scale,
• vegetation at the river banks,
• various structures of the river bed,
• surrounding area,
• land use, cultivation,
• housing estates
• road ways.

In addition to these visual objects, various attributes are retrievable from a database. These include hydrological data, data about the water quality, land ownership data or data about the zoobenthos of the river and its structure (e.g., naturalness of its banks, number of barricades, shading, depth and width erosion). All this data can be queried in a typical GIS or database manner.

By exploring the virtual reality visually and retrieving database information, the planner can assess the quality of the flood plain and evaluate the necessity for redevelopment measures. For example the planner, who in fact could be more than just one person, is confronted with an elongated river course. He/she discovers that there is no width erosion at all, just try a small number of barricades, no drift wood and the river temperature is too warm. The planner must find a solution which takes into account buildings, roads or land ownership while planning the natural redevelopment of the river. Therefore, the planner *edits* the flood plain model in order to try out different planning scenarios and uses different interaction tools from a tool box to manipulate spatial objects with his/her bare hands. In this manner, he/she grabs river sections to bend them out of their original shapes and specifies a new river course with meanders. Creating the meander, the planner might have two options. If old river structures exist, he/she can reconnect an old meander to the course. If not, measures can be introduced which will lead to the growing of the meander. During the model alterations, the plausibility of all interactions is checked. For example, it will be checked if the new river course were directed uphill. In this case, the system would reject the modification. By editing river sections, the planner tries to encourage the erosion processes. Erosion is a characteristic feature of a natural river course with a high diversity of structures.

The following step relates to the vegetation along the river banks which is important for wildlife (e.g., birds), shading (prevents from high water temperatures) and as a natural protection against excessive erosion. The planner can grab trees, groups of trees or bushes from a wide pool of vegetation elements and move them close to the river. This way the planner designs a new flood plain model. He/she re-edits it, until a role model is defined which fits her/his interdisciplinary demands.

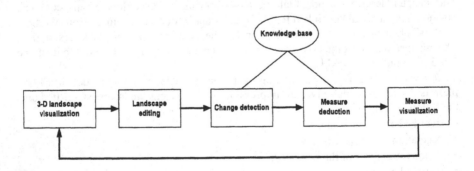

Fig. 1. User workflow

As soon as a planning scenario finds consensus with other planners, the system analyzes the modified virtual model, detects the changes (original/edited model), and deduces measures to be carried out to achieve the specified objectives in the real world. To perform this step, a knowledge base starts to work. It compares the starting point with the new role model in order to detect and analyze all changes. The changes serve as input for the rule base which deduces measures to be taken into account for a sustainable river restoration and maintenance.

Measures can be displayed in various ways. Measures such as 'planting of bank coppice', 'toleration of depth and width erosion', 'destruction of the bottom sealing', or 'rebuilding of bottom and bank stabilization' could be visualized as cartographic symbols or pictograms. Since the river course is divided into 100 m sections, the symbols and pictograms will be placed at the corresponding river sections. Measures that refer to one specific object are displayed near this object. A sewage pipe which has to be deleted from the river will be crossed out, so that the planner knows what to do and exactly where to do it. Additionally, a list with further instructions could be visualized. It includes information about appropriate species (e.g., tree species) to use and secondary measures such as 'ask farmer X for interest in land conversion'. This textual measure explanation includes also a list of effected thematically attributes such as water quality, if a waste water pipe is cut from the river.

Knowledge Base and Inference Engine

Measure deduction requires expert knowledge. A catalog containing various measures for sustainable river maintenance builds the basis for the knowledge base. This catalog includes measures such as 'planting of bank coppice', 'reconnection of old/cutoff arms', 'toleration of depth and width erosion', 'conversion of bordering arable farm land into grassland' or 'destruction of the bottom sealing' [19].

For instance, the placement of meanders at a river course invokes rules that induce measures that could be executed in practice. The following (simplified) example shows some rules for the deduction of measures in order to archive a meander at a river course.

```
if historic water course is known
then

    if Attribute('property can be bought')
    then Measure('rebuilding of old water course')

    if Measure('rebuilding of old water course')
    then Measure('initial planting of bank coppice')
         Measure('creation of bank buffer zones')
         Measure('toleration of depth and width erosion')
    endif

else
```

```
if Attribute('river profile.width') /
   Attribute('river profile.depth') ≤ 2.0
then Measure('broadening of river profile')

if Attribute('indigenous trees') is valid upstream
then Measure('placement/toleration of deadwood')
else Measure('placement of troubling stones')

...

endif
```

The example contains both thematic and spatial conditions (see conditions set in italics) and changes that trigger measure deductions. To specify such state changes, the user edits the landscape model visually. The measures deduced by the inference engine are displayed (see figure 2). Note, that this could result in set of contradictory measures and corresponding explanations.

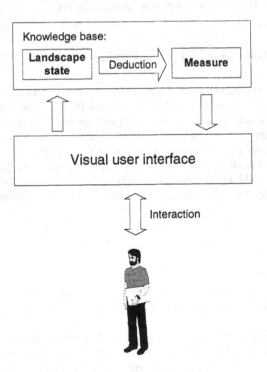

Fig. 2. Knowledge base and visual user interface

User Interface Specification

We can conceive different layers of representation here: the user's mental representation, the external representation, i.e. the displayed image, and the data model used to implement the system (cf. [21]). Visualization is used considering two different aspects. On the one hand, the task is to generate a visual representation of the ideas the planner has in mind. On the other hand, the objects held in the spatial database and deduced measures have to be presented visually (see figures 2 and 3). In the project described here, visualization plays a central role as a human-computer interface (cf.[18]) that facilitates input and output of planning ideas.

In addition to change detection (chapter 6) and knowledge bases (chapter 4), the user interface design is a challenge for the landscape editing paradigm. The components of the user-computer interface were defined using the four-level language model suggested by [9].

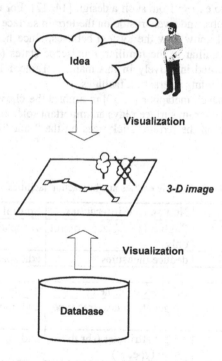

Fig. 3. Role of visualization

The *conceptual design* defines the key application concepts. This level incorporates the user's mental model of the high-level interaction. Here, the model consists of the overall landscape, landscape states, spatial and thematic entities, a set of (textual) facts and rules, and measures. A prototype system will include spatial entity classes to handle surfaces describing terrain, single trees, shrub groups, river courses, and coverages holding land parcel information (e.g., land use, ownership).

The relations between these main elements are as follows: A landscape object knows various states S_i. One of these states describes the current state of the landscape (S_0). Further states S_i, $i \neq 0$, may define planning scenarios. A landscape state is composed of spatial entities. In the following, we will use the term geo-object instead of spatial entity. The landscape is linked to the facts and rules holding knowledge about the spatial, temporal and thematic relations between the spatial entities as well as about the measures that have to be deduced to realize the specified state. Since these rules might be valid for different landscapes, they are not part of the landscape, but are associated with it.

The user can edit the visual portion of the landscape by creating geo-objects, changing the spatial extent or positions of geo-objects that already are part of the landscape, or modifying their appearance. The interface design is based on the sand table metaphor, i.e. the user works standing in front of a table with tangible and movable items. Users will expect the interface to behave according to what their experience has taught them to expect from such a design [14, 17]. For example, spatial objects such as trees, shrubs, and rivers reside on the terrain surface ("gravitational constraint"). The user will know how the system behaves, since he/she can establish a mapping from the unfamiliar to the familiar. Landscape states (especially: planning scenarios) can be specified intuitively in this manner. Table 1 lists the basic entity classes and the corresponding interaction facilities.

Note that the workbench metaphor [1, 30] resembles the chosen sand table. Since the non-planar, editable terrain surface plays an important role, and the planner wants to sketch river courses on the terrain, stick trees on the "sand" etc., we favored the sand table metaphor.

Table 1. Basic entities and interaction facilities

Entity class	Non-spatial interaction	Spatial interaction
Landscape	(high-level object control only)	via spatial entities
Landscape state	deduce measures	edit spatial entities
Spatial entities:		
Terrain	(not necessary here)	mould
Tree	set/get attributes (tree type, ...)	add, move, resize, remove
Shrub group	set/get attributes (shrub group type, ...)	add, move, mould, remove
River course/sections	set/get thematic attributes (bank/bottom stabilization,...)	course editing (place meanders, create curves at river sections, ...)
Flood plain	set/get thematic attributes (substance concentrations, ...)	enlarge (or reduce) extent
Land parcel coverage	set/get thematic attributes	split / merge polygons

	(e.g., change land use)	
Knowledge base:		
Facts and rules	(textual) editing, querying	-
Measures	(deduce "on button-click")	Visualization

The *semantic design* specifies detailed functionality of the system. Here, functional requirements are described. The signatures of the operations that have to be implemented were specified for the envisioned application. On this level, especially the meanings conveyed by the input commands and the display (i.e., computer output) have to be defined. Moreover, we took into account which semantic errors might occur.

A structural approach has been proposed to handle metaphors in interface design [6]. For example, a formal approach based on algebraic specifications was described by [15]. To specify the "electronic" sand-table substitute, the terrain object must be distinguished from the other geo-objects. This way, the "gravitational constraint" can be formulated. Consequently, this constraint constitutes the distinction from related categories such as the 2-D electronic desktop or the workbench metaphor mentioned above.

The implementation of the envisioned user interface will not work if the equations given in the specification do not hold at editing time. For example, moveable objects reside on the terrain surface. There are many more equations that are part of a complete specification, e.g. a tree may not be taller than the tree's size at its maximum age, water has to flow downhill, and a tree's crown and the soil below the terrain surface may not overlap. It has to be defined how constraint infringements are handled at editing time.

Apart from the sand-table metaphor, some additional metaphors are needed to provide the required editing facilities to the user. The landscape editor we've designed comprises a box containing geo-object templates. To instantiate a geo-object, a template can be taken out of this box, which is located beside the actual landscape visualization. Moreover, so-called *handles* (or *grips*), as known from various CAD and drawing programs, allow geometry editing (e.g. [10, 2]). For example, the vertex of a polyline defining a river course can be picked and moved. Another way to define a new river course would be a manipulation based on a "modeling clay metaphor". The user can deform the river course like a modeling clay sausage. Note that there are many more metaphors inherent in the system such as visual buttons that can be punched to trigger off certain events (e.g. [24]) etc.

The *syntactic design* defines the sequence of inputs and outputs, i.e. the grammatical structure of the "tokens" used to articulate the semantic concept [13]. The operations specified on the semantic level can be decomposed into elementary interaction units. The higher-level operations are composed of these units.

The interaction with geo-objects will be performed in the VR environment. We use 3-D stereoscopic output on a projection table. Since the user's head and hand movements are tracked, he/she can interact with the visualized objects as if they were real objects located in space in front of him/her. Object selection and manipulation are realized using the hand-held stylus metaphor. To start an editing command, the user has to click at the geo-object he/she wants to manipulate. For this, the hand-held stylus with its (physical) button is used. Subsequently, the manipulation can be done, e.g.

using the grips mentioned above. The type of tokens used for input are actions of the following types: 'click on geo-object', 'select geo-object template', 'set initial position', 'hit button "X" ', 'digitize position', and various editing actions.

The maintenance of the facts and rules needed for measure deduction and necessary to perform the plausibility checks mentioned above, requires an environment that is suitable to handle textual information. The deduced measures will be displayed in the visual environment. Cartographic symbols, signatures and variables will be used as output tokens.

Finally, the *lexical design* determines, how the inputs and outputs are actually formed from primitive hardware operations.

In the VR environment, low-level primitive inputs are the movement of the head and the hand (in the environment described in chapter 2, there are video-tracked infrared LEDs on the shutter glasses and on the stylus the user is holding in his/her hands) and the triggering of events by activating a button fixed on the stylus. The output are sets of rendering primitives that assemble geo-objects, cartographic elements, or UI elements. Table 2 summarizes the four-level design described above.

Table 2. User interface design following FOLEY and VAN DAM's [9] four-level language model

	Objects	Operations
Conceptual level	• landscape, landscape states, and geo-objects on the sand table • facts & rules (plausibility rules and measures) • planning documents (texts, maps, ...), cartographic output elements	• state editing facilities • measure deduction & visualization
Semantic level	• concrete classes corresponding to the conceptual objects	• complete list of "virtual" (in the software-technical sense) object methods
Syntactic level	• geo-objects: Directly manipulable visual objects (shapes, buttons, ...) • knowledge base: text	• geo-objects: Selection, point location • knowledge / measures: text / cartographic elements
Lexical level	• visualization: Shutter glasses, stylus • knowledge base: as known from text-editors	• visualization: Head and hand movement, button activation • knowledge base: as known from text-editors

Coupling of Knowledge Base and Visual User Interface

The editing of geo-objects might lead to changes in the landscape state. In order to deduce measures, these changes have to be detected by the system. These changes also trigger affected rules. Consequently, new measures will be deduced. These measures will be presented using cartographic design facilities. For this, information about the geo-objects to which the measures refer is needed.

Table 3. Examples for geo-objects triggering measures

Geo-object	Event/Interaction	Relevant changes	Possible measures
Tree	Add a new tree	coordinates, size	Placement of trees, eventually erasure of bank stabilization
River section	Set water quality	change in water quality	All measures which help to improve water quality
River course	Place meander	coordinates, curvature, topology	Planting, toleration of erosion, creation of buffer zones, etc.

The rules held in the knowledge base determine which changes have to be detected after an editing session. These changes may refer to geometric, topological or thematic characteristics. Table 3 shows examples of how geo-object modifications may induce measures. The rule conditions define the task that has to be done by a change detection algorithm.

Consequently, the approach presented requires the combination of

- interactive 3-D real-time visualization
- spatial and thematic query facilities
- a knowledge base and an inference engine.

Existing 3-D real-time rendering libraries such as OpenGL [32] offer the primitive input and output facilities that are needed to implement the user-interface on the lexical and syntactic level. The main work to be done is to establish the link to the other architectural components. Concerning the data models, these components are usually incompatible: 3-D rendering libraries are based on rendering primitives such as triangles/polygons, textures etc. [10]. Sophisticated spatial and thematic queries, require data-models that include topological information and handle thematic information (e.g., GIS technology). Finally, the facts and rules held in the knowledge bases are put into the language of logics, which usually is represented as text. Ways to set up integrated systems are suggested by [4], [5] or [26].

It is known that the data model mismatches might cause difficulties (e.g., erroneous visualizations, see [27]). One of the reasons for this is that the application objects

As mentioned above, it is very important to maintain semantic consistency at editing time. Moreover, there may be additional constraints that may affect spatial or thematic constraints; e.g., a planned meander may not intersect a housing estate.

Conclusions

The approach presented suggests a new way of traversing planning processes. The interface design is based on a sand table metaphor which enables a very intuitive interaction. Visualization is no longer an additional feature, but becomes an essential part in the processes of problem formulation and decision-making. The interaction facilities described enable consensus-based planning processes in which planners can play out different scenarios. With the implementation of expert knowledge expansion of common knowledge-based spatial decision support systems into a knowledge-based measure suggestion system becomes possible [19]. This step enables planning processes to become more transparent and comprehensible.

The landscape editing paradigm introduced necessitates semantic plausibility checking at editing time. The rules held in the knowledge-based measure deduction component define the task that has to be done by a convenient change detection algorithm.

We have started to implement a prototype system based on the 3-D visualization framework MAM/VRS [7] and a "virtual" GIS component [3]. A prototype rule-base coupled to a 2-D GIS, is also available [20].

There is, however, much research still to be done. One of the research issues is to find out to what extent the knowledge from the participating disciplines (river ecology, landscape planning, hydraulic engineering, etc.) can be formalized considering all crucial spatial and thematic interdependencies. The issue, to what extent the proposed system will effect the quality of the decisions is unresolved. In this paper we focused on the processing of qualitative knowledge. The authors are aware of the role of quantitative processes and the huge potential of the integration of numerical simulation models.

Moreover, fuzzy data have to be processed to model the investigated landscapes properly, because the knowledge base deceives an exactness which in fact may not be given at all. It is not just spatial heterogeneity, but temporal and thematic variablity that makes fuzzy-sets necessary (cf. [11, 16]). Finally, temporal aspects (landscape development) have to be considered for a comprehensive landscape state description.

Acknowledgements

We would like to thank U. Streit, C. Uhlenkueken, L. Bernard, and A. Hitchcock from the Institute for Geoinformatics at Muenster University, and the Minsterium für Schule und Weiterbildung, Wissenschaft und Forschung des Landes Nordrhein-Westfalen for their support.

References

1. Agrawala, M., A.C. Beers, B. Fröhlich, P. Hanrahan, I. McDowall & M. Bolas (1997): *The Two-User Responsive Workbench: Support for Collaboration Through Individual Views of a Shared Space.* Proceedings SIGGRAPH '97, http://www-graphics.stanford.edu/papers-/twoviewer.

2. Autodesk, Inc. (1992): *AutoCAD Release 12, Reference Manual.* San Rafael, CA: Autodesk.

3. Bernard, L., B. Schmidt & U. Streit (1998b): *AtmoGIS - Integration of Atmospheric Models and GIS.* Proceedings of the 8th International Symposium on Spatial Data Handling (SDH '98) in Vancouver, Canada, pp. 267-276.

4. Bernard, L., B. Schmidt, U. Streit & C. Uhlenküken (1998a): *Managing, Modeling, and Visualizing High-Dimensional Spatio-Temporal Data in an Integrated System.* GeoInformatica, Vol. 2, No. 1, Norwell, MA: Kluwer Academic Publishers, March 1998, pp. 59-77.

5. Buehler, K. & L. McKee (1996): *The OpenGIS Guide - Introduction to Interoperable Geoprocessing.* Technical report, Open Geodata Interoperability Specification (OGIS), Open GIS Consortium, Inc.

6. Carroll, J.M., R.L. Mack & W.A. Kellogg (1988): *Interface Metaphors and User Interface Design.* In M. Helander, ed.: Handbook of Human-Computer Interaction, Elsevier, pp. 67-85.

7. Döllner, J. & K. Hinrichs (1999): *An Object-Oriented Approach for Integrating 3D Visualization Systems and GIS.* Computers & Geosciences, special issue "Geoscientific Visualization", Elsevier Science, in press.

8. Dorfmüller, K. & H. Wirth (1998): *Real-Time Hand and Head Tracking for Virtual Environments Using Infrared Beacons.* In N. Magnenat-Thalmann & D. Thalmann, eds.: Modelling and Motion Capture Techniques for Virtual Environments. Lecture Notes in Computer Science, 1537, Berlin: Springer, pp. 113-127.

9. Foley, J.D. & A. van Dam (1982): *Fundamentals of Interactive Computer Graphics.* Reading, MA: Addison-Wesley, pp. 217-243.

10. Foley, J.D., A. van Dam, S.K. Feiner & J.F. Hughes (1996): *Computer Graphics : Principles and Practice.* 2nd ed., Reading, MA: Addison-Wesley.

11. Grabaum, R. & U. Steinhardt, eds. (1998): *Landschaftsbewertung unter Verwendung analytischer Verfahren und Fuzzy-Logic.* UFZ-Bericht Nr. 6/1998, Leipzig: Umweltforschungszentrum Leipzig-Halle.

12. Higuchi, T. (1989): *The Visual and Spatial Structure of Landscapes.* Massachusetts Institute of Technology (MIT), MIT Press paperback edition.

13. Jacob, R.J.K. (1999): *User Interfaces.* Encyclopedia of Computer Science, 4th ed., ed. by D. Hemmendinger, A. Ralston & E. Reilly, Macmillan Reference Ltd., 1999, in press.

14. Kuhn, W. (1992): *Paradigms of GIS Use.* 5th International Conference on Spatial Data Handling, Charleston, SC, pp. 91-103.

15. Kuhn, W. & A.U. Frank (1991): *A Formalization of Metaphors and Image-Schemas in User Interfaces.* In D.M. Mark & A.U. Frank, eds.: Cognitive and Linguistic Aspects of Geographic Space, Kluwer, pp. 419-434.

16. Lutze, G. & R. Wieland (1997): *Fuzzy in der Landschaftsforschung und –modellierung.* In R. Grützner, ed. (1997): Fortschritte in der Simulationstechnik : Modellierung und Simulation im Umweltbereich. Braunschweig: Vieweg, pp. 233-247

17. Mark, D. (1992): *Spatial Metaphors for Human-Computer Interaction.* 5th International Conference on Spatial Data Handling, Charleston, SC, pp. 104-112.

18. Medyckij-Scott, D. (1994): *Visualization and Human-Computer Interaction in GIS.* In H.M. Hearnshaw & D.J. Unwin, eds.: Visualization in Geographical Information Systems, Chichester: Wiley.

19. Möltgen, J. & A. Hitchcock (1998): *A GIS Application for the Derivation of Measures to Maintain and Restore Lowland Rivers.* Proceedings of the 8th International Symposium on

Spatial Data Handling (ed. by T.K. Poiker & N. Chrisman), Vancouver, Canada, 1998. International Geographical Union, pp. 247-255.

20. Möltgen, J. & H. Pundt (1998): *Regelbasierte GIS-Werkzeuge zur Maßnahmenherleitung in der Gewässerpflege*. In J. Strobl & F. Dollinger, eds.: Angewandte Geographische Informationsverarbeitung (AGIT '98), Heidelberg: Wichmann.

21. Norman, D.A. (1991): *Cognitive Artifacts*. In J. Carroll, ed.: Designing Interaction: Psychology at the Human-Computer Interface, Cambridge Series on Human-Computer Interaction 4, Cambridge, UK: Cambridge University Press, pp. 17-38.

22. Rizzoli, A.E. & W.J. Young (1997): *Delivering Environmental Decision Support Systems: Software Tools and Techniques*. Environmental Modelling & Software 12(12), pp. 237-249.

23. Schmidt, B., U. Streit & C. Uhlenküken (1999): *Zur Einsetzbarkeit von Workbench-Umgebungen für geowissenschaftliche und planerische Fragestellungen*. In J. Strobl & T. Blaschke, Hrsg.: Angewandte Geographische Informationsverarbeitung XI (AGIT '99), Heidelberg: Wichmann, pp. 482-489.

24. Serra, L., T. Poston, Ng H., Chua B.C. & J.A. Waterworth (1995): *Interaction Techniques for a Virtual Workspace*. ICAT/VRST '95, Japan, http://www.informatik.umu.se-/~jwworth/vrst95-1.html

25. SpatialViSC-Initiative (1998): Projektbeschreibungen im Rahmen der fächerübergreifenden Arbeiten zu "SpatialViSC". University of Münster, Germany, http://ifgi.uni-muenster.de/3_projekte/spatial_visc/workbench_main.html.

26. Story, P.A. & M.F. Worboys (1995): *A Design Support Environment for Spatio-Temporal Database Applications*. Proceedings COSIT '95, Lecture Notes in Computer Science, 988, Springer, pp. 413-430.

27. Uhlenküken, C., B. Schmidt & U. Streit (1999): *Visual Exploration of High-Dimensional Spatial Data: Requirements and Deficits*. Computers & Geosciences, special issue "Geoscientific Visualization", Elsevier Science, in press.

28. van House, N.A., M.H. Butler & L.R. Schiff (1998): *Cooperative Knowledge Work and Practices of Trust: Sharing Environmental Planning Data Sets*. ACM 1998 Conference Proceedings on Computer Supported Work.

29. van Voris, P., W.D. Millard, J. Thomas & D. Urban (1993): *TERRA-Vision - The Integration of Scientific Analysis into the Decision Making Process*. International Journal of Geographic Information Systems, 7, pp. 143-164.

30. Wesche, G., J. Wind, W. Heiden, F. Hasenbrink & M. Göbel (1997): *Engineering on the Responsive Workbench*. Proceedings of the 8th Eurographics Workshop on Visualization in Scientific Computing, April 28-30, 1997, Boulogne sur Mer, France.

31. Wherrett, J.R. (1996): *Visualization Techniques for Landscape Evaluation : Literature Review*. Macaulay Land Use Research Institute (MLURI), Aberdeen, Scotland, http://bamboo.mluri.sari.ac.uk/~jo/litrev.

32. Woo, M., J. Neider & T. Davies (1997): *OpenGL Programming Guide*. 2nd ed., Addison-Wesley.

33. Zhu, X., R. G. Healey, et al. (1998): A Knowledge-Based Systems Approach to Design of Spatial Decision Support Systems for Environmental Management. Environmental Management 22(1), pp. 35-48.

A Framework for Integrating GIS and Digital Images

Zarine Kemp

Computing Laboratory
University of Kent
Canterbury, Kent CT2 7NF, UK
z.Kemp@ukc.ac.uk

Abstract. Digital images are potentially a rich source of spatially referenced information but often their use in GIS is restricted; either because internal representations do not allow access to content-dependent information or do not provide adequate context-dependent information and functionality for querying and retrieval. This paper proposes a generic, extensible, object-oriented framework for achieving seamless integration of GIS and digital images.

1 Introduction

Since the advent of geographic information systems (GIS), they have been used in a wide range of disciplines as generic tools for spatial data management and analysis. Some of these application areas, generally referred to as environmental information systems, are very reliant on the availability of large volumes of remotely sensed data of increasing spatial and spectral resolution. The requirement to extract meaningful information from these image datasets has resulted in parallel developments in image processing techniques. However, experience has shown that the use of satellite imagery for environmental spatiotemporal analyses achieves best results when it is combined with other operationally derived datasets, both spatial and aspatial [9], [34]. While recent hardware and software developments have helped, the problems inherent in managing spatial data from diverse sources at different scales and different underlying formats have proved a stumbling block to effective analysis.

From the systems point of view, some integration has occurred with GIS providing access to separate database, cartographic and image processing components that are coupled in some way to provide facilities for transferring data between them. The technological challenge for GIS is the development of a model whose semantic capabilities enable canonical representations of complex images in terms of spatiotemporal objects and their behaviour [23]. The problem of seamlessly integrating images in GIS is part of the larger problem (cogently discussed in [6]) of the mismatch between spatial paradigms at the user end and the diverse representational and functional solutions provided by the GIS. This paper concentrates on the data server component of an integrated GIS but argues that due to the special requirements for handling digital images, an extensible infrastructure with additional functionality is required. The conceptual data model and architecture described takes account of the considerably greater functionality required to store, view, index and manage heterogeneous data than would be the case with conventional data management. The

P.Agouris and A.Stefanidis (Eds.): ISD'99, LNCS 1737, pp. 153-167, 1999 complexities include powerful indexing, searching and display capabilities which can be computationally expensive if content-based searching is required for image data. In some cases the search may be fuzzy or based on incomplete information, so alternative retrieval mechanisms may have to be provided.

The rest of the paper is organised as follows. Section 1.1 introduces an environmental application to illustrate the diverse image management requirements of GIS. Section 2 presents a high-level view of the functionality required to integrate image sets into GIS. Section 3 discusses a metadata model that enables spatiotemporal data to be searched and retrieved in a GIS environment. Section 4 introduces design issues relevant to image modelling and management and discusses an implementation environment for realising the system. Section 5 concludes the paper with suggestions for further research directions.

1.1 Motivating Example

The rationale for integrating images and GIS is introduced through the example presented in this subsection. Although the scenario is based on a real application, it serves to illustrate the generic requirements for managing images within GIS. Figure 1 presents part of the conceptual data model for an environmental GIS for monitoring marine biodiversity (BioMar), using the UML graphical notation.

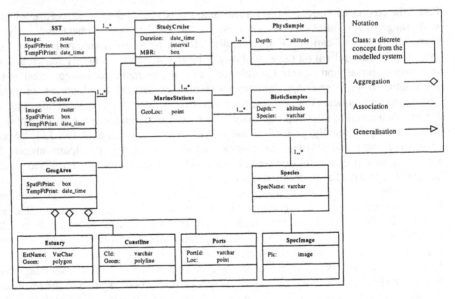

Fig. 1. Conceptual data model (BioMar)

Only the main entities have been depicted and those attributes that represent the spatiotemporal properties of the model. The diagram focuses on the structural rather than the behavioural aspects of the objects.

We present a brief description of the data model in Figure 1. The operational data sets are collected during research study cruises in different geographical areas at specific sampling points. The measurements pertain to aspects of the marine environment; these environmental values are located in space-time via the geo-temporal variables of the cruise and marine station entities. The biological data related to plankton species are often associated with images of species to help scientists with the identification of biotic samples. Other image sets representing marine variables are derived from satellite images representing sea surface temperatures (SST), ocean colour (OC) and so on. These images are located in space-time by the spatiotemporal footprints attached to to each object. In addition, the GIS includes geographical data in vector format such as coastlines, ports and areas of interest such as estuaries and spawning areas which are specified as aggregations of other geoobjects. It should be noted that the data model depicted in Fig. 1 is a *logical* model as viewed from the user's perspective establishing relationships between the entities. It may frequently be the case that the datasets are in separate, distributed data repositories rather than in one integrated database. In the such a situation, the underlying system would include additional software modules to present an abstracted logical view to the user. The provision of such a capability is beyond the scope of this paper and will not be considered further.

Consideration of the example application suggests that systems that integrate GIS and images exhibit the following characteristics:
- most entities of interest have dispositions in space and through time, one or both of these being central to most analyses,
- data originate from diverse sources: mapping agencies, remote sensors, and field observations, and are therefore heterogeneous,
- data sets may also be derived, either by interpolation or the application of biological and physical process models
- data types used to represent the variables are of various structures, which require internal mapping and transformation to achieve consistency for analysis.

Thus, flexible models are required to enable the spatial semantics of objects to be expressed. Several standards have been proposed for this purpose including [8], [25], [26], [29]. Here we assume a set of spatial abstract types conforming to a standard, to enable spatial properties to be expressed at the object and the attribute level.

2   Images in GIS

It follows from the previous section that a GIS which integrates images along with generic data types requires to provide additional functionality for:
- representation of various types of images such as satellite images, photographs etc.
- image processing capabilities to extract content-based features,
- indexing mechanisms based upon image features, spatial and temporal attributes as well as application domain relevant semantics,
- query and retrieval involving all types within the data model: spatial objects of raster as well as vector types as well as aspatial attributes.

To enable image objects to be seamlessly integrated into spatiotemporal analysis requires them to be associated with additional metadata to enable querying and retrieval. These metadata objects can be thought of as annotation, abstracts or cues to enable the content and semantics of images to be queried. Spatial data standards such as OpenGIS suggest similar roles for metadata. Figure 2 illustrates the use of metadata at different abstraction levels to achieve progressively increasing knowledge-based image representation.

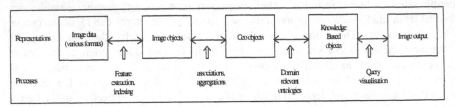

Fig. 2. Image representations at different abstraction levels in a GIS

As an aside, it should be noted that thematic mapping from space based sensors is one of the major uses of remote sensing. There is a substantial amount of research into the problem of classification and spatial generalisation based on satellite images [33] which are outside the scope of this paper. Likewise, effective presentation and visualisation of georeferenced image data, although an important component of the computational pipeline, is not considered further.

2.1 Content-Based Searching

The major difference between image and other data types is the problem of content-based indexing and retrieval. Consequently, a system that integrates images with GIS has to include these additional capabilities. The recent explosive growth in digital image database systems has been supported by corresponding research into the computational problems of content-based indexing and retrieval techniques for images. Here we present a brief survey in the context of their relevance to GIS.

Image management methods range from generic ones that apply to all types of images as described in [5], [24], to highly domain specific ones as in [2], [7]. These techniques can be categorised in different ways, generally reflecting the mechanism used to represent the content of images for querying and indexing. The text-based approach, which uses keywords, cues, or similar alphanumeric descriptors to characterise image content provides an accurate and effective means of generating image indexes. However, the major disadvantage is that it does not lend itself to automated techniques and requires user-mediated capture of index values. On the other hand, the image property based approach uses intrinsic visual properties of an image to extract a set of features which are used to generate query indexes. These automated techniques have been successfully used in image database systems such as Virage, QBIC and VisualSEEk [4], [14], [30] especially in the context of datasets consisting of photographic images. Despite their limitations, these techniques can be useful and are easy to embed in a GIS.

We have adopted a hybrid strategy in our system; we use generic feature based techniques where applicable, customised methods where absolutely necessary, both augmented by alphanumeric descriptions in the form of metadata objects associated with spatial objects at different levels of abstraction. The reasons for this design decision are as follows. The generic techniques have been shown to work reasonably well in different application domains with varying collections of images. This is a useful characteristic in situations such as the GIS application described in section 1.1 which consists of several different image sets each with its particular requirements for analysis and display. The algorithms are relatively easy to include in a GIS and can be used to achieve initial partitioning of the data space at the image level. We briefly survey the core feature-based techniques that are of relevance to GIS/image integration in the context of our example application.

Generic properties such as colour, texture and shape are used to represent normalised patterns of image content. For example, a colour histogram is a vector $<h_1, h_2, ... h_n>$ where each element h_j represents the number of pixels of colour j in the image. The resultant feature vectors for all the properties are used to construct indexes for subsequent querying. In generic image databases, the query usually takes the form of a candidate or query image that is compared with those in the dataset, the result being a small subset of images that are most similar to the query image; the similarity score is based on a distance measure. For example, colour histograms are typically compared using the sum of absolute value of differences or the sum of squared differences.

A useful extension is to allow for the property of image coherence [27]. In this case, the colour histogram is not just a measure of the number of pixels of a particular colour but also a measure of the extent to which the colour constitutes a coherent region. This enables the feature vector to capture some spatial information about an image, i.e. it emphasises where contiguous areas of a particular colour exist within an image. In our application, queries on the colour feature have proved to be successful in locating images representing sea surface temperatures (SST) where the *'temperature values > 10C exist'* or where *'temperature values >10C consist of >50% of the image'*.

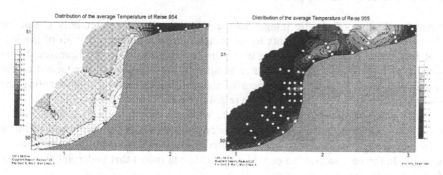

Fig. 3. Sea surface temperature data in the example application

Note that in some cases where satellite images are processed to reduce multispectral measurements to one unique parameter (as in the case of NDVI), in our model a metaobject would be associated with the image to provide a textual mapping to the pixel values. Figure 3 illustrates how SST images may be selected and visualised.

Texture analysis is concerned with low level, high frequency patterns in the image. Texture elements, small uniform intensity regions, can be analysed by shape and relative placement to extract information about image contents. In the context of the application, the texture feature can be used for image sets of ocean turbulence and in combination with other features to achieve a more accurate similarity measure.

The generic shape feature in general purpose image management frameworks can be of use in particular domains. They rely on shape characterization techniques such as the *gestalt* algorithm in the Excalibur Image Database of Informix [12]. One of the major entities in the application domain is plankton species which consist of images of line drawings as illustrated in Figure 4. During the development of the system the shape feature vector was explored to provide a species identification capability for marine biologists. However, this feature proved to be of limited use as biological species identification depends on morphological characteristics rather than shape. Instances of the same species vary in shape depending on stage of growth and gender, thus generating a lot of false positives during the retrieval process. The only solution in such cases is to provide a customised, interactive interface as part of the retrieval function.

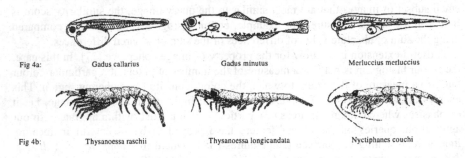

Fig 4a: Gadus callarius   Gadus minutus   Merluccius merluccius

Fig 4b: Thysanoessa raschii   Thysanoessa longicandata   Nyctiphanes couchi

Fig. 4. Images for species identification based on shape

Another feature of generic image feature indexing which is potentially useful for GIS is the ability to attach weights to the image feature primitives. Not all of the low level features may be equally relevant to 'similarity' measures in all domains. Some systems such as Virage enable the user to specify the weights to be attached to the feature primitives to enable refinement of the similarity measure, thus enabling the 'resembles' function to be tailored to the requirements of specific image sets.

The conclusion drawn from experiments with the prototype is that at the image object level, image feature vectors can be used successfully for querying and retrieval of entities of type image. Only where required, special purpose algorithms need to be included. In the next section we consider the metadata model that underpins the design of the integrated image/GIS.

3   A Metadata Model for Images

In the context of spatial information, several metadata standards have been proposed such as the American FGDC/Standards for Digital Geospatial Metadata [13] and the European catalogue of Data Sources (CDS). These have concentrated on the use of metadata from the perspective of globally distributed spatial data libraries, linked to web-based access. The discussion in the previous section as well as proposals such as the one presented in [3] suggest that image objects need to be associated with appropriate metadata for content-based and semantic searching. These metadata objects have been described as image attributes and categorised as 'content-based' or 'content-independent', 'domain-dependent' or 'domain-independent' and 'data driven' or 'application driven' [22].

   The metamodel described in this section embodies a functional perspective on metadata. Conceptually, metadata objects may be considered as a hierarchy of objects which partition the search space spatially and thematically at multiple levels of abstraction. Different metadata objects are associated with different levels of the hierarchy according to their purpose and function. This partitioning provides an efficient mechanism for browsing, querying and retrieval and also mirrors the user's search requirements. The inclusion of domain determined ontologies helps to reduce the gap between the implemented model and user reality. A conceptual view of the metadata model is shown in figure 5. This model can be used in most integrated image/GIS to enable flexible searching and querying of the image objects.

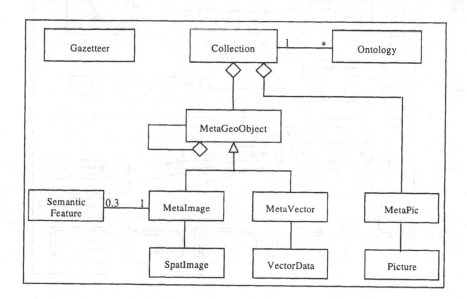

Fig. 5. Conceptual metadata model

The first (top) level of the metadata model comprises domain-dependent metadata. It contains the *Collection* class, which is a concept inherited from the library community, a standalone *Gazetteer*, which consists of pairs of location names and spatial coordinates, and an *Ontology* class which consists of a vocabulary specific to a particular domain and the relationship between associated concepts such as synonyms and thesauri. A *Collection* can be viewed as a cluster of objects that relate to the same knowledge domain. Hence, users can, at a high level of abstraction, browse through existing collections in order to narrow the search and increase precision without losing recall. *Collection* is an aggregation of *MetaGeoObjects*. Attributes in a collection include title, descriptive annotation, originator, date of creation, duration, overall spatial and temporal footprints of the underlying data sets. The second level down the hierarchy consists of *MetaGeoObjects* and their subclasses. The class contains attributes and methods that are applicable to all subobjects. Among those attributes are spatial and temporal footprints, name, collector and annotation. The *MetaGeoObject* class implements a *part_of* relationship which allows nested metadata to be described and composite objects modelled. Moreover, a MetaGeoObject can be an aggregation of vector data types such as points, lines and polygons. Each respective subclass is associated with type dependent. The *MetaImage* subclass contains metadata such as format, image resolution, a thumbnail representation of the image, image size, lineage etc. The third level contains the different data types with their respective data. At that level, large objects such as images, are stored and maintained.

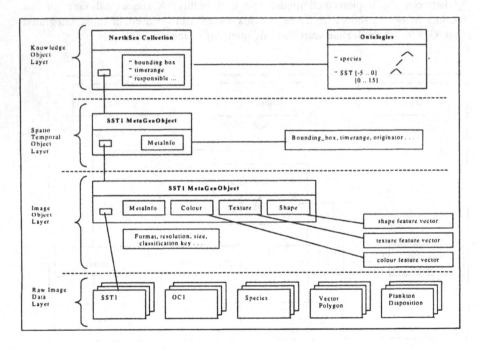

Fig. 6. Instantiation of metadata objects

Figure 6 depicts a possible instantiation of the metadata model. For example at the Image Object level, an SST image object will contain attributes such as size, format, resolution and lineage as well as feature attributes which have been automatically extracted and indexed when the image was input to the database. Note that the model can be extended to include other multimedia types such as text (e.g. reports) or video. Thus, the retrieval mechanism operates in a flexible way. Using metadata objects at the top level of the hierarchy users can pose queries by concepts, spatial footprints, time and collections. Alternatively, users can specify a narrower spatial bounding box, use a specific temporal interval or even query the annotation keywords. Using metadata at the bottom level, users can pose queries using the attributes associated with specific base data types.

4   Image Types in GIS: Implementation Issues

In this section we proceed to consider how the concepts discussed earlier for integrating images in GIS may be embodied in a GIS platform. From the implementation perspective, factors affecting image type specifications can be broadly categorised as (a) media type dependent and (b) application dependent. The total type specification of an image entity, namely its structure and behaviour, will be defined by an interaction between these two aspects. Thus, an image entity will be defined partly by virtue of its medium type, namely *image*, and partly by the role of that image in the conceptual model of the particular GIS application. Figure 7 below illustrates this concept. The base *image* type is considered to be analogous to the basic built-in types of integers, reals, chars, etc.; thus, an image type definition can be expressed by a template such as:

Image type   <name>

Representation
                <structural definition>
Operations
                <functional definition>

The base type specification: includes the image and the associated metadata objects as described in the previous subsection. The operations consist of functions that are fundamental to the capture, manipulation and output of image data: operations applied to all or a selected subset of pixels, filtering, and geometric transformations between coordinate systems, format and type conversion etc.

Application-dependent functionality: just as important in a GIS, are the application level semantics associated with such an object. These are a reflection of the role played by an image object in the overall conceptual model of the GIS, and are governed by factors such as:
-   whether the object is spatially referenced or not in the overall schema,
-   whether the application requires the image data to be merely displayed or to participate in content-based retrieval,
-   whether the query style is exact match or interactive browsing.
For example, in the GIS for marine environmental monitoring, an image of a particular species of zooplankton may be simply associated with the entity *plankton*, to be displayed as a descriptive attribute depicting the appearance of a particular instance of the entity. In this case, additional functionality is not required. If, however, the application has a requirement for content-based querying of the plankton image dataset, then an interactive interface is required to prompt the user for the required morphometric measurements to enable identification to be made [15]. Consider the example of another entity, *SST*, which is a set of images with spatial and temporal

footprints held in its associated metadata object. The *SST* entity could be queried in exact match mode on its space and time attributes or the contents of image values by evaluating a query image against the stored feature vector index. The same GIS includes spatial data in vector format identifying spawning areas of major fish species; a query involving an intersection *of 'spawning areas'* and *'SST values > n'* would require the spatial overlap operator to take account of the different underlying spatial representations.

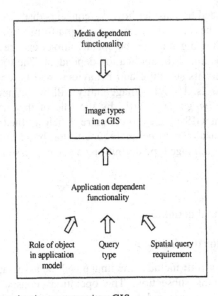

Fig. 7. Factors which determine image types in a GIS

A taxonomy of query types enables evaluation of the proposed image data model as suggested in [17]. In our GIS relevant query types are:

- *exact match*: these are typical SQL type queries and may involve objective attributes of images such as date of image capture or collection name. Sets of images for visualising temporal change can also be retrieved.
- *query by browsing*: these retrievals may involve semantic attributes of images and result in a candidate set being returned to the user. This query style helps to constrain the search space, enabling the user to continue browsing or using the intermediate results to formulate another query.a Alternatively, the user may browse a set of image abstractions (thumbnail sketches) and navigate to a required object.
- *spatial query*: these take several forms depending on the underlying representation of the spatial object. For example, retrieving an image by querying the spatial footprint of an image set is straightforward. Queries involving one or more image sets may involve map algebra type boolean operations to enable required image subsets to be retrieved.
- *spatial queries involving joins:* between image and vector spatial types or different vector types require a library of built-in spatial operations to cover all possible combinations of geometric primitives. Retrieval by querying spatial and aspatial attributes, in any combination and permutation of attribute type is of greatest

relevance in a GIS. Thus, encapsulated methods for the efficient creation and update of appropriate spatial indexes is a requirement for all the base types.

Note that image types can be queried in many other ways, for example the spatial disposition of subobjects within an image (*'subobj a to-left-of subobj b'*) as in [30]; by using shape based queries to retrieve objects from topographic datasets [2]; locating spatial image objects in a conceptual problem space [21], [28].

The preceding discussion on issues that inform the design and implementation of images in GIS suggests that adaptive multiple representations of image types are required. Figure 8 below illustrates a typical image type hierarchy that addresses the requirements of the diverse image entities in the marine GIS.

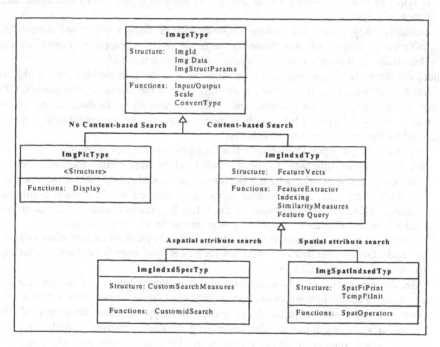

Fig. 8. Conceptual hierarchy for image types

4.1 Object-Oriented Design and Implementation

Various researchers have noted two important aspects of building GIS for environmental systems: first, the need for integration of GIS and images [18] and second, the difficulties entailed when simulation and process models need to be integrated in a GIS [1]. Consequently, our perspective on GIS/image integration is a catholic one encompassing data management, process modelling, flexible query and retrieval and visualisation. Integrated GIS and image systems can be built using a range of software platforms with different mechanisms for coupling the software components. For example, an ecological multimedia GIS was built using a proprietary GIS (ArcInfo) and extended to handle images and other multimedia objects using AML and C [16]. In another case, a slightly more flexible image capability was built into a GIS using the Illustra object-relational database [19] for image storage and management and C++ and Tcl/tk for the interfaces and visualisation [23].

It has been widely accepted that with the advent of object-oriented technology, and object-oriented/object-relational databases, various software components can be truly integrated instead of merely coexisting [31]. To achieve this, the development environment needs to be extensible and customisable:

- extensibility: as seen in the previous section, the built-in object types in a GIS cannot anticipate or provide all the types and functionality require for images. What is required is the capability of declaring user defined types, UDTs and associated functions UDFs.
- customisability: given the unique requirements of each application, monolithic software platforms are unsuitable; a range of plug-in components such as the DataBlades in Informix provide a solution to the problem [10].

There are therefore compelling reasons to indicate that the framework must be object-oriented. Experiments indicated that the requirements of the marine environmental GIS could be met by using the capabilities of a next-generation database management system such as Informix [20] which provides most of the computational support required for the implementation as follows:

- The basic image types available to the GIS developer must be *encapsulated*; this enables a clean interface to be provided while hiding the media-dependent complexity. For example, a base type for images would include the data structures to hold the raw data, and if spatial indexing is required would include a suitable indexing engine to build and maintain the index. It is important that these details are hidden from the GIS user to enable convenient interfaces to be provided.
- Provision of image and spatial types and associated operators as first class objects, and multidimensional indexing methods such as R-trees greatly facilitate the task of building an integrated GIS [32].
- Effective description of image content and metadata requires full support for the *aggregation* abstraction which enables objects of multiple types to be composed into complex 'container' objects. It is easier to support these structures if the compositional capabilities of the underlying paradigm provide complex pointer structures and type constructors for collections, lists, tuples, sets, and relations, as in the object-oriented model.
- The powerful object-oriented concept of *inheritance*, which enables extensibility and software reusability enables the construction of new object types on top of an existing hierarchy. The system provides base image and types and 'hooks' for the GIS designer to extend the base types. To accommodate the domain-dependent requirements for content-based retrieval and querying requires a mixture of declarative and procedural representations; this capability is provided via a set of compiled functional objects.
- Emerging standards: One of the problems that has bedevilled GIS in the past was the multiplicity of spatial representations tied to proprietary software which resulted in loose coupling between spatial and aspatial components. Now that the standard SQL:1999 is about to see the light of day, features specifically required for GIS/image integration will become part of standard query languages [11]. Given an

underlying object-oriented model image representations, SQL statements can be used to include image handling functionality in the GIS interface to:
- specify an entity with the appropriate image type
- insert instances of image objects
- extract feature vectors and insert into associated metadata objects
- query image entities using feature vectors
- express spatiotemporal queries involving spatial joins on different spatial object types
- query metadata objects at higher abstraction levels to provide a browsing, user-mediated style of interaction.

The discussion in this section has concentrated on the specific requirements for integrating modelling, specification and retrieval of images in GIS in a seamless manner. It is assumed that these capabilities are embedded in a generic environment for modelling and designing GIS applications.

5   Conclusions

Completely transparent integration of GIS and heterogeneous image types is a goal that has yet to be achieved. However, we believe that an object-oriented data management infrastructure is a promising starting point. The prototype that is being developed demonstrates that:
- images can be manipulated and queried in conjunction with other spatial and aspatial data types
- mechanisms for plugging in customised indexing and retrieval methods allow for flexible interpretation of image management requirements
- different image sets in a GIS can be managed according to application specific requirements
- it is necessary to provide core image management functionality, subsetting/chunking, changing   resolution, compression etc., to enable images to be integrated into an application model
- for most GIS applications inclusion of user-mediated metadata functionality is required.

There several issues that need to be addressed: these include mechanisms for automating the capture of the semantic, domain-dependent metadata, flexible user interfaces that enable structured querying as well as the navigational, fuzzy-match retrieval paradigm that is a more natural method of interacting with image datasets and the degradation in performance of GIS as a consequence of integrating huge volumes of data digital images and associated metadata objects. A GIS application design methodology and appropriate tools is needed to guide users in designing applications by reusing the underlying spatial and image type specifications. An intelligent visualisation module which is responsive to the retrieval taxonomy in section 4 is also a longer term goal.

Acknowledgements

The author would like to thank Informix Inc. for the generous provision of a licence to use the Informix Universal server, under the University Grants Program. Thanks are also due to Claudio de Souza Baptista for help with Informix.

References

1. Abel D., Taylor K. and Kuo D. (1997), Integrating Modelling Systems for Environmental Management Information Systems, *SIGMOD Record*, Vol 26, No 1, March 1997.
2. Agouris P., Stefanidis A. and Carswell D. (1998), Digital Image Retrieval Using Shape Based Queries, *Proceedings of SDH'98, The 8th International Symposium on Spatial Data Handling*, Poiker T. and Chrisman N. (Eds.), Vancouver, Canada, July 1998.
3. Anderson J.T. and Stonebraker M. (1994), SEQUIOA 2000 Metadata Schema for Satellite Images, *SIGMOD Record*, Vol. 23, No. 4.
4. Bach J.R., Fuller C., Gupta A., Hampapur A., Horowitz B., Humphrey R., Jain R. and Shu C-F, (1996), The Virage Image Search Engine: An open framework for image management, *The Proceedings of the SPIE Conference: Storage and Retrieval of Still Image and Video Databases*, Vol. 2670, pp 76-87.
5. Bergman L.D, Castelli V. and Li C-S. (1997), Progressive Content-Based Retrieval from Satellite Image Archives, *D-Lib Magazine*, October 1997, ISSN: 1082-9873.
6. Burrough P.A. and Frank A. (1995), Concepts and paradigms in spatial information: are current geographical systems truly generic?, *International Journal of Geographical Information Systems*, Vol. 9, No. 2, 101-116.
7. Chen H, Smith T.R. Larsgaard M.L, Hill, L.L. and Marshall R. (1997), A Geographical Knowledge Representation System for Multimedia Geospatial Retrieval and Analysis, *International Journal of Digital Libraries*.
8. Clementini E. and Felice P. (1994), Object-Oriented Modelling of Geographic Data, *Journal of the American Society of Information Science*, Vol. 45, No.9, pp 669-679.
9. Cowan D.D.,Koch P.M., Mayfield C.I. and Swayne D.A (1996), An Information Framework for Environmental Research and Management, *Environmental Software Systems*, Denzer R., Russell D. and Schimak G. (Eds.), Chapman Hall, London, ISBN 0 412 73730 2.
10. Dessloch S. and Mattos N. (1997), Integrating SQL Databases with Content-specific Search Engines, *Proceedings of the 23rd VLDB Conference*, Athens, Greece, 528-537.
11. Eisenberg A. and Melton J. (1999), SQL: 1999, Formerly known as SQL3, *SIGMOD Record*, Vol 28, No 1, March 1999.
12. Excalibur (1997), The Excalibur Image Datablade Module, User's Guide, Version 1.1.
13. FGDC (1995), Content Standards for Digital Geospatial Metadata, *Federal Geographic Data Committee*, 1995.
14. Flickner M., Sawhney H., Niblack W. et al (1995), *IEEE Computer*, September 1995.
15. Froese R., Papasissi N, (1989), The Use of Modern Relational Databases for the Identification of Fish Larvae, *The Journal of Applied Ichthyology*, Vol. 6, pp 37-45.
16. Groom J. and Kemp Z. (1995), Generic multimedia facilities in geographic information systems, *Innovations in GIS 2*, Fisher P. (Ed), Taylor & Francis, London, ISBN 07484 0269-1.
17. Modelling and Retrieval for a Class of Image Database Applications, *Multimedia Database Systems: Issues and Research Directions*, Subrahmanian V. and Jajodia S. (Eds.), Springer-Verlag, Berlin, ISBN: 3-540-58710-1.

18. Hartnall T. (1994), Laser-Scan Limited, Cambridge UK, Environmental Management through Integration of Remote Sensing and GIS, *Proceedings of GIS 94*, Birmingham, UK, 17-18 May.

19. Illustra Documentation (1994), Illustra Information Technologies Inc., Oakland, CA 94607.

20. Informix (1997), Informix Answers Onlione – Product Documentation, version 1.91.

21. Jones C.B., Taylor C., Tudhope D. and Beynon-Davies P. (1997), Conceptual, spatial and temporal referencing of multimedia objects, *Advances in GIS Research II*, Kraak M-J and Molenaar M. (Eds.), Taylor & Francis, London, ISBN: 0 7484 0591 7.

22. Kashyap V., Shah K. and Sheth A. (1996), Metadata for Building the Multimedia Patch Quilt, *Multimedia Database Systems: Issues and Research Directions*, Subrahmanian V. and Jajodia S. (Eds.), Springer-Verlag, Berlin, ISBN: 3-540-58710-1.

23. Lombardo D. and Kemp Z. (1997), Towards a model for multimedia geographical information systems, *Innovations in GIS 4*, (Ed.) Zarine Kemp, Taylor & Francis, London.

24. Ogle V.E, and Stonebraker M. (1995), Chabot: Retrieval from a Relational Database of Images, *IEEE Computer*, Vol 28, No 9, September 1995.

25. OpenGIS Consortium, The OpenGIS Abstract Specification- Topic 11: Metadata, 1999.

26. Parent C., Spaccapietra S., Zimanyi E., Donini P., Plazanet C. and Vangenot C. (1998), Modelling Spatial Data in the MADS Conceptual Model, *Proceedings of SDH'98, The 8th International Symposium on Spatial Data Handling*, Poiker T. and Chrisman N. (Eds.), Vancouver, Canada, July 1998.

27. Pass G, Zabih R, and Miller J. (1996), Comparing Images Using Color Coherence Vectors, *ACM Multimedia 96 Proceedings*, Boston, MA (The Fourth ACM International Multimedia Conference), November 18-22, 1996, Wendy Hall, T.D.C. Little, ISBN 0-89791-871-1.

28. Ruggles C.N. (1992), Structuring image data within a multi-media information system, *International Journal of Geographical Information Systems*, Vol 6, No 3, 205-222.

29. SAIF 1995, British Columbia Specifications and Guidelines for Geomatics Spatial Archive and Interchange Format: Formal Definition, *SAIF Info, Surveys and Resource mapping Branch, BC Ministry of Environment, Lands and Parks*, BC, Canada, Release 3.2.

30. Smith J.R. and Chang S-F. (1996), VisualSEEK: a fully automated content-based image query system, *ACM Multimedia 96 Proceedings*, Boston, MA (The Fourth ACM International Multimedia Conference), November 18-22, 1996, Wendy Hall, T.D.C. Little, ISBN 0-89791-871-1.

31. Stenzel H, Carson G.S, Herman I. and Kansy K. (1994), PREMO – An Architecture for the Presentation of Multimedia Objects in an Open Environment, *Multimedia/Hypermedia in Open Distributed Environments*, Herzner W. and Kapper F. (Eds), Springer-Verlag, June 1994.

32. Stonebraker M, Frew J, Gardels K. and Meredith J. (1994), The SEQUOIA 2000 Storage Benchmark, in Readings in Database Systems, (Ed.) Stonebraker M, Kaufman M, San Mateo, California.

33. Wilkinson G.G. (1996),A review of current issues in the integration of GIS and remote sensing data, *Int. J. Geographical Information Systems*, Vol 10, No 1, 85-101.

34. Wright D, and Goodchild M. (1997), Data from the Deep: Implications for the GIS Community, *IJGIS, International Journal of Geographical Information Science*, Vol. 11, No. 6.

On Ontology in Image Analysis

Thomas Bittner and Stephan Winter

[1] Department of Computing Science
Queen's University at Kingston
bittner@cs.queensu.ca
[2] Department of Geoinformation
Technical University, Vienna
winter@geoinfo.tuwien.ac.at

Abstract. Object reconstruction from remote sensed images is an actual research topic in computer vision, photogrammetry, and spatial information science. One of the most interesting related questions is the modeling of the uncertainty of knowledge gained by such a process. For a better understanding of the different sources and aspects of uncertainty, indeterminacy, vagueness, and the relations between them, a better understanding of the underlying ontological and epistemological foundations of imaging is necessary.

An important aspect is to make the relationships between the objects in the world that are observed, for example, by means of remote sensing, and fiat objects created from the remote sensed data by means of spatial analysis explicit. Both kinds of objects are linked to each other by observation and analysis processes. The process of spatial analysis has three basic components which are modeled in this paper as mappings between fiat objects of different kind. We show that vagueness in the definition of fiat objects involved in this process results in indeterminacy of location of those objects. Definitorial vagueness and location indeterminacy of location result in uncertainty about the truth of conclusions about existence, properties, and location of objects in the world derived from knowledge about fiat objects created by spatial analysis.

1 Introduction

Object reconstruction from remote sensed images is an actual research topic in computer vision, photogrammetry, and spatial information science. One of the most interesting related questions is the modeling of the uncertainty of knowledge gained by such a process. Recent proposals include fuzzy sets (Molenaar & Cheng 1998) and rough sets (Worboys 1998a, Worboys 1998b).

Beyond the modeling of uncertainty for spatial analysis, we feel the need to describe ontological and epistemological aspects involved in the process of imaging. In order to get a better understanding of the different sources and aspects of uncertainty, indeterminacy, vagueness, and the relations between them, a better understanding of the underlying ontological and epistemological foundations of imaging is necessary.

We start from the distinction between bona fide and fiat objects (Smith 1995). Roughly, bona fide objects are spatial objects in physical reality which

P. Agouris and A. Stefanidis (Eds.): ISD'99, LNCS 1737, pp. 168–191, 1999.
© Springer-Verlag Berlin Heidelberg 1999

exist independently of human cognition. Examples are the planet Earth, islands, lakes. Fiat objects are created by human cognition. Examples are legal fiats like political subdivisions, land property, or — of central concern for this paper — fiat objects created by spatial analysis of remote sensed data.

We show that the process of spatial analysis has three basic components, which are modeled as mappings between fiat objects of different kinds. We relate vagueness in the definitions of fiat objects involved in this process to different kinds and sources of uncertainty. We show that vagueness in the definition of fiat objects results in indeterminacy of location of those objects.

An important aspect is to make the relationships between the objects in the world that are observed, for example, by means of remote sensing, and fiat objects created from the remote sensed data by means of spatial analysis explicit. This will provide the basis for a discussion about the truth of conclusions about existence, properties, and location of objects in the world derived from knowledge about analysis created objects.

This paper is structured as follows. We start with a short review of remote sensing and spatial analysis performed on remote sensed data (Section 2). In particular we introduce a running example which will be used to illustrate the discussion in the remainder of this paper. In Section 3 we review and introduce ontological foundations. Formal models of location in space are reviewed in Section 4. These models provide the basis of the formalization provided in this paper. In Section 5 fiat objects created during processes imaging and remote sensing are discussed and formal representations are provided. This results in the discussion of the ontological status and adequate formalization of fiat objects created by spatial analysis in Section 6. The conclusion are given in Section 7.

2   The Principle of Remote Sensing

This section gives a short wrap up of remote sensing and image processing. It provides the starting point for the ontological investigation in the later sections.

2.1   The Physical and Geometrical Model

Remote sensing is an observation technique based on sensors for spectral reflectance, registering radiation typically in optical, infrared, thermal or microwave band (Kraus 1988). The sensors are single, or ordered in lines or in rectangular arrays, however, in any case recordings are combined to two-dimensional raster images. The rectangular shape of each sensor element g_i is mapped by a central projection onto a region G_i on the earth surface, i.e., the shape of G_i is not necessarily a rectangle due to terrain elevation and image orientation. Nevertheless, the property that $\bigcup_i g_i$ forms a partition is preserved for $\bigcup_i G_i$.

It is common to call the physical sensor element as well as the raster image element a *pixel*. Physically, the sensitive area of each pixel is not identical to its rectangular shape. The area on the earth surface corresponding to the sensitive area of a pixel is called sometimes *instantaneous field of view* I (Bruegger 1995). The set $\bigcup_i I_i$ does not form a partition.

In principle, each pixel g_i registers the number of photons received in a time interval. The resulting intensity value, denoted also by g_i, represents the mean reflectance over I_i:

$$g_i = \int I_i \, \mathrm{d}t$$

For simplicity it is assumed generally that $\int I_i \stackrel{!}{=} \int G_i$. This assumption causes some (radiometric) uncertainty. Other radiometric uncertainty results from the complex and dynamic relation between surface object and reflectance, involving perspective, lighting, and surface properties, and also from the atmospherical disturbances, electronical noise and other physical limitations.

The geometry of the raster image is that of a central projection. The parameters of the mapping function between g_i and G_i are known only imprecise, so that the assignment of the value of g_i to the area of G_i is (geometrically) uncertain, too. The other source of geometric uncertainty is the regular discretization of the imaging sensor, which does not fit to partitions of space on the earth surface.

Some effects causing uncertainty are systematic and can be rectified. The remaining effects, together with the model errors in rectification, accumulate inseparably, requiring models of imaging and of image interpretation coping with uncertainty. These effects are assumed to be independent and randomly distributed. Then the observed intensity values can be interpreted as results of stochastic processes (Baarda 1967). A stochastic process is an *a-priori* indeterminate process that is characterized by a distribution. If there are many and independent elementar effects the distribution of the process is a Gaussian (central limit theorem) (Koch 1988).

The intensity value of g_i gives now some evidence to represent reflection of a class of surface objects with specific properties (color, e.g.). Evidence is expressed in terms of probability. The probabilities for all classes which are expected to be observed in the image are used to determine the object (class) at G_i. This determination is called image classification.

2.2   Classification of Remote Sensing Images

With the rectified image at hand, one is interested in information about type and properties of objects on the earth surface in the covered area. The information is extracted by visual or automatic image *interpretation* (Kraus 1988):

- Visual interpretation is made by an expert who exploits spectral features, patterns, textures, and knowledge about natural and man-made features. — Human interpretation is still too complex to be transferred to a computer.
- For the automatic image interpretation pixel-wise multispectral classification is preferred, exploiting pixel attributes only: the n intensity values at each pixel correspond to a point in an n-dimensional space. In this space, all

points are grouped in clusters. The clusters are matched with object classes, with some *a-priori* or interactively given knowledge.

The multispectral classification assumes also stochastic variations of intensity values, characterizing the assignment of a pixel to a class by a probability which is derived from the centrality in the cluster. However, as discussed before, uncertainty concerns variations of individual objects from a class prototype as well as all the geometric and radiometric random effects on the signal.

With a probability value for each class, a pixel is assigned to the class of the maximum likelihood. One can post-process a classified image to get individual objects. Image segmentation combines connected pixels of the same class label to components. Each connected component refers to an object. Boundaries of objects look crisp, but they are not, due to uncertain assignments of pixels to classes.

2.3   An Example

The running example for this paper shall be height images, as derived from laser scanning (Krzystek 1991). Such remote sensed images are specific in so far as they represent distances in their pixel values. The distances are derived by the run-time an emitted laser pulse needed to be received again. Usually the distance is rectified to the elevation of the terrain, given the height of the sensor. Our discussion for the effects causing (stochastic) uncertainty still remains valid.

A problem from practice is investigated by Molenaar *et al.* (Cheng, Molenaar & Bouloucos 1997, Molenaar & Cheng 1998): they deal with the classification of *foreshore*, *beach*, and *foredune* from terrestrial height measurements as well as from remote sensed height images.

For laser scanning images, the error of measurement can be evaluated in a system calibration (Krzystek & Wild 1992). The result can be applied for statements about the uncertainty of the height values of each pixel, e.g., by a standard deviation σ.

The second category of uncertainty concerns the class definition. Molenaar *et al.* define the three classes by the height intervals (in m): *foreshore* (-6,-1); *beach* (-1, 2); *foredune* (2, 25). Because definitions vary in between some limits from expert to expert, Molenaar *et al.* handle the variation by a fuzzy definition of the classes, using a trapezoidal membership function (Klir & Folger 1988) for each class. A trapezoid needs four parameters: start and end point of uphill line, and start and end point of downhill line. In contrast to the crisp definition, a fuzzy definition of the classes is now: *foreshore* (-8.0, -4.0, -1.6, -0.6); *beach* (-1.6, -0.6, 1.5, 2.5); *foredune* (1.5, 2.5, 22, 28), with the cross-over points at the crisp boundaries (Fig. 1 (A-C)).

If a height value is uncertain and its classification is fuzzy, the two must be compounded. Molenaar *et al.* calculate a convolution of fuzzy membership function and likelihood function, leading to a belief function (Klir & Folger 1988) that determines the uncertainty of each pixel belonging to the different classes. The classification is visualized with its belief values in Figure 1 (D).

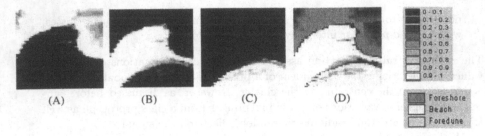

Fig. 1. The three fuzzy landscape classes (a-c), and the compound classification (d). (The figures are taken from Molenaar & Cheng 1998, with the kind permission of the authors).

3   Spatial Objects and Location

3.1   Spatial Objects

Aspects of Ontological Categorization. Following Smith & Mark (1998), we assume that in the ontological characterization of geographic reality three basic aspects are involved:

1. aspects characterizing *what* spatial objects are,
2. aspects characterizing *where* spatial objects are located, i.e., aspects of embedding of spatial objects into geographic space, and
3. aspects of scale.

In the remainder we use the notion of 'spatial object' to refer to objects characterized by those aspects.

The 'What'. What spatial objects are is characterized to a certain degree by their observable properties. Every object has its unique identity. During its existence every object preserves its identity even if its properties change. In order to characterize spatial objects with respect to what they are beyond observable properties we consider their identity, and:

- The compositional structure of their constituent object-parts.
- Modes of their existence within physical reality and with respect to human cognition.

The Where. Aspects characterizing *where* objects are located, and relationships between *what* objects are and *where* they are, have been investigated in spatial sciences for centuries. Surveyors deal with the question where things are located on Earth (Moffitt & Bouchard 1987). Geography deals with the relationships between what things are and where they are (Abler, Marcus & Olson 1992). In this paper aspects characterizing *where* spatial objects are, are captured by the notion of location. Location is formalized as a relation between spatial objects and regions of space.

Aspects of Scale. Aspects of scale refer to the classification of spatial objects with respect to size relative to observability and modes of observation by human beings. There is a whole class of literature that deals with different classifications in this respect. An overview can be found in (Freundschuh & Egenhofer 1997). Spatial objects of geographic scale, considered in this paper, are larger than the human body and cannot be perceived within a single perceptual act. Examples are cities, mountains, or lakes.

Bona Fide and Fiat Objects. Spatial objects do not only have constituent object-parts, they also have boundaries, which contribute much more to their ontological make-up as do object-parts (Smith & Mark 1998). One fundamental distinction characterizing *what* spatial objects are is based on the classification of boundary parts. This results in the distinction between objects with *bona fide* and objects with *fiat* boundaries.

Bona fide boundaries "... are boundaries *in the things themselves*. They would exist (and did already exist) even in the absence of all delineating or conceptualizing of our ... part. Bona fide boundaries are boundaries which exist independently of all human cognitive acts - they are a matter of qualitative differentiations or discontinuities of the underlying reality." (Smith 1995, p. 475) Examples are surfaces of extended objects like tennis balls, plants, the surface of Earth, and the shore line separating water and sand in Example 2.3.

Fiat boundaries " ... are boundaries which exist only in virtue of different sorts of demarcations effected cognitively by human beings. Such boundaries lie entirely skew to all boundaries of *bona fide* sort (as in the case of the boundaries between Utah and Wyoming). They may also, however (as in the case of Indiana and Pennsylvania), involve a combination of fiat and *bona fide* portions, or indeed they may be constructed entirely out of *bona fide* portions which however, because they are not themselves intrinsically connected, must be glued together out of heterogeneous portions in fiat fashion in order to yield a boundary that is topologically complete. " (Smith 1995, p. 476) Examples are many state and provincial borders, country lines, property lines, borders of postal districts, boundaries of soil-types.

The classification of boundaries generalizes to the objects they bound. Bona fide objects are topologically closed bounded by a fiat boundary. Examples are human beings, the planet Earth, lakes, highways. Fiat objects are bounded either by bona fide boundaries of different sorts glued together by human cognition or are at least partly bounded by boundaries of fiat sort. Examples are 'The North Sea', 'The Rocky Mountains', political subdivisions, land property.

3.2 Fiat Objects

Fiat objects can be classified with respect to the way human conceptual demarcations carve out fiat objects, i.e., create fiat boundaries, in physical reality. Those conceptual demarcations differ in the degree in which they *specify* what the objects they *create* are and where they are located. In the context of this paper we discuss three kinds of fiat objects:

1. Consensus Fiats
2. Measurement and Observation Fiats
3. Spatial Analysis Created Fiats

Consensus Fiats. "Consensus fiats may be products of informal consensus, reflecting for example usage as this evolves informally over time. Bays, peninsulas, etc., are parts of spatial reality, physical parts of the world itself. But they are parts of reality that would not be there absent corresponding linguistic and cultural practices of demarcation and categorization" (Smith & Mark 1998, p. 316). Consequently, human concepts represented and shared by means language 'carve out', i.e., create, fiat objects in physical reality. The definitions of those concepts are often subject to vagueness (Smith 1995), i.e., those definitions only vaguely specify *what* the spatial objects they create are and *where* they are located.

Fiats Created by Observation and Measurement Processes. Human beings create fiat objects during their interaction with physical reality. Visual observation of physical reality creates fiat boundaries all the time, e.g., the horizon bounding the 'visual field' (Smith 1995), my body axes create fiat boundaries separating the fiat objects 'the world in front of me', 'the world in my back', left and right of me and so on. What those objects are and where they are located is well defined in each moment of time but their location changes all the time.

Measurement is a specific and precise form of observation. Measurement processes create fiat objects, which regions form partitions[1] of space and time (Carnap 1966, Bittner 1999a)[2]. Consider the measurement of time. The measuring process, i.e., the use of a clock to measure temporal extension, creates fiat temporal objects, which regions partition the time line. Those temporal objects are located at time intervals bounded by 'clock-ticks'. Of central concern for this paper are fiat objects on the surface of Earth created by remote sensing processes. The boundaries of those fiat objects are created by geo-referencing of pixels of remote sensed raster images[3]. Other examples are fiat objects created by sample data and interpolation (Example 2.3).

Fiats Created by Spatial Analysis. The process of creating fiat objects by spatial analysis assumes a measuring process that creates a set of fiat objects, which form a regional partition of Earth[4]. Based on those *sets* of *simple* fiat

---

[1] Regional partitions are sets of regions which intersect only at their boundaries and which sum up the whole space.

[2] Smith & Mark (1998) call those fiats "mathematical fiats that are artifacts of a certain technology."

[3] In the context of this paper we see geo-referencing as an idealized process, i.e., we abstract from aspects causing radiometric and geometric uncertainty, which were discussed in Section 2.1.

[4] Prototypical examples of those processes are imaging in remote sensing and sampling of point data followed by interpolation operations (Sect. 2.3).

objects we can define, i.e., create, *complex* fiat objects as sums of primitive fiat cell objects.

For example, each fiat cell object, which was created by a measuring process, is characterized by a number of values which refer to some kind of measurement, e.g., a certain number of photons of certain wavelength measured by a particular raster sensor. We now can define sums of raster-cell-fiats which values satisfy certain conditions, for example, having received a certain number of photons with a particular wave length within a certain time interval, or, as in case of the example in Section 2.3, having registered the same run-time of single photons. Corresponding to practice in image classification (Section 2.2), the conditions often are formulated weaker, allowing a range of pixel values to be summed up. We will discuss the process of creating fiat objects by means of spatial analysis extensively in Section 6.

On Defining Fiat Objects

Definite Fiats. Consider legal fiats such as political subdivisions or land property, fiats created by measuring processes, or fiats created by point interpolation operations. The definition of those objects contains the specification of the *exact* region of space at which those objects are located[5]. In all cases the exact regions are often defined and stored in terms of semi-algebraic or semi-linear formulas (non-linear or linear polynomials) (Kanellakis, Kuper & Revesz 1990). In the case of land property those definitions are stored in property records. In the case of fiat objects created by remote sensing the exact regions are implicitly given in terms of the geo-referencing of raster images. In the case of point interpolation, the equivalence classes defined in the attribute domain induce a unique regional partition of the underlying space[6] and hence define the exact regions of the corresponding partition forming fiat objects.

Definite fiat objects, which explicitly contain the definition of their exact region of space, are the only kinds of spatial objects for which human beings can know exact location. Since the boundaries of those fiats are usually not observable in physical reality there exist rules and procedures that allow to determine the location of those boundaries and mark them such that they become observable. A very significantly marked legal boundary, for example, was the Berlin Wall separating East and West Berlin during the Cold War. May me, you marked the boundary of your property in order to separate it from your neighbor's property.

Vaguely defined fiats. Consider fiat objects like mountains, hills, valleys, ridges, or capes. " ... we can all agree that they are real, and that it is obvious where the top of a mountain or the end of a cape is to be found. But where is the boundary

---

[5] The notion of location as a relation between spatial objects and regions of space will be discussed in the next section.

[6] Assuming continuous distribution functions describing the spatial distribution of the attribute value. See for example (Laurini & Thompson 1994).

of Cape Flattery on the island inside? Where is the boundary of Mount Blanc among its foothills?" (Smith & Mark 1998, p. 316) The human concepts and definitions that bring those fiat objects into existence do not specify their boundary locations. Consequently, we cannot apply rules and measurement in order to make those boundaries observable. Any human being can complete the definitions and draw the boundary of her or his 'Mount Blanc' or 'Cape Flattery'. The vagueness of concepts bringing fiat objects into existence cause indeterminacy of location. " ...if you point to an irregularly shaped protuberance in the sand and say 'dune', then the correlate of your expression is a fiat object whose constituent unary parts are comprehended (articulated) through the concept dune. The vagueness of the concept itself is responsible for the vagueness with which the referent of your expression is picked out. Each one of a large verity of slightly different and precisely determinate aggregates of molecules has an equal claim to being such a referent." (Smith & Mark 1998, p. 315)

Often, the vague definition might be strong enough to identify regions of space which are part of the object's exact region, which overlap the object's exact region, or where no parts of the object are located. This often allow us to draw boundaries around a 'certain' core and 'certain' exterior. Doing so we create a regional partition consisting of three concentric regions similar to those shown in Figure 2. The boundary of the vaguely defined object is located somewhere between the core and the exterior[7].

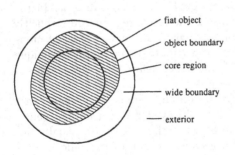

Fig. 2. A vaguely defined fiat object

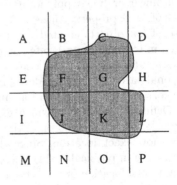

Fig. 3. Rough Location in a Regular Raster.

3.3   Location

Exact Location. Every spatial object is exactly located at a single region of space in each moment of time (Casati & Varzi 1995). This region may be a simple

---

[7] For an extended discussion see (Cohn & Gotts 1996).

region of three dimensional space, for example, think of your body and the region of space it carves out of the air. The exact region of a spatial object may be a complex region, consisting of multiple regions of three dimensional space, as in the case of the exact region of the Hawaiian islands. The exact region may be a complex region, consisting of multiple regions of two dimensional space, as in the case of the representation of the Hawaiian islands on a paper map. Notice that even in this case we distinguish between the spatial object 'Representation of the Hawaiian islands' consisting of several layers and blends of paint and the region of space it carves out of the map space.

Spatial change refers to the fact that spatial objects can be located at different regions of space at different points in time. This implies a concept of absolute space, i.e., regions of space do not move, shrink, or grow. Spatial objects can move, shrink, grow. This makes them being located at different regions of space at different moments of time. See for example (Borgo, Guarino & Masolo 1996).

Rough Location. Rough location describes the location of spatial objects within sets of regions of space that form regional partitions (Bittner 1999b). Rough location is characterized by sets of relationships between *parts* of the object's exact region and *parts* of partition regions. Consider Figure 3, which shows the rough location of a spatial object, o, with a non-regular shaped region, which is located within a raster-shaped regional partition. The raster shaped regional partition, G, might be created, for example, by remote sensing. Rough location can be represented by upper and lower approximation sets[8]. The lower approximation set, $\underline{o}$, of the object, o, with respect to the partition, G, is the set of all raster regions, $g \in G$, that are part of the exact region of o. The upper approximation set, $\overline{o}$, is the set of all raster regions that overlap the exact region of the object, o.

$$\underline{o} = \{K\}$$
$$\overline{o} = \{B, C, D, E, F, G, H, I, J, K, L, N, O, P\}$$

In this paper we distinguish three kinds of rough location:

1. *Overlap sensitive* rough location, which is characterized by overlap and non-overlap relations between exact regions of spatial objects and partition regions. This corresponds to upper approximation sets.
2. *Containment sensitive* rough location, which is characterized by part-of and non-part-of relations between exact regions of spatial objects and partition regions. This corresponds to lower approximation sets.
3. *Overlap & containment sensitive* rough location, which is characterized by pairs of upper and lower approximation sets.

---

[8] The notions of lower and upper approximation sets come from rough set theory (Pawlak 1982) and were applied to the spatial domain for example by Worboys (1998a) and Bittner (1999b).

Consider Figure 2. The overlap & containment sensitive rough location of the vaguely defined fiat object o in the regional partition consisting of three concentric regions, called core, wide boundary, and exterior can be represented the lower and upper approximation sets $\underline{o} = \{core\}$ and $\overline{o} = \{core, wide\_boundary\}$. Notice, that the rough location of the vague defined object in this regional partition is well defined and determinate. The notion of rough location allows to abstract from the indeterminacy of location caused by the vagueness of the object definition.

4   Modeling Location

4.1   Modeling Exact Location

Spatial objects and regions of space have compositional structure. We model spatial objects, regions of space, and their compositional structure using the Boolean algebra (Halmos 1963, Stell & Worboys 1997) of regular closed sets (Requicha 1977). Regular closed sets are sets which are equal to the closure of their interior. Regular closed point sets model regions of space (Gotts 1996). They are topologically well formed in that sense that they do not contain isolated points or infinitely thin 'spikes'. In a Boolean algebra join, $\vee$, and meet, $\wedge$, operations are defined, which are interpreted as (regularized[9]) union and intersection of regular closed sets.

Let O be the Boolean algebra of spatial objects and R be the Boolean algebra of regions of space. Since every spatial object is exactly located at a single region of space at each moment of time we can define a function, r, mapping spatial objects onto regions of space:

$$r : O \to R$$

The mapping r is a bijection in the domain of bona-fide objects but not in the domain of fiats. This is due to the fact that no two physical objects can be located at the same region of space in the same moment of time. It is not a bijection in the domain of fiat objects, since fiat objects of *different kind* can be located at the same region of space in the same moment of time (Casati & Varzi 1995). For example, the objects 'City of Vienna' and 'Federal State Vienna' are located at the same region of space in every moment of time.

Obviously, the mapping, r, is by no means computable. Furthermore as discussed, for example, by Bittner (1999a), for most spatial objects we cannot even know the exact region of space at which they are located. Nevertheless we know that for every spatial object the exact regions exists and hence, the mapping, r, exists. Consequently, we can use the notion $r(o)$ to refer on a formal level to the exact region of the object $o \in O$.

---

[9] See (Gotts 1996) or (Requicha 1977).

4.2   Approximating Regions of Space

We now review the notion of relationship mappings which was originally introduced by Bittner & Stell (1998). In this paper we use relationship mappings in order to model rough location of analysis created fiat objects within the regional partition created by the underlying measurement process.

Overlap Sensitive Approximation. Let the set $\Omega_\exists = \{\Diamond, 0^\Diamond\}$ be a set of ways elements $g \in G$ can relate to an element $r \in R$. The function $p_\exists$ is a relationship function defined as:

$$p_\exists : G \times R \to \Omega_\exists; \quad p_\exists(g,r) = \begin{cases} \Diamond & \text{if } \exists a \preceq g(a \preceq r) \\ 0^\Diamond & \text{otherwise} \end{cases}$$

The mapping $p_\exists(g,r)$ returns the value $\Diamond$ if and only if the regions g and r overlap.

The relationship function, $p_\exists$, induces an approximation function $\alpha_\exists$:

$$\alpha_\exists : R \to \Omega_\exists{}^G; \quad \alpha_\exists(r) =_{def} g \mapsto p_\exists(g,r)$$

The symbol $\Omega_\exists{}^G$ denotes a set of functions from G to $\Omega_\exists$. The mapping $\alpha_\exists$ assigns to each $r \in R$ a function $(G \to \Omega) \in \Omega_\exists{}^G$. Consider figure 3. The set of regions $G = \{A, B, C, \ldots, P\} \subset R$ forms a regional partition of the plane. The gray non-regular shaped region, $r \in R$, is located in the regional partition G. The graph[10] of the approximation function $(\alpha_\exists R) : G \to \Omega_\exists$ approximating the region, r, with respect to the partition, G is:

G	A	B	C	D	E	...
$\Omega_\exists$	$0^\Diamond$	$\Diamond$	$\Diamond$	$\Diamond$	$\Diamond$	...

Containment Sensitive Approximation. Containment sensitive approximation is represented by approximation mappings $\alpha_\forall$, which are defined based on relationship functions $p_\forall$:

$$p_\forall : G \times R \to \Omega_\forall; \quad p_\forall(g,r) = \begin{cases} \Box & \text{if } \forall a \preceq g(a \preceq r) \\ 0^\Box & \text{otherwise} \end{cases}$$

The mapping $p_\forall(g,r)$ returns the value $\Box$ if and only if g is a subset of r. The relationship function, $p_\forall$, induces an approximation function $\alpha_\forall$:

$$\alpha_\forall : R \to \Omega_\forall{}^G; \quad \alpha_\forall(r) =_{def} g \mapsto p_\forall(g,r)$$

The approximation function $\alpha_\forall$ assigns to each $r \in R$ a function $(G \to \Omega_\forall) \in \Omega_\forall{}^G$. Consider figure 3. The graph of the approximation function $(\alpha_\forall r) : G \to \Omega_\forall$ is:

G	A	B	...	K	L	...
$\Omega_\forall$	$0^\Box$	$0^\Box$	...	$\Box$	$0^\Box$	...

---

[10] The graph of a mapping explicitly lists the set of tuples forming the mapping.

Overlap & Containment Sensitive Approximation. We now define the overlap & containment sensitive value domain Ω_3 as pairs of containment and overlap sensitive value domains $\Omega_\forall$ and $\Omega_\exists$:

$p_3(g,r)$	$p_\forall(g,r) = \Box$	$p_\forall(g,r) = 0^\Box$
$p_\exists(g,r) = \Diamond$	$(\Box, \Diamond)$	$(0^\Box, \Diamond)$
$p_\exists(g,r) = 0^\Diamond$	-	$(0^\Box, 0^\Diamond)$

The relationship function p_3 applied to region r and partition region g returns $(\Box, \Diamond)$ if and only if g is a part of r. It yields $(0^\Box, \Diamond)$ if g and r overlap, without g being a part of r, and $(0^\Box, 0^\Diamond)$ otherwise. Assuming $\forall g \in G(g \neq \bot)$ the case '$p_\forall(g,r) = \Box$ and $p_\exists(g,r) = 0^\Box$' cannot occur (Bittner & Stell 1998).

The relationship function, p_3, induces an approximation function α_3 as discussed above. Consider figure 3. The graph of the approximation function $(\alpha_3 r)$: $G \to \Omega_3$ is:

G	A	B	...	K	L	...
Ω_3	$(0^\Box, 0^\Diamond)$	$(0^\Box, \Diamond)$	...	$(\Box, \Diamond)$	$(0^\Box, \Diamond)$	...

4.3 Modeling Rough Location

In this section, so far, we discussed how spatial regions can be approximated with respect to regional partitions. Those approximations can be represented formally by means of approximation functions derived from relationship functions. The notion of location refers to relation between spatial objects, $o \in O$, and regions of space, $r \in R$. In order to model rough location using approximation functions we define location mappings as:

$$loc : O \to \Omega^G; \quad (loc\ o) =_{def} (\alpha \circ r)o$$

The function $r(o)$ refers to the exact region of the object $o \in O$. The operator $\circ$ refers to the composition of α and r defined as $(\alpha \circ r)o = \alpha(r(o))$.

Lower and upper rough approximations of the object, o, discussed in Section 3, can easily be defined in terms of the overlap & containment sensitive location mappings $loc_3 : O \to \Omega_3{}^G$ by writing $\underline{o} = \{g \in G \mid ((loc_3\ o)g) = (\Box, \Diamond)\}$ and $\overline{o} = \{g \in G \mid ((loc_3\ o)g) = (\Box, \Diamond)$ or $((loc_3\ o)g) = (0^\Box, \Diamond)\}$.

5 Modeling Definite Fiat Objects

Fiat objects are created in the human mind. In the scientific realm definite fiat objects are created by exact definitions. Consequently, humans can have exact and complete knowledge about those definite fiat objects.

5.1 Defining Classes of Definite Fiats

Let A be an attribute domain ranging over classificatorial, ordering , or quantitative concepts. In abstract domains we can use concepts like real numbers in our definitions without considering issues of observability and measureability. The only assumption we have is that these definitions need to be expressible by finite means of formal language.

Let $A_1, \ldots, A_n$ be a finite number of attributes. $\phi(A_1, \ldots, A_n)$ is a class of fiat objects that are completely characterized by the attribute vector $A_1, \ldots, A_n$ and a set of formula ϕ, which characterize the class of objects $\phi(A_1, \ldots, A_n)$ in terms of attribute values $(a_1, \ldots, a_2) \in A_1 \times \ldots \times A_n$. Since we are in abstract, fiat domains it is possible to completely characterize classes of objects by finite number of attributes and finite number of formula.

Consider, for example, the class of definite fiat objects called 'land property'. Objects of this kind are classified by attributes like property Id, owner, the object's exact region, land use, etc. The region of the object might be specified by semi-algebraic formulas like linear polynomials. There might be formulas constraining possible values the attributes can take. For example the attribute domain owner should range over valid names of human beings that are alive.

5.2 Definite Fiat Objects

Let $v = (a_1, \ldots, a_n) \in A_1 \times \ldots \times A_n$, be a vector of attribute values characterizing a spatial object $o \in O$. In fiat domains we can assume that v completely characterizes the object o up to its identity. Since o is a spatial object the region $r(o)$ at which o is exactly located exists.

In definite fiat spatial domains, the exact spatial location, i.e., the exact region of the object, is often a defining property (think of land property). In this case, one of the attribute domains ranges over regions of space. The knowledge about the kind of the object, i.e., the class it belongs to, and knowledge about its exact location at a certain moment in time is sufficient to fix the object's identity. This is due to the fact that no two spatial objects of the same kind can be located at the same region of space at the same moment in time (Casati & Varzi 1995). In database systems the identity of a spatial object is often handled explicitly by identifiers and handled as attribute value.

Since the attribute value vector, v, uniquely determines the object, o, we can write $r(v)$ to refer to the region at which the object, o, is located exactly. We use the notion of a pair to refer to a definite fiat objects with its attributes and its exact location region:

$$o = (v, r(v)). \tag{1}$$

Suppose the class of objects $O' \subset O$ is characterized by attributes $A_1, \ldots, A_n$ where A_1 ranges over regions. The function $r(v)$ simply yields the attribute value $v_1 \in A_1$, i.e., $r(v) = v_1$.

A certain class of regularity shaped regions can be represented finitely by means of semi-algebraic formulas. The representation of spatial objects by a finite number of attributes $A_1, \ldots, A_n$ where A_i ranges over semi-algebraic formulas was discussed, for example, by Paredaens, Van den Bussche & Van Gucht (1994).

5.3   Definite Fiats forming Regional Partitions

Let $\phi(A_1, \ldots, A_n) = \{o_1, \ldots, o_m\}$ be a set of definite fiat objects. Every object $o_i \in \phi(A_1, \ldots, A_n)$ is characterized by a attribute n-tuple $(a_1, \ldots, a_n)$. Assume the regions of the objects $o_1, \ldots, o_m$ sum up the whole space, i.e., $r(o_1) \vee \ldots \vee r(o_m) = U$. Since the objects $o_1, \ldots, o_m$ are of the same kind, their exact-location-regions cannot overlap (Casati & Varzi 1995). Consequently, the set of regions $\{r(o_1), \ldots, r(o_m)\}$ forms a regional partition of space. Under these assumptions, the set of objects $\phi(A_1, \ldots, A_n)$ can be modeled as mapping.

$$c : \{r(o_1), \ldots, r(o_m)\} \to A_1 \times \ldots \times A_n$$

If we assume that the region of space is a defining property of objects in class $\phi(A_1, \ldots, A_n)$ and A_1 ranges over a set of regions forming a partition of space, then the mapping can be written as $c : A_1 \to A_2 \times \ldots \times A_n$. Under the additional assumption that A_1 ranges over regions representable by semi-algebraic formulas the mapping, c, representing the class of objects $\phi(A_1, \ldots, A_n)$, has the signature $c : \Gamma(x_1, \ldots, x_d) \to A_2 \times \ldots \times A_n$. In this formula $\Gamma(x_1, \ldots, x_d)$ is a set of semi-algebraic formulas with d variables representing the particular regional partition of the space of dimension d.

5.4   Definite Fiats Created by Measuring Processes

Measuring processes create regional partitions of the underlying domain. Examples are time intervals bounded by clock-ticks in the case of time measurement (Carnap 1966), or raster cells on Earth in the case of remote sensing (Section 2). Let $G = \{g_1, \ldots, g_n\}$ be a regional partition created by a remote sensing process. At each partition region attribute values $a_1, \ldots, a_k$ are observed or measured. The measuring process yields the set of fiat objects $O = \{o_1, \ldots, o_n\}$ of kind $\phi(A_1, \ldots, A_k)$ with partition $G = \{r(o_1), \ldots, r(o_n)\}$. The objects are brought into existence by applying Definition 1 in the mind of the human being performing the measurement. Each single object is created by defining $o_i =_{def} (v_i, g_i)$, where $v_i = (a_1, \ldots, a_k)$ is the vector of attribute values measured at region g_i. Due to the partition structure of the regions of the created objects, O, the outcome of a measurement process can be represented as a mapping $c : G \to A_1 \times \ldots \times A_k$.

Consider the example in Section 2.3. At each pixel, i, exactly one attribute a_1^i was measured over the area g_i on Earth: the run-time of a photon on the distance sensor-Earth-sensor. Consequently, the objects, O, are of kind 'photon run-time measured to a region on Earth'. These objects are characterized by a single attribute value run_time and a region of space g_i. The definite fiat object, o_i, is created by applying Definition 1, i.e., $o_i =_{def} (run\_time_i, g_i)$. The set of fiat objects, O, created by the whole measurement process is represented by the mapping $c : G \to Photon\_Run\_Time$. The attribute $Photon\_Run\_Time$ ranges over values run_time. For example, the beginning of the graph of the mapping c is:

G	g_{11}	g_{12}	$\ldots$
$Photon\_Run\_Time[ns]$	4822	4826	$\ldots$

6 Modeling Fiats Created by Spatial Analysis

A special kind of fiat spatial objects are objects created by spatial analysis. Assume a set of fiat objects $O = \{o_1, \ldots, o_n\}$ of kind $\phi(A_1, \ldots, A_k)$ represented by the mapping $c : G \rightarrow A_1 \times \ldots \times A_k$ with $G = \{r(o_1), \ldots, r(o_n)\}$. This set might be created, for example, by a measuring process such as remote sensing as discussed in the previous section. In spatial analysis fiat objects are created in a process that has three basic components, which are modeled as mappings between different kinds of fiat objects:

1. Measuring processes yield sets of definite fiat objects forming regional partitions carrying certain attribute values representing the outcome of the measuring process. Examples are attribute values representing measured heights, strength of radiation, wavelength of measured radiation, or run time length of photons. The mapping *transform_attributes* transforms those attribute values into attribute values characterizing classes of fiat objects. For example, the measured run time of photons can be transformed into the attribute domain 'elevation height' which can be used to define classes of fiat objects like foreshore, shore, or foredune.

   In general, mappings *transform_attributes* are of signature $(G \rightarrow A_1 \times \ldots \times A_k) \rightarrow (G \rightarrow B_1 \times \ldots \times B_l)$ transforming tuples $((g_i \mapsto (a_1^i, \ldots, a_k^i))$ into tuples $(g_i \mapsto (b_1^i, \ldots, b_l^i))$.

2. There are mappings *classify_location*, which yield values $\omega \in \Omega$ characterizing the mode of location of an object, o, at a particular partition region, g_i, depending on a given input, $(b_1^i, \ldots, b_l^i)$, related to this region. Possible modes of location are overlap sensitive, containment sensitive, or overlap & containment sensitive location.

   Mappings *classify_location* are of signature $(G \rightarrow B_1 \times \ldots \times B_l) \rightarrow (G \rightarrow \Omega)$, i.e., they return the value ω depending on the input vector $(b_1, \ldots, b_l)$ for each $g_i \in G$.

3. There are mappings *create_object_attributes*, which compute attribute values for the created fiat object from the attribute values of the measurement created objects, for example, the average elevation hight for the new object from the 'elevation height' of the raster cells at which it is located.

   In general, mappings *create_object_attributes* computing the attribute values of the new object are of signature $(G \rightarrow B_1 \times \ldots \times B_l) \rightarrow B_1 \times \ldots \times B_m$.

The whole creative human process of creating fiat objects of kind $\pi(B_1, \ldots, B_m)$ by spatial analysis is modeled as a mapping, *analyze*, transforming a mapping representation of a measurement process into the new, analysis created, fiat object: *analyze* $: (G \rightarrow A_1 \times \ldots \times A_k) \rightarrow ((B_1 \times \ldots \times B_m), (G \rightarrow \Omega))$. The fiat object is modeled as a pair consisting of an n-tuple of attribute values and a location mapping representing rough location in the underlying regional partition, i.e., $o = ((b_1, \ldots, b_m), (\text{loc } o))$. We are now discussing those components in detail and give more examples.

6.1 Transforming Measured Attributes

Creating fiat objects by means of spatial analysis assumes the definability of those fiat objects of kind $\pi(B_1, \ldots, B_m)$ in terms of sets of fiat objects of kind $\psi(B_1, \ldots, B_l)$. Consider, for example, remote sensing. The measuring process creates fiat objects of kind $\phi(A_1, \ldots, A_k)$, which attributes range, for example, over the intensity of radiation of a certain wavelength emitted by the surface of Earth, or the run time of photons emitted by a laser and reflected from the surface of Earth. Assume we are interested in finding places on Earth belonging to the class foreshore as discussed in the example in Section 2.3. Molenaar *et al.* defined the class of fiat objects *foreshore* of kind $\pi(terrain\_elevation)$ in terms of terrain elevations values within the interval of $-6m$ to $-1.1m$, i.e., $(-6m \leq b \leq -1.1m) \in \pi(B)$. The observations from remote sensed images are photon run times; they must be transformed into relative heights with respect to sea level on Earth. This is a two step process. Firstly: At each pixel exactly one attribute a_1 was measured over the area g_i, the run-time of a photon. Multiplied with the speed of light, the kind of the attribute is (double) *distance*. Secondly: Relative height with respect to sea level on Earth is computed by subtracting the distance from (given) sensor height.

We define the mapping $transform\_attributes$: $(G \rightarrow Photon\_Run\_Time)$ $\rightarrow (G \rightarrow terrain\_elevation)$. It transforms the attribute run_time into the attribute $terrain\_elevation$ for every partition element $g \in G$. For example, the photon run-time $a_1 = 4822ns$ measured at location g_{11} is transformed into the attribute value $b_1 = -5.49m$ of kind $terrain$ $elevation$ which remains assigned to location g_{11}.

The mapping $transform\_attributes$ creates a set of fiat objects of kind $\psi(terrain\_elevation)$ which members are co-located with fiat objects of kind $\phi(Photon\_Run\_Length)$. Sets of fiat objects of kind $\psi(terrain\_elevation)$ will be used to create objects like foreshores of kind $\pi(terrain\_elevation)$ by spatial analysis. This is discussed in the next section.

6.2 Creating Fiat Objects

Defining Classes of Analysis Created Objects. Measurement processes, such as remote sensing or point sampling, create sets of definite fiat objects of kind $\phi(A_1, \ldots, A_k)$. Those are transformed into objects of kind $\psi(B_1, \ldots, B_l)$. The attribute domains, $B_1, \ldots, B_l$, create the attribute space $B_1 \times \ldots \times B_l$. Every possible instance, $(b_1, \ldots, b_l)$, is interpreted as the coordinate of a point in this attribute space. In the context of concrete measurement those attribute points are not arbitrarily distributed. They form clusters (Section 2.2). The underlying assumption of spatial analysis is that those clusters in the attribute space correspond to classes of objects in reality (Kraus 1990). Classes of fiat objects created by spatial analysis are defined such that they correspond to clusters in the attribute space.

Consider the example of a terrain elevation image (Section 2.3). We profit from the natural shape of foreshore, beach and dune, which can be separated in the height profile (Fig. 4 left). With that property elevation yields a good selectivity of height clusters. The histogram of an elevation image, i.e. the function accumulating the frequency the occurrences of elevation values, shows a three-modal distribution (Fig. 4 right). Each mode[11] corresponds to one object class.

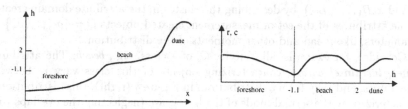

Fig. 4. A height profile through typical beach terrain (*left*), with h: terrain elevation, and x: direction of profile. — The histogram of the remote sensed image (*right*), with h: terrain elevation, and r, c: the image indices.

Creating Fiat Object Instances. Spatial objects are characterized by aspects specifying *what* they are and *where* they are located (Section 3). What fiat objects are, is characterized by their attribute values, $(b_1, \ldots, b_l)$. For fiat objects created by spatial analysis these attribute values are derived from *sets* of attribute values $(b_1, \ldots, b_k)$ belonging to a cluster in the attribute space $B_1 \times \ldots \times B_l$. The location of fiat objects created by spatial analysis, is characterized by their rough location within the regional partition, G, created by the underlying measurement process.

We define spatial analysis created objects of kind $\pi(B_1, \ldots, B_m)$, which is based on a measuring process that yields the set O of kind $\phi(A_1, \ldots, A_k)$ as pair containing an attribute vector $(b_1, \ldots, b_m) \in B_1 \times \ldots \times B_m$ and a location mapping of signature $(\text{loc } o) : G \to \Omega^{12}$,

$$o =_{def} ((b_1, \ldots, b_m), (\text{loc } o)).$$

Consequently, the act of creating a fiat object, o, consists of two components:

1. The computation of the attribute vector $(b_1, \ldots, b_l)$ from the attributes $(a_1^i, \ldots, a_k^i)$ of objects $o_i \in O$ created by the measuring process.
2. The computation of the rough location representation, $(\text{loc } o)$, of o

---

[11] We speak of three *modes* meaning a robust concept of local frequency maxima.
[12] Ω can be either Ω_3 or Ω_v

Both components perform operations on the mapping representation of the underlying measuring process, $c : G \rightarrow A_1 \times \ldots \times A_k$. The process of creating fiat object by spatial analysis is modeled by the mapping *analyze*:

$$analyze \quad : \quad (G \rightarrow A_1 \times \ldots \times A_k) \rightarrow ((B_1 \times \ldots \times B_m), (G \rightarrow \Omega))$$

$$analyze\ c =_{def} ((create\_object\_attributes \circ transform\_attributes)\ c),$$

$$((classify\_location \circ transform\_attributes)\ c)$$

Attributes. The mapping $create\_object\_attributes : (G \rightarrow B_1 \times \ldots \times B_l) \rightarrow B_1 \times \ldots \times B_m$ computes a single attribute tuple for the analysis created fiat object of kind $\pi(B_1, \ldots, B_m)$, by describing the cluster in the attribute domain created by the attributes of the set of measurement created objects $O = \{o_1, \ldots, o_n\}$ by parameters, like mean and other moments of the distribution.

Consider, for example, all objects, O, of a class, e.g., *beach*. The attributes values, *terrain_elevation*, characterizing objects of this class vary in between some limits, and they form a distribution. In Figure 4 (right), this distribution is characterized by the second mode of the histogram (neglecting the overlaps with continuing distributions of *foreshore* and *dune*). A multi-modal distribution is separated ideally at (robust) local minima, so in this case we decide to separate at $-1.1m$ and $2m$, forming a beach-cluster of $[-1.1m \ldots 2m]$. The histogram function in this interval can be used now to describe the distribution of beach objects, e.g., by a mean and a standard deviation.

Rough location. The rough location representation of a fiat spatial object, o', of kind $\psi(B_1, \ldots, B_l)$ within a regional partition, G, created by a set of objects, O, of kind $\phi(A_1, \ldots, A_k)$, is defined as the application the composition of the mappings $transform\_attributes$ and $classify\_location$ to the mapping c:

$$(loc\ o') \quad : \quad G \rightarrow \Omega$$

$$(loc\ o') =_{def} (classify\_location \circ transform\_attributes)\ c.$$

We already discussed the mapping c, representing the outcome of the measuring process, and the mapping $transform\_attributes$ transforming those results into attribute domains that can be used to define fiat objects in terms of clusters within these attribute domains. The mapping $classify\_location$ finally creates the location mapping representation of the analysis created object within the underlying regional partition.

6.3   Classifying Location

We now discuss the mapping $classify\_location$. It performs a classification of partition elements, $g_i \in G$, characterized by an attribute n-tuple $(b_1^i, \ldots, b_m^i)$, with respect to the class definition, $\pi(B_1, \ldots, B_m)$, of the fiat object to be constructed. The classification is based on the class definition of the fiat object in terms of clusters in the attribute space $B_1 \times \ldots \times B_m$. Clusters in the attribute space do not necessarily have sharp and well defined boundaries (See Section

2.3). This has the consequence that we need to distinguish crisp and vague class definitions.

Crisp class definitions correspond to clusters on the attribute domain with well defined boundaries. Vague class definitions correspond to clusters with ill defined boundaries. In the remainder of this section we show that

- crisp class definitions cause the classification process of the partition elements to yield containment sensitive rough location, and
- vague class definitions cause the classification process of the partition elements to yield overlap & containment sensitive rough location.

Crisp class definitions. Let *classify_location* be the mapping

$$classify\_location \ : \ (G \to B_1 \times \ldots \times B_l) \to (G \to \Omega_\forall)$$

$$classify\_location(g_i \mapsto (b_1, \ldots, b_l)) = \begin{cases} (g_i \mapsto \Box) \text{ if} \\ \quad containment\_condition(b_1, \ldots, b_l) \\ (g_i \mapsto 0^\Box) \text{ otherwise} \end{cases}$$

The condition *containment_condition* needs to be expressed formally in terms of constraints on the values of attribute l-tuples, $(b_1, \ldots, b_l)$. Those constraints describe the clusters in the attribute domain, which define the class of the object to be constructed.

Regarding to the spatial extent, i.e., the *where*, these constraints define conditions that are assumed to be sufficient to postulate that:

- *given* an input value $(b_1, \ldots, b_l)$ related to region g_i
- *then* we postulate that there exists an analysis created fiat object, o, of kind $\psi(B_1, \ldots, B_l)$ such that the region g_i is part of the exact region of the object o, i.e., $((loc_\forall \ o) \ g_i) = \Box$.

With crisp class definitions, only containment and non-containment classifications occur. Consequently, the mapping *classify_location* yields containment sensitive rough location. The exact region of the analysis created fiat object $r(o)$ coincides with the sum of partition regions for which the 'containment condition' holds.

Consider the example in Section 2.3. The attribute value $b_1 = -5.49m$ of the pixel g_{11} (remember the discussion in section 6.1) is contained in the interval, $[-6m, -1.1m]$, characterizing objects of class foreshore crisply. In terms of the mapping *classify_location* this is expressed as:

$$classify\_location \ : \ (G \to terrain\_elevation) \to (G \to \Omega_\forall)$$

$$classify\_location(g_i \mapsto b) = \begin{cases} (g_i \mapsto \Box) \text{ if } -6m \leq b \leq -1.1m \\ (g_i \mapsto 0^\Box) \text{ otherwise} \end{cases}$$

Vague class definitions. We now consider vague definitions of classes of fiat objects. Vague definition means that there are no sharp boundaries of clusters in the attribute space $B_1 \times \ldots \times B_m$. Vague class definitions result in overlap & containment sensitive rough location of the corresponding object instances in regional partitions created by the the underlying measurement processes. Let *classify_location* be the mapping

$$classify\_location : (G \to B_1 \times \ldots \times B_l) \to (G \to \Omega_3)$$

$$classify\_location(g_i \mapsto (b_1, \ldots, b_l)) = \begin{cases} (g_i \mapsto (\square, \Diamond)) \text{ if} \\ \quad containment\_condition(b_1, \ldots, b_l) \\ (g_i \mapsto (0^\square, \Diamond)) \text{ if} \\ \quad overlap\_condition(b_1, \ldots, b_l) \\ (g_i \mapsto (0^\square, 0^\Diamond)) \text{ otherwise} \end{cases}$$

The conditions *containment_condition* and *overlap_condition* need to be expressed formally in terms of constraints on the values of attribute l-tuples, $(b_1, \ldots, b_l)$. We already discussed the containment condition in the context of crisp class definitions above. The *overlap_condition* defines conditions that are sufficient to postulate that:

- given an input value $(b_1, \ldots, b_l)$ related to region g_i
- then we postulate that there exists an object o of kind $\psi(B_1, \ldots, B_l)$ such that the region g_i and the exact region of the object o overlap but g_i, is not a part of the object's exact region. i.e., $((\text{loc}_3 \, o) \, g_i) = (0^\square, \Diamond)$.

The distinction of three modes of location rather than two reflects the vagueness of the class definition and corresponds to the location of vague defined fiat objects in concentric regional partitions consisting of a core region an exterior region and a wide boundary between them (Fig. 2)[13]. In the case of rough location in regional partitions the *core* region is formed by those partition elements which are classified as $(\square, \Diamond)$, the *exterior* is formed by partition regions classified as $(0^\square, 0^\Diamond)$, and the *wide_boundary* is formed by partition elements classified as $(0^\square, \Diamond)$.

Consider the example in Section 2.3. The membership in a the class *foreshore* was defined by a trapezoidal function with breakpoints at $(-8m, -4m, -1.6m, -0.6m)$. In terms of the mapping *classify_location* this is expressed as follows:

$$classify\_location : (G \to terrain\_elevation) \to (G \to \Omega_3)$$

$$classify\_location(g_i \mapsto b) = \begin{cases} (g_i \mapsto (\square, \Diamond)) \text{ if } -4m \leq b \leq -1.6m \\ (g_i \mapsto (0^\square, \Diamond)) \text{ if } -8m \leq b < -4m \text{ or} \\ \quad -1.6m < b \leq 0.6m \\ (g_i \mapsto (0^\square, 0^\Diamond)) \text{ otherwise} \end{cases}$$

In the vague definition of the class *foreshore*, the pixel with an attribute $b_1 = -5.49m$ satisfies the 'overlap condition', but not the 'containment condition' of the class *foreshore*: $classify\_location(g_{11} \mapsto -5.49m) = (g_{11} \mapsto (0^\square, \Diamond))$.

---

[13] Notice that Fig. 2 is an idealization. In general, the partition regions may be complex regions consisting of multiple disconnected parts.

7 Conclusions

The purpose of spatial analysis performed on data resulting from measurement in physical reality is to identify objects, o', in physical reality that satisfy certain conditions. The process of spatial analysis yields objects, o, that are created by classification and other analysis operations. They are of fiat sort since they are the result of a human classification and analysis process. They are roughly located within the underlying regional partition, G, created by the measuring process. The exact location of the fiat spatial object o is unknown if o is subject to definitorial vagueness.

In the process of spatial analysis fiat objects are created in a process that has three basic components, which were modeled as mappings.

1. The mapping $transform\_attributes : (G \to A_1 \times \ldots \times A_k) \to (G \to B_1 \times \ldots \times B_l)$ transforming sets of fiat objects created by measurement or observation processes and represented by mappings of signature $c : (G \to A_1 \times \ldots \times A_k)$, into a set of co-located fiat objects represented by mappings of signature $d : (G \to B_1 \times \ldots \times B_l)$. Their attribute values form cluster in the attribute space $B_1 \times \ldots \times B_l$. Those cluster provide the basis for the definition of the final, analysis created object of kind $\pi(B_1, \ldots, B_m)$.

2. The mapping $classify\_location : (G \to B_1 \times \ldots \times B_l) \to (G \to \Omega)$ which yields the mapping representation, $(\text{loc } o) : (G \to \Omega)$, of the rough location of the analysis created fiat object within the regional partition, G, created by the underlying measurement process.

3. The mapping $create\_object\_attributes : (G \to B_1 \times \ldots \times B_l) \to B_1 \times \ldots \times B_m$ computing the attribute values of the new object.

The whole creative human process of bringing fiat objects of kind $\pi(B_1, \ldots, B_m)$ into existence by means of spatial analysis, is modeled as a mapping, $analyze$: $(G \to A_1 \times \ldots \times A_k) \to ((B_1 \times \ldots \times B_m), (G \to \Omega))$. This mapping transforms a mapping representation, c, of a measurement process into the new, analysis created, fiat object, i.e., $analyze\ c = (b_1, \ldots, b_m, (\text{loc } o))$.

It is important to distinguish fiat objects created by spatial analysis and the objects in the world they are supposed to correspond to. Both objects are related to each other in that sense that the radiation emitted by the measured object 'object in the world' caused sensor response during the remote sensing process which was recorded and caused fiat objects created by the remote sensing process to have certain attribute values. The fiat object 'object created by spatial analysis on remote sensed data' was created by performing spatial analysis on those objects. Obviously both objects, the measured object 'object in the world' and the fiat object 'object created by spatial analysis on remote sensed data', are different in nature and related to each other in the sense that the fiat object 'object created by spatial analysis on remote sensed data' *owes its existence* to:

- the existence of the object 'object in the world',
- the existence of a measuring act such as remote sensing, and
- the existence of a creative human act of spatial analysis.

Subject of ongoing research are the following questions:

- What is the justification to derive conclusions about bona fide and fiat objects in reality from knowledge about fiat objects created by spatial analysis?
- How does the *vagueness* of definitions of analysis created objects and the *indeterminacy* of their location relate to *uncertainty* about the truth of conclusions about the corresponding bona fide and fiat objects in physical reality?

Acknowledgements

The research of the first author was financed by the GEOIDE network. This support is gratefully acknowledged.

References

Abler, R., Marcus, M. & Olson, J. M., eds (1992), *Geographer's Worlds*, Rutgers University Press New Brunswick, New Jersey.

Baarda, W. (1967), *Statistical Concepts in Geodesy*, Vol. 2, Netherlands Geodetic Commission, Delft.

Bittner, T. (1999a), On ontology and epistemology of rough location, *in* 'Spatial information theory - Cognitive and computational foundations of geographic information science, COSIT 99', number 1661 *in* 'Lecture Notes in Computer Science', Springer Verlag, Hamburg, Germany.

Bittner, T. (1999b), Rough Location, Ph.d., Technical University Vienna, Department of Geoinformation.

Bittner, T. & Stell, J. G. (1998), 'A boundary-sensitive approach to qualitative location', *Annals of Mathematics and Artificial Intelligence* **24**, 93–114.

Borgo, S., Guarino, N. & Masolo, C. (1996), Towards an ontological theory of physical objects, *in* 'Computational Engineering in System Applications (CESA 96)'.

Bruegger, B. P. (1995), Theory for the integration of scale and representation formats: Major concepts and practical implications, *in* A. U. Frank & W. Kuhn, eds, 'Conference on Spatial Information Theory', Vol. 988 of *Lecture Notes in Computer Science*, Springer, pp. 291–310.

Carnap, R. (1966), *An Introduction to the Philosophy of Science*, Dover Publications, INC., New York.

Casati, R. & Varzi, A. (1995), 'The structure of spatial localization', *Philosophical Studies* **82**(2), 205–239.

Cheng, T., Molenaar, M. & Bouloucos, T. (1997), Identification of fuzzy objects from field observation data, *in* S. C. Hirtle & A. U. Frank, eds, 'Spatial Information Theory (COSIT '97)', Vol. 1329 of *Lecture Notes in Computer Science*, Springer, Laurel Highlands, PA, pp. 241–259.

Cohn, A. & Gotts, N. (1996), The 'egg-yolk' representation of regions with indeterminate boundaries, *in* P. Burrough & A. Frank, eds, 'Geographic Objects with Indeterminate Boundaries', GISDATA Series II, Taylor and Francis, London.

Freundschuh, S. & Egenhofer, M. (1997), 'Human conceptions of spaces: Implications for gis', *Transactions in GIS*.

Gotts, N. M. (1996), An axiomatic approach to topology for spatial information systems, Technical Report 96.25, School of Computer Studies.

Halmos, P. (1963), *Lectures on Boolean Algebras*, D. van Nostrand Company, Princeton, New Jersy.

Kanellakis, P., Kuper, G. & Revesz, P. (1990), Constraint query languages, *in* '9th ACM PODS', pp. 299–313.

Klir, G. J. & Folger, T. A. (1988), *Fuzzy Sets, Uncertainty, and Information*, Prentice Hall, Englewood Cliffs.

Koch, K. R. (1988), *Parameter Estimation and Hypothesis Testing in Linear Models*, Springer, Berlin.

Kraus, K. (1988), *Fernerkundung*, Vol. 1, Ferd. Dümmlers Verlag.

Kraus, K. (1990), *Fernerkundung*, Vol. 2, Ferd. Dümmlers Verlag.

Krzystek, P. (1991), Fully automatic measurement of digital elevation models, *in* 'Proceedings of the 43rd Photogrammetric Week, Stuttgart', pp. 203–214.

Krzystek, P. & Wild, D. (1992), Experimental accuracy analysis of automatically measured digital terrain models, *in* W. Förstner & S. Winter, eds, 'Robust Computer Vision', Wichmann, Karlsruhe, pp. 372–390.

Laurini, R. & Thompson, D. (1994), *Fundamentals of Spatial Information Systems*, The APIC series, Academic Press.

Moffitt, F. & Bouchard, H. (1987), *Surveying*, Harper & Row, Publishers, New York.

Molenaar, M. & Cheng, T. (1998), Fuzzy spatial objects and their dynamics, *in* D. Fritsch, M. Englich & M. Sester, eds, 'ISPRS Commission IV Symposium "GIS Between Visions and Applications"', Vol. 32/4 of *International Archives of Photogrammetry and Remote Sensing*, Stuttgart, pp. 389–394.

Paredaens, J., Van den Bussche, J. & Van Gucht, D. (1994), Towards a theory of spatial database queries, *in* 'Thirteenth ACM SIGACT-SIGMOD-SIGART Symposium on Principles of Database Systems', Minneapolis.

Pawlak, Z. (1982), 'Rough sets', *Internat. J. Comput. Inform* **11**, 341–356.

Requicha, A. A. G. (1977), Mathematical models of rigid solid objects, Technical Memorandum TM 28, University of Rochester, College of Engineering & Applied Science.

Smith, B. (1995), On drawing lines on a map, *in* A. Frank & W. Kuhn, eds, 'Conference on Spatial Information Theory, COSIT', Vol. 988, Springer, Semmering, Austria.

Smith, B. & Mark, D. M. (1998), Ontology and geographic kinds, *in* 'Proc. Int. Symposium on Spatial Data Handling, SDH'98', Taylor and Francis, Vancouver.

Stell, J. & Worboys, M. (1997), The algebraic structure of sets of regions, *in* S. Hirtle, A. Frank & K. Kuhn, eds, 'Conference on Spatial Information Theory, COSIT'97', Springer.

Worboys, M. F. (1998*a*), 'Computation with imprecise geospatial data', *Computers, Environment and Urban Systems*.

Worboys, M. F. (1998*b*), 'Imprecision in finite resolution spatial data', *Geoinformatica*.

Relational Algebra for Spatial Data Management

N.A. Lorentzos[1], N.Tryfona[2], and J.R. Rios Viqueira[1]

[1] Informatics Laboratory, Agricultural University of Athens
Iera Odos 75, GR 11855 Athens, Greece
{lorentzos, rios}@aua.gr

[2] Computer Science Department, Aalborg University
Fredrik Bajersvej 7E, DK-9220 Aalborg, Denmark
tryfona@cs.auc.dk

Abstract. An extension to the relational model is defined for the management of spatial data. The model adopts a radically new methodology for the formalization of three spatial data types, *point*, *line* and *surface*, based on a definition for *spatial quanta*. A relational algebra is next defined whose operations are closed and their result is defined uniquely. Most important, the operations represent adaptations of others that had been used in previous research for the modeling of temporal data. Hence, the model applies uniformly to the management of conventional, spatial and temporal data.

1 Introduction

Commercial systems lack an underlying formal theory for the homogeneous handling of both spatial and conventional data [8]. As a consequence, the handling of spatial data is based on the separate processing of the geographic and non-geographic attributes (see for example [4]). They also lack a powerful language for query formulation, hence they necessitate a lot of programming. To overcome these limitations, numerous research approaches have been undertaken in recent years, concerning various aspects of spatial data. Topological relations between spatial objects are addressed in [3], [7]. Characteristics of an SQL extension for the management of spatial data are investigated in [6]. Issues related to the building of spatial databases are identified in [22]. However, the representation and management of spatial data is by itself a non-trivial problem. A typical example is the intersection of two surfaces, which is, in the general case, a set of surfaces or lines or points or combinations of them. Similar problems are identified in operations regarding the union or difference of pieces of spatial data. Considering therefore *point*, *line* and *surface* as primitive data types (which is close to human intuition) may result in the definition of non-closed operations. To overcome this problem, some approaches consider more complex data types, such as *sets of surfaces* [2], [10], [11]. In spite of this, in [25] it is argued that, whatever sophisticated and generic data model is defined, there will always be a lack of support for some particular spatial data types.

In terms of defining a spatial database model, various alternatives have been investigated: Extensions to the relational and the nested relational model are proposed in [2] and [6], respectively. Object-oriented approaches have been proposed in [10], [24]. A relational extension with object-oriented characteristics is proposed

P.Agouris and A.Stefanidis (Eds.): ISD'99, LNCS1737, pp. 192-208, 1999

in [5]. Spatial models, other than relational or object-oriented, are defined in [1], [23]. Finally, a many-sorted algebra is defined in [11]. The above diverge approaches witness that the definition of primitive spatial data types and the formalization of operations between them have proved to be most challenging problems.

The present paper proposes an extension to the relational model that is based on *spatial quanta*. Only the three primitive spatial data types that are close to human intuition are considered, *point*, *line* and *surface*. Relational algebra operations are also defined, which are closed and their result is defined uniquely. The model enables the uniform representation and handling of both spatial and conventional data. Most important, the formalism did not actually require the definition of new operations, it only had to adapt accordingly operations that had been defined in previous research for the management of *interval* (and subsequently *temporal*) data [13] (in this present work we restrict only to the management of spatial data).

The remainder sections of this paper can be summarized as follows: A formalism for *spatial quanta* is provided in Section 2. An extension to the relational model is formalized in Section 3. The advantages of the model are outlined in Section 4. Concluding remarks and further research are discussed in the last section.

2   Formalism for Spatial Data

In this section we provide a quantum-based formalism for spatial data. For our purposes, we denote by R the set of real numbers and by $I_m = \{1, 2, ..., m\}$, $m > 0$, a subset of the integers.

2.1 Spatial Quanta

Quantum Points: The set of *quantum points* is defined as

$$Q_{POINT} = \{(i, j) \in I_m^2\}.$$

Geometrically, each element in Q_{POINT} can be interpreted as a dot on a plane. Since this set is finite, each of its elements can be identified uniquely by an integer. Hence, Figure 1 depicts the geometric interpretation and the identifier integer of the elements of Q_{POINT}, in the case that $m = 15$. This value of m will be considered fixed in all the subsequent examples.

Now let $p \equiv (i, j) \in Q_{POINT}$. We then adopt the following notation and terminology for the points below:

$$p_N \equiv (i, j+1) \quad (p_N \text{ is to the } north \text{ of p}).$$
$$p_S \equiv (i, j-1) \quad (p_S \text{ is to the } south \text{ of p}).$$
$$p_E \equiv (i+1, j) \quad (p_E \text{ is to the } east \text{ of p}).$$
$$p_W \equiv (i-1, j) \quad (p_W \text{ is to the } west \text{ of p}).$$
$$p_{NE} \equiv (i+1, j+1) \quad (p_{NE} \text{ is to the } northeast \text{ of p}).$$
$$p_{NW} \equiv (i-1, j+1) \quad (p_{NW} \text{ is to the } northwest \text{ of p}).$$
$$p_{SE} \equiv (i+1, j-1) \quad (p_{SE} \text{ is to the } southeast \text{ of p}).$$
$$p_{SW} \equiv (i-1, j-1) \quad (p_{SW} \text{ is to the } southwest \text{ of p}).$$

Points p_N, p_S, p_E, p_W are called *neighbors of* p. *Corner points* are called the points p, p_E, p_{NE} and p_N. As an example, consider p = 33, in Figure 1. Then its neighbors are $33_N = 48$, $33_S = 18$, $33_E = 34$ and $33_W =32$. Also, 32, 33, 48, 47 are corner points.

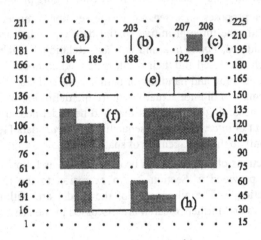

Fig. 1. Spatial quanta and spatial objects.

Quantum Lines: Let p, q $\in$ Q_{POINT} be two neighbor points, one of which is to the east of the other (i.e. the coordinates of one of them are (i, j) whereas those of the other are (i+1, j)). Then the set

$$ql_{p,q} \equiv \{(x, y) \in R^2 \mid i \leq x \leq i+1 \wedge y = j \}.$$

is called a *pure horizontal quantum line*. Similarly, if one of them is to the north of the other (i.e. their coordinates are (i, j) and (i, j+1)) then

$$ql_{p,q} \equiv \{(x, y) \in R^2 \mid x = i \wedge j \leq y \leq j+1\}.$$

is called a *pure vertical quantum line*.
As can be deduced from the definition, $ql_{p,q} = ql_{q,p}$. As is also obvious, a *pure quantum line* (i.e. either a *pure horizontal* or a *pure vertical quantum line*) consists of an infinite number of R^2 elements. A pure quantum line can geometrically be interpreted as a line segment with *edges* the points p, q $\in$ Q_{POINT}. Figures 1(a) and 1(b) show two pure quantum lines, $ql_{184,185}$ and $ql_{188,203}$.
If Q_{PL} denotes the set of all *pure quantum lines* (horizontal or vertical) then

$$Q_{LINE} = Q_{PL} \cup Q_{POINT}$$

is called *the set of all quantum lines*. Since $Q_{POINT} \subset Q_{LINE}$, every element in Q_{POINT} is called a *degenerate quantum line* (*quantum line degenerated to a point*).

Quantum Surfaces: Let p, q, r, s $\in$ Q_{POINT} be a clockwise or a counter-clockwise order of four corner points (i.e. their coordinates are (i, j), (i+1, j) (i+1, j+1) and (i, j+1)). Then

$$qs_{p,q,r,s} \equiv \{(x, y) \in R^2 \mid i \le x \le i+1 \land j \le y \le j+1 \}.$$

is called a *pure quantum surface*.

By definition, $qs_{p,q,r,s}$, $qs_{q,r,s,p}$, $qs_{s,r,q,p}$ etc are equivalent notations of the same pure quantum surface. It is also true that a pure quantum surface consists of an infinite number of R^2 elements. A pure quantum surface can geometrically be interpreted as a square whose *corners* are the points p, q, r, s $\in Q_{POINT}$ and whose *sides* are the four quantum lines $ql_{p,q}$, $ql_{q,r}$, $ql_{r,s}$, and $ql_{s,p}$. Figure 1(c) depicts a pure quantum surface, $qs_{192,193,208,207}$.

If Q_{PS} denotes the set of all *pure quantum surfaces* then

$$Q_{SURFACE} = Q_{PS} \cup Q_{LINE}$$

is called *the set of all quantum surfaces*. Since $Q_{LINE} \subset Q_{SURFACE}$, every element in Q_{LINE} is called a *degenerate quantum surface*. More precisely, if q $\in Q_{SURFACE}$ and it is also true that q $\in Q_{LINE} - Q_{POINT}$ then q is a *quantum surface degenerated to a quantum line*. If q $\in Q_{SURFACE}$ and it is also true that q $\in Q_{POINT}$ then q is a *quantum surface degenerated to a quantum point*.

Quanta: An element either in Q_{POINT} or in Q_{LINE} or in $Q_{SURFACE}$ is called a (*spatial*) *quantum*.

2.2 Spatial Data Types

To provide formal definitions of spatial data types, some notation and terminology is first introduced.

$Q_{PL\&PS} \equiv Q_{PL} \cup Q_{PS}$ denotes the set of *pure quantum lines* and *pure quantum surfaces*.

Q_{GEO} denotes any of the sets Q_{POINT} or Q_{LINE} or $Q_{SURFACE}$.

If q $\in Q_{GEO}$ then *set*(q) is defined as

$$set(q) = \begin{cases} \{q\} & \mid q \in Q_{POINT} \\ q & \mid otherwise \end{cases}$$

For example, $set(1) = \{1\}$, $set(ql_{1,2}) = ql_{1,2}$ and $set(qs_{1,2,17,16}) = qs_{1,2, 17,16}$ (Figure 1).

Power(A) denotes the set of all possible subsets of a set A.

Connectivity: If A $\in$ *Power*($Q_{PL\&PS}$) - $\{\varnothing\}$ then we say that *A is connected* if and only if for every $s_1 \in$ A and for every $s_2 \in$ A there exists a sequence $q_1 \equiv s_1$, q_2, q_3, ..., $q_n \equiv s_2 \in$ A such that $q_i \cap q_{i+1} \ne \varnothing$ for all i = 1,2, ..., n-1.

As an example, $1 = \{ql_{138,139}, ql_{139,140}, ql_{140,141}, ql_{141,142}\}$ in Figure 1(d) is connected. The same is also true for the spatial objects in Figures 1(e)-1(h). Based on the above, the following spatial data types (*DT*) are now defined.

DT1.   POINT = $\{\{p\} \mid p \in Q_{POINT}\}$.

The elements of this set are said to be of a *POINT data type*. By definition, a point is a set of a single element. Given for example 1, 2, …, 225 ∈ Q_{POINT}, {1}, {2}, …, {225} are of a POINT type. The geometric interpretation of an element in POINT is defined as a dot in the plane i.e. it is identical to that of the elements in Q_{POINT}. Note that a point was defined as a set because, as a spatial data type, it is mainly incorporated in set operations, as will be seen in Section 3.

DT2.   LINE = POINT ∪ {S | S ∈ *Power*(Q_{PL}) - {∅} ∧ S is connected}.

The elements of this set are said to be of a *LINE data type*. The geometric interpretation of a line is defined as the union of the geometric interpretations of all its elements. By definition, a point is also a line. An element in LINE − POINT is called a *pure line*. One such line is l = {$ql_{138,139}$, $ql_{139,140}$, $ql_{140,141}$, $ql_{141,142}$} in Figure 1(d). Similarly, pure lines are the spatial objects in Figures 1(a), 1(b) and 1(e). An element in POINT is called a *degenerate line* or a *line degenerated to a point* (points {1}, {2}, …, {225}).

DT3.   SURFACE = POINT ∪ {S | S ∈ *Power*($Q_{PL\&PS}$) - {∅} ∧

S is connected ∧

($\forall$ q_1 ∈ S) ($\forall$ q_2 ∈ S) (q_1 ⊄ q_2)}.

The elements of this set are said to be of a *SURFACE type*. The geometric interpretation of a surface is defined as the union of the geometric interpretations of all its elements. By definition, a point is also a surface and the same is also true for a line. An element in SURFACE that consists solely of pure quantum surfaces is called a *pure surface* (consider for example the set of quantum surfaces that compose each of the spatial objects in Figures 1(c), 1(f) and 1(g)). Figure 1(g) depicts a *surface with one hole*. An element in SURFACE, which is also in LINE is called a *degenerate surface*. It can be either a *surface degenerated to a line* (consider for example the set of quantum lines in each of the Figures 1(a), 1(b), 1(d) and 1(e)) or a *surface degenerated to a point* (consider for example {1}, {2}, …, {225}). Finally, a surface consisting of both pure quantum surfaces and pure quantum lines is called a *hybrid surface* (consider for example the set of quanta that compose the object in Figure 1(h)).

From the above, it follows that POINT ⊂ LINE ⊂ SURFACE. In the sequel GEO is used to denote any of the data types POINT or LINE or SURFACE. An element in any of these sets is said to be a *geo* or *spatial object*. As is obvious, a geo object is defined in a unique way and has a unique geometric interpretation.

2.3 Spatial Predicates and Functions

Clearly, a whole series of spatial predicates and functions can be defined. Here we restrict to the definition of only those that are used in the remainder sections. Their definition is an adaptation of those that have been given in [13] for the modeling of *interval* (and subsequently *temporal*) data. For ease, we define that

$$rank(\text{POINT}) = 0,$$
$$rank(\text{LINE}) \ \ = 1,$$
$$rank(\text{SURFACE}) = 2.$$

Given also a spatial object g, its data type is denoted by *domain*(g). Now consider g_1, $g_2 \in$ GEO, not necessarily of the same data type. Then we define the following:

Predicate cp: It enables identifying whether two spatial objects *overlap*. Formally,

$$g_1 \ cp \ g_2 \Leftrightarrow (\exists \ q_1 \in g_1) \wedge (\exists \ q_2 \in g_2) \wedge (set(q_1) \cap set(q_2) \neq \varnothing).$$

In [13] this predicate is called *common points*. In various spatial and temporal data modeling approaches it is usually called *overlaps*. For example,

$$\{1\} \ cp \ \{l_{1,2}\},$$
$$\{l_{1,2}, l_{2,3}\} \ cp \ \{s_{1,2,17,16}, s_{16,17,32,31}\}$$

evaluate to *True* whereas

$$\{1\} \ cp \ \{2\},$$
$$\{l_{1,2}, l_{2,3}\} \ cp \ \{l_{4,5}\}$$

evaluate to *False*.

Unary Predicates: They enable identifying spatial objects of a particular type. Given for example a geo object g, some predicates are the following:

$$is\_point(g) = True \quad \text{if and only if } g \subseteq Q_{\text{POINT}}.$$
$$is\_pure\_line(g) = True \quad \text{if and only if } g \subseteq Q_{\text{PL}}.$$
$$is\_pure\_surface(g) = True \quad \text{if and only if } g \subseteq Q_{\text{PS}}.$$

For example,

$$is\_point(\{3\}), is\_pure\_line(\{ql_{1,2}, ql_{2,3}\})$$

evaluate to *True* whereas

$$is\_point(\{ql_{1,2}\}), is\_pure\_line(\{qs_{1,2,17,16}\}).$$

evaluate to *False*.

Function merge: It returns a new spatial object, composed of quanta of two other overlapping spatial objects. Formally, if $g_1 \ cp \ g_2$, then $g \equiv merge(g_1, g_2)$ is defined as

$$g = (g_1 \cup g_2) - \{q \mid (q \in g_1 \cup g_2) \wedge (\exists \ q \in g_1 \cup g_2) \wedge (set(q) \subset set(q \ ))\}$$

and the domain of g is that one whose rank satisfies

$$rank(domain(g)) = max(rank(domain(g_1)), rank(domain(g_2))).$$

As an example,

$$merge(\{1\}, \{l_{1,2}\}) = \{l_{1,2}\}.$$
$$merge(\{l_{1,2}, l_{2,3}\}, \{s_{1,2,17,16}, s_{16,17,32,31}\}) = \{l_{2,3}, s_{1,2,17,16}, s_{16,17,32,31}\}.$$

Data type transformation functions: They transform between spatial data types. Some of them are the following:

Let {p} be a spatial object of any GEO type. Then it is defined that

$$to\_point(\{p\}) = \begin{cases} \{p\} \in \text{POINT} & | \; is\_point(\{p\}) = True \\ \\ undefined & | \; is\_point(\{p\}) = False \end{cases}$$

Functions *to_line* and *to_surface* can be defined in an analogous way.

3   Relational Modeling of Spatial Data

Based on the GEO types defined in the previous section, we are now ready to show how spatial objects can be incorporated in the relational model. As is shown, all GEO data types can be represented in a uniform way. A set of relational operations is also defined that are closed and their result is defined uniquely.

3.1   Data Structures

A relation is defined in the known way, except that the underlying domain of an attribute can now be of some GEO type. $R(A_1, A_2, ..., A_n)$ or $R(\mathbf{A})$ denotes a relation scheme with attributes $A_1, A_2, ..., A_n$. As an example, let

R(Name | CHAR(20), G | SURFACE)

be the relation in Figure 2(a). It consists of three tuples, one for a lake, another for a river and a third for a spring. The geometric interpretation of its data is given in Figure 2(b).

Relations $R_1(A_1, A_2, ..., A_n)$ and $R_2(A_1, A_2, ..., A_n)$ are *union-compatible* if attributes $R_1.A_i$ and $R_2.A_i$ have the same underlying domain, for $i = 1, 2, ..., n$. Note that if $R_1.A_i$ and $R_2.A_i$ are of some GEO type, they are union-compatible even if $rank(domain(R_1.A_i)) \neq rank(domain(R_2.A_i))$. This is due to the fact that POINT $\subset$ LINE $\subset$ SURFACE. In the sequel, G (perhaps subscripted) is used to denote the name of an attribute of some GEO type. Note also that the notation $R(\mathbf{A}, G)$ does not necessarily imply that G is the last attribute of R. For simplicity reasons, the majority of the examples that follow consider relations of the form $R(G)$.

3.2   Relational Algebra Operations

The following rules apply to the relational algebra operations that are defined below:

1. One unary operation, *Compute*, returns a relation with more attributes that those of the original relation. The underlying domain of each new such attribute matches the domain of the result that is returned by the respective function, which is involved in *Compute*.

2. For the remainder unary operations as well as the binary operations *Product* (i.e. *Cartesian Product*) and *Join*, the domain of each attribute of the result relation matches the respective domain of the attribute of the original relations.

3. The input relations, R_1 and R_2, in the remainder binary operations must be union-compatible. If the result relation contains an attribute G of some GEO data type, then the domain of G matches that one whose rank satisfies the property

$$max(rank(domain(R_1.G)), rank(domain(R_2.G))).$$

R

Name	G
Marathon lake	g1
Aoos river	g2
Crystal spring	g3

(a)   (b)

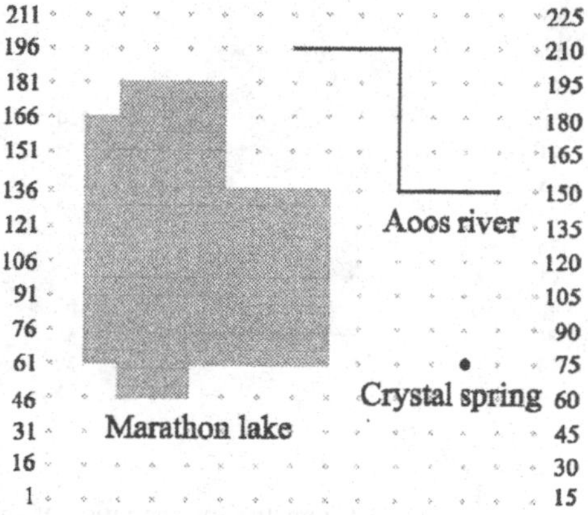

Fig. 2. Relation with spatial data and their geometric interpretation.

The set of relational algebra operations includes all the well-known algebraic operations of the conventional relational model. The most important are summarized below.

Union:	$U = R_1$ *Union* R_2	
Except:	$E = R_1$ *Except* R_2	
Intersect:	$I = R_1$ *Intersect* R_2	
Project:	$P = Project[\mathbf{A'}](R)$	$\varnothing \neq \mathbf{A'} \subseteq \mathbf{A}$
Product:	$P = R_1$ *Product* R_2	
Select:	$S = Select[F](R)$	(F is a well-formed formula)
Join:	$J = R_1$ *Join*$[F]$ R_2	($\equiv Select[F](R_1$ *Product* R_2))

Note that the first three operations should not be confused with relevant *spatial operations* that are usually defined is spatial data models. As an example, if $R_1(G)$ and $R_2(G)$ are the relations of spatial objects whose geometric interpretations are shown in Figures 3(a) and 3(b) then $U = R_1$ *Union* R_2 consists of so many tuples as the number of distinct tuples in both R_1 and R_2. The remainder operations are defined as follows.

Compute: It is an operation that enables the incorporation of functions [12]. Formally, consider $R(\mathbf{A})$ and the functions $f_1, f_2, \ldots, f_m$ that are defined respectively in terms of the sets of attributes $\mathbf{A_1}, \mathbf{A_2}, \ldots, \mathbf{A_m} \subseteq \mathbf{A}$. Then

$$C = Compute[C_1 = f_1(\mathbf{A_1}), C_2 = f_2(\mathbf{A_2}), \ldots, C_m = f_m(\mathbf{A_m})](R)$$

returns a relation with scheme $C(A, C_1, C_2, ..., C_m)$ and content

$$\{(a, c_1, c_2, ..., c_m) \mid ((a) \in R) \land (c_1 = f_1(a_1) \land c_2 = f_2(a_2) \land ... \land c_m = f_m(a_m))\}.$$

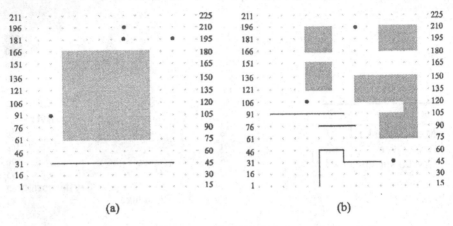

(a)   (b)

Fig. 3. Geometric interpretation of spatial data of two distinct relations.

As an example, assume that a relation scheme is

$$R(A \mid INTEGER, B \mid INTEGER, G_1 \mid SURFACE)$$

and that all the values recorded in G_1 are surfaces degenerated to points. Then

$$C = Compute[D = A+B, G_2 = to\_point(G_1)](R)$$

has scheme

$$C(A \mid INTEGER, B \mid INTEGER, G_1 \mid SURFACE, D \mid INTEGER, G_2 \mid POINT)$$

and consists of the tuples

$$\{(a, b, g_1, a + b, to\_point(g_1)) \mid (a, b, g_1) \in R\}.$$

The next two operations had specially been defined for the management of *interval* (and subsequently *temporal*) data and had been shown to be closed [13]. The definition of their application to relations containing spatial data is given below. Hence, they still remain closed.

Unfold: It *decomposes* a geo object g into all its *sub-objects* $\{g_i\}$, where g_i is a spatial quantum. For each sub-object a new tuple is produced in the result relation. Formally, let $R(A, G)$ be a relation scheme and let

$$U = Unfold[G](R).$$

Then the scheme of the result relation is $U(A, G)$ and its extension is defined as

$$U = \{(a, \{g_i\}) \mid (a, g) \in R \land g_i \in Q_{GEO} \land (\exists g_i' \in g)(set(g_i) \subseteq set(g_i'))\}.$$

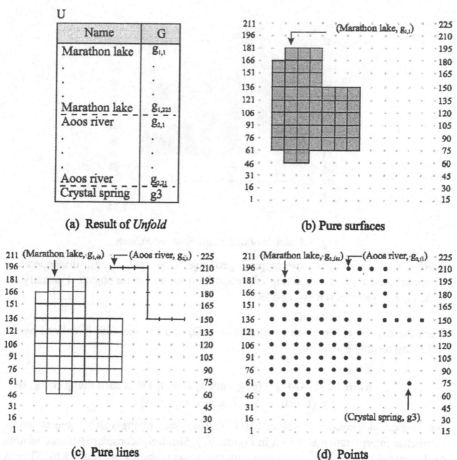

(a) Result of *Unfold*

(b) Pure surfaces

(c) Pure lines

(d) Points

Fig. 4. Result of operation *Unfold* and respective geometric interpretation.

As an example, consider the relation in Figure 2(a), consisting of the spatial objects whose geometric interpretation is given in Figure 2(b). Then the result relation of operation U = *Unfold*[G](R) is given in Figure 4(a). Each $g_{i,j}$ value that is recorded in attribute G of this relation is of the form {q}, where q is a quantum. The geometric interpretation of these $g_{i,j}$ is shown in Figures 4(b)-4(c). More precisely, Figure 4(b) (Figure 4(c), Figure 4(d)) shows the geometric interpretation of those $g_{i,j}$ whose respective quanta are pure quantum surfaces (pure quantum lines, points). Note that if *domain*(R.G) = POINT then *Unfold*[G](R) ≡ R.

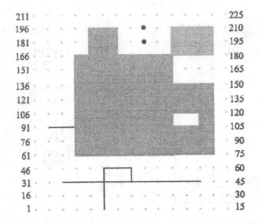

Fig. 5. Example of operations *Fold* and *PUnion*.

Fold: Given a family of overlapping geo objects g_1, g_2, ..., g_n, this operation *composes* a new object, consisting of the spatial quanta of these objects. Formally, let $R(A, G)$ be a relation scheme and let

$F = Fold[G](R)$.

Then the scheme of the result relation is $F(A, G)$ and its extension is defined by the following recursive algorithm:

$F = R$;

while there exist $t_1 = (a, g_1)$ and $t_2 = (a, g_2) \in R$ such that g_1 *cp* g_2 **do**
$F = (F - \{t_1, t_2\}) \cup \{(a, merge(g_1, g_2)\}$.

As an example, consider relation $R_1(G)$ that consists of the spatial objects whose geometric interpretation is shown in Figure 3(a). Similarly, consider $R_2(G)$ consisting of the spatial objects whose geometric interpretation is shown in Figure 3(b). Then R $= R_1$ *Union* R_2 consists of all the tuples in either R_1 or R_2. Then *Fold*[G](R) consists of 4 tuples, one tuple for each of the spatial objects in Figure 5. As the example shows, if a point overlaps with either a pure line or a pure surface, it does not appear in the result relation, it is *absorbed* by the latter. Similarly, the portion of a pure line that overlaps with a pure surface is *absorbed* by the latter. Note that if *domain*(R.G) = POINT then *Fold*[G](R) $\equiv$ R.

PUnion: It *composes* new spatial objects. Each of them consists of the overlapping quanta of the spatial objects of two distinct relations. Formally, let $R_1(A, G)$ and $R_2(A, G)$ be two union-compatible relations, where $R_1.G$ and $R_2.G$ are not necessarily of the same GEO type. Then the scheme of

$PU = R_1$ *PUnion*[G] R_2

is $PU(A, G)$ and its content is that one obtained by the composite operation

Fold[G](*Unfold*[G](R_1) *Union* *Unfold*[G](R_2)).

As an example, let R_1 and R_2 consist of the spatial objects in Figures 3(a) and 3(b), respectively. Then R_1 *PUnion*[G] R_2 consists of the spatial objects in Figure 5. The observations on *Fold*, that regard the absorbing of a spatial object from another, also apply to this operation. Hence, the example shows that *PUnion* covers all the possible cases of a *spatial union* between two geo objects, in a way that matches user requirements. Note that if the $domain(R_1.G) = domain(R_2.G) = POINT$ then

$$R_1 \; PUnion[G] \; R_2 \equiv R_1 \; Union \; R_2.$$

PExcept: It produces new spatial objects. Each of them consists of those overlapping quanta of the spatial objects of a relation R_1 which are not quanta of some spatial object of a relation R_2. Formally, consider $R_1(A, G)$ and $R_2(A, G)$, where $R_1.G$ and $R_2.G$ are not necessarily of the same GEO type. Then the scheme of

$$PE = R_1 \; PExcept[G] \; R_2$$

is PE(**A**, G) and its content is that one obtained by the composite operation

$$Fold[G](Unfold[G](R_1) \; Except \; Unfold[G](R_2)).$$

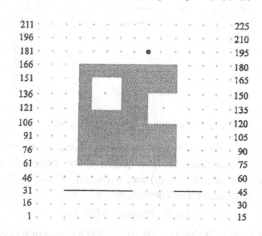

Fig. 6. Example of operation *Pexcept*.

As an example, assume again that R_1 and R_2 consist of the spatial objects in Figures 3(a) and 3(b), respectively. Then PE = R_1 *PExcept*[G] R_2 consists of the spatial objects in Figure 6. If q_1, q_2 are quanta, $(\{q_1\}) \in R_1$, $(\{q_2\}) \in R_2$ and $\{q_1\}$ overlaps with $\{q_2\}$ then the example demonstrates the following interesting cases:

If $\{q_1\} \in$ POINT and $\{q_2\} \in$ POINT   then $\{q_1\} \notin$ PE.

If $\{q_1\} \in$ POINT and $\{q_2\} \in$ LINE   then $\{q_1\} \notin$ PE.

If $\{q_1\} \in$ POINT and $\{q_2\} \in$ SURFACE   then $\{q_1\} \notin$ PE.

If $\{q_1\} \in$ LINE   and $\{q_2\} \in$ POINT   then $\{q_1\} \in$ PE.

If $\{q_1\} \in$ LINE   and $\{q_2\} \in$ LINE   then $\{q_1\} \notin$ PE, where $\{q_1\} \subseteq$ $\{q_2\}$.

If $\{q_1\} \in$ LINE   and $\{q_2\} \in$ SURFACE   then $\{q_1\} \notin$ PE, where $\{q_1\} \subseteq \{q_2\}$.

If $\{q_1\} \in$ SURFACE and $\{q_2\} \in$ POINT   then $\{q_1\} \in$ PE.

If $\{q_1\} \in$ SURFACE and $\{q_2\} \in$ LINE   then $\{q_1\} \in$ PE.

If $\{q_1\} \in$ SURFACE and $\{q_2\} \in$ SURFACE then $\{q_1\} \notin$ PE, where $\{q_1\} \subseteq \{q_2\}$.

The same observation also applies to the elements of two spatial objects. Hence, the example shows that *PExcept* covers all the possible cases of a *spatial difference* between two geo objects, in a way that matches user requirements. Note that if the domain of G is POINT in both R_1 and R_2 then R_1 *PExcept*[G] $R_2 \equiv R_1$ *Except* R_2.

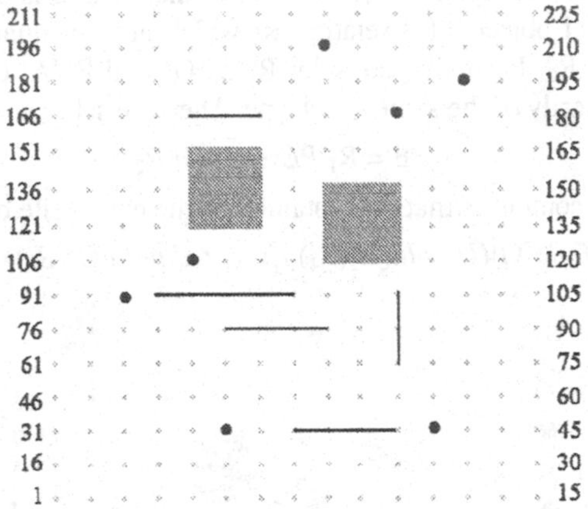

Fig. 7. Example of operation *Pintersect*.

PIntersect: It also produces new spatial objects. Each of them consists of those overlapping quanta that are also common quanta of the spatial objects of two distinct relations. Formally, consider $R_1(A, G)$ and $R_2(A, G)$, where $R_1.G$ and $R_2.G$ are not necessarily of the same GEO type. Then the scheme of

$$PI = R_1 \text{ } PIntersect \text{ } [G] \text{ } R_2$$

is PI(A, G) and its content is that one obtained by the composite operation

$$Fold[G](Unfold[G](R_1) \text{ } Intersect \text{ } Unfold[G](R_2))$$

As an example, assume again that R_1 and R_2 consist of the spatial objects in Figures 3(a) and 3(b), respectively. Then R_1 *PIntersect*[G] R_2 consists of the spatial objects in Figure 7. As the example shows, *PIntersect* covers all the possible cases of a *spatial intersection* between two geo objects, in a way that matches user requirements. Note that if the domain of G is POINT in both R_1 and R_2 then R_1 *PIntersect* [G] $R_2 \equiv R_1$ *Intersect* R_2.

Using the above operations, it is obvious that many queries can be replied. One example is *'retrieve that part of the intersection of the spatial objects in Figure 3(a) with those in Figure 3(b), which are of a point type'*. If R_1 and R_2 are the respective relations, that contain these objects, the operations are:

$$PI = R_1 \text{ } PIntersect[G] \text{ } R_2$$
$$S = Select[is\_point(G)](PI)$$
$$C = Compute[G_1 = to\_point(G)](S)$$
$$P = Project[G_1](C)$$

In this sequence of operations, *Compute* is used in order to transform the result into POINT data type.

4   Advantages

The advantages of the proposed model can be summarized as follows:

1. *Closed algebraic operations:* The result of every relational algebra operation is always a relation. Hence, the algebra is not many-sorted.

2. *No need to define new algebraic operations:* Except the traditional relational algebra operations, all the others that have been defined in the present paper (i.e. *Fold, Unfold* etc) are actually adaptations of previous ones [12], [13] that had been defined for the management of interval (and subsequently temporal) data.

3. *Establishment of association between spatial objects and relations:* It has been shown that spatial objects can be recorded as attribute values of relations.

4. *Establishment of association between algebraic operations and operations between spatial objects:* Operations on spatial objects can be seen as algebraic operations on relations.

5. *Uniformity of operations:* A unique set of operations is used for the management of both conventional and spatial and temporal data (for the management of temporal data see [13]).

6. *Closeness to human intuition:* This is justified by an outline of some characteristics of the model that match human intuition:

    (i) By definition, lines and surfaces contain an infinite number of points.

    (ii) Lines are not defined as arcs, therefore they do not have either *begin* or *end* points.

    (iii) A line is treated as a degenerate surface and a point is treated as either a degenerate line or as a degenerate surface, depending on the user requirements.

7. *Capability to Define Complex Spatial Objects:* Certain applications require the management of complex spatial objects consisting, for example, of both surfaces and lines and points. Clearly, such objects can directly be represented in the proposed model. Moreover, these objects can be decomposed into their constituent parts (pure surfaces, pure lines and points), by applying the relational algebra operations that have been defined in conjunction with appropriate predicates. This functionality accords with human intuition, since people occasionally consider exclusively either complex spatial objects or their individual constituent parts, depending on the application requirements. As has been shown (last example in Section 3), the model inherits this capability.

8. *User friendliness:* In our opinion, this is justified by the following:

    (i) The model is close to human intuition.

    (ii) Its formalism has been based on the relational model, which is being used for the development of the majority of commercial applications.

5 Conclusions

An extension to the relational model has been formalized for the management of spatial data. The model enables the manipulation of spatial data by the application of algebraic operations to relations. All these operations are closed and their result is defined uniquely. Regarding relevant research work, the following similarities have been identified in the literature.

Work on the incorporation of operations *Fold* and *Unfold* [12], [13] for the management of spatial data has also been reported in [17], [18]. However, the fundamental differences of [17], [18] from the present work are the following. Quanta are not considered, but five spatial data types are introduced. One of these types is *point* whereas the remainders are of the form *sets of points*. Hence, the two approaches differ in the data types. Operations *Fold* and *Unfold* are defined but, as opposed to the present paper, *Unfold* always returns points. As a consequence, *Fold* and *Unfold* are considered only at the conceptual level and the operations are applied to relations consisting of an infinite number of tuples.

An extension to relational algebra is also defined in [9]. The approach incorporates a definition that resembles that of the *pure quantum surface*, defined in the present paper. Nothing relevant to the definition of pure quantum lines or points is formalized though. Consequently, lines and points are not incorporated in [9]. *Surfaces* are not defined as in the present paper, since the relevant data type reminds of *set of surfaces*. Two operations, *compose* and *decompose*, have functionality similar to *fold* and *unfold*, defined in the present paper, yet there are differences between the functionality of these two sets of operations.

A similar observation, regarding the use of objects resembling the *pure quantum surfaces* of the present paper is incorporated in [26]. However, the objectives of [26] are fully different from those of the present paper. In particular, it develops a *hybrid-raster* representation aiming at incorporating the 9-intersection model, proposed in [7], in raster-based applications. Hence, neither spatial data types nor algebraic operations are defined in [26].

Regarding the formalism provided in Section 2, especially Sections 2.1 and 2.2, there are some similarities with relevant definitions given in the areas of Computational Geometry, Computer Graphics, Image Processing and Spatial Data Structures. For example, the term *discrete* or *quantized space* is introduced in [14], where such a space is defined as a *finitely presented Abelian Group* that satisfies certain properties. The term *pure quantum surface*, introduced in the present paper, could be associated to what is commonly called *pixel* [16], [21]. If we restrict to pixels, the terms *4-connected* and *8-connected sets* are defined in [21] and equivalent respective definitions are *(d-)connected* [15] and *(i-)connected sets* [16]. From these definitions, the terms *8-connected* [21] and *i-connected set of pixels* [16] correspond to what has been defined in the present paper as *pure quantum surface*. It should be noted however that the term *connectivity* that is introduced in the present paper concerns, in addition, a set that is composed of both pure quantum surfaces and pure quantum lines. Definitions for *4-connected* and *8-connected points* can also be found in [19], [20]. As opposed to the formalism of the present paper, infinite sets are mainly considered in all these approaches. For example, [19] considers the set of all I^2 points and [21] considers an *infinite background*. We are not aware of any approach in which a *2-d point* data type is defined as a set of a single element, as in the present paper. As should finally be obvious, none of the approaches in these areas of research aims at the definition of a relational algebra for the management of spatial data.

Further research includes the investigation of the spatial properties of the operations defined in the present paper and the incorporation of optimization techniques. The result of this investigation will be considered in conjunction with relevant research results in other relevant research areas, e.g. [14], [15], [16], [19], [20], [21], [22], before an implementation of the proposed model is undertaken.

Acknowledgement

This work has been supported by the European Union, TMR Project CHOROCHRONOS (FMRX-CT96-0056). The first of the authors devotes this paper to both sides of the innocent and heroic people of Yugoslavia.

References

1. Benoit, D., Voisard A.: A Unified Approach to Geographic Data Modeling, Technical Report 9316, University of Munich (LMU), (1993).

2. Chan, E.P.F., Zhu, R.: QL/G - A Query Language for Geometric Data Bases, Proc. First International Conference on GIS, Urban Regional and Environmental Planning, Samos, Greece, (1996) 271-286.

3. Clementini, E., Felice P., Oosterom, P.V.: A Small Set of Formal Topological Relationships Suitable for End-User Interaction, Advances in Spatial Databases, Third International Symposium, SSD93, D. Abel and B. C. Ooi (eds.), Lecture Notes in Computer Science 692, Springer-Verlag, Singapore, (1993) 227-295.

4. Delis, V., Hadzilacos, T., Tryfona, N.: An Introduction to Layer Algebra, Proc. 6th International Symposium on Spatial Data Handling (SDH 94), (1994) 1020-1041.

5. DeWitt, D.J., Kabra, N., Luo, J., Patel J.M., Yu, J.: Client-Server Paradise, Proceedings of the 20th International Conference on Very Large Data Bases, (VLDB 94), J. B. Bocca, M. Jarke, C. Zaniolo (eds.), Morgan Kaufmann, Santiago de Chile, Chile, (1994) 558-569.

6. Egenhofer, M. J.: Spatial SQL: A Query and Presentation Language, IEEE Transactions on Knowledge and Data Engineering 6(1), (1994) 86-95.

7. Egenhofer, M. J., Herring, J. R.: Categorizing Binary Topological Relations Between Regions, Lines, and Points in Geographic Databases, Technical Report, Department of Surveying Engineering, University of Maine, (1990).

8. ESRI, Arc/Info User s Guide, Environmental Systems Research Institute, Redlands, CA (1991).

9. Gargano, M., Nardelli E., Talamo, M.: Abstract Data Types for the Logical Modeling of Complex Data, Information Systems 16(6), (1991) 565-583.

10. Günther, O., Riekert, W.: The Design of GODOT: An Object-Oriented Geographic Information System, IEEE Data Engineering Bulletin 16(3), (1993) 4-9.

11. Güting, R.H., and Scheneider, M.: Realm-Based Spatial Data Types: The Rose Algebra, Very Large Data Bases Journal 4, (1995) 100-143.

12. Lorentzos, N.A., Johnson, R.G.: Extending Relational Algebra to Manipulate Temporal Data, Information Systems 13(3), (1988) 289-296.

13. Lorentzos, N.A., Mitsopoulos, Y.G.: SQL Extension for Interval Data, IEEE Transactions on Knowledge and Data Engineering 9(3), (1997) 480-499.
14. Mylopoulos, J., Pavlidis, T.: On the Topological Properties of Quantized Spaces. I. The Notion of Dimension, Journal of the ACM 18(2), (1971) 239-246.
15. Mylopoulos, J., Pavlidis, T.: On the Topological Properties of Quantized Spaces. II. Connectivity and Order of Connectivity, Journal of the ACM 18(2), (1971) 247-254.
16. Pavlidis, T.: Algorithms for graphics and image processing, Computer Science Press, 1982.
17. van Roessel, J.W.: An Integrated Point-Attribute Model for Four Types of Areal Gis Features, Proc. 6th International Symposium on Spatial Data Handling 1 (SDH'94), T. C. Waugh, R. G. Healey (eds.), Edinburg, Scotland, UK, (1994) 127-144.
18. van Roessel, J.W.: Conceptual Folding and Unfolding of Spatial Data for Spatial Queries. In: Towards SQL Database Extensions for Geographic Information Systems, V. B. Robinson, H. Tom (eds), National Institute of Standards and Technology Report NISTIR 5258, Gaithersburg, Maryland, (1993) 133-148.
19. Rosenfeld, A.: Connectivity in Digital Pictures, Journal of the ACM, 17(1), (1970) 146-160.
20. Rosenfeld, A, and Pfaltz, P.: Sequential Operations in Digital Image Processing, Journal of the ACM 13(4), (1966) 471-494.
21. Samet, H.: Applications of Spatial Data Structures, Computer Graphics, Image Processing and GIS, Addison Wesley 1990.
22. Samet, H., Aref, W.G.: Spatial Data Models and Query Processing, Modern Database Systems: The Object Model, Interoperability, and Beyond, Won Kim (ed.) ACM Press and Addison-Wesley, (1995) 338-360.
23. Scholl, M., Voisard, A.: Thematic Map Modeling, Design and Implementation of Large Spatial Databases (SSD 89), Lecture Notes in Computer Science 409, Springer-Verlag, Berlin, (1989) 167-190.
24. Voigtmann, A., Becker, L., Hinrichs, K.: An Object-Oriented Data Model and a Query Language for Geographic Information Systems, Report 15/95-I, Institut fór Informatik, Westf Wilhelms-Universitöt, Mónster, (1995).
25. Waterfeld, W., Schek, H-J.: The DASDBS Geokernel - An Extensible Database System for GIS, Three-Dimensional Modeling with Geoscientific Information Systems, A. K. Turner (ed.), Kluwer Academic Publishers, Netherlands, (1992) 69-84.
26. Winter, S., Frank, A.U.: Functional Extensions of a Raster Representation for Topological Relations, Interoperating Geographic Information Systems, A. Vckovski, K. Brassel, H.-J. Schek, (eds.), Lecture Notes of Computer Science 1580, Springer-Verlag, Berlin, (1999) 293-304.

Data Access

Integrating GIS and Imagery Through XML-Based Information Mediation

Amarnath Gupta, Richard Marciano, Ilya Zaslavsky, and Chaitanya Baru

San Diego Supercomputer Center, 10100 Hopkins Drive, La Jolla, CA 92093-0505
{gupta,marciano}@sdsc.edu, zaslavsk@rohan.sdsu.edu,
baru@sdsc.edu

Abstract. In this paper, we investigate a mediation-based approach to integrating information from geospatial information sources such as GIS's and databases of geo-referenced imagery. This approach is based on the use of XML to represent the information at the sources, by exporting XML Document Type Definitions (DTD's) associated with each source, and employing XML-based query languages to query integrated views of information at the mediator. Our goal is to enable users to issue a single query to the mediator, and provide the capability to return a result that seamlessly combines information from multiple sources. This paper describes issues in designing such a mediated system for geospatial data. Our notion of mediation for geospatial data is the "logical integration" of data achieved by creating correspondences between related spatial information, similar to the way mediation is done in "standard" databases. Thus, this notion of mediation does not depend on the development of spatial algorithms that operate on images or vector data and achieve "physical integration" through techniques such as image *conflation*. However, the mediator architecture does allow for the integration of physical integration techniques. The paper discusses issues related to *wrapping* of GIS and other geospatial sources and issues in querying such sources using an XML-based query language.

1   Introduction

Integration of information from distributed, heterogeneous information sources is an active area of research in the database community. The research efforts have mainly concentrated on sources such as collections of web documents, relational databases and text files. In the domain of spatial information systems, researchers have studied integration architectures, issues and problems in semantic interoperability and information integration concepts for spatial data [11,16,17]. Some recent approaches [14,15,19] have applied information integration methodology from the database community to spatial information systems. In this paper, we propose a mediation-based approach for integrating information from two types of information sources, viz. spatial information systems such as GIS and searchable databases of geo-referenced imagery. As in [14,19], our goal is to enable users to issue a single query in order to search multiple information sources and, in return, receive a combined result incorporating data from across these sources. Similarly, we would like to

P.Agouris and A.Stefanidis (Eds.): ISD'99, LNCS1737, pp. 211-234, 1999

provide authenticated and authorized users the ability to update sources. This paper describes the architecture of a mediation-based system and steps through the query evaluation procedure in an such a system. We emphasize that the notion of "integration" addressed in this paper does not rest on the development of spatial algorithms that operate on images or vector data and achieve "physical integration" (e.g., see [11]) through techniques like image conflation, as described in, say, [11]. Instead, we aim to attain "logical integration" by creating correspondences between related spatial information similar to non-spatial mediation systems [10]. We demonstrate how existing physical integration techniques can fit into our information association methodology. However, the development of such methods is not the focus of this paper.

1.1 Background

Various interoperability approaches and architectures have been discussed for distributed geographic processing and spatial data integration. Reviews of GIS interoperability and integration efforts are provided in [16, 19, 28, 29]. GIS standardization efforts in a number of countries have resulted in the development of standard specifications for data exchange, including SDTS (U.S.), FEIV (France), ALK (Germany), and SAIF (Canada) [30]. These specifications must contend with *de facto* commercial spatial data interchange standards, such as ESRI's E00 files and shapefiles, MapInfo's MIF/MID, and AutoCAD's dxf. Being relatively new, the former standards have not significantly affected data in legacy spatial information sources. At the same time, these new standards have not linked themselves with emerging standards for Web-based data interchange such as SGML and XML.

GIS integration efforts for supporting spatial data interoperability can be broadly categorized as follows:
- **Cataloguing of geographic sources** (or any sources/datasets), using *locational identifiers*. The Alexandria Digital Library, which supports spatial range queries on a variety of resources, is an example of this approach [ADL];
- **Developing gateways between databases**, by defining universal schemas and persistent views over a variety of data sources .
- **Data warehousing.** Sometimes referred to as the "eager approach" to data integration [14]. The OpenGIS Consortium efforts and related research resulted in the development of GIS interoperability standards based on this model, and in a series of national-level initiatives in the U.S. (via FGDC) and European countries. With several prototypes and testbeds developed (such as the OpenMap testbed [27]), research has focused on semantic and physical interoperability between selected sources. However, experiments of mapping selected GIS data models – Arc/Info, MGE and SPRING - to OpenGIS standard have demonstrated lack of formal standard definition which results in ambiguity and competing alternatives [26]. This approach is efficient for relatively small number of sources with known structure.
- **Mediator-based systems.** Similar to the concept of federated database (also called multidatabases). These systems support homogeneous views (in a common data

model) over heterogeneous data sources. Multidatabases are generally based on the client-server model with a middleware system (e.g. based on CORBA or COM) connecting the client and server layers. Mediator systems are based on a 3-level architecture, which include a "foundation" layer (databases with *wrappers*), a mediation layer (which supports exchange of queries and results between wrapped legacy data sources and applications), and an application/user interface layer [10]. The advantage of this architecture is its modularity and scalability. These systems support combining query results from individual sources rather than combining the data. In addition, the use of a semistructured data model at the mediator enables the modeling of sources with no structure or implicit structure. Examples of such semi-structured mediator-based systems include TSIMMIS [1,8], DISCO [23], and Information Manifold [22]. An example of the use of this approach for geospatial data is the Aquarelle project [INRIA] and the research described in [24] and [25]. Accessing geo-referenced SGML-structured information via the Web within the framework of this system is being explored at the time of writing of this paper [31].

Hybrid approaches combining features of the above architectures have also been proposed. For example, a GIS mediation/warehousing architecture described by [13] is built on four layers: the *application* layer (handles end-user requests), the *abstract services* layer (maintains a uniform view of overall system, i.e. a virtual database), the *concrete services* layer (maintains views of precise operations for each system and manages distribution of tasks between systems), and the *system services* layer (invokes services to specialized systems).

1.2 Creating Integrated Views

An important issue in mediation is the specification of "logical equivalence" relationships among data from different sources. Assume two information sources A and B, as shown in Figure 1. Source A organizes its information elements in the form of a tree while source B organizes its information in the form of a graph.

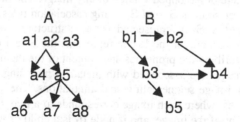

Fig. 1. Information sources A and B are tree- and graph-structured, respectively

The information integration issue relates to defining a *logical* source, say C, from A and B. Source C may never be physically *materialized*, but only generated "on-the-fly". Creating C requires the definition of rules on the original sources such that the elements of C may be defined as a logical association between elements of A and B. In this example, the rules may be:

1. Equate the element *a3* in A with the element *b1* in B
2. Do not include *b5* or any of its descendants in B, in C
3. Make a child of *a5* in A, whose value is greater than 7, also a child of *b4* in B
4. Label elements *a1* to *a8* in A as *c1* to *c8* in C. Also, label elements *b2* to *b4* in B to *c9* to *c11* in C

The resulting "integrated" information source is shown in Figure 2. Note that not all elements of the original sources need appear in the integrated view of the information (e.g. element b5). Information integration is achieved using a set of "association rules".

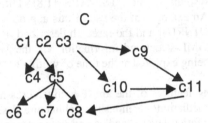

Fig. 2. In the integrated source C, elements and relationships from sources A and B have been integrated according to specific association rules

1.3 Integrating Geospatial Information Sources

Consider two information sources S_1 and S_2, shown in Figure 3, where S_1 is a GIS containing themes such as *soil map, parcel map, digital elevation map* and *transportation network map* of Southern California, and S_2 is an image library containing geo-referenced satellite images, aerial images and property photographs, and associated metadata such as timestamps of images, of different regions in Southern California. Assume that the image library is managed by a DBMS, which is able to provide a complete or a cropped version of any image. The information source S_3 is a view defined over sources S_1 and S_2, using association rules to integrate data across sources. Suppose that S_1 is represented as a tree-structured source using an R-tree, for example, where a node of the R-tree represents the extent of a theme, with additional metadata describing the properties and content of the theme. For the source S_2, assume that the images are associated with metadata including metadata related to image classification, image segmentation, and annotations. The view exported by source S_2 is a set of trees, where each image corresponds to a tree. Each node of this tree represents a segment of the image, and if node n_1 is a child of node n_2 it implies that the segment represented by n_1 is contained within the segment represented by n_2.

The structure of S_3 is a graph, where the nodes of tree-structured views of S_1 and S_2 are connected through a number of equivalence relations. These relations may be established by rules that specify inter-object associations including, (1) *containment conditions,* e.g., the extent of image object node n_3 in S_2 is covered by theme node n_5 in S_1, (2) *spatial or temporal joins,* (3) *logical associations,* e.g., both items refer to the city of San Diego.

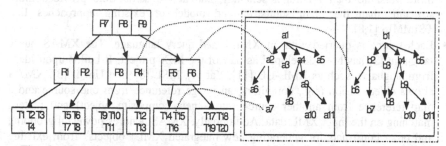

Fig. 3. The structure of the integrated information source. Note the dashed associations between the R-tree-structured representation of the GIS source and the set of image sources.

2   Architecture of an XML-Based Spatial Mediator

As described before, mediator-based systems employ a 3-level architecture consisting of the application (client) level, the mediator level, and the wrapper level. Wrappers serve as translators to convert data and query requests between the data model of the underlying information source and the model supported by the mediator. In our approach, we employ an XML-based data model at the mediator level. We extend the mediator of the MIX (*Mediation of Information using XML*) project [MIX] to support spatial sources as well. In the MIX system, the result of any query is an XML document. For queries issued on GIS and image sources, the result document may contain text, tables, figures, images, vector graphics and maps. Thus, the mediator should be able to deal with all of these types of information using the XML framework. In general, the MIX mediator receives a user query, fragments the query according to the capabilities of the sources, and sends the fragments to the appropriate sources. As the sources return their individual results to the mediator, the mediator integrates these result fragments into a single combined result and sends that back to the user.

2.1 The MIX Framework

Following are the key aspects of the MIX system:
- Each source exports a model of the information it contains in the form of an XML DTD. Data is exported as XML documents which subscribe to the DTD. For both GIS and image sources, the wrapper has to undertake the task of transforming the underlying information into XML. We use XML DTDs as a structural description (in effect, a schema) of the data exchanged by the components of the mediator architecture. The wrappers produce documents that conform to the associated DTD. As described in the next section, the GIS wrapper constructs the DTD by using the "catalog" information in the GIS. The schema provided by a DTD is

more versatile than relational schemas, and at the same time provides more structure than the plain semistructured model of existing approaches like TSIMMIS [1,8].

- Each source is queried with an XML-based query language. The XMAS query language [2] has been developed as part of the MIX project. It builds upon ideas from languages such as XML-QL [11], Yat [4], MSL [8], and UnQL [3]. XMAS allows object fusion (e.g., combining an image reference from one source and a map reference from another source into a new composite object) and pattern matching on the input XML data. Additionally, XMAS features powerful grouping and order constructs for generating new integrated XML "objects" from existing ones. The grouping operation can be used to arrange the same information in different ways.

- The query evaluation and integration process may be viewed as generation of a *virtual XML document*. As mentioned before, the output of a query in the MIX framework is an XML document. While it may be possible to materialize this document in one-shot, we provide the flexibility to produce this document in a browsing or navigational mode. In this mode, the user issues an XMAS query, and gets back only a "virtual" unmaterialized result. As the user navigates through the result, the system progressively expands the unvisited parts of the document.

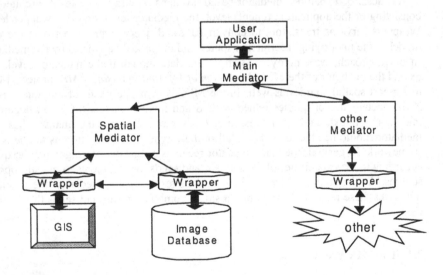

Fig. 4. All the links shown in this figure communicate through XML for data and XMAS for queries. The inter-wrapper links communicate by exchanging binary information if needed

2.2 Extending the MIX Framework for Spatial Data

Figure 4 shows the components of the MIX mediator system specialized for handling spatial information. The XMAS query from the user application is issued to the so-called "main mediator."

The main mediator receives the query containing both the non-spatial and spatial components. It applies a set of rules to identify the spatial part of the query, which it routes to the spatial mediator. In our example, all the query clauses refer to map and image information, thus the entire query is directed to the spatial mediator.

2.3 An Example Spatial Query

As a running example in this paper, we will use the following query based on sources S_1 and S_2 mentioned in the previous section.

Query: Using (a) the *Total Assessed Value (TAV)* (i.e. land price + improvement estimate) of the parcel maps of the regions in San Diego specified as *Carmel Valley* in the 1998 *Police Service Regions* of San Diego, and (b) aerial imagery of the regions and photographs of house properties in those regions, produce the following table:

Table 1. Output of example query

Year	TAV > $500K	$300K< TAV <$500K	$200K< TAV <$300K	$100K< TAV <$200K	TAV <$100K
1975	Join TAV map of qualified parcels with aerial photo of the same regions	Property pictures of five most expensive properties in the same regions	Same conditions as in Column 1		
1980					
1985	Same conditions as for Year 1975				
1990					
1995					

Processing this query requires:
- finding the region corresponding to "Carmel Valley" from the Police Service Regions of 1998
- for each specified year, classifying this region into the five land price ranges as shown, and generating one map per range
- for each map in a given range, overlaying it on top of the appropriate aerial image of Carmel Valley

- for each sub-region, identifying house properties in the region, ranking them by price, and choosing the top five photos
- arranging the information in the requested tabular form, as shown

The query produces a table of 25 maps and 25 sets of house photographs. We chose this particular query in order to show that the query output need not always be a single map. In this case, it is a table of 25 maps. The query demonstrates the need for the mediator to decompose a single query into multiple simpler queries to be executed by the GIS. The query also requires physical integration (the images from the image source need to be fetched and overlaid onto the TAV map) and logical integration, exercised through the join conditions on the aerial images and maps and on the property picture addresses and the qualifying regions in the GIS.

Grouping of the results according to time and value range is achieved using the powerful grouping construct available in the XMAS query language [2]. In the example XMAS query shown in the next subsection, we illustrate how reserved namespaces (i.e., a set of tag names) can be used to tailor XMAS to process data in different domains, e.g. the spatial domain. This query also illustrates the power of the virtual XML document concept. In this example, the query result contains 50 properties in Carmel Valley. The user may be interested in further examining the textual metadata of only, say, the first 20 of these and, further, may retrieve the images of only three properties. The virtual document concept will avoid unnecessary computation of the entire result set.

2.3.1 An Example XMAS Query

The XMAS version of the example query is shown below. Rather than explaining each step of the query, we point to a few key elements:

1. The notation *mix:<tagname>* refers to tags in a reserved namespace, which the mediator is aware of. Thus, the mediator recognizes the type of data and has specific ways of handling that data type. For example, *mix:region* would not be expected to have, say, a *length* attribute.
2. The query is directed to the mediator without specifying the location of any source. The reserved namespace tag *mix:source* (line 10), is used to indicate which definition of "Carmel Valley" should be employed.
3. The function *category(price,totalValueCategory)* (line 43), is a function that examines the total assessed value of a parcel in the parcel map and assigns the parcel to the correct bracket.
4. The output table is defined by grouping the results first by year (using the notation {$y} on line 37) and then by total assessed value ({$c} on line 36) within the year.
5. Wherever the same variable (e.g., $r) is used multiple times, it has to bind to the same constant. Thus, the aerial image, corresponding to $r on line 23, and the map object, corresponding to $r on line 10, must be of the same region, and the address of the property (line 32) must belong to the parcels satisfying the category condition.
6. The spatial predicate *within(region1,region2)* (line 46) is used without any software dependent syntax. We assume here that the user can enquire from the mediator what the supported functions are and how they can be invoked. For

example, if one of sources underneath the mediator may support another function centroid_within(region1, region2), the mediator will export the function and the user has to know which is suited for a query.

7. The predicate *display_order(mapData1, mapData2)* (line 49) is procedural and specifies that mapData1(corresponding to a theme) should be overlaid on mapData2. In case multiple mapData were involved, the mapData elements would be presented as a nested list in the form—display_order(mapData1, (mapData2,mapData3)).

```
1.  answer = construct $A
2.  where
3.  $A:<table>
4.  <row>
5.     <year>$y</>
6.       <totalValueCategory>$c
7.         <totalValue>$tv</>
8.         <mapColumn>
9.             <mix:map>
10.               <mix:region mix:source=$s1>$r
11.                 <mix:regionName>$n</>
12.             </>
13.             <mix:mapData>$md1
14.               <mix:dataName>$d1</>
15.               <mix:dataValue>$tv</>
16.               <mix:region>$r2</>
17.               <mix:date>$y</>
18.             </>
19.             <mix:mapData>$md2
20.               <mix:datatype>$dt
21.                 <mix:resolution>$res</>
22.             </>
23.             <mix:region>$r</>
24.             <mix:date>$y</>
26.             </mix:map>
27.         </mapColumn>
28.     <pictureColumn orderby=$p orderType=asc topN-5>
29.             <mix:image>
30.               <mix:dataName>$d3</>
31.               <price>$p</>
32.               <address>$a</>
33.               <mix:date>$y</>
34.             </>
35.         </>
36.       </totalValueCategory> {$c}
37.     </year>{$y}
38.  </row>
39.  </table>
40.  in http://some.mediator.url
41.  and
42.  belongsTo($y, (1975,1980,1985,1990,1995)) and
43.  category($tv,$c) and  ($s1 =
44.  "San_Diego.Police_Service_Region") and ($n =
45.  "Carmel Valley") and ($md1= "Parcel Map") and
```

```
46.   ($d1= "total assessed value") and within($r2,$r)
47.   and ($md2 = "imagery") and ($dt= "aerial") and
48.   ($res <= 16m) and ($d3 = "property photo") and
49.   mapsTo($a,$r2) and display_order($md1,$md2)
```

3   Wrapping Spatial Information Sources

In general, queries received by wrappers can be classified as *direct*, *logically equivalent*, or *indirect queries* [1]. A *direct query* is a request that can be satisfied by a primitive operation provided by the underlying information source. *Indirect queries* are those that are not supported by the underlying information source, thus the wrapper itself must have the computational capability to produce the required results. For example, a source may not be able to compute the correlation coefficient of a sequence of number pairs, thus the wrapper would have to perform that computation. Finally, *logically equivalent queries* are those that cannot be directly processed by the source, however, it is possible to rewrite the input query into one or more other queries to the underlying source which, in effect, can answer the original query. For example, the query, "For each census tract in San Diego that has over 30% minority population, find the zip code boundaries that intersect with it," may require multiple requests to a GIS source to identify the census tracts and then intersect with the zip code regions. However, it is possible to write the GIS script to generate the necessary result, thus, this is an example of a logically equivalent query. The task of the wrapper is further complicated for such queries since it may have to *compose* a program from smaller modules to produce the result. In this paper, we focus primarily on direct and logically equivalent queries, and provide only a simple example of indirect queries.

A key feature that distinguishes GIS sources from many other sources studied in the mediation literature is that most GIS sources are *stand-alone, interactive* systems. At best, interoperability is supported only within the same family of software products and not across federated, heterogeneous GIS sources. A GIS serves the roles of a database system (for spatial data), a computation source (e.g., for network flow optimization), and a presentation source (e.g., surface generation and mosaic creation), and is not usually equipped with a generic query language for declarative access. A GIS wrapper overcomes this problem by maintaining an internal model, including schema as well as instance information of a given source, and simulating the necessary ad hoc interface. The wrapper functions by first transforming the query/result into this internal model.

3.1 The Internal Schema of the GIS Wrapper

Most GIS sources recognize various map layers (e.g. coverage and themes) and a large body of common operations such as overlay and spatial intersections. These ubiquitous objects and functions can be considered as a simple typed algebra (as has been done more than once since 1983 D. Tomlin's Map Algebra [32]). For a specific GIS source the wrapper has to know how the types and functions in its algebra maps to the types and functions in the source. The wrapper assumes that there are at least 2 kinds of functions: boolean returning functions and object returning functions. An example of the latter is, say, the function *within*(region1, region2) written in ArcView Avenue script, where region1 is a theme object and region2 is region object, and the function is called #FTAB_RELTYPE_ISCOMPLETELYWITHIN, and needs to be invoked as:

region1.SelectByTheme(region2, #FTAB_RELTYPE_ISCOMPLETELYWITHIN, 0, #VTAB_SELTYPE_NEW).

Using the MapBasic syntax of MapInfo, the same function would be written as:

SELECT * FROM Region1 WHERE OBJ ENTIRELYWITHIN Region2.OBJ

The results returned are mapped back to internal types and hence are easily translated into XML. All additional types and operations supported by a GIS system will have to be layered on top of the simple algebra.

The GIS wrapper models every GIS source as having a **collectionObject** at the top level followed by **themeObject** and a **dataObject**, at the next level below. A collectionObject represents a group of co-registered themeObjects. A themeObject has the subtypes:

- **themeMap**: a binary blob that represents a map produced by the underlying GIS as the result of an operation. Each themeMap object has an identifier, a resolution and an extent. It may contain additional metadata, such as the time when the theme was created. A themeObject can be instantiated as a map.
- **table**: a representation of attribute information associated with a GIS theme in the form of a possibly nested table. Each table object has an identifier and a list of column names. A nested table is represented by treating a column name as a named list instead of a singleton name.
- **themeProperties**: a set of properties that describe an aggrgegate of the data contained in the theme. For example, for each type of dataObject in a theme, it will contain information like the number of information items in the theme, the spatial granularity of a cell, indexes implemented if any, existing topology if any, and so forth.

A dataObject represents the type of information associated with any theme. Each data object maintains its spatial extent, and has a reference to the table in the themeObject related to it. It may additionally have information on the valid time of the underlying data and accuracy of the data items. For many common GIS applications, the set of dataObject subtypes includes:

- **regionObject**: representing a 2D polygonal object in a theme
- **curveObject:** representing open or closed polylines in a theme
- **networkObject**: representing a graph possibly consisting of intersecting polylines
- **pointObject**: representing a feature that is represented in a theme as a point object
- **matrixObject**: representing a feature where every element in an array is associated with a value

The purpose of defining object types, like those described above, is to facilitate the translation of an XMAS query into syntactically well-formed queries in the language of the underlying GIS, and to convert the results returned from the GIS into a well-formed XML structure. These object types can be specialized, using inheritance, when developing wrappers for specific GIS systems. For example, the wrapper of a specific GIS, may have chosen to define an object, say, networkObject, as a transportation. For every built-in or user-extended type a list of function signatures is also defined. For example, for curveObject, the spatial intersection is defined as: intersect(curveObject, regionObject) and so on. The function signatures are needed so that the parameters specified therein can be made visible to the mediator[1] and be used to formulate valid XMAS queries. This also enables the wrapper system to be extensible so that if a specific GIS system permits some special function (e.g., water drainage computation for a digital elevation model) or object type, it can be simply exported to the mediator.

3.2.1 Catalog Extraction

The catalog is the schema information of the GIS source, which the wrapper exports to the spatial mediator as an XML DTD. It also maintains an internal version of the catalog to translate XMAS queries into GIS queries. In this paper, we use ArcView from ESRI as an illustrative example to discuss catalog services and query translation.

An example XML DTD for the GIS catalog is given below:

```
<!ELEMENT arcview_project (views|tables|scripts)* >
<!ELEMENT views (view)* >
<!ELEMENT view (projection|units|themes)* >
 <!ATTLIST view name CDATA #IMPLIED>
<!ELEMENT projection (#PCDATA)* >
<!ELEMENT units (#PCDATA)* >
<!ELEMENT themes (theme)* >
<!ELEMENT theme (assoc_table|threshold|extents)* >
 <!ATTLIST theme name CDATA #IMPLIED>
<!ELEMENT assoc_table (#PCDATA)* >
<!ELEMENT threshold EMPTY >
 <!ATTLIST threshold val CDATA #IMPLIED>
<!ELEMENT extents (bottom|left|top|right)* >
<!ELEMENT bottom (#PCDATA)* >
<!ELEMENT left (#PCDATA)* >
<!ELEMENT top (#PCDATA)* >
<!ELEMENT right (#PCDATA)* >
<!ELEMENT tables (table)* >
<!ELEMENT table (col)* >
<!ATTLIST table name CDATA #IMPLIED>
<!ELEMENT col EMPTY >
 <!ATTLIST col alias CDATA #IMPLIED>
 <!ATTLIST col type CDATA #IMPLIED>
 <!ATTLIST col width CDATA #IMPLIED>
 <!ATTLIST col decimal CDATA #IMPLIED>
```

[1] This actually happens during a registration procedure, but such operational details are omitted in this paper

```
<!ELEMENT scripts (script)* >
<!ELEMENT script EMPTY >
 <!ATTLIST script name CDATA #IMPLIED>
```

In a given GIS instance, we distinguish between a base theme set **B** and view theme set **V** as follows. A theme *b* is a base theme if it has only one of the subtypes of dataObject (e.g., if it only contains regionObjects) or if the wrapper engineer designates it to be a base theme. A theme *v* is a view theme if it has been created based upon a set of base themes $\{b_i\}$, such that the information in *v* is strictly a subset of the information in $\cup_i\{b_i\}$. The intuition behind making this distinction is that it is more optimal if query can be answered from a view theme rather than a base theme, since a view theme is equivalent to materialization, and reuses precomputed expensive spatial predicates on the same base data set. In order to recognize a theme as a view theme we employ the following. Assume that the projects in the system comprise universe of themes[2]. We traverse the project structure of ArcView and identify all themes referenced by it. For themes that have creation scripts, we identify the names of other themes, and arrange them to form a dependency graph of themes which is maintained by the wrapper. All themes with no incoming edges in the graph are placed in **B** and the others are placed in **V**. If a theme does not have a creation script it is placed in **B**. Hence in the worst case, every theme is treated as basic. In addition to this labeling, the wrapper engineer has the ability to specify for each view theme how the view was derived. The derivation needs to state which attributes (spatial or otherwise) were used to derive the view and what restriction condition was applied on the respective attributes. While it is difficult to extract this derivation information automatically, such a specification can enhance the efficiency of query processing. To see why this is so, consider a user query that looks for the ethnic distribution of all census tracts that overlap "Carmel Valley". Let us suppose the wrapper has identified two themes whose tables have the attributes "census tract number" and population. If it is known a priori that one of those two themes has already been restricted (subset) based on another attribute (e.g., median income greater than $25,000), then this information can be used to discard that theme, because the theme will not produce a complete answer (since it does not have the records corresponding to the population having median income less than $25,000). In the absence of such view information, the wrapper has to use other heuristics, such as selecting the theme with a higher record count. We will revisit this issue in a later section.

For each theme object we create a catalog record having the XML DTD structure shown before. Note how the internal schema of the wrapper has been used in constructing and that the themes are labeled as base and view. This basic structure can be augmented by any additional information that can be extracted by traversing the project structure. For example, for ArcView, if a satellite image stored as a layer will have the additional attributes such as "bandstatistics". Instead of simply exporting a set of theme DTDs to the mediator, we organize them into a container document by first creating an R-tree corresponding the spatial extents of the themes and then generating the XML document from the R-tree, as shown in Figure 3. Note that an internal node of the R-tree only induces a nesting in the

---

[2] It is very easy to include themes not referenced by any project in the universe.

XML document, without producing material data. The reason for having the R-tree representation at the spatial mediator is to gain efficiency during query processing. It is very likely that in order to choose the candidate sources for a query the mediator will need to ask, "which are the themes that provide some information in the user specified rectangle of interest?" Having the R-tree index within the mediator saves the trouble of going back to the information sources.

In addition to the containment relation and the derivation dependency graph, the wrapper may maintain other indices to connect the themes. One important thread is to place all themes in a temporal order, based on the valid time (i.e., the time when the data items were valid) of the theme. In case of themes valid over an interval of time the temporal order may be implemented through a data structure like the interval tree.

3.2 Wrapping an Image Library

Image sources may have both metadata-based retrieval and content-based retrieval capabilities [21]. The objective in wrapping image libraries is to provide access via a uniform interface to complete or partial digital images, as well as image features and other associated metadata.

3.2.1 The internal model for image sources

In general, image wrappers recognize the following object types associated with images:

- **image**: an image is associated with a set of standard metadata, e.g. its dimensions, format and pixel depth (bits per pixel). Images may be multiband, and could be retrieved one band at a time or up to three bands together. Standard image operations include cropping, rotation, and changing brightness and contrast. A spatial image is a specialization of image that must additionally have a georeference and resolution.

- **image mask**: a mask is a pixel chain within a bounding box, with specified coordinates. The purpose of a mask is to represent a segment produced by an image processing operation. The purpose of treating an image mask as a distinct data type is to separate the segment and its properties from the image. This allows an image to be associated with multiple segments produced by different operations that can be transferred across different components of the integrated system such as from the image library to a GIS wrapper.

- **image feature**: an image feature is a representation of an image property such as texture in a photograph or concrete region in a satellite image, that is computed by some analysis operation. Each instance of a feature is associated with an image mask that localizes the area over which it was computed. For convenience, a feature instance is associated with additional metadata such as the name of the feature and the parameter values used to compute it. We expect that image libraries will provide similarity functions based on features (e.g., it can request all images having some segment with texture similar to a given texture [20]).

- **scene graph**: scene graph, a term used in the VRML and MPEG-4 literature, represents a tree-like decomposition of a real or virtual scene, using a well-defined system of node types. We do not use all the features of a scene graph like the image transformation specifications. In our usage, a leaf node in the scene graph stands for a "unit region" in the image whose property can be described by a set of simple image features. We also keep the provision that the region defining a leaf node can be described by a shape property (e.g., "a circular area"), where the property belongs to an allowed type in VRML and MPEG-4 scene graphs. An internal node is constructed using the containment relation, as shown in Figure 2.

4   Evaluation of Spatial Queries

The task of the spatial mediator is to parse the spatial subquery, of a given query, and generate the associated evaluation plan. The spatial mediator is required to, (1) fragment the subquery between information sources and determine the order of execution of each fragment, (2) use the schema and capability information exported by each source to rewrite subquery fragments such that each source is able to evaluate the rewritten fragments, and (3) send each rewritten fragment to the corresponding source, collect the results from each source and return the combined result to the application mediator.

4.1   Query Planning at the Mediator

In this section, we sketch the typical sequence of steps executed by the spatial mediator. The exact sequence and details of each step will vary depending on the actual query. In the following, we refer back to the query example discussed in Section 2.3.1.

1. **Determine Map Request**: The tag *mix:map*, in line 9 of the XMAS query, specifies that the output of the query should be a map. The spatial mediator then expects to know which geographical area needs to be mapped, and which variables should be used to produce the map.
2. **Identify Map Region**: The next tag *mix:region*, on line 10, specifies the region to be mapped and informs that this region can be found in the source theme called, "Police Service Region" within the provenance of "San Diego". In this example, we assume that the information mapping the region to the theme is also available in the GIS itself. The mediator searches the DTD exported by the GIS wrapper and determines that the "San Diego City" theme has an associated table called "Police Service Region", and that the table has a polygon as a field.
3. **Produce Wrapper Query Condition for Map Region**: Line 11 identifies the *regionName* variable, $n, and line 44 specifies that its value must be "Carmel Valley". The mediator also knows that the tag *regionName* maps to the field name *srvRgn* in the "Police Service Region" table of the source GIS. Thus, it places the query condition *srvRgn= "Carmel Valley"* in the query fragment to be sent to the GIS wrapper.

4. **Identify Map Attribute 1,** *total assessed value*: The tag, *mix:mapData* on line 13, specifies the element to be mapped. As before, this data element is identified with a query condition on the "total assessed value" field of the table in the "Parcel Map" theme. But in this case, several "Parcel Map" themes are found, each associated with a different year. The mediator picks the years corresponding to the query by inspecting the DTD for the Parcel Map themes. We will show in the next section how the year gets associated with the theme in the DTD provided by the wrapper. Since 5 years (thus, 5 themes) are requested, the mediator produces 5 (almost identical) copies of all query conditions gathered so far, and treats them as *independent subqueries* to be sent to the GIS wrapper.

5. **Produce Wrapper Query Condition for Map Attribute,** *total assessed value*: The *total assessed value* attribute must satisfy the function category(price,totalValueCategory) and the results must be grouped into columns based on category value. Since there are 5 possible categories that each parcel map can belong to, a map needs to be produced for each. Thus, the mediator issues 5 "related" queries to the wrapper for each independent subquery mentioned above.

6. **Identify Map Attribute 2,** *imagery*: The next tag, *mix:mapData* on line 19, specifies the next element to be mapped. This element is an aerial map in the image library and must satisfy query conditions on the year, the resolution and the georeference to identify images for the query. The mediator has the DTD exported by the image wrapper. Whether the query can be safely answered is unspecified at this point since the region specifying the georeference is not computed yet. Thus, the mediator forms a partial query for the image wrapper.

7. **Formulate Query Fragments for Wrapper**: The *mix:map* tag on line 9 has a corresponding end tag on line 26. The mediator produces one independent and several dependent query fragments for the subquery represented by the *mix:map* element.

8. **Determine Image Request**: Similar to the map request, the mediator verifies that the necessary tables and field names exist in the DTD specified by the image library. It uses a rule to determine that the predicate *mapsTo(address, parcel region)* on line 48 is to be performed in two steps: first, obtain the address block from the Parcel Map table in the GIS source, second, formulate a range query on the street number in the image library.

9. **Determine Query Execution Plan**: The query is executed in the following order:
   1. Determine the extent of the Carmel Valley region.
   2. Use the extent to find corresponding aerial images of the region in the image library.
   3. Validate that there exist images of the region at the specified resolution. If there are images at multiple resolutions, use a rule to choose the finest resolution image covering the entire map region.
   4. Initiate transfer of the image from the image library to the GIS[3].
   5. Execute the map retrieval query (which produces 25 sets of results), and determine the parcels. Also, fetch the address block of the parcel, since that will be required in a later part of the query.
   6. Formulate the image query including the sorting.

---

[3] Assuming for now that the image and the GIS layer can be aligned.

4.2 Examples of a Rewritten Query Fragment

As mentioned before, a query fragment is a portion of the spatial query that is rewritten to match source capabilities. Each fragment is sent to an individual wrapper. This rewritten fragment contains the table and field names, structures, and functions supported by the source. We illustrate this in the following paragraphs.

- **Determine the boundary of the region Carmel Valley**

```
ans1 = construct $R
where
<ArcView_Projects>
            <theme name = $n1>
            </theme>
            <tables>
              <table name=$n2>
                <col name=$n3>$v1</>
                <col name=$n4>$v2
$R:              <extents>
                    <top>$t</>
                    <bottom>$b</>
                    <left>$l</>
                    <right>$r</>
                  </extents>
                </col>
              </table>
            </tables>
</ArcView_Projects>
in http://wrap.gis.url
and ($n1= "sdcity.shp") and ($n2 = "Attributes of
sdcity.shp") and ($n3 = "Police Service Region") and
($v1 = "Carmel Valley") and ($n4= "Shape") and
getExtentTop($v2,$t) and getExtentBottom($v2,$b) and
getExtentRight($v2,$l) and getExtentLeft($v2,$r).
```

After the rewriting, the tags in a fragment match those in the source, which also makes it easier to convert to the native language of the source. The output of the query, $R, is the extents (bounding rectangle) of the desired region.

- **Produce a map overlaying the Parcel Map and Aerial image**

Assume that we have obtained the georeferenced aerial image from the image library, which is aligned with the other GIS layers. Assume that this image is stored in the GIS as the file *"carmelimage"*. We show one of the five independent queries that are sent to the wrapper. Here, the year of the parcel map is fixed.

```
ans1 = construct $M
where
$M:        <mix:map>
<ArcView_Projects>
                <theme name = $n1>$t1
                <extents>
                    <top>$t</>
                    <bottom>$b</>
                    <left>$l</>
```

```
                    <right>$r</>
                  </extents>
                </theme>
                <theme name = $n2 >$t2</>
                <theme name =$n3 >$t3</>
                <tables>
                  <table name=$n4>
                    <col name=$n5>$v1</>
                    <col name=$n6>$v2</>
                  </table>
                </tables>
      </ArcView_Projects>
      </mix:map>
      in http://wrap.gis.url
      and ($n1= "sdcity.shp") and ($t = 3.62482e+006) and ($b
      = 3.6225e+006) and ($l = 481477) and ($r = 481477) and
      ($n2 = "sdparcels95.shp") and ($n3 = "carmelimage") and
      ($n4 = "Attributes of  sdparcels95.shp") and ($n5 =
      "total  assessed value") and ($v1 > 500000) and ($n6=
      "address block") and display_order($t3,($t2,$t1)).
```

Here the extents from the first theme are used to limit the map produced to the area extracted from the previous query. Also, the response to the query is a map, which is returned by reference as a URL where the image will be available.

4.3 Spatial Equivalence at the Spatial Mediator

Several mismatches may occur when combining the image and GIS sources. The spatial mediator incorporates rules to handle such mismatches and establish spatial equivalence between corresponding entities. It is not our intent to create an exhaustive set of rules for all equivalence conditions that may need to be included for any arbitrary combination of spatial sources. We believe the mediator needs to be extensible and the designer of a specific system will have the responsibility of including new rules. Once a rule is defined and registered, the mediator will have an engine to check the preconditions of the rule and execute the rule. In this section we briefly discuss the architectural extension to accommodate such rules, the structure of an equivalence rule and how it impacts the query evaluation plan.

We keep the feature alignment problem out of the scope of this paper. In Figure 6 we show two processes that cooperate with the mediator and wrapper to execute spatial and numeric data conversion. The Spatial Data Converter converts spatial data from one projection system to another. It is controlled by the mediator, but transfers

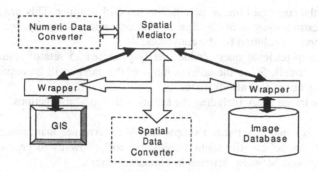

Figure 6. A revised architecture of the system to account for impedance mismatch between information sources

information between the wrappers. The numeric data converter helps the negotiation process between the wrappers and the mediator.

Suppose the GIS layer of the "Police Service Region" and "Parcel Map" layers are in UTM projection, while the image data of the San Diego region is from the USGS 7.5 quad and is unprojected in geographic coordinates (we call this projection = "geographic" here). This will produce the following changes in the query evaluation steps outlined in Step 9 of Section 4.

Determine Query Execution Plan: The query planner formulates and executes in the following order:

1. First determine the extents of boundary of the region Carmel Valley from the GIS.
2. Check <projection> and <units> tags of the returned result and determine the projection used by the GIS source.
3. Look up rules to find that what image tag or attribute the tag <projection> of GIS source maps to. At this step the mediator discovers that the <projection> tag in the GIS source corresponds to the "projection" attribute of the <mix:image> tag.
4. Look up at the schema of the image sources and finds the values of the attribute "projection". At this point the mediator finds that all georeferenced images have the "projection" attribute set to "geographic".
5. Convert coordinates if necessary. For our example, it fires a rule of the form:
6. projection(georaphic, coordX, coordY) :- projection(UTM, coordX1, coordX2), UTM2geo(coordX1, coordX2, coordX, coordY).
7. The predicate geo2UTM invokes the Numeric Data Converter to execute the requisite conversion. As a side effect the mediator uses an image transfer rule and determines that "geo2UTMImage" is the conversion routine for the spatial data.
8. Use the new extents to find the aerial image of the region in the image library.
9. Validate the query that images of the region exist at the requisite resolution.
10. If there are images at multiple resolutions for the region, it uses a rule to chose the finest resolution image covering the entire map region.
11. Initiate transfer of the image from the image library to the GIS. At this point is already known that the image must be transformed before sending it to the GIS system using the "geo2UTMImage" routine. The spatial data converter is the

invoked and the converted image is routed to the GIS wrapper. This process was chosen to illustrate the use of the Spatial data converter. In reality, we need to select a cost optimal solution for the conversion.

12. Execute the map retrieval query (which really produces 25 sets of results), and determine the parcels. Since the address block of the parcel will be required in a later part of the query, it is also fetched.

13. Formulate the image query including the sorting and "top 5" instructions.

Although the example here treats a simple case of equivalence management at the spatial mediator, we believe the same architecture will allow us to perform more involved reconciliation between different information sources.

Table 3. Portion of the sample result for the example query (TAV is total assessed value).

Year	TAV > $500K		$300K < TAV < $500K
1975			
1980			

4.3.1 Execution of an XMAS Query Fragment on a GIS

As discussed earlier, portions of the query execution plan which get passed down to the spatial wrapper need to be converted into a query language native to the underlying GIS system. This subsection builds on the running example and sketches a possible solution for a GIS system like ArcView. The underlying principle is that primitive GIS spatial operations can be invoked and composed into larger programs.

A logically equivalent Avenue script is generated whereby primitive spatial operations can be composed to form more complex programs. Let us illustrate this process with the formulation of two consecutive spatial queries: (1) restrict the parcel map to the Carmel Valley neighborhood, (2) using this more focused parcel map, locate all homes whose total assessed value is greater than $500,000.

Essentially here we are querying the underlying GIS system to extract the parcel data that will be overlaid onto an aerial photography. This corresponds to partially filling in one of the cells of the result document for the example query.

- Query (1) can be accomplished by invoking a primitive request called **QueryThemeByTheme**, which takes as input parameters (*ThemeObject, SearchTheme, spatialRelationship*). In our example query the *ThemeObject* would be the parcel map, the *SearchTheme* would be a boundary theme for Carmel Valley, and the *spatialRelationship* would constrain the selection using the *"Within"* operator.

- Query (2) can be accomplished by invoking a simple primitive request called **QueryThemeByExpression**, which takes as input parameters (*ThemeObject, QueryExpression*). The query expression would be *"[total assessed value] > 500000"*, assuming an attribute field named "total assessed value" in the *ThemeObject*'s associated attribute table.

- The overall GIS query would combine (1) and (2) in the following manner:

  av.Run("SetEnvironment",
  {parcelTheme="Parcel Map", selectionTheme="Carmel Valley Police Service Region",
  relation="Within", expression="[total assessed value] > 500000")

  av.Run("QueryThemeByTheme", {parcelTheme, selectionTheme, relation })
  av.Run("QueryThemeByExpression", { parcelTheme, expression })

  Av.Run is the standard Avenue call to run an Avenue script with arguments from within an Avenue script. The "SetEnvironment" Avenue script takes as arguments a list of attribute/value pairs where the attribute is the name of a variable that will be initialized to the associated value.

- Let us detail the first of these two primitive requests in Avenue. **QueryThemeByTheme** would be written as:

```
Region1 = self.Get(0);
Region2 = self.Get(1);
Relationship = self.Get(2);
Rel = av.Run( "Lookup", Relationship );
Distance = self.Get(3);
if (Distance = null) then
      Distance = 0;
Region1.SelectByTheme( Region2, Rel, Distance, #VTAB_SELTYPE_NEW )
Region1 = av.Run( "SaveSelection" )
```

The "SaveSelection" Avenue script transforms a selection bitmap into a Theme object.

5   Discussion

This paper presented an architecture and a logical schema for Web-based spatial information mediation using XML. We have traced a sample query integrating imagery and GIS sources, through its evaluation at the spatial mediator and dispatching to XML-wrapped geodata sources, where query fragments are translated to the language of the source and executed. We believe that, while a first step in the development of scalable and extensible spatial data mediation systems, this exercise helped us elucidate areas of complications which create the context for future research. These proposed research areas include:

- Development of rules and a cost model for selecting spatial data sources in the spatial mediator. Metadata for each source will describe the source's capabilities, such as size of data, data quality, indexing, available format and projection conversion and alignment routines, the monetary price of retrieving particular data, etc. This information will allow the mediator to estimate which sources need to be queried, in what order, where the retrieved data fragments need to be assembled (i.e. which source should be designated as a "collector" source), etc.
- Development of a general cost model for parsing, evaluating, and distributing queries, and for assembling the results.
- Incorporation of physical integration (alignment) management capabilities in the architecture of the mediator system, and in query planning at the mediator. An "intelligent" alignment mediator will maintain a semantic graph of "alignable layers". This graph will demonstrate, for example, that linework from a soil map and a vegetation map, a vegetation map and a land use map, a coastline map and a political boundaries map should closely align. By contrast, any alignment between a vegetation boundaries and a road network, for example, will have lower alignment priorities, if any. Development of such a semantic graph requires research into persistent landscape features that "show through' multiple geographic layers, and may form the strongest links in the graph.
- Incorporation of data quality issues in the context of information mediation, in particular, inferring the desired accuracy level of geodata sources based on the target query accuracy. The inferred expected accuracy of sources will be used by the spatial mediator in query planning, and become a component of the query cost model.
- Balancing the automated and manual procedures in the process of human interaction with the spatial mediator system. This will be important when we need to put a human in the loop for performing computations in mediated GIS systems.
- Supporting geographic analysis "workflow" as a sequence of spatial queries to the mediator system. This will require preserving intermediate query results, in XML form, at some URLs, so that they can be used as a source for subsequent queries.
- Scalability analysis of the mediation of multiple GIS and imagery sources.
- Supporting alternative mechanisms to associate names with geographic objects. This will address the problem that in general, there may be a many-to-many mapping between the names and geographic objects

References

[1] Y. Papakonstantinou, A. Gupta, H. Garcia-Molina, J. D. Ullman: A Query Translation Scheme for Rapid Implementation of Wrappers. DOOD 1995: 161-186. http://www.cse.ucsd.edu/~yannis/papers/querytran.ps

[2] C. Baru, A. Gupta, B. Ludäscher, R. Marciano, Y. Papakonstantinou, P. Velikhov, A. Yannakopulos: XML-Based Information Mediation with MIX. *Proceedings of the SIGMOD'99* (to appear). http://www.npaci.edu/DICE/Pubs/sigmod-demo99.pdf

[3] P. Buneman, S. B. Davidson, M. F. Fernandez, and D. Suciu. Adding Structure to Unstructured Data. In 6th Intl. Conference on Database Theory (ICDT), LNCS 1186, pp. 336-350, Delphi, Greece, 1997. Springer.

[4] S. Cluet, C. Delobel, J. Simeon, and K. Smaga. Your Mediators Need Data Conversion! In Proceedings of the 1998 ACM SIGMOD International Conference on Management of Data, pp. 177-188, 1998.

[5] M. J. Carey, L. M. Haas, V. Maganty, and J. H. Williams. PESTO: An Integrated Query/Browser for Object Databases. In Intl. Conference on Very Large Data Bases (VLDB), pp. 203-214, 1996.

[6] M. F. Fernandez, D. Florescu, J. Kang, A. Y. Levy, and D. Suciu. STRUDEL: A Web-site Management System. In ACM Intl. Conference on Management of Data (SIGMOD), pp. 549-552, 1997.

[7] B. Ludascher, R. Himmer oder, G. Lausen, W. May, and C. Schlepphorst. Managing Semistructured Data with FLORID: A Deductive Object-Oriented Perspective. Information Systems, 23(8), 1998.

[8] Y. Papakonstantinou, S. Abiteboul, and H. Garcia-Molina. Object Fusion in Mediator Systems. In Intl. Conf. on Very Large Data Bases (VLDB), 1996.

[9] Y. Papakonstantinou and P. Velikhov. Enhancing Semistructured Data Mediators with Document Type Definitions. In Intl. Conference on Data Engineering (ICDE), Syndey, Australia, 1999 (to appear).

[10] G. Wiederhold. Mediators in the Architecture of Future Information Systems. *IEEE Computer*, 25(3):38-49, 1992.

[11] P. M. Mather, Map-image registration accuracy using least-squares polynomials. *Int. J. Geographical Information Science* 9:543-554, 1995.

[12] XML-QL: A Query Language for XML. W3C note, http://www.w3.org/TR/NOTE-xml-ql, 1998.

[13] A. Voisard and H. Schweppe. Abstraction and Decomposition in Interoperable GIS. *International Journal of Geographic Information Science* 12(4), Taylor and Francis, June 1998.

[14] A. Voisard and M. Juergens. Geographic Information Extraction: Querying or Quarrying? In *Interoperating Geographic Information Systems*, M. Goodchild, M. Egenhofer, R. Fegeas and C. Kottman (Eds.), Kluwer Academic Publishers, New York, 1999.

[15] K. Stock and D. Pullar. Identifying Semantically Similar Elements in Heterogeneous Spatial Databases using Predicate Logic Expression. In Proc. Interoperating Geographic Information Systems, Second International Conference, INTEROP '99, Andrej Vckovski, Kurt E. Brassel, Hans-Jörg Schek (Eds.), Zurich, Switzerland, March 10-12, 1999.

[16] D. J. Abel, Towards integrated geographical information processing. *Int. J. Geographical Information Science* 12:353-371, 1998.

[17] H. Kemppainen. Designing a Mediator for Managing Relationships between Distributed Objects. In Proc. Interoperating Geographic Information Systems, Second International Conference, INTEROP '99, Andrej Vckovski, Kurt E. Brassel, Hans-Jörg Schek (Eds.), Zurich, Switzerland, March 10-12, 1999.

[18] S. Shimada and H. Fukui. Geospatial Mediator Functions and Container-based Fast Transfer Interface in SI3CO Test-Bed. In Proc. Interoperating Geographic Information Systems, Second International Conference, INTEROP '99, Andrej Vckovski, Kurt E. Brassel, Hans-Jörg Schek (Eds.), Zurich, Switzerland, March 10-12, 1999.

[19] T. DeVogele, C. Parent and S. Spaccapietra, On spatial database integration. *Int. J. Geographical Information Science* 12:335-352, 1998.

[20] W. Y. Ma, " NETRA: A Toolbox for Navigating Large Image Databases," Ph.D. Dissertation, Dept. of Electrical and Computer Engineering, University of California at Santa Barbara, June 1997.

[21] A. Gupta, S. Santini, and R. Jain, "In Search of Information in Visual Media", *Communications of the ACM*, December 1997, vol. 40 (No. 12): 35:42.

[22] A. Levy, A. Rajaraman and J. Ordille: Querying Heterogeneous Information Sources Using Sources Descriptions. *Proceedings of VLDB*, 1996: 251-262.

[23] A. Tomasic, L. Raschid, P. Valduriez: Scaling Access to Heterogeneous Data Sources with DISCO. *IEEE Transactions on Knowledge and Data Engineering*, Vol. 10, No. 5, 1998: 808-823.

[24] S. Shimada, H. Fukui: Geospatial Mediator Functions and Container-based Fast Transfer Interface in SI^{3}CO Test-Bed. In Proc. Interoperating Geographic Information Systems, Second International Conference, INTEROP '99, Andrej Vckovski, Kurt E. Brassel, Hans-Jörg Schek (Eds.), Zurich, Switzerland, March 10-12, 1999, pp. 265-276.

[25] Y.A. Bishr, H. Pundt, C. Rüther: Proceeding on the Road of Semantic Interoperability - Design of a Semantic Mapper Based on a Case Study from Transportation. In Proc. Interoperating Geographic Information Systems, Second International Conference, INTEROP '99, Andrej Vckovski, Kurt E. Brassel, Hans-Jörg Schek (Eds.), Zurich, Switzerland, March 10-12, 1999, pp. 203-215.

[26] G. Camara, R. Thome, U. Freitas, A.M.V. Monteiro: Interoperability In Practice: Problems in Semantic Conversion from Current Technology to OpenGIS. In Proc. Interoperating Geographic Information Systems, Second International Conference, INTEROP '99, Andrej Vckovski, Kurt E. Brassel, Hans-Jörg Schek (Eds.), Zurich, Switzerland, March 10-12, 1999, pp 129-138.

[27] C.B. Cranston, F. Brabec, G.R. Hjaltason, D. Nebert, H. Samet: Interoperability via the Addition of a Server Interface to a Spatial Database: Implementation Experiences with OpenMap, In Proc. Interoperating Geographic Information Systems, Second International Conference, INTEROP '99, Andrej Vckovski, Kurt E. Brassel, Hans-Jörg Schek (Eds.), Zurich, Switzerland, March 10-12, 1999, pp. 115-128.

[28] Y. Bishr: Overcoming the semantic and other barriers to GIS interoperability. *Int. J. Geographical Information Science* 12, 1998: 299-314.

[29] R. Laurini: Spatial multi-database topological continuity and indexing: a step towards seamless GIS data interoperability. *Int. J. Geographical Information Science* 12, 1998: 373-402.

[30] Geographic Data Exchange Standards: http://www2.echo.lu/oii/en/gis.html

[31] V. Christophides, M. Scholl and A.-M. Vercoustre: Querying Heterogeneous Semi-Structured Data.   ERCIM   News   No.   33   –   April   1988. http://www.ercim.org/publication/Ercim_News/enw33/scholl.html

[32] C. D. Tomlin: Geographic Information Systems and Cartographic Modeling, 1990, Englewood Cliffs, NJ: Prentice Hall.

The ATREE: A Data Structure to Support Very Large Scientific Databases*

Pedja Bogdanovich and Hanan Samet

Computer Science Department and Center for Automation Research and Institute for
Advanced Computer Studies
University of Maryland, College Park, MD 20742, USA

Abstract. The datasets generated by satellite observations and super-computer simulations are overwhelming conventional methods of storage and access, leading to unreasonably long delays in data analysis. The major problem that we address is the slow access, from large datasets in archival storage, to small subsets needed for scientific visualization and analysis. The goal is to minimize the amount of storage that has to be read when a subset of the data is needed. A second goal is to enhance the accessibility of data subsets by applying data reduction and indexing methods to the subsets. The reduced format allows larger datasets to be stored on local disk for analysis. Data indexing permits efficient manipulation of the data, and thus improves the productivity of the researcher. A data structure called the ATREE is described that meets the demands of interactive scientific applications. The ATREE data structure is suitable for storing data abstracts as well as original data. It allows quick access to a subset of interest and is suitable for feature-based queries. It intrinsically partitions the data and organizes the chunks in a linear sequence on secondary/tertiary storage. It can store data at various resolutions and incorporates hierarchical compression methods.

1 Introduction

Present day and future supercomputer simulations and observations by satellites and other monitoring devices produce very large data sets. These datasets are overwhelming conventional methods of storage and access, leading to unreasonably long delays in data analysis. Because of this, the speed of processors is no longer an issue in scientific applications—the management of terabytes of data is the major bottleneck.

Future hardware technology developments will certainly help the situation. Data transfer rates are likely to increase by as much as an order of magnitude, as will tape and cartridge capacities. However, new supercomputers and massively-parallel processor technologies will allow scientists to calculate at finer spatial

---

* This work was supported in part by the Department of Energy under Contract DEFG0592ER25141, the National Aeronautics and Space Administration under Fellowship Grant NGT-30130, and the National Science Foundation under Grant IRI-9712715.

P. Agouris and A. Stefanidis (Eds.): ISD'99, LNCS 1737, pp. 235–248, 1999.
© Springer-Verlag Berlin Heidelberg 1999

and temporal resolutions, and thus generate more data. Most of the data generated by models and experiments must reside on tertiary devices, and only a subset of that data will usually be of immediate interest. The effective management of large amounts of scientific data will therefore be an ongoing concern.

Interactive analysis and visualization applications frequently require rapid access to relatively small subsets of this data. Current commercial database management systems (DBMSs) provide inadequate support [15]. The primary reasons are: Conventional DBMSs do not adequately support data abstractions such as spatio-temporal data arrays. The indexing methods they provide are inappropriate for this type of data, making proximity queries, and operations based on spatial and temporal ranges, very expensive. Current DBMSs do not support tertiary storage. They only support secondary storage (i.e., disks), which is not sufficient for the massive data generated and analyzed in scientific applications.

The initial thrust of this research is to solve problems such as those faced by climate model researchers being unable to easily access previously stored data. The methods described here may benefit various scientific and engineering applications in areas identified as Grand Challenges. Examples of areas that use large-scale multidimensional simulation programs and analysis methods are seismic studies, oil reservoir modeling, climate modeling, fluid turbulence, vehicle dynamics, and hazardous waste management. This research uses global climate modeling as a concrete example of an application area that can take immediate advantage of our solutions and determine their effectiveness. We fully expect to be able to generalize our work to other Grand Challenge areas, or to any application or experimental area requiring fast access to small subsets within large collections of scientific data.

The major problem we wish to address is the slow access to small subsets of large datasets in archival storage needed for visualization and analysis. The goal is to minimize the amount of storage that has to be read when a subset of the data is needed. A second goal is to enhance the accessibility of data subsets by applying data reduction and indexing methods to the subsets. The reduced format will allow larger datasets to be stored on local disk for analysis. Data indexing will permit efficient manipulation of the data, and thus improve the productivity of the analyst.

In this paper, we introduce a data structure called the ATREE which achieves the goals listed above. Section 2 describes typical raster data, as well as the concept of abstracts. Section 3 describes the ATREE data structure, Section 4 describes our algorithms, and Section 5 describes the user interface.

2   Raster Data

Our research focuses on raster data. Raster data is used to represent multidimensional vector field data, sampled at discrete points. Such data is generated by satellite observations and supercomputer simulations.

Raster data is the most voluminous data type encountered in Global Change Research. For example, a single Landsat Thematic Mapper image is 300 megabytes. Other satellites beam down on the order of terabytes of data per day [5].

Raster data is also generated by a climate modeling simulations. A climate simulation model is run for a simulation period of 30 years. At every 3–6 hours of simulation time the state of the model is dumped out. The resulting dataset consists of a number of *variables*. A variable is a multidimensional array of values of the same type. More precisely, a variable is a multidimensional vector field, most often a scalar field. That is, each variable is a multidimensional array corresponding to a certain spatio-temporal domain. The first characteristic of the data is that the number of dimensions is quite small, usually at most four. Typical dimensions are *longitude* × *latitude* × *height* × *time*. Typical variables are air temperature and wind velocity defined over these dimensions. The number of variables in a dataset is also relatively small, up to several hundred. However, the volume of data for each variable is large because the spatio-temporal extent of the data is large. In the case of climate modeling data, this results from a large number of samples in the temporal coordinate.

A typical dataset contains from several gigabytes to several terabytes of data. Hence, this data is typically kept on tertiary devices (Exabyte tapes, OD's, etc.). In order to analyze the data, it is downloaded to a local disk.

Operations on raster data fall into one of two categories:

Spatial extraction: extracting a subset of values corresponding to a hyper-rectangular region of multidimensional space (i.e., subsetting and slicing). Examples of higher-level operations that rely on spatial extraction are browsing, data visualization, and statistical analysis of data. Such operations are also known as window queries (e.g., [2]).

Feature queries: i.e., value searching. Example: "find all regions which contain a hurricane". Typically this type of query accesses large portions of the data sets, but the answers are small.

Figure 1 shows a three-dimensional set of raster data.

Abstracts

In order to deal with terabyte data sets, we introduce a storage management technique called *abstracts*. Other Grand Challenge projects such as Sequoia 2000 [16] have also proposed the use of abstracts [7]. Abstracts involve extraction of certain "essential" parts of the original data. Abstracts can be seen as precomputed answers to anticipated queries, or precomputed data that helps answer a class of queries. Abstracts are several orders of magnitude smaller than the original data sets.

A data set can have multiple abstracts associated with it, each corresponding to a different "essential" part of the data set. Thus, each abstract is a different view of the data. What the abstracts are really depends on the data and on the *context* in which the data is used. Note that an abstract need not produce the same kind of information as does the original data. Another way to view an abstract is as a secondary index into the original data since abstracts let us quickly position into the original data.

Abstracts have many benefits. If a query can be answered from an abstract, then the bandwidth increases and the response time decreases. Since abstracts are several orders of magnitude smaller than the original data set, abstracts can be kept in secondary storage instead of in tertiary storage. Hence, the speedup is cumulative (smaller size + faster storage device), and may even be greater since caching can now be effectively employed. Compressing datasets using lossy compression methods, such as hierarchical compression [4], is one example of data abstraction. Another example is the use of multiresolution data structures [Salem92]. In this case, a collection of abstracts is represented at different levels of detail.

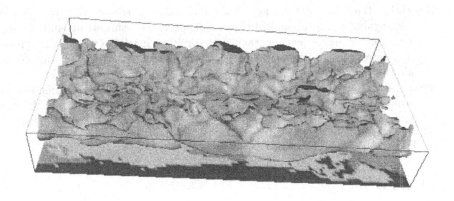

Fig. 1. Iso-surface of one slice in the temporal dimension of a wind-velocity vector field (raster data) generated by a climate modeling simulation.

3   The ATREE Data Structure

The ATREE data structure is an extensible data structure suitable for the storage of original data sets, as well as abstracted data sets. The main features of the ATREE are:

- The ATREE data structure is a multidimensional indexing data structure. Spatial indexing allows quick access to data based on its spatial location.
- Data is partitioned into chunks according to the principle of spatial locality. The size and shape of the chunks is chosen according to the expected usage of the data.
- Data chunks are organized (laid out) on archival storage according to the expected usage of the data. For example, if Morton codes [8,12] are used, then data chunks are stored on secondary/tertiary storage devices according to the principle of spatial locality.
- The data structure allows for hierarchical compression techniques to be applied (both lossy and non-lossy). Note that unlike traditional compression techniques, this data structure allows for direct indexing into compressed data. This means that only chunks of data that are accessed by the user are decompressed.
- The ATREE data structure can store multiresolution data.
- The data structure allows for non-spatial information to be included, which facilitates quick retrieval of data based on non-spatial attributes (e.g., crop types).

The ATREE data structure is an extension of the region quadtree data structure [13,12]. We describe the ATREE data structure below.

3.1   Subdivision Scheme

Unlike the region quadtree which always subdivides quadrants into exactly four disjoint sub-quadrants, the blocks corresponding to the region nodes of the ATREE, called *orthants*, are subdivided along pre-specified coordinates at each level of the tree. (The same coordinates are subdivided for all the orthants at the same level.) At least one coordinate has to be subdivided at each level of decomposition. When an orthant is subdivided along a coordinate, it is subdivided into two halves. Figure 2 represents a four-level deep ATREE.

For example, we can implement KD-trees [3] by defining subdivision of orthants to be performed on different coordinates (cyclically) at each level. Region quadtree-like decomposition can be achieved by an ATREE when the orthants are subdivided along all coordinates at each level.

The benefits of this approach in comparison with the region quadtree approach are as follows:

- Region quadtrees are not suitable for storing data with non-square extents since the leaf nodes also have non-square extents. This is desirable in cases where one coordinate has many more samples than the others. The ATREE subdivision scheme allows data with non-square extents to be stored.

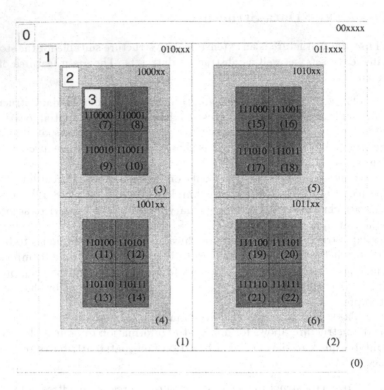

Fig. 2. Shape of a four level ATREE: The root orthant is subdivided along the x-coordinate, the first-level orthants are subdivided along the y-coordinate, and the second-level orthants are subdivided along both the x and y coordinates. Binary numbers represent a location code encoding of the orthant, and the numbers in parentheses represent orthant ordinal numbers for the encoding used.

- Multidimensional generalizations of the region quadtree are impractical even for moderately high dimensions due to the high fan-out factor (2^d). The subdivision criterion used by the ATREE provides fine control over the fan-out factor at each level of the structure.
- Orthants specify how data is chunked. By controlling the subdivision scheme, we can control the shape of the data chunks.

3.2   Location Codes

Since the data is to be stored in memory, it is often necessary to linearize it so that is is ordered and can be accessed. In order to linearize multidimensional data, a location code scheme is used. The linearization process maps hyperrectangles to integers. We use the function lc. In particular, $k = \mathrm{lc}(r)$ where r is a hyperrectangle corresponding to some orthant in the subdivision, and k is the orthant's number. The function lc has to be 1-1 and onto since lc^{-1} must be defined.

Location codes based on Morton order (also known as Z-order [9]) linearize multidimensional space so that the orthants which are spatially close tend to have their location code numbers close. However, the ATREE data structure allows for any consistent location code scheme to be used. By using different location code schemes, we can specify how orthants (data chunks) are laid out on archival storage.

For example, consider a multiresolution representation of data in which we store both leaf and non-leaf nodes. Nodes deeper in the tree refine the data from higher levels. In this case we might want to have a breadth-first arrangement of nodes in order to have data clustered on a per-level basis. This is easily achieved by using a location code scheme which first encodes the depth of the node and then its bit-interleaved top-left corner. Figure 2 illustrates one such encoding. The encoded values of orthant nodes are given as binary numbers. Symbol 'x' represents a "don't care" value. The depth is encoded in the first two bits and the remaining bits form the Morton encoding for the bottom-left orthant corner. Note that orthants which lie on the same level have ordinal numbers which are close.

3.3 Transformation Function

A transformation function specifies what is actually stored with each ATREE orthant node. It is applied to both internal and leaf nodes of the tree. By storing data in non-leaf orthant nodes we get a pyramid [17], termed the sc APyramid, variant of the ATREE data structure. This allows data to be stored at different resolutions—orthants near the root of the tree contain low resolution data, and as we descend the tree, the data is refined further.

Note that in order to facilitate data retrieval, the inverse of the transformation must exist. Let $d = t(o)$, where o is a subset of the original data corresponding to some orthant, t is a transformation function, and d is the data returned by the transformation function, i.e., the data that is actually stored on the disk. Now, let t^{-1} be the inverse of the transformation function, that is, the function that takes raw data retrieved from the disk and returns data *corresponding* to the original untransformed data. Ideally, $o = t^{-1}(t(o))$ but this need not to be the case, such as, for example, in the case of lossy compression.

The transformation function can also specify non-spatial data that is to be stored with each orthant. This information can be used to aid in answering non-spatial queries.

3.4 Subdivision Criterion

The subdivision criterion specifies how deeply we go in subdividing orthants. If the ATREE does not store internal nodes and if the transformation function is the identity function, then the subdivision criterion effectively specifies the size of data chunks stored on the disk. In this case, one of the approaches that we employ is to stop subdividing space as soon as the data associated with the orthant is of a certain size (leaf-orthant-data-size). In order to maximize performance when data is stored on secondary storage devices, we will use the size of a virtual memory page size as the size of the leaf orthant data. For tertiary devices, bigger chunks are appropriate, e.g., we may use the size of the platter.

As another example, consider a transformation function which is a lossy transformation. Assuming that transforming data corresponding to smaller spatial extents leads to more accurate transformed data, a subdivision criterion might inverse-transform the data returned by the transformation function and compare it with the original data. If the accuracy is greater than a certain prescribed accuracy, the criterion is not satisfied. In this way we can directly control the level of accuracy achieved.

Figure 3 shows a two-dimensional ATREE decomposition of map data. We used the following subdivision criterion: we stop subdividing orthant nodes as soon as all the values within a node are equal, all the way to the pixel size, if necessary (as in region quadtrees). Typically we do not subdivide data that to such a fine level of detail. In practice, we use some of the subdivision criteria described above.

Fig. 3. Region quadtree-like subdivision criterion: Stop subdividing orthant nodes as soon as all the values within a orthant are equal.

4   Algorithms

In this section we describe some ATREE algorithms.

4.1   Build

The build operation takes the raw data in some standard format (DRS, NetCDF, HDF) and builds an ATREE. The input parameters for the build operation are also the parameters that define the ATREE:

1. Shape: defines the subdivision scheme to be used. Recall that the subdivision scheme determines the spatio-temporal regions to which the subdivision criterion and the transformation function will be applied.
2. Location code scheme: defines the layout of the data on archival storage. Recall that the location code scheme should be chosen according to the expected access pattern of the dataset. For example, for multiresolution data structures we want some breadth-first location codes, since we want to cluster data on a per-level basis.
3. Transformation function: defines what is actually stored with each node, e.g., the data reduction technique that is being used. This is determined by the actual data and its intended scientific use.
4. Subdivision criterion: defines the level of detail stored in the data. This is determined by the required level of detail or accuracy.
5. Optional metadata function: other information that we may wish to associate with a node.

Below, we describe the top-down and bottom-up build algorithms.

Top-Down Build Algorithm. The idea behind the top-down build algorithm is to start from the root orthant node and then recursively subdivide as needed. The top-down build algorithm is given in Figure 4.

Starting from the root orthant node,

1. Apply the subdivision criterion to the orthant node.
2. If the criterion is not satisfied, then the orthant node is a leaf node. In this case, apply the transformation function to the subset of data corresponding to the orthant node, and store the data returned.
3. If the criterion is satisfied, then the orthant node is an internal node. Subdivide the node and recursively apply the procedure to the descendant nodes. In the case of an APYRAMID, data is stored with internal nodes as well.

Fig. 4. Top-down build algorithm.

The top-down approach may be impractical since it may be hard to apply a transformation function to orthant nodes with large spatio-temporal extents (that is, nodes near the top of the tree) since the amount of the data associated with these nodes is large. However, the top-down build algorithm may be used for the APYRAMID, since the transformation function has to be applied to all the orthant nodes anyway.

Bottom-Up Build Algorithm. The idea behind the bottom-up build algorithm is to start from the deepest possible level of the tree and merge. The bottom-up build algorithm is given in Figure 5.

Start from the deepest possible level of the tree and generate all the leaf orthant nodes. The process proceeds by repeating the following procedure for each level of the tree:

1. For every mergeable group of sibling nodes, generate a parent node.
2. Apply the subdivision criterion to the parent node. If the criterion is not satisfied, then remove all the descendant nodes.

(The algorithm is implemented as a post-order tree traversal.)

Fig. 5. Bottom-up build algorithm.

4.2   Subset Algorithm

The subset operation extracts data from an ATREE that corresponds to a given extent. In addition to the subset extent, the subset operation also requires an *accuracy test function* to be specified. The accuracy test function returns **TRUE** if the data stored with a current orthant is accurate enough; otherwise, it returns **FALSE**, meaning that we need to go deeper in the tree. The subset algorithm is given in Figure 6.

Starting from the root orthant node,

1. If the orthant's extent does not intersect the subset's extent, then return.
2. If there is no data stored with the orthant node, then skip to step 4.
3. Retrieve the data stored with the orthant node. Apply the accuracy function. If it returns **TRUE**, or if the node is a leaf node, then inverse-transform the data, and extract and return the data that is within the subset's extent.
4. Recursively apply this procedure to all the children of the current orthant node, and return the union of the returned values.

Fig. 6. Subset algorithm.

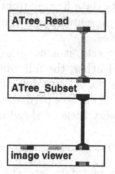

Fig. 7. Simple AVS network which displays a spatio-temporal subset of original raster data.

The performance of subsetting depends on what location code scheme is used since the bottleneck is disk/tape retrieval. Recall that the location code scheme defines how the data is clustered on the archival storage. Hence the location code scheme should be chosen according to the anticipated access pattern of datasets so that the subset operation is executed as efficiently as possible.

4.3 Value Search Algorithms

A *search object* needs to be specified as an input parameter of the content search operation. It is a generic representation of the feature that we are searching for. A content search algorithm returns the (hyper-rectangular) regions of an ATREE that contain the search object. In addition to a search object, a *test function* needs to be specified. The test function takes a search object and an orthant node and returns one of: **NO**, meaning that the object is not present in the region corresponding to the orthant node; **REGION**, which represents a subextent of the orthant that contains the feature; and **MAYBE**, meaning that we need to go deeper in the search to obtain an answer.

5 User Interface

The ATREE data structure is implemented as a C++ object library. Currently, the ATREE uses a B-Tree as its underlying storage mechanism.

We have also implemented a suite of AVS [1] modules to operate on ATREEs. AVS employs the boxes-and-arrows visual programing paradigm. Each AVS module represents some high level operation and is graphically represented by a box. Functionally, a module is a Unix process with a number of input and output arguments, called input and output ports. An output port of one module can be connected to an input port of another module, provided that the port types match. This connection is graphically represented by a colored line (arrow) between modules. The line represents data flowing from the first module into the second, and the color of the line represents the data type. Figure 7 is an example of a simple AVS network of modules.

Given the sizes of ATREE data sets, it is not possible to pass a whole data set from one module to another. Rather, the following approach is taken. The ATREE object library implements the ATREE data structure as permanent objects (in the OO sense). Only a reference to a permanent ATREE object is passed between two modules, so there is very little overhead in communication between modules.

We have implemented the following modules:

Build. Input to this module is a raw data set. The output from this module is the reference to the new ATREE object. In addition, this module takes a number of parameters which specify how the resulting ATREE is built. These parameters include Subdivision Scheme, Split Criterion, Transformation Function, and Location Code object specifications.

Subset. This module is a basic spatial query. The input to this module is a hyperrectangle, and the output is a data set corresponding to the specified spatial domain.

There are two versions of this module. The first version outputs another ATREE as the result of this operation, and the second version outputs a multidimensional field in standard AVS format. This field can be then piped into any other AVS module that takes field data as input for further analysis and visualization.

Composite. This module is a spatial join operation (e.g., [14]). The input is two ATREEs which are combined into a single data sets: $d_3(x) = f(d_1(x), d_2(x))$ where d_1 and d_2 are input data sets, d_3 is an output data set, $x \in$ domain(d_1) $\cup$ domain(d_2), and f is the composite function.

There are two versions of this module. The first version outputs another ATREE. The second version outputs an AVS field.

Figure 8 shows the AVS network used to generate Figure 1.

6   Conclusion

Objectives of research in global change are to study, predict, and understand changes, both natural and anthropogenic, in the Earth system [6]. This requires improvements in observations, models, and information systems. Our research addresses improvements in information systems—that is, the development of a data structure to facilitate the construction of a database management system that efficiently indexes and accesses large data-sets.

To summarize, we believe that the ATREE data structure meets the demands of interactive scientific applications used in global change research, i.e., data analysis and visualization. The ATREE data structure will permit global change

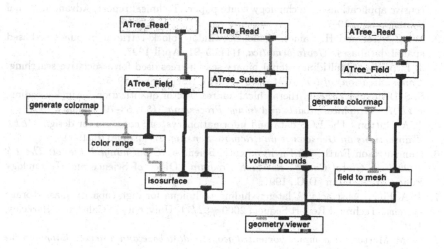

Fig. 8. AVS network used to generate a three-dimensional iso-surface shown in Figure 1.

scientists to store large amounts of data such as the data generated by satellite observations. In particular, the ATREE data structure is suitable for storing abstracts as well as original data. It can store data at various resolutions. It intrinsically partitions data and organizes the chunks in a linear sequence onto secondary/tertiary storage. It allows quick access to a subset of interest, and is suitable for feature-based queries.

There are a number of directions for future research. They include comparisons with other methods and simulations of storing ATREEs on tertiary storage. Note that a top-down build algorithm is useful for many compression algorithms. However, the drawback is a need to have all data accessible at once. Hence, it is worhtwhile to experiment with bottom-up and hybrid build algorithms. A bottom-up algorithm is a local process. It starts from smallest orthant nodes and merges the nodes as it moves up the tree to process larger nodes. A hybrid build algorithm is a combination of the top-down and bottom up build algorithms.

It is also worthwhile to investigate how to implement feature-based queries. Examples of such queries are: "Find all spatio-temporal regions that contain a hurricane" or "Find all spatio-temporal regions which exhibit the El-Niño pattern". In addition, experiments with different compression techniques (e.g., DCT [11], wavelet transforms [10]) would be worthwhile.

References

1. Gaining insight through data visualization – the competitive advantage for data intensive applications — technology white paper. Technical report, Advanced Visual Systems, Inc., 1997.
2. W. G. Aref and H. Samet. Efficient window block retrieval in quadtree-based spatial databases. *GeoInformatica*, 1(1):59–91, April 1997.
3. J. L. Bentley. Multidimensional binary search trees used for associative searching. *Communications of the ACM*, 18(9):509–517, September 1975.
4. S. S. Dixit and Y. Feng. Hierarchical address vector quantization for image coding. *CVGIP—Graphical Models and Image Processing*, 1(53):63–70, January 1991.
5. J. A. Dutton. The EOS data and information system: concepts for design. *IEEE Transactions on Geoscience and Remote Sensing*, 27(2):109–116, 1990.
6. Committe on Earth and Environmental Sciences. *Our Changing Planet: The FY 1992 U.S. Global Change Research Program.* Office of Science and Technology Policy, Washington, D.C., 1991.
7. J. A. Fine. Abstracts: A latency-hiding technique for high-capacity mass-storage systems. Technical Report Sequoia 2000 #92/11, University of California, Berkeley, 1992.
8. G. M. Morton. *A computer oriented geodetic data base and a new technique in file sequencing.* IBM Ltd., Ottawa, Canada, 1966.
9. J. A. Orenstein and T. H. Merrett. A class of data structures for associative searching. In *Proceedings of the Third ACM SIGACT-SIGMOD Symposium on Principles of Database Systems*, pages 181–190, Waterloo, Canada, April 1984.
10. W. H. Press. Wavelet transforms. *Harward-Smitsonian Center for Astrophysics*, (Preprint No. 3184), 1991.
11. K. R. Rao and P. Kip. *Discrete Cosine Transform—Algorithms, Advantages, Applications.* Academic Press, Inc., London, 1990.
12. H. Samet. *Applications of Spatial Data Structures: Computer Graphics, Image Processing, and GIS.* Addison-Wesley, Reading, MA, 1990.
13. H. Samet. *The Design and Analysis of Spatial Data Structures.* Addison-Wesley, Reading, MA, 1990.
14. H. Samet and W. G. Aref. Spatial data models and query processing. In *Modern Database Systems, The Object Model, Interoperability and Beyond*, W. Kim, ed., pages 338–360. ACM Press and Addison-Wesley, New York, NY, 1995.
15. H. Shoshani. Properties of statistical and scientific databases. In *Statistical and Scientific Databases*, Z. Michalewicz, ed. Ellis Horwood, February 1991.
16. M. Stonebraker, J. Frew, and J. Dozier. The sequoia 2000 project. In *Proceedings of the 3rd International Symposium on Large Spatial Databases, SSD'93*, Singapore, June 1993.
17. S. L. Tanimoto. Image transmission with gross information first. *Computer Graphics and Image Processing*, 9(1):72–76, January 1979.

Improving High-Dimensional Indexing with Heuristics for Content-Based Image Retrieval

Yongjian Fu and Jui-Che Teng

Department of Computer Science
University of Missouri-Rolla
{yongjian,jteng}@umr.edu

Abstract. Most high-dimensional indexing structures proposed for similarity query in content-based image retrieval (CBIR) systems are tree-structured. The quality of a high-dimensional tree-structured index is mainly determined by its insertion algorithm. Our approach focuses on an important phase in insertion, that is, the tree descending phase, when the tree is explored to find a host node to accommodate the vector to be inserted. We propose to integrate a heuristic algorithm in tree descending in order to find a better host node and thus improve the quality of the resulting index. A heuristic criteria for child selection has been developed, which takes into account both the similarity-based distance and the radius-increasing of the potential host node. Our approach has been implemented and tested on an image database. Our experiments show that the proposed approach can improve the quality of high-dimensional indices without much run-time overhead.

1 Introduction

Visual data management has attracted increasing attention as more and more digital images, videos, and graphics, have become available on-line. One focus in the visual data management is the content-based image retrieval (CBIR), that is, the access of images based on their visual features such as color, shape, texture, spatial relationship, and so on [5]. The CBIR technology has wide applications in medical image management, multimedia systems, digital library, GIS, and many other systems.

In order to perform CBIR, images are processed and their visual features are extracted and stored with the images in an image database. Therefore an image can be represented as a feature vector in a feature space. A user then may give a query image and look for similar images. The features of the query image are extracted and are compared with those of other images in the database. Similar images which are decided based on some similarity metrics, such as the distance between the feature vectors of the images, are returned as the result of the query.

Such kind of queries are termed as similarity queries [12]. Unlike traditional database queries where an exact match is sought, similarity queries search for similar images to a query and the search is called similarity search. Like in traditional database systems, indexing structures may be built on the data to

P. Agouris and A. Stefanidis (Eds.): ISD'99, LNCS 1737, pp. 249–267, 1999.
© Springer-Verlag Berlin Heidelberg 1999

facilitate similarity queries. An index will group images in the database with similar features to speed up similarity search.

Several high-dimensional indexing structures for similarity query have been proposed including SS-tree [12], SS$^+$-tree [10], SR-tree [8], X-tree [2], and M-tree [3]. These structures extend previous multidimensional structures such as R-tree [6], R*-tree [1], and KD-tree [4], by enhancing nodes and entries with feature statistics specifically required by similarity search.

The biggest problem with these structures is that there is overlapping among the nodes which would affect search efficiency and accuracy as well as storage cost. Different approaches have been attempted to reduce the overlapping, but most of them focus on data structure and node splitting strategy.

In this paper, the problem of overlapping is examined and a different approach is proposed to solve the problem. We focus on the insertion algorithm of the indexing structures because that is where the overlapping is introduced. We propose to integrate a heuristic algorithm, beam search, in the insertion algorithm in order to improve the quality of the indexing and thus improve similarity search performance.

The approach has been implemented and tested on an image database. Our experiments show that the integration of beam search in insertion can improve the quality of indexing and query without incurring much overhead.

The rest of the paper is organized as follows. In Section 2, related work and background in similarity query and similarity search are described. Our approach is introduced in Section 3. Experiments and explanations are presented in section 4. Related issues are discussed in Section 5 which also gives some directions for future work. Section 6 concludes the paper.

2   Similarity Query and Similarity Search

The modules involved in CBIR are illustrated in Fig. 1. When a user sends a query through the user interface, the query processing module will search for images satisfying the query condition and return them through the user interface. The query processing may need help from an index built on image features which are extracted and stored with the images in the image database.

There are three modes in which users may interact with a CBIR system: browsing, query-by-example, and query-by-attributes.

- In browsing mode, the user scans through the images sequentially to find interesting images.
- In query-by-example mode, the user gives an image and asks for images similar to it. The given image is called the query image which can be an image from the database or a sketch the user draws.
- In query-by-attributes mode, the user specifies the visual attributes, such as color distribution, of the images interested.

Of course, a user can switch mode in search for the target images. For example, one may first browse through the images to find an image that is close to what one is looking for and use that as a query image.

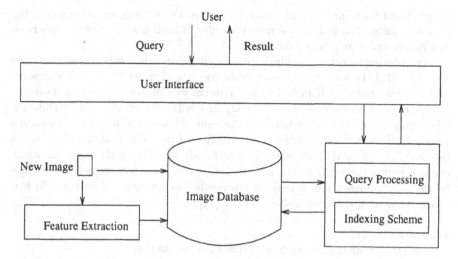

Fig. 1. Modules in content-based image retrieval

In query-by-example mode, the features of the query image are extracted using image processing techniques and submitted to the query processor as a vector. In query-by-attributes mode, a vector is given by the user. Therefore, to the query processor, these two modes are identical. In this paper, we assume the feature vector is already obtained. The browsing mode does not need indexing and thus is not discussed in this paper.

For the purpose of indexing and query processing in CBIR, images are often represented by their visual features. Each image is represented as a vector in the multidimensional vector space where each dimension represents a feature. Indexing structures are built on these vectors to facilitate the query processing. The design of indexing structures in CBIR systems is greatly influenced by the following two characteristics.

One prominent characteristic of image features is their high dimensionality. The dimensionality of feature vectors can easily run up to tens, and sometimes hundreds, which poses challenges for earlier indexing structures, such as B^+-tree, R-tree [6], and KD-tree [4]. The data structures need to be space efficient and provide fast insertion and search algorithms.

Another characteristic of CBIR systems is the fuzzy nature of queries. Usually, users cannot give a precise description of what they are looking for, or they have only a rough idea of the images they are looking for, but do not know exactly. In other words, they are interested in approximations instead of exact matches.

Most high-dimensional indexing structures for CBIR are tree-structured. Starting with an empty tree, an index is built on the vectors by inserting vectors one by one. When a user gives a query image, its features are extracted and searched with the help of the index. Images that are similar to the query image based on some (dis)similarity metrics on the vectors are returned to the user as results. The indexing structures differ in their node structure, insertion algorithm, and search algorithm.

An indexing structure for similarity search, SS-tree, was introduced by White and Jain [12]. In an SS-tree, each node consists of a set of entries and some information about itself including the number of children it has and its depth (height). In a nonleaf node, each entry refers to one of the node's children. The entry stores the total number, the centroid and radius of the bounding sphere, and the variance, of the vectors in the subtree rooted at the child, and a reference to the child. Each entry in a leaf node stores a single image, in which the centroid is the feature vector of the image and the reference is to the image. In their implementation, a node is represented as an array of entries which is represented by a structure called SSElem [12].

```
struct SSElem {
    SSElemPtr child_array_ptr;// pointer to child
    int immed_children;      // number of children in array
    int total_children;      // number of children in subtree
    int height;              // height above leaf
    int update_count;        // counter for update
    float radius;            // radius of bounding sphere
    float variance;          // sum of squared dist. from centroid
    float centroid[DIM];     // vector or mean
    char data[DATA_SIZE];    // closest immediate child
};
```

A simple SS-tree for two-dimensional feature vectors is illustrated in Fig. 2. Fig. 2(a) shows the vectors in feature space, and Fig. 2(b) shows the data structures in the SS-tree to represent them.

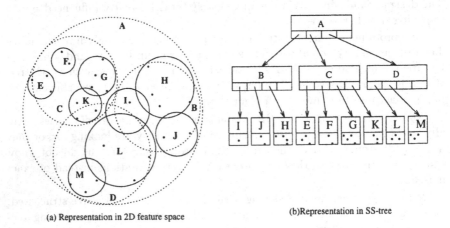

(a) Representation in 2D feature space

(b)Representation in SS-tree

Fig. 2. A simple SS-tree

An SS-tree is initialized with the root node and an empty child which is a leaf. When a vector is inserted into an SS-tree, it descends down from the root to a leaf node choosing the closest child along the path according to a (dis)similarity metric. If there is an empty entry in that leaf, the vector is put there and the information is updated along the path up to the root. Otherwise, the overflowing node is split and a new node is created. Some entries are moved to the new node whose representing entry will be re-inserted in a similar procedure.

One problem with SS-tree is the overlapping of the bounding spheres of nodes, which gets worse when the dimensionality increases. Several approaches have been proposed to overcome the problem. SS^+-tree [10] extends SS-tree by introducing a clustering method, the k-means algorithm, in node splitting to reduce overlapping. SR-tree [8] combines SS-tree and R^*-tree such that an entry contains both bounding rectangle and bounding sphere of the vectors. X-tree [2] introduces supernode to avoid node splitting as much as possible. A supernode is a nonleaf node with extra entries to accommodate alienated entries in order to reduce overlapping among the nodes. M-tree [3] includes the distance between the parent node to each child in the entry. Based on the property of metric space, M-tree may improve the search speed by reducing the number of distance calculations.

In this paper, we take a different approach to reduce the overlapping. If we look at the insertion algorithm of SS-tree, it consists of two phases: tree descending and node splitting. In tree descending, we traverse from the root to a leaf node, called *host*. Node splitting takes place when an entry needs to be added to a full node, i.e, a node whose entries are all used. Previous algorithms such as SS^+-tree [10] and M-tree [3] focus on splitting strategies. We look at the tree descending in the insertion algorithm in this paper.

It is obvious that SS-tree follows a single path in tree descending, i.e, starting from the root, the best child of the current node is followed. The best child is the one with the smallest weighted Euclidean distance between the new vector and the centroid of the child. This is illustrated in Fig. 3 where the dotted line denotes the path SS-tree follows.

However, this simple method may miss the best host. This is illustrated in Fig. 4(a), where A and B are nonleaf nodes of the root, $A1, A2, A3, A4$ are leaf nodes and children of A, and $B1, B2$ are leaf nodes and children of B. The new vector, p, will choose node B at the higher level and $B1$ as the host, even though $A3$ is the closest leaf node to p and thus a better host.

A heuristic algorithm, beam search, is introduced in tree descending to search for the best host and thus to reduce the overlapping. Instead of choosing a single child for descending, m children are followed. According to the similarity metric, the best m child nodes of the root are explored. The best m children of these nodes are then selected and the process continues until the leaf nodes are reached.

Moreover, we examine another factor that affects the tree descending, i.e., the criterion for choosing children to explore. It is not enough to use the distance between the new vector and the child as the only clue. An example is given in Fig. 4(b), where the new vector, p, is closer to $A1$, but would better be inserted

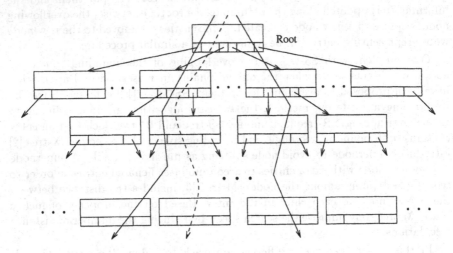

Fig. 3. Tree descending

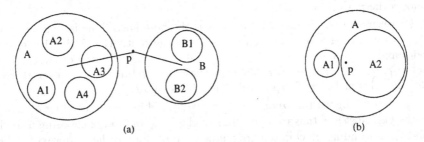

(a)   (b)

Fig. 4. Insertion of new vector

into $A2$ which causes less overlapping. We propose a weighted average of two measures as the child selection criterion in tree descending which subsumes the simple criteria used in previous algorithms. Our approach is explained in detail in the next section.

3   Building High Quality Indices

It is clear that the insertion algorithm plays a key role in the shaping of the overlapping among the nodes. In order to reduce overlapping, several approaches have looked into the node splitting strategies in insertion [10, 3]. As pointed out earlier, another important phase in insertion is tree descending. The tree descending process can be viewed as the search for the best host of the vector in the indexing tree.

A lot of tree searching algorithms are available, including depth-first, breadth-first, best-first, A*, iterative deepening, as summarized in [14]. They all find the best host eventually. However, in the worst case, these algorithms will search the entire tree, which is prohibitive when the tree size is large.

On the other extreme, SS-tree and many others follow a single path in descending whose time complexity is linear to the height of the tree. But they may easily miss the best host as discussed earlier.

In our approach, the beam search algorithm is adapted as a compromise between time complexity and indexing quality. Beam search algorithm can be briefly explained as follows. Detailed algorithm can be found in [14]. A priority queue which can hold m elements is initialized with only the initial state, where m is given by users. All of the elements in the queue are popped and states immediately reachable from these elements are pushed into the queue. The procedure continues until the queue is empty or the goal is reached.

The beam search algorithm is integrated into the insertion algorithm. At each level, we explore the best m nodes based on a selection criterion. Initially, m children of the root are selected. The best m children of the root's children are then explored. The process stops when we reach the leaf nodes. Obviously, this gives us a greater chance to find a better host than in SS-tree, while still keeping the time complexity linear to the height of the tree. The beam search based algorithm is illustrated in Fig. 3 where the solid lines denote the paths explored by the algorithm when m is two.

The selection criterion is a weighted average of two measures. For a vector p, the cost function for inserting p into a node n , $f(n,p)$, is defined as:

$$f(n,p) = w_1 * d(n,p) + w_2 * \Delta r(n,p) \tag{1}$$

where w_1, w_2 are adjustable weights, $d(n,p)$ is the weighted Euclidean distance from n to p, and $\Delta r(n,p)$ is the increase of radius of n if p is inserted. The intuitive idea is that a host should be as close to p and increase its radius as small as possible. Therefore, the smaller $f(n,p)$ is, the better it is to insert p into n.

This criterion generalizes the ones used in SS-tree and M-tree. If w_1 and w_2 are set to 1 and 0, respectively, it is the same as in SS-tree. M-tree uses a criterion in which w_1 is 1 and w_2 is ∞. The use of the criterion gives us more flexibility in picking hosts and thus tuning the algorithm. When $w_1 > w_2$, it will generate tighter nodes. On the other hand, a larger w_2 will result in less overlapping of nodes.

Obviously, SS-tree can be viewed as a special case of our approach where m, w_1, and w_2 are set to 1, 1, and 0, respectively. While other methods extend SS-tree in splitting strategy, we generalize it in tree descending. Moreover, our method can be applied to other high-dimensional tree-structured indices as well.

The node and entry structures implemented in our experiments are shown in Fig. 5. Unlike the implementation in [12], we clearly distinguish node structure and entry structure. This adds flexibility and readability in coding. Moreover, the separation reduces the storage cost because the information of a node, including height and number of immediate children, can be stored just once in the node, rather than repeated in all of its entries. Besides, a pointer to parent node is added which is useful for updating information in ancestors when a vector is inserted.

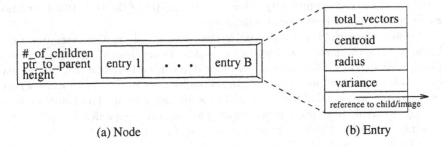

(a) Node   (b) Entry

Fig. 5. Node and entry structures

3.1 Algorithm for Insertion

The insertion algorithm is outlined below. The tree is initialized with the root node and an empty leaf child of the root. The value of m used in beam search is predefined by a user. A split strategy similar to that of SS-tree is used in which entries are partitioned to minimize the variance in the dimension which has the biggest variance before splitting.

```
(1)   insert(r: node, p: entry)      // insert p into a tree rooted at r
(2)      initialize a priority queue, Q, and an array N[m]
(3)      for each child n of r do
(4)         add (n, f(n,p)) into Q
(5)      while Q is not empty      // descending
```

(6) $N[1] \leftarrow \text{pop}(Q)$
(7)   if $N[1]$ is a leaf or at the same level as p //found the host
(8) $host \leftarrow N[1]$
(9)   break
(10) $k \leftarrow 1$ //number of nodes to explore
(11)   while Q is not empty and $k < m$
(12) $k \leftarrow k + 1$
(13) $N[k] \leftarrow \text{pop}(Q)$
(14)   empty Q
(15)   for $i = 1$ to k do
(16)   add all child nodes of $N[i]$ into Q
(17)   if $host$ has an empty entry
(18)   add p into $host$ and modify bounding spheres
(19)   else
(20)   split $host$, create a new node s
(21)   move some entries to s, modify bounding spheres
(22)   create an entry e to represent s, insert(r, e) //re-insert new node

The priority queue Q holds the nodes with the smallest $f(n, p)$'s. Obviously, the descending process from step 2 to 12 has a time complexity of $O(mBh)$ where B is the maximal number of entries in a node called *branching factor*, and h is the height of the tree. It is achievable since the priority queue can be built after all elements are added.

3.2 Algorithm for Similarity Search

Given a query image, its features are extracted and sent to the search algorithm to find similar images. There are two kinds of queries, range query and nearest neighbor query. In a range query, users are looking for all images within certain similarity range of the query image, usually measured by the distance of their feature vectors. In a nearest neighbor query, users are looking for k most similar images, called nearest neighbors, to the query image.

Actually, these two kinds of queries can be unified into a single query type and handled by a general algorithm. Given an integer k and a range d, the algorithm finds k closest neighbors with in the distance d to the query image. When k is infinite, this becomes a range query. When d is infinite, this is a nearest neighbor query.

An algorithm is presented below which is a revised version of the one in [13] with some minor errors fixed. Starting at the root node, it progressively goes down the tree, pruning the nodes which do not contain answers. When a leaf node is reached, its entries are put into a priority queue which holds up to k elements as potential answers.

(1) search(r: node;   // the root of the indexing tree
           k: integer;   // number of neighbors to return
           d: distance;   // maximum distance to the query image

```
              q: vector;)          // features of the query image
(2)   max_d = d;
(3)   initialize an intermediate queue IQ and an answer queue RQ
(4)   IQ ← r
(5)   while IQ is not empty
(6)       next node n ← pop(IQ)
(7)       if n is nonleaf
(8)           for each child c of n
(9)               if dist(c, q) − r(c) ≤ max_d {    //c may contain answer
(10)                  insert c into IQ
(11)                  if dist(c, q) + r(c) < max_d   // c surely contain answer
(12)                      and RQ is full {           // found k answers already
(13)                      max_d = dist(c, q) + r(c); //reduce
(14)                      remove all nodes x in IQ if d(x, q) − r(x) < max_d
(15)                      }
(16)                  }
(17)      else                                       // leaf node
(18)          for each child c of n
(19)              if dist(c, q) ≤ max_d {            // c maybe an answer
(20)                  insert c into RQ
(21)                  if RQ overflow {               // has k + 1 elements
(22)                      pop(RQ)
(23)                      x = top(RQ)                //peek top element in queue
(24)                      max_d = min(max_d, dist(x, q));
(25)                      remove nodes x in IQ if d(x, q) − r(x) < max_d
(26)                      }
(27)                  }
```

In the algorithm, $dist, r$, and max_d are distance function, radius, and maximal distance from q to be a potential answer, respectively. The priority queues arrange nodes according to their distances to q, with the furtherest one at the top of IQ and the closest one at the top of RQ.

4   Performance Study

The indexing structure and the insertion and search algorithms have been implemented and tested on an image database consisting of 800 images each containing a single object. Extensive experiments have been conducted to study the tree quality and running time of our approach. The tests are done on a Sun Ultra1 workstation with 64MB memory running Solaris 2.5. The image features used in the experiments are discussed in the next subsection, followed by results of the experiments.

4.1   Image Features

The image features used in the experiments fall into three categories: moment invariants, geometry, and Fourier descriptors. Currently in our system, the features are computed off-line with a Matlab program and stored in a file. All the features are normalized and grouped together into a single vector.

Moment Invariants Hu [7] introduced the use of a set of moment invariants based on nonlinear combinations of low-order two-dimensional *Cartesian moments* for pattern recognition. Those features are invariant under image translation, scaling and rotations.

The two-dimensional Cartesian moment, m_{pq}, of order $(p+q)$ of a $N \times N$ gray-scale image $f(x, y)$ over a finite region R is defined as

$$m_{pq} = \int \int_R x^p y^q f(x, y) dx dy \cong \sum_{x=1}^{N} \sum_{y=1}^{N} x^p y^q f(x, y) \qquad (2)$$

where the sum is taken over all the $N \times N$ pixels in the image. The centroid $(\overline{x}, \overline{y})$ of $f(x, y)$ is defined by $\overline{x} = m_{10}/m_{00}$, $\overline{y} = m_{01}/m_{00}$. The translation-invariant central moments of order $(p+q)$ are obtained by placing origin at the centroid $(\overline{x}, \overline{y})$:

$$\nu_{pq} = \int \int_R (x - \overline{x})^p (y - \overline{y})^q f(x, y) dx dy \cong \sum_{x=1}^{N} \sum_{y=1}^{N} (x - \overline{x})^p (y - \overline{y})^q f(x, y). \qquad (3)$$

In order to obtain the scale-invariants, we define $\mu_{pq} = \nu_{pq}/\nu_{00}^{1+(p+q)/2}$, $p+q \geq 2$ where $\nu_{00} = m_{00} = N$. And also, rotation-invariant features can be constructed from the ν_{pq}s. By using these functions, Hu [7] derived seven moment invariants:

$M_1 = \mu_{20} + \mu_{02}$

$M_2 = (\mu_{20} - \mu_{02})^2 + 4\mu_{11}^2$

$M_3 = (\mu_{30} - 3\mu_{12})^2 + (3\mu_{21} - \mu_{03})^2$

$M_4 = (\mu_{30} + \mu_{12})^2 + (\mu_{21} + \mu_{03})^2$

$M_5 = (\mu_{30} - 3\mu_{12})(\mu_{30} + \mu_{12}) \times [(\mu_{30} + \mu_{12})^2 - 3(\mu_{21} + \mu_{03})^2] +$
$\qquad (\mu_{03} - 3\mu_{21})(\mu_{03} + \mu_{21}) \times [(\mu_{03} + \mu_{21})^2 - 3(\mu_{12} + \mu_{30})^2]$

$M_6 = (\mu_{20} - \mu_{02}) \times [(\mu_{30} + \mu_{12})^2 - (\mu_{21} + \mu_{03})^2] + 4\mu_{11}(\mu_{30} + \mu_{12})(\mu_{03} + \mu_{21})$

$M_7 = (3\mu_{21} - \mu_{03})(\mu_{30} + \mu_{12}) \times [(\mu_{30} + \mu_{12})^2 - 3(\mu_{21} + \mu_{03})^2] +$
$\qquad (\mu_{30} - 3\mu_{12})(\mu_{21} + \mu_{03}) \times [(\mu_{03} + \mu_{21})^2 - 3(\mu_{12} + \mu_{30})^2]$

Geometry Several simple metrics have been used to measure the geometric properties of objects such as area and perimeter. However, these simple measures are scale and size dependent and thus not suitable for similarity search. We first explain some terms below, then give a list of features used in our experiments.

The *area* of an object is expressed as the total number of pixels in the object. The object's *perimeter* is the number of pixels traversed around the boundary of the object starting at an arbitrary initial boundary pixel p_i and returning to the initial pixel. The centroid μ is the center of gravity for this object, by averaging the coordinates of each pixels in the object. The *bounding rectangle* is the smallest rectangle enclosing the object. A *convex hull* is the minimal convex covering of an object. The radii of gyration, R_{max} and R_{min}, are dynamically equivalent lengths of an object along the directions of axes passing the centroid of the object with zero cross-correlation. The maximum Feret's diameter F_{max} is defined as the longest distance between any two points on the object's perimeter. F_{min} is the width of the object perpendicular to F_{max}. The equivalent circular diameter F_{ecd} is the diameter of an equivalent circular with the same area as the original object.

- *Eccentricity* or *elongation* is defined as:

$$\frac{(\mu_{20} - \mu_{02})^2 + 4\mu_{11}}{area}.$$

- *Extent* or *rectangularity* is defined as the ratio of the area to the bounding rectangle which equals to $F_{max} \times F_{min}$.
- *Form factor* is defined as

$$\frac{\pi \times area}{4 \times perimeter \times perimeter}.$$

- *Roundness* or *compactness* is defined as the ratio of F_{ecd} to F_{max}.
- *Anisometry* is the ratio of R_{max} to R_{min}.
- *Bulkiness* is defined as

$$\frac{12.566 \times R_{max} \times R_{min}}{area}.$$

- *Convexity* is defined as the ratio of perimeter of convex hull to perimeter.
- *Solidity* is defined as the ratio of area to the area of convex hull.
- *Circular variance*, the proportional mean-squared error with respect to solid circle, is defined as

$$\frac{1}{N\mu_r^2} \sum_i (\|p_i - \mu\| - \mu_r)^2$$

where μ_r is the mean radius, $\frac{1}{N} \sum_i \|p_i - \mu\|$.
- *Elliptic variance*, the proportional mean-squared error with respect to solid ellipse, is defined as

$$\frac{1}{N\mu_{r_c}} \sum_i (\sqrt{(p_i - \mu)^T C^{-1}(p_i - \mu)} - \mu_{r_c})^2$$

where $\mu_{r_c} = \frac{1}{N} \sum_i \sqrt{(p_i - \mu)^T C^{-1}(p_i - \mu)}$, and C is the covariance matrix, $\frac{1}{N} \sum_i (p_i - \mu)(p_i - \mu)^T$.
- *Euler number* is defined as difference between the numbers of connected regions and of holes in an object.

Totally, 11 features are used to measure the object geometry.

Fourier Descriptors By expanding the boundary of a two dimensional object into the frequency domain, Fourier transformation generates a complete set of complex numbers, called *Fourier descriptors* [15], which represent the frequency contents of the boundary of the object. These descriptors are invariant to scaling, rotation, translation, and mirror reflection.

The boundary of a closed shape is a sequence set of successive boundary points T derived from some boundary tracing algorithms. A boundary point $P(x, y)$ is then measured by its curvature function $k(s)$. The parameter s is the path length of the boundary from the initial point P_0 to the current point P. The complex domain of $k(s)$ may be expressed in terms of a pair of cyclic waveforms, the real part, $x(s)$, and the imaginary part, $y(s)$, as

$$k(s) = x(s) + iy(s) \tag{4}$$

which is periodic over the perimeter length T and gives a complete description of the measured shape boundary. By expanding it into Fourier domain, we could obtain the following discrete Fourier series:

$$k(s) \cong \frac{1}{T} \sum_{n=0}^{T-1} c(n) \exp\left(i\frac{2\pi s}{T}n\right), \qquad 0 \le s \le T - 1 \tag{5}$$

where the coefficients $c(n)$, known as *Cartesian Fourier descriptors*, are obtained from

$$c(n) = \sum_{s=0}^{T-1} k(s) \exp\left(-i\frac{2\pi n}{T}s\right), \qquad 0 \le n \le T - 1. \tag{6}$$

Using this method for Fourier descriptors, a truncated series of the curvature function $k(s)$ approximates the original shape. The lower frequency descriptors contain the information of a general key shape. The higher frequency descriptors contain the information about its smaller variant details. By increasing the wave number n, the Fourier descriptors could find more and more fine details of the boundary. In our experiments, a value of 20 is used for n, i.e., the most significant 20 values of $k(s)$ are used as image features.

4.2   Experiments

Several parameters affect the performance of our approach, including m, w_1, w_2, and B. They are listed in Table 1. Different combinations of these parameters are tested to examine their effects on three performance measures: the insertion time, the number of leaf nodes. and the average radius of leaf nodes.

Insertion Time The total insertion time for different m is shown in Fig. 6. We test values from 1 to $B/2$ for m. Note not all values of m apply to all values of B. The weights are set to $w_1 = 1$ and $w_2 = 0$. Under this setting, SS-tree is the special case where $m = 1$.

Table 1. Parameters in algorithms

Parameter	Meaning
B	maximum number of children in a node (branching factor)
m	number of children explored in beam search
w_1	weight for distance
w_2	weight for radius increase

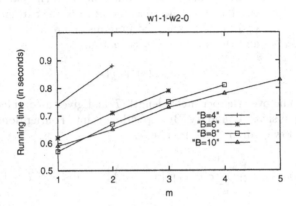

Fig. 6. Insertion time for different values of m

From Fig. 6 it can be observed that the insertion time increases when m grows for a given B. Since the insertion time includes splitting time, it is not always linear to m, but it increases almost linearly with m. For the same m, the time decreases when B increases except when $B = 10$ and $m = 1$. This is probably because the height of tree decreases as B increases, but when B is big, the benefit is offset by the fact that it have to search more children at each level.

Fig. 7 shows the insertion time for different weights of w_1 and w_2 with respect to the branching factor B. The value of m is set to 2 which is the most commonly used value. Similar patterns have been discovered for other values of m. The insertion time increases when B increases because of smaller tree height, but not much when B is large because of more children at each node. The insertion time increases with w_2, especially when B is small. This is because the bigger the w_2, the more emphasis is put on radius increase. This has the tendency to insert the new vector into bigger nodes, which in turn causes more splits and running time. It is interesting to notice that when w_1 is nonzero, the differences are much smaller than when w_1 is zero. It can be concluded that the distance should be taken into consideration when selecting children.

Number of Leaf Nodes The number of leaf nodes in the resulting tree is also computed in our experiments as a measure of tree quality. Our tests show a

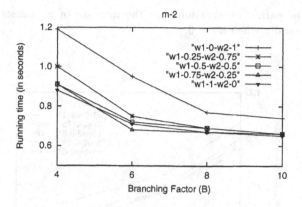

Fig. 7. Insertion time for different weights

tree with smaller number of leaf nodes also have smaller total number of nodes. Besides storage benefit, a smaller tree with fewer node also speeds up search.

The number of leaf nodes for different B is shown in Fig. 8. Again, the weights are set to $w_1 = 1$ and $w_2 = 0$ so that SS-tree is included. When B is small, the beam search reduces the number of leaf nodes. It actually generates more leaf nodes when $B = 10$. This is probably because the beam search algorithm misses the best hosts when B is large. Another interesting finding is that increasing m does not necessarily reduce the number of leaf nodes.

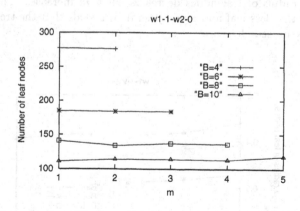

Fig. 8. Number of leaf nodes for different values of m

The effect of weights on the number of leaf nodes is shown in Fig. 9. The value of m is set to 2. The number of leaf nodes increases when w_2 increases.

This echos the earlier observation that the increase of w_2 causes more nodes splitting, especially when $w_1 = 0$.

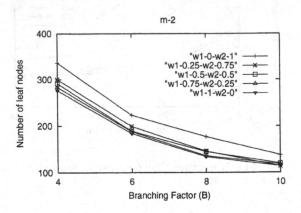

Fig. 9. Number of leaf nodes for different weights

Average Radius of Leaf Nodes Another measure of tree quality is the average radius of leaf nodes which reflects the compactness of leaf nodes.

The average radius of leaf nodes generated for different m is shown in Fig. 10. The average radius of leaf nodes decreases when m increases. This, combined with the fact that less leaf nodes are generated, reveals that the tree is in better shape with beam search.

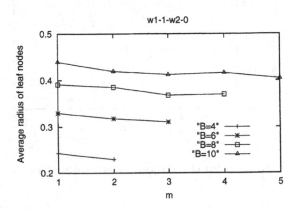

Fig. 10. Average radius of leaf nodes for different values of m

As shown in Fig. 11, the average radius of leaf nodes is the smallest when w_1 and w_2 have non-zero values. This is interesting to notice as it reveals that some mixture of distance and radius increase are more desirable than both extremes when w_1 or w_2 is 0. Generally, equal weights with $w_1 = w_2 = 0.5$ generate good results. Investigation is being conducted to learn more about the weights for different situations.

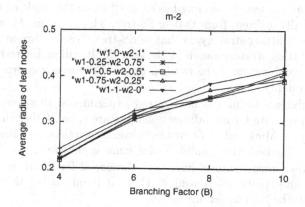

Fig. 11. Average radius of leaf nodes for different weights

To summarize, the quality of the tree is improved with beam search since the number of leaf nodes and average radius of leaf nodes decrease. The increase in total insertion time is insignificant. This demonstrates the advantages of our approach.

5   Discussion

It is assumed that query performance is much more important than update performance and update is much less frequent than query [12]. The same assumptions are taken in this paper. Therefore, it is worth to trade time in insertion/update for better query performance. However, in cases when the update is frequent and costly, the m in the beam search should be reduced, or even degrade to 1 which is equivalent to SS-tree. The introduction of the beam search algorithm, therefore, gives extra flexibility in indexing.

Another issue with indexing structures for similarity search is concurrency control when locking mechanism is used in the image database. The root node has to be exclusively locked during updating. This will not cause serious performance degradation in most cases since most CBIR systems have infrequent updates and they are usually done in batch mode when user querying is not so active. Besides, the strict consistency requirements may be relaxed in some cases. For example, missing one target image by reading a dirty node is not a serious problem, if, say,

20 images are returned. It should be pointed out that the introduction of beam search in our approach does not induce extra burden compared with SS-tree because both have to lock the root node.

Some possible future extensions of our work are discussed below.

- The two key factors in insertion are tree descending and node-splitting strategy. As we have discovered through our experiments, the introduction of beam search in tree descending has some effect on the resulting tree, but not dramatically different from that of SS-tree. This is mainly because we used the same splitting strategy as that of SS-tree. We are currently evaluating other splitting strategies such as those in [3]. It will be interesting to study how the combination of the two can improve the insertion process and thus the tree quality.
- The Euclidean distance is used in our experiments. However, it is not always appropriate for high-dimensional feature space. Other similarity metrics, such as Minkowski's L^p distance, cosine distance, and normalized correlation, may be better candidates for some applications.
  Many other image features have been developed for CBIR, including color, texture, and spatial relationship[5, 11, 9]. It is interesting to apply our approach to the broader feature space.
  Since our approach is independent of similarity metric and image features, it can be applied to other similarity metrics or image features with little modification.
- The effectiveness of beam search in insertion will be more apparent when the tree is deep. This is because the best host will also be hidden deep down the tree and our approach will have advantage to find it than others like SS-tree. The nest step in our research is to expand the image database so that we can evaluate our approach in a larger database.

6   Conclusion

The problem of overlapping in high-dimensional indexing structure has been examined. A novel approach is proposed to solve the problem by introducing a heuristic algorithm, the beam search method, in tree insertion. When a new vector is inserted, the beam search will explore several children in order to find a better host. This will improve the quality of the indexing and thus improve similarity search performance. In addition, a heuristic child selection criterion is developed which takes into account both the distance and the increase of radius when searching for best hosts.

Our experiments on a image database show that the integration of beam search in insertion can improve the quality of indexing and query without incurring much run-time overhead. Besides, the effects of parameters on the indexing results are also studied. Finally, related issues and future directions of the research are discussed.

References

1. N. Beckmann, H.-P. Kriegel, R. Schneider, and B. Seeger. The R*-tree: An efficient and robust access method for points and rectangles. In *Proc. 1990 ACM-SIGMOD Int. Conf. Management of Data*, pages 322–331, Atlantic City, NJ, June 1990.

2. S. Berchtold, D. Keim, and H. Kriegel. The X-tree: an index structure for high-dimensional data. In *Proc. 22nd VLDB*, pages 28–39, Mumbai, India,, 1996.

3. P. Ciaccia, M. Patella, and P. Zezula. M-tree: an efficient access method for similarity search in metric spaces. In *Proc. 23rd VLDB*, pages 426–435, Athens, Greece, 1997.

4. J. H. Friedman, J. H. Bentley, and R. A. Finkel. An algorithm for finding best matches in logarithmic expected time. In *ACM Trans. on Mathematical Software*, pages 209–226, Vol. 3, Sept. 1977.

5. V. Gudivada and V. Raghavan. Content-based image retrieval systems. In *IEEE Computer*, pages 18–22, Vol 28, No. 9, 1995.

6. A. Guttman. R-tree: A dynamic index structure for spatial searching. In *Proc. 1984 ACM-SIGMOD Int. Conf. Management of Data*, June 1984.

7. M.-K. Hu. Pattern recognition by moment invariants. *Proc. IRE*, 49, Sept. 1961.

8. N. Katayama and S. Satoh. The SR-tree: an indexing structure for high-dimensional nearest neighbor queries. In *Proc. ACM SIGMOD Int. Conf. on Management of Data*, pages 369–380, Tucson, Arizona, 1997.

9. P. Kelly, T. Cannon, and D. Hush. Query by image example: the CANDID approach. In *Proc. Storage and Retrieval for Image and Video Databases III*, pages 238–248, SPIE Vol. 2420, 1995.

10. R. Kurniawati, J. Jin, and J. Shepherd. The SS+-tree: an improved indexing structure for similarity searches in a high-dimensional feature space. In *Proc.*, pages 110–120, SPIE Vol. 3022, 1997.

11. W. Niblack, R. Barber, W. Equitz, M. Flickner, E. Glasman, D. Petkovic, P. Yanker, C. Faloutsos, and C. Taubin. The QBIC project: Querying images by content using color, texture, and shape. In *Proc. Storage and Retrieval for Image and Video Databases*, pages 173–187, SPIE Vol. 1908, 1993.

12. D. White and R. Jain. Similarity indexing with the SS-tree. In *Proc. 12th IEEE Int. Conf. on Data Engineering*, pages 516–523, New Orleans, Louisiana, 1996.

13. D. White and R. Jain. Algorithms and strategies for similarity retrieval. In *Technical Report, Department of Computer Science and Engineering*, University of California, San Diego, 1997.

14. P. Winston. *Artificial Intelligence (2nd Ed.)*. Addison-Wesley, 1984.

15. C. T. Zahn and R. Z. Roskies. Fourier descriptors for plane closed curves. *IEEE Trans. on Computers*, 21:269–281, March 1972.

Representation and Interactive Manipulation of Massive CAD Databases

Andy Wilson, Dinesh Manocha, and Ming C. Lin

Department of Computer Science, University of North Carolina, CB #3175, Sitterson Hall, Chapel Hill, NC 27599-3175, USA

{awilson,dm,lin}@cs.unc.edu
http://www.cs.unc.edu/~geom/mmc
http://www.cs.unc.edu/~walk

Abstract. Many applications of computer-aided design (CAD) and scientific visualization involve representing and manipulating large CAD databases. Structural and mechanical designers often create models of ships, oil platforms, spacecraft, and process plants that are composed of hundreds of thousands of parts and take many gigabytes of storage space. Furthermore, their model complexity exceeds the interactive visualization and manipulation capabilities of current high-end graphics systems. Different applications like multi-disciplinary design reviews, simulation-based design and virtual prototyping desire the ability to directly perceive and manipulate such large models at interactive frame rates (i.e., more than 20 frames a second). However, current algorithms and systems are unable to handle such large databases at interactive rates. In this paper, we describe algorithms to automatically partition and order large CAD databases for interactive walkthroughs and proximity queries. These include techniques to localize the computations such that the algorithms use a relatively small and bounded memory footprint.

1   Introduction

Three dimensional spatial databases, composed of tens of millions of geometric primitives, are frequently used to represent models of large CAD environments like powerplants, submarines, airplanes, urban environments etc. The geometric primitives may correspond to polygons, spline patches, CSG or Boolean combinations of primitives and other procedural representations. In terms of size, they correspond to tens of gigabytes of data. For many virtual prototyping and CAD-based applications, we need capabilities for *interactive walkthroughs* of such large datasets as well as performing *proximity queries* at interactive rates. In this paper, we present representations and database management techniques to support such capabilities on massive CAD databases.

P. Agouris and A. Stefanidis (Eds.): ISD'99, LNCS1737, pp. 268–285, 1999
© Springer-Verlag Berlin Heidelberg 1999

Figure 1: Interactive collision detection and tolerance verification
between a user and the pipes in the power plant using IMMPACT.

1.1   Interactive Walkthrough

As part of a design review, it is useful to inspect portions of a CAD model before it is
actually constructed. In the past, this has been done primarily with pre-computed fly-
throughs along specified paths. These deliver high visual quality, but at the expense of
long computation and no way to interact with the model in real time. Current high-end
graphics systems, however, have enough rendering power to display a model
consisting of roughly 50,000 – 80,000 polygons at 20 frames per second. By allowing
the designers to control the viewpoint from which the model is rendered, we can
achieve an interactive walkthrough that permits inspection of any area of interest,
whether or not it has been specified beforehand. However, detailed models of
complex objects can require much more than 80,000 polygons to represent them. See
Figure 2 for examples of some large CAD databases. Furthermore, over the last few
years the size of CAD databases produced by the design process appears to be
growing faster than the storage and rendering capacities of high-end graphics systems.
In this paper, we describe techniques to address some of these problems. These
include allocating rendering resources based on two criteria:

- Do not even attempt to render anything that will not be ultimately visible.
- Objects far from the user's viewpoint need not be rendered in full detail, if at
  all.

We divide a large CAD database into virtual cells that partition the space the user can
move through. At runtime, we use these cells to determine which parts of the model
need to be rendered in full detail and which parts can be replaced by a low complexity
approximation. The virtual cells also allow us to keep only a portion of the database
in the main memory at any time. A more detailed description, including the
implications for memory management, is given below.

1.2   Interactive Proximity Queries

Another part of the design process is collision checking or tolerance verification, where parts of a CAD database are tested for overlap or proximity. These tests are performed on pairs of objects. The performance of such queries is can be accelerated by using hierarchical data structures (such as bounding volume hierarchies). Examples of such hierarchies include trees of spheres, axis-aligned bounding boxes and oriented bounding boxes. However, these hierarchies require considerable memory, often occupying up to five times the size of the original CAD database. As a result, it is hard to fit them into main memory of current high-end graphics systems. In this case, we encode the spatial relationships between different objects in the database in an *overlap graph*. The tests specified by the overlap graph can be ordered to reduce both the size of the computation and the time spent waiting for disk I/O.

1.3   Main Contributions

We have generalized the concept of cells and portals for architectural models to spatial databases that do not admit a natural spatial subdivision. This allows us to process models of arbitrary size for real-time visualization so long as sufficient storage is available for auxiliary data. We have also introduced the concept of *overlap graphs* that allow us to break a set of proximity queries down to groups of manageable size. Finally, we have developed systems that implement both of these algorithms and demonstrate their performance on the model of a coal-fired power plant composed of more than 15 million triangles.

CAD Database	Approximate number of parts
Automobile	20,000
Boeing 777	5,000,000
Aircraft Carrier	20,000,000

Fig. 2. Sample sizes of some CAD databases. Each part may be represented by a few hundred to a few thousand polygons for a total database size in the tens or hundreds of gigabytes.

2   Related Work

There is considerable work on managing large data sets corresponding to architectural models, CAD models, terrain models as well visualization data sets.

For architectural models, Teller et al. proposed techniques to compute a spatial subdivision of cells using a variant of the k-D tree data structure [TS91][Tel92]. After subdivision, cells and portals are identified and used for visibility computation. Based on this spatial representation, Funkhouser et al. [FST92][FS93] construct an adjacency graph over the leaf cells of the spatial subdivision. As part of a runtime system, they keep in memory only that portion of the model which is visible from the current observer's viewpoint or that might become visible in future frames and use a pre-fetching scheme to load geometry needed for nearby viewpoints. Teller et al. [TFFH94] also proposed an algorithm for partitioning and ordering large polygonal environments for radiosity computations. They use visibility information to partition the environment into subsets and order the computation to minimize the number of reads and writes. Bukowski and Séquin [BS97] also used visibility preprocessing, spatial decomposition and database management techniques to integrate architectural walkthrough systems with simulators (e.g. fire simulators).

For large CAD models, Aliaga et al. [Ali98] partition the model into virtual cells. At run time they ensure that the geometry and texture information associated with the current cell(s) is in main memory and use pre-fetching algorithms to prepare neighboring cells. Avila and Schroeder [AS97] use a dynamic loading strategy to load objects and their LODs (levels of detail) from a database. Cox and Ellsworth [CE97] have presented application-control demand paging algorithms for visualizing large data sets from computational fluid dynamics.

3   Interactive Walkthrough

In this section, we describe the method of virtual cells as applied to interactive walkthroughs and memory management for large CAD databases. To allow interactive walkthrough of a CAD database composed of tens of millions of polygons, we attempt to reduce both the size (measured in number of objects) and the complexity of the data which must be rendered at any frame. The reduction in size is achieved via culling techniques, described below, that use a division of the model into virtual cells and information about the user's view to quickly discard most of the objects. Furthermore, we pre-compute LODs of objects that are contained inside the cells and dynamically choose among different LODs as a function of viewpoint. We also use occlusion culling algorithms to cull away portions of the model not visible from the current viewpoint inside the cell. More details are given in [Ali98].

3.1   Virtual Cells

The use of cells and portals for pre-computing visibility in architectural models is a well-known technique [Airey90,FST92,Luebke95]. It allows a system to quickly determine visible geometry from any given viewpoint by traversing a graph in which each node is a cell (usually corresponding to a room in the architectural model) and each edge is a portal (such as a door or a window) connecting two cells. By annotating the nodes with the geometry inside the corresponding cells, the potentially visible set (PVS) for a given viewpoint may be quickly assembled. The cells-and-portals technique relies on a high degree of occlusion between adjacent cells to limit the depth of the traversal.

We observe, however, that many interesting CAD databases such as power plants, submarines, outdoor models or automobile engines do not exhibit this occlusion. In a power plant, for example, there are well-visited walkways from which most or all of the structure of the dense, complex piping is in view at once. In such an environment, cells and portals will not yield a useful bound on the size of the potentially visible set.

We have generalized the method of cells and portals to allow the imposition of an occlusion relation, specified by a set of *virtual cells*, on CAD databases of arbitrary size and structure. A virtual cell is constructed in such a way that the data contained within the cell fall within the rendering and memory capacity of the host workstation. Furthermore, the portions of the model outside the cell can be rendered in a small and constant amount of time regardless of their actual complexity. The generation of virtual cells is performed as a preprocess, and proceeds as follows:

1. Subdivide objects in the CAD database into sub-objects of uniform size.
2. Specify (via user input or some heuristic) areas of interest where the user would like to be able to maneuver. We use the notion of a *viewpoint emphasis function* to describe areas of higher importance [Ali98].
3. Automatically place points within those areas of interest to serve as the centers of virtual cells. Compute cell boundaries from these points.
4. For each cell center, compute the dimensions of a rectilinear box to optimize both the image fidelity as well as the rendering speed for viewpoints within the box. This is the *cull box* for a particular cell. Typically, the cull box for a particular cell is several times larger than the virtual cell itself.
5. Construct a list of all of the objects (or object chunks) which fall inside each cull box. Attach that list to the corresponding cell.
6. For each virtual cell, render the portion of the model outside the cull box and store the results as an inexpensive image-based representation. This will be used to replace the rest of the model at runtime.

Database subdivision and cell generation typically takes a few minutes for large models composed of millions of polygons. Constructing the image-based representations takes significantly longer (a few hours or tens of hours, depending on model complexity) and may be updated incrementally once an initial solution is available.

3.2   Runtime Culling and Rendering

The user's view of the database at any given frame is constructed from the potentially visible geometry for the current virtual cell and the corresponding far-field representation. To find the set of objects that will actually be rendered, we apply the following culling techniques during each frame:

- Cell Culling: Discard every object that does not intersect the cull box for the current virtual cell. The objects which pass this test are exactly the potentially visible set for the current virtual cell; since this was computed as a preprocess, a table lookup suffices.

- View Frustum Culling: Discard every object in the PVS (potentially visible set) that falls outside the current view frustum.
- Occlusion Culling: Attempt to find and discard objects that are occluded by other objects in the scene.

Objects which pass all of the culling steps are rendered at an appropriate level of detail. The portion of the database which falls outside the current cell is approximated by rendering the image-based far-field representation.

3.3   Runtime Memory Management

At a minimum, only the objects that will actually be drawn in a given frame need to reside in memory at render time. Since these objects are part of the PVS for the current cell, we have a bound on their size and therefore their rendering time. This bound is computed as one of the parameters to the cell construction process. However, if we keep only the data for the current cell in memory, we will have to stop when moving between cells to load newly visible objects. We avoid this by speculatively pre-fetching model data for nearby cells chosen via user motion prediction.

3.3.1   Pre-fetching

We manipulate the portions of the model in memory with a prefetch algorithm and data cache. At regular intervals, the motion predictor is used to generate a list of cells likely to be visited in the near future. Data for these cells are loaded according to the algorithm in Figure 3. The prefetching task is implemented as a free-running process to permit overlapped rendering and data fetching. Objects loaded from disk are maintained in a model data cache. When the cache fills, old objects are evicted using a least-recently-used replacement policy.

```
Figure 3. Prefetch Algorithm for MMR system.

COMPUTE PREFETCH NEEDS:
 Find user's current cell C
 Find set of nearby cells N (via prediction)

IMMEDIATE NECESSITIES:
 Look up geometry G required to render C
  If not loaded, page G into memory from disk

SPECULATIVE PREFETCHING:
 For all cells n∈N use prediction rules to
 enumerate in order of increasing distance
 from viewpoint:
  Look up geometry G and far-field data T
   needed to render cell n
  Append G onto geometry prefetch queue
  Append T onto auxiliary prefetch queue
 While C remains constant:
  Page in geometry G and far-field reps T
   from queues
```

3.3.2 Motion Prediction

We observe that user motion falls into two general patterns: staying in one area to examine some feature of the database in detail, or moving quickly to get from one area to another. If the user is staying in one area, then cells surrounding the current viewpoint are more likely to be visited. If the user is moving quickly, then cells in a straight line along the direction of motion are likely to be visited. In general, a smooth transition between these two modes might be desirable, but in practice a simple threshold is adequate: since the user's velocity is limited, we can make the changeover in time to stay ahead of the needed data.

4   Interactive Proximity Queries

In this section, we describe database management and query ordering techniques to perform interactive proximity queries in massive CAD databases. For many CAD applications, the designers would like to test for accessibility of parts and feasibility of the entire design in addition to being able to walk through the artifact. Furthermore, it should be possible to reach, manipulate and extract nearly any part of the model for inspection and repair. Any system which supports such tasks needs to be able to perform interactive *proximity queries* between modeled objects. The set of queries required for such applications include:

- Collision detection – given two or more objects, determine if a geometric contact has occurred between them.
- Distance computation – if two objects are disjoint, find the minimum Euclidean distance between them.
- Tolerance verification – given a threshold value, test whether the separation of two selected objects is less than this threshold distance.

We exploit the pairwise nature of collision detection by encoding a series of proximity queries to be performed on a particular database as the processing of an *overlap graph*. Partitioning and manipulating the overlap graph allows us to evaluate a series of proximity queries using significantly less memory than would be required to hold the entire database and auxiliary data structures. Furthermore, ordering the traversal of the overlap graph permits pre-fetching of geometry to be used for subsequent queries. We apply a similar technique based on motion prediction to handle memory management in dynamic situations where the total sequence of proximity queries is not known in advance.

4.1   Overlap Graph

We cast the sequence of proximity queries as the processing of an overlap graph. The nodes in the overlap graph correspond to individual objects in the database, and proximity information between a pair of objects is represented as an edge between the corresponding nodes. Proximity detection throughout the environment is performed by traversing the edges in the overlap graph in a specified order, performing the proximity test specified by each edge, and marking that edge with the result of the test. Furthermore, with each node of the graph, we associate a weight that corresponds to the memory required by a bounding volume hierarchy for that object. It varies as a linear function of the number of polygons corresponding to the object and the constant factor varies based on the particular bounding volume (e.g. sphere, axis-aligned bounding box or oriented bounding box). The weight associated with any subgraph is computed by adding the weights of all the nodes of that subgraph.

In the worst case, where all objects in the world overlap all other objects, the overlap graph may contain $O(V^2)$ edges, where V is the number of vertices. Fortunately, such configurations are rare in large databases composed of tens of thousands of objects. We minimize the number of proximity tests that must be performed at runtime by only adding those edges to the overlap graph that are likely to represent actual contacts. Specifically, we annotate each node in the graph with the axis-aligned bounding box (AABB) of its corresponding object, then add edges only between nodes whose bounding boxes overlap. These bounding boxes can be computed with a single pass through the database, during which each object is loaded exactly once and then immediately discarded. For collision detection, we use the minimum-volume AABB for each object. For tolerance verification and distance computations, we add an appropriate offset. For dynamic environments, we use incremental algorithms to re-compute the bounding boxes for all objects undergoing motion or being added to the environment.

An overlap graph is mainly useful in applications where expensive queries such as interference detection between geometric objects, or perhaps set intersection between large groups of line segments, are evaluated between pairs of objects. If each individual query is inexpensive (i.e. a test between a single pair of axis-aligned bounding boxes), it may be faster to dispense with the graph construction and resort to a simpler algorithm.

4.2   Graph Partitioning and Refinement

We use depth-first search to compute all the connected components of the overlap graph and the weight of each connected component. In many large environments, finding components with relatively small weights is rare. Objects typically have wildly varying sizes (e.g. very long pipes in a powerplant), are arranged in close proximity to one another, or may even consist of multiple disjoint parts. As a result, the weight of each connected component may be too large to fit into the memory cache. We therefore partition the overlap graph into *localized subgraphs*. Our criteria for partitioning are as follows:

- The weight of each localized subgraph should be less than the size of the memory cache M.
- The number of edges crossing between localized subgraphs should be minimized.

Based on this partitioning, we order the computations to minimize the number of disk accesses. The problem of computing an optimal partition that minimizes both disk accesses and the number of edges crossing between localized subgraphs is NP-complete. A number of approximation algorithms have been proposed, including spectral partitioning algorithms, geometric partitioning algorithms and multi-level schemes. Refer to [KK97] for a brief survey. Our approach for graph partitioning makes use of three sub-algorithms.

Algorithm 1. Decomposing Objects: We decompose objects with high polygon count or whose bounding volumes overlap with a large number of other bounding volumes into two or more sub-objects. For each sub-object we create a separate node in the overlap graph.

Algorithm 2. Separately Handling High Valence Nodes: We identify a set of nodes with high valence such that their total weight is less than the capacity of the memory cache M. By swapping the objects represented by neighbor nodes into the memory cache one at a time, all the proximity queries represented by edges incident to high valence nodes are computed. These edges can then be removed from the overlap graph. Note that this requires at most one load of each object in the component. We then decompose the resulting graph using multi-level partitioning algorithms.

Algorithm 3. Multi-Level Graph Partitioning: This involves three phases: coarsening, partitioning, and ordering or uncoarsening [HL93][KK97]. To coarsen the graph, we use the weights of the vertices and ensure that the size of the partition of the coarse graph is within a small factor of *M*. After coarsening, a bisection of this much smaller graph is computed, and then this partitioning is projected back towards original graph (the finer graph). At each step of the graph uncoarsening, the partition is further refined. The overall process involves the following three phases:

- **Coarsening Phase**: The graph G_0 is transformed into a sequence of smaller graphs $G_1, G_2, ..., G_m$ such that $V_0 > V_1 > ... > V_m$.
- **Partitioning Phase**: A 2-way partition P_m of the graph $G_m = (V_m, E_m)$ is computed which partitions V_m into two parts, each containing half the vertices of G_0.
- **Uncoarsening Phase**: The partition P_m of G_m is projected back to G_0 by going through intermediate partitions $P_{m-1}, P_{m-2}, ..., P_1, P_0$. At each of these steps, the partition is further refined as highlighted in [HL93]. Since the finer graph has more degrees of freedom, such refinements usually decrease the edge-cut.

Finally, the edges that link objects in different partitions, and along with the incident nodes, form a new graph that we call the *cut graph*. We compute its connected components and recursively apply the three sub-algorithms. We repeat them until we can decompose the overlap graph into localized subgraphs, $L_1, L_2, ..., L_k$, such that the weight of each subgraph is less than *M*.

4.3   Runtime Ordering and Traversal

Given the localized subgraphs L_i, we traverse each subgraph to check its component objects for proximity. The traversal is rooted at the node with the greatest number of edges and proceeds in a breadth-first fashion, with neighboring nodes visited in descending order of their valences.

During traversal, object geometry and bounding-volume hierarchies are cached in main memory. By looking ahead to the next few proximity tests to be performed (on the basis of the graph representation), we are able to prefetch geometry and compute bounding volume hierarchies in advance. After the traversal of each subgraph terminates, memory used by its component objects is released, so that it can be reused by subsequent traversals.

4.4   Dynamic Environments

In many scenarios, the user may move objects or add or delete objects from the database. We treat these objects as floating nodes in the overlap graph. For each floating node, we maintain a list of potential overlaps with objects in the rest of the world. These lists are updated and evaluated each time the node moves. The potential-overlap lists are maintained using AABBs and a sweep-and-prune algorithm [CLMP95] to use coherence between time steps. For the overlapping pairs, the bounding volume hierarchies are constructed in a lazy manner and used for performing the proximity queries corresponding to edges in these lists.

4.5   Memory Management

The algorithm uses temporal and spatial coherence to prefetch geometry from the CAD database using one processor while it is performing queries on the other processors. For static environments, it makes use of the ordering specified by the edges of the localized subgraphs to prefetch the geometry. For dynamic objects, the algorithm estimates the object's velocity. On the basis of the velocity and time interval used for prediction, it expands the AABB of moving objects by an appropriate offset. The algorithm prefetches the geometry corresponding to all the nodes overlapping with the „expanded" bounding boxes.   Bounding volume hierarchies are not stored in the database, as it is faster to recompute them when objects are loaded than to store them on disk and load them into memory.

5   Implementation and Performance

We have built two systems, MMR (Massive Model Renderer) [Ali98] and IMMPACT (Interactive Massive Model Proximity and Collision Tester) [WLML99], incorporating the methods described above. In this section, we give a brief description of each system and its performance on a CAD model of a coal-fired power plant containing 15 million polygons.

5.1   MMR

Our MMR system is written in C++, using OpenGL and GLUT. We tested its performance on an SGI Onyx2 with four 195 MHz R10000 processors, two gigabytes of main memory, and Infinite Reality graphics with two RM6 boards and 64MB of texture memory. The system uses modified Erikson and Manocha's [Erikson99] simplification to compute static levels of detail for the objects in the database, and textured depth meshes (TDMs) to approximate the distant geometry. We use one processor to render the current frame and two to prepare for the next frame. On the fourth processor, an asynchronous process fetches TDMs and objects data for nearby cells. Figure 5 illustrates frame rates achieved by our system with all acceleration techniques enabled, and Figure 8 shows its performance for various cache sizes. Memory management techniques have saved us over 90% of the 1.3GB needed to hold the entire model in memory. Furthermore, we can use auxiliary data structures (like textured depth meshes taking about 50GB space) for rendering acceleration.

5.2   IMMPACT

Our test model, the coal-fired power plant, consists of many complex piping structures that are axis-aligned. Spheres are not a good approximation for this type of geometry. Since the user can only interact with a small portion of the massive model at a time (due to size differential), most parts of the massive model can be assumed to be stationary. Furthermore, OBBs require more storage than AABBs in general and one of our goals is to minimize the frequency of disk access. Therefore, we have used AABBs as the bounding volumes in performing queries on the power plant. To reduce the memory overhead, the hierarchies are constructed lazily and are not fully traversed during interference tests. Only the root of the tree is created during initialization, and construction of further levels is deferred until some interference test accesses them.

The combination of bounding volume hierarchies and model geometry required 200 bytes per triangle (using double-precision arithmetic). This allowed us to choose a conservative cache size of 160 megabytes, enough to hold some 800,000 triangles. Object decomposition during the graph processing was based on k-d tree decompositions of objects in the CAD database. For graph partitioning, we used a public domain implementation of a multi-level graph partitioning algorithm, METIS [KK97], available from the University of Minnesota.

Our graph partitioning and refinement algorithms try to minimize the number of disk accesses. We applied the partitioning sub-algorithms to the power plant model with several different cache sizes. In Fig. 7, we show the number of triangles loaded from the disk as a function of the cache size. For a small cache for 150K triangles (i.e. 30MB), we need to load each triangle 60 times from the disk on average. However, with a cache of 800K triangles (i.e. 160 MB) we load each triangle about 4.2 times on average. Notice that we would need more than 3.2GB to load the entire model and its bounding volume hierarchy.

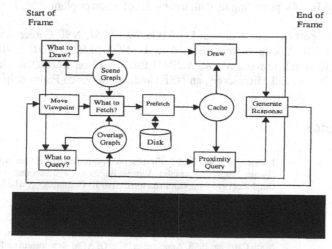

Figure 4: System pipeline for IMMPACT proximity tester.

More detailed information about the implementation of IMMPACT is given in [WLML99].

6   Conclusions

We have presented methods for ordering and localizing computations in massive CAD databases in order to satisfy some bound on the size of the working set. For interactive walkthroughs, we have generalized the method of cells and portals to handle environments in which there is little occlusion via construction of virtual cells. For interactive proximity queries, we cast the processing of a model as the construction and traversal of an overlap graph. We have implemented our algorithms as part of two systems, MMR and IMMPACT. They can process a model of a coal-fired powerplant using a 160 megabyte working set, whereas the database consisting of the original model and associated data structures take tens of gigabytes.

Our plans for future work include extending the method of virtual cells to be able to automatically place cell centers in a CAD database without user intervention. We also plan to extend both virtual cells and overlap graphs to handle dynamic environments in which many objects are moving.

Acknowledgements

We are grateful to Stefan Gottschalk for providing us with a framework to implement different bounding volume hierarchies [Got99] and to Eric Larsen for jointly developing the IMMPACT system. The MMR Walkthrough system has been jointly developed with Dan Aliaga, Fred Brooks, Jon Cohen and other members of the UNC Walkthrough group. We are also also grateful to James Close and Combustion Engineering Inc. for providing us with the model of a power plant.

Supported in part by ARO Contract DAAH04-96-1-0257, NSF Career Award CCR-9625217, ONR Young Investigator Award (N00014-97-1-0631), NIH/National Center for Research Resources Award 2P41RR02170-13 on Interactive Graphics for Molecular Studies and Microscopy, an NSF Graduate Research Fellowship, and Intel.

References

[Airey90]   J. Airey, J. Rohlf, and F. Brooks. Towards Image Realism with Interactive Update Rates in Complex Virtual Building Environments. In Computer Graphics (1990 Symposium on Interactive 3D Graphics), pp. 41-50, ACM Press, 1990.

[Ali98]   Aliaga et al. A framework for real-time walkthroughs of massive models. Technical Report TR98-013, Department of Computer Science, University of North Carolina, 1998. Appeared in Proc. Of ACM Symposium on Interactive 3D Graphics.

[AS97]   Lisa Sobierajski Avila and William Schroder. Interactive visualization of aircraft and power generation engines. In IEEE Visualization 97, Roni Yagel and Hans Hagen, eds., pp. 83-486. IEEE, November 1997.

[BCG+96]   G. Barequet, B. Chazelle, L. Guibas, J. Mitchell, and A. Tal. Boxtree: A hierarchical representation of surfaces in 3d. In *Proc. Of Eurographics '96*, 1996.

[BS97]   Richard Bukowski and Carlo H. Sequin. Interactive simulation of fire in virtual building environments. In *SIGGRAPH 97 Conference Proceedings*, pp. 35-44, ACM SIGGRAPH, 1997.

[Cam91]   S. Cameron. Approximation hierarchies and s-bounds. *In Proceedings. Symposium on Solid Modeling Foundations and CAD/CAM Applications*, pp. 129-137, Austin, TX, 1991.

[Cam96]   S. Cameron. A comparison of two fast algorithms for computing the distance between convex polyhedra. *IEEE Transactions on Robotics and Automation*, 13(6):915-920, December 1996.

[CE97]   Michael B. Cox and David Ellsworth. Application-controlled demand paging for Out-of-Core visualization. In *IEEE Visualization 97*, Roni Yagel and Hans Hagen, eds., pp. 235-244. IEEE, November 1997.

[CLMP95]   J. Cohen, M. Lin, D. Manocha, and M. Ponamgi. I-Collide: An interactive and exact collision detection system for large-scale environments. In *Proc. of ACM Interactive 3D Graphics Conference*, pp. 189-196, 1996.

[Erikson99]   C. Erikson and D. Manocha. GAPS: General and Automatic Polygon Simplification. Technical Report TR98-033, Department of Computer Science, University of North Carolina, 1998. To appear in Proc. of ACM Symposium on Interactive 3D Graphics, 1999.

[FS93]   T. A. Funkhouser and C. H. Sequin. Adaptive display algorithm for interactive frame rates during visualization of complex virtual environments. In *Proc. of ACM SIGGRAPH '93*, pp. 247-254, ACM SIGGRAPH, 1993.

[FST92]   T. A. Funkhouser, C. Sequin, and S. Teller. Management of large amounts of data in interactive building walkthroughs. In *Computer Graphics (1992 Symposium on Interactive 3D Graphics)*, volume 25, pp. 11-20, ACM, 1992.

[GJK88]   E. G. Gilbert, D. W. Johnson, and S. S. Keerthi. A fast procedure for computing the distance between objects in three-dimensional space. *IEEE Journal of Robotics and Automation*, volume RA-4:193-203, 1988.

[GLM96]   S. Gottschalk, M. Lin, and D. Manocha. OBB-Tree: A hierarchical structure for rapid interference detection. In *Proc. of ACM SIGGRAPH '96*, pp. 171-180, ACM SIGGRAPH, 1996.

[Got99]   S. Gottschalk. *Collision Queries using Oriented Bounding Boxes*. PhD thesis, University of North Carolina, Department of Computer Science, 1999.

[HL93]   B. Hendrickson and R. Leland. A multi-level algorithm for partitioning graphs. Technical report SAND93-1301, Sandia National Laboratory, 1993.

[Hub93]   P. M. Hubbard. Interactive collision detection. *In Proceedings of IEEE Symposium on Research Frontiers in Virtual Reality*, October 1993.

[JC98]   D. Johnson and E. Cohen. A framework for efficient minimum distance computation. *IEEE Conference on Robotics and Automation*, pp. 3678-3683, 1998.

[KGL+98]   S. Krishnan, M. Gopi, M. Lin, D. Manocha, and A. Pattekar.   Rapid and accurate contact determination between spline models using shelltrees. In *Proc. of Eurographics '98*, 1998. To appear.

[KHM+96]   J. Klosowski, M. Held, J. S. B. Mitchell, H. Sowizral, and K. Zikan. Efficient collision detection using bounding volume hierarchies of k-dops.   In SIGGRAPH '96 Visual Proceedings, page 151, ACM SIGGRAPH, 1996.

[KK96]   G. Karypis and V. Kumar.   A fast and high quality multilevel scheme for partitioning irregular graphs. *SIAM Journal on Scientific Computing*, pp. 269-278, 1996.

[Luebke95]   D. Luebke and C. Georges, Portals and Mirrors: Simple, Fast Evaluation of Potentially Visible Sets, in Proc. of ACM Interactive 3D Graphics Conference, ACM Press, 1995.

[LC91]   M. C. Lin and John F. Canny.   Efficient algorithms for incremental distance compuation. In *IEEE Conference on Robotics and Automation*, pp. 1008-1014, 1991.

[LG98]   M. C. Lin and S. Gottschalk.   Collision detection between geometric models: A survey. In *Proc. of IMA Conference on Mathematics of Surfaces*, 1998.

[Qui94]   S. Quinlan.   Efficient distance computation between non-convex objects.   In *Proceedings of International Conference on Robotics and Automation*, pp. 3324-3329, 1994.

[RH94]   J. Rohlf and J. Helman.   Iris Performer: A high performance multiprocessor toolkit for realtime 3D graphics. In *SIGGRAPH '94 Conference Proceedings*, pp. 381-394, ACM SIGGRAPH, 1994.

[Sei90]   R. Seidel.   Linear programming and convex hulls made easy.   In *Proc. 6th Annual ACM Conference on Computational Geometry*, pp. 211-215, Berkeley, California, 1990.

[Tel92]   S. J. Teller.   *Visibility Computations in Densely Occluded Polyhedral Environments*. PhD thesis, CS Division, UC Berkeley, 1992.

[TFFH94]   S. Teller, C. Fowler, T. Funkhouser, and P. Hanrahan. Partitioning and ordering large radiosity computations. In *SIGGRAPH '94 Conference Proceedings*, pp. 443-450, ACM SIGGRAPH, 1994.

[TS91]   S. Teller and C. H. Sequin.   Visibility preprocessing for interactive walkthroughs. In *SIGGRAPH '91 Conference Proceedings*, pp. 61-69, ACM SIGGRAPH, 1991.

[WLML99]   A. Wilson, E. Larsen, D. Manocha and M. C. Lin.   IMMPACT: A System for Interactive Proximity Queries in Massive Models. Technical Report TR98-031, Department of Computer Science, University of North Carolina, 1998.   To appear in Proc. of Eurographics 1999, Milan, Italy.

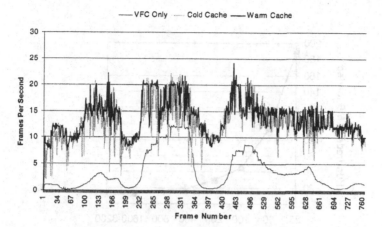

Figure 5: Power plant model frame rates achieved by the MMR system with view-frustum culling only, a cold cache and a warm cache.

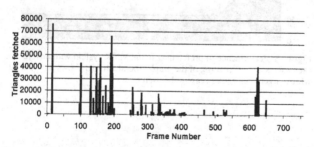

Figure 6: Temporal distribution of I/O for recorded path in MMR system.

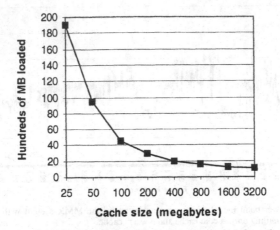

Figure 7: This graph highlights the data fetched from the disk during graph partitioning and refinement algorithm in IMMPACT as a function of cache size. While a small cache size (< 250K polygons) results in a very high number of disk accesses, the algorithm is able to efficiently partition the model and perform proximity queries with a cache size of 800K polygons. The model is composed of more than 15 million triangles.

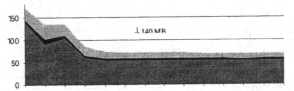

Figure 8: Performance of prefetching in the MMR system with different cache sizes. The flattening of the graph around 140MB shows the point at which larger cache sizes cease to be useful.

Figure 9: Proximity queries between an avatar and the power plant model. IMMPACT takes a few milliseconds to perform these queries.

Figure 10: CAD model of a coal-fired power plant with more than 15 million triangles. The model consists of more than 1800 objects and takes more than 1.3GB on disk.

Conquest: CONcurrent QUEries over Space and Time

Silvia Nittel, Kenneth W. Ng, and Richard R. Muntz

Computer Science Department
University of California
Los Angeles, CA 90095-1596
{silvia,kenneth,muntz}@cs.ucla.edu

Abstract. The need and opportunity to efficiently find patterns and features in the vast and growing scientific data sets of today is apparent. In this paper, we present an extensible and distributed query processing system called Conquest (CONcurrent QUEries over Space and Time) which delivers high performance for non-traditional database query applications. Conquest is composed of three components: *query management subsystem*, *query execution engine* and *user-interface subsystem*. Both operation and data parallelism are supported for high-performance query execution. Scientists can arbitrarily introduce their familiar well-known raster and vector geometry data types to the Conquest data model as well as particular algorithms - so-called operators - for specific applications. Tools are available to help support these new data types and operators so that a developer can focus on programming his/her core logic of algorithms without paying a penalty to deal with the novel execution environment's features.

1   Introduction

With the vastly growing availability of satellite raster data sets, either from commercial or government satellites, the need and opportunity to efficiently mine these data sets for specific phenomenon or features (e.g., weather patterns and their impact on other areas of the earth) becomes more apparent. Scientists would like to find patterns and features in large satellite raster data sets, relate their results to other data sets, and share their findings with specialists in closely related fields to collaborate on a larger scientific task. For example, at UCLA's NASA-sponsored ESP^{2}Net project [ESP98], scientists from the Atmospheric Science and Oceanography Department at the Jet Propulsion Lab (JPL), the Scripps Institute in San Diego, and the Department of Atmospheric Science at the University of Arizona collaborate on the task of convection detection and tracking over the Western Pacific. This group of scientists is also interested in the influence of convection on the rainfall events over the West Coast of the United States. Typical tasks include mining ISCCP DX and CL data sets for cloud coverage and movement, and extracting such features in the form of vector

P. Agouris and A. Stefanidis (Eds.): ISD'99, LNCS 1737, pp. 286–307, 1999.
© Springer-Verlag Berlin Heidelberg 1999

data (polygons). Results are used as input for follow-up studies which temporally and spatially relate the cloud coverage occurrences to rainfall events on the U.S. West Coast.

To perform such raster image analysis and feature discovery tasks efficiently, the following requirements for a support tool exist: (1) a data model that supports a large variety of both raster data types such as coverages and vector geometry data types (points, lines, polygons), (2) high-level query specification capabilities, and (3) a processing architecture that provides for high performance of query execution necessary for the vast amounts of data that are often processed during a query. Furthermore, such a tool should provide an extensible data model that allows users to define their own data types, and it should also allow for extensible query processing in the sense that a scientist can define his/her own algorithms (i.e. operators) for a particular feature extraction task.

Due to the huge amount of data that is normally processed for feature discovery and extraction, non-data flow oriented languages and systems are not particularly efficient for this kind of massive data processing. In a non-data flow environment, an operator performs a computation only when all its operands are available and then outputs its result. This one-time activation is a severe restriction to massive data processing. In particular, for large data sets it is important to avoid writing intermediate results to secondary storage. Using, however, a data flow paradigm makes it difficult for scientists or programmers to write operators since they are commonly more accustomed to programming in a procedural language rather than in a data flow or functional programming language. Also, writing operators in a procedural language makes it easier to 'wrap' available data analysis legacy code instead of re-writing it within a dataflow language.

At the UCLA Data Mining Laboratory, we have developed and introduced Conquest [St95,Sh96a]. Conquest provides a data model that supports both raster and vector geometry data types, and also allows a scientist to define his/her own data types and operators. Conquest provides a graphical user interface to compose and execute queries as shown in Figure 2. For the execution of queries, the approach taken in Conquest is to use a data streaming scheme; here, *streams* of data objects instead of single data items are constantly exchanged between operators, i.e. an operator repeatedly executes as long as there is more data to be consumed from its input.

Based on the data streaming paradigm, Conquest parallelizes a query execution by (a) distributing operators to different processors and (b) replicating an operator (".cloning") to several operator instances and splitting the original input stream among these identical instances. Based on available resources, a query is compiled, optimized, and executed in a workstation farm environment. However, highly efficient, parallelized materialization of a data flow diagram on a Von Neumann architecture is not trivial since it is hard to analyze the behavior of a data flow diagram before actually executing it. For example, it is often difficult to know the resource availability (memory, CPU, I/O, communication, etc.), data selectivity, and other run-time properties of each operator and data flow link in advance. To alleviate the problem and provide for improved efficiency, Conquest uses a dynamic re-optimization scheme which collects run-time information, makes predictions of query and system behavior, and re-configures a query execution plan based on cost prediction on-the-fly during runtime [Ng98,Ng99a].

Conquest places a strong emphasis on support for writing and integrating operators into the environment. Scientists often have large amounts of data analysis legacy code available that they would like to easily integrate into the environment. The legacy code might be written in different programming languages which should, nevertheless, be usable in Conquest. Given the complex environment of Conquest, the task of writing an operator is not simple. Therefore, several choices have been made to simplify this task: (1) the programming interface for *user-defined operators* in Conquest has been designed to be object-oriented and procedural in contrast to the parallel, data streaming based execution environment. (2) Conquest provides the operator development tool *opGen* which automates the task of integrating an operator written in a native programming language with the execution environment of Conquest. *opGen* separates the system code from the operator logic, and generates the system code automatically for an operator. The design of opGen was based on Design Patterns [Ga95]. A Conquest operator developer implements his/her algorithm according to its procedural description, i.e. mapping one or more input data objects to one or more output data objects, and can choose a procedural language that he/she is accustomed to, or can use the programming language that had been used for already existing data analysis code.

A scientific data mining tool such as Conquest also has to be able to work in a heterogeneous, distributed workstation environment, possible using a wide-area network, to make use of all available processing power in a typical scientists' environment and enable collaboration. Evolved and re-implemented over several generations, the recent version of Conquest is implemented using Iona's CORBA implementation OrbixWeb 3.1 which is used to provide location and platform transparency for query execution. The current version of Conquest runs at UCLA, JPL (Pasadena), HRL (formerly known as Hughes Research Laboratory) (Malibu), the Scripps Institute (San Diego) and at the University of Arizona (Tucson).

The remainder of this paper is organized as follows. An overview of the Conquest system is given in Section 2. Section 3 presents the approach taken in Conquest to integrate user-defined operators into the parallel execution environment. Section 4 describes capabilities of Conquest regarding user-defined data types, the integration of heterogeneous data sources, and data formats into the Conquest environment, as well as specific issues regarding the exchange of data between platforms and machines. Related work is discussed in Section 5, while Section 6 presents our conclusions.

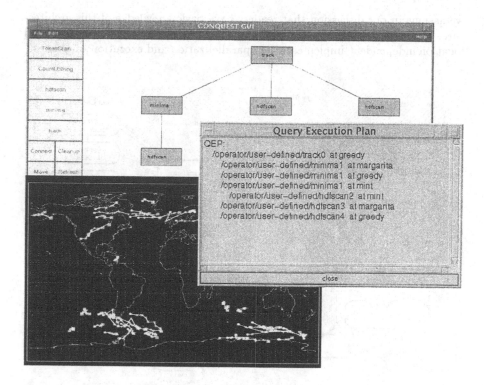

Fig. 1. A typical Conquest query execution

2   The Conquest System Architecture

The overall system architecture of Conquest is shown in Figure 2. The system consists of three parts: the *query management subsystem*, the *query execution engine*, and the *query user interface subsystem*. The query execution system is responsible for the distributed, parallel execution of a scientific query. The query user interface supports composition of scientific queries graphically, and execution of these queries without programming effort. The query management subsystem performs the compilation and optimization of a query, and includes the system catalog (or registry), and the system measurement module for this task. The latter is used for dynamic re-optimization of long-running queries which is also performed by this subsystem. We will discuss each of these three subsystems in the following sections. The current implementation of Conquest is based on the Common Object Request Broker Architecture (CORBA) [Ob98][1], and

---

[1] The system we choose is IONA's OrbixWeb 3.0, which is a Java-based CORBA implementation [Io97]. Conquest is primarily written in Java.

we assume in our discussion that readers have basic knowledge of this architecture. The use of CORBA as an underlying infrastructure allows for platform and location independent implementation, parallelization and execution of queries.

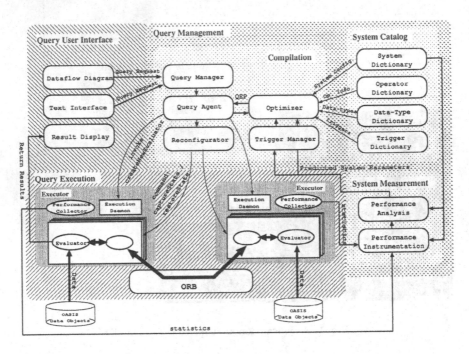

Fig. 2. The Conquest system architecture.

2.1 Query Management Subsystem

The *query manager* is a well-known CORBA object within Conquest, and for Conquest clients, and interacts with the front-end graphical or textual user interface to accept requests to execute queries. Upon receiving a query request, which is internally expressed as an algebraic expression, the query manager creates a *query agent* which is responsible for executing and answering this particular query. The query agent sends the algebraic expression to the *query optimizer* which generates a query execution plan (QEP) [Sh96b,Ng99b]. To materialize and execute the query execution plan, the query agent contacts several execution daemons each of which runs on either a local or remote host machine. Using CORBA, Conquest easily supports a distributed execution that allows to include remote sites for query execution, because remoteness of an execution server is transparent to the query agent. Remote sites are normally used if they contain data required by a query. This avoids staging the data to a local machine. An execution daemon is constantly running on all host machines that are registered within Conquest; each daemon listens to requests of a query agent. The execution daemon dynamically starts local *execution servers* on request which are also CORBA objects[2]. An execution server starts several *evaluators*, and sets up the communication between evaluators according to the query execution plan. An evaluator is responsible for executing *one* Conquest operator according to a data streaming paradigm. For performance reasons, evaluators are implemented as pure Java processes (not as more heavy-weight CORBA objects).

The query agent plays a central role over the life cycle of a query evaluation. This component is responsible for coordinating the re-optimization and re-configuration of a query; it monitors the evaluators so that in case of an evaluator crash, the query is either reconfigured or aborted. Furthermore, it responds to the requests forwarded from the GUI or client to pause, restore, and abort the query under execution (scientific queries are typically long-running), and it kills the related evaluators when the query is finished or aborted.

The *optimizer, reconfigurator* and *trigger manager* cooperate to implement the triggered run-time re-optimization [Ng99a]. The trigger manager evaluates trigger rules registered in the *trigger dictionary* to determine whether a run-time optimization should be performed or not. Run-time re-optimization of queries is one of Conquest's novel features which we will not explain in detail here. However, to perform run-time re-optimization, operators have to be equipped to provide certain information and interfaces to the environment to allow this task. Detailed information can be found in [Ng98] and [Ng99a].

The system catalog maintains both system configuration information and various dictionaries such as the system configuration database, the operator dictionary, the user-defined type (UDT) dictionary, as well as the trigger dictionary. The system catalog is a tree-structured database, and collaborates with other parts of the Conquest system via a CORBA interface. The system measurement module provides *instrumentation* and *analysis* services needed mainly for optimization and re-optimization tasks. The instrumentation service collects various system and query performance information, and the analysis service predicts the system information using mean-based forecasting methods, which compute averages of collected parameter values over a certain period as the forecasted value [Wo97]. More sophisticated algorithms for performance prediction are under development.

2.2 Query Execution Engine

The query execution engine is the core of the Conquest system. It loads user-defined operators and other user-defined entities[3], and organizes the "pipelines"

---

[2] An execution daemon actually maintains a pool of shared and unshared execution servers to reduce the response time due to launching an execution server.

[3] When we say "user-defined," we really mean "user-extensible," because there are system built-in operators and other built-in entities. The Conquest system treats built-in operators/entities just like other user-defined operators/entities.

between these operators to realize the user-specified query according to the query data flow diagram (input from the optimizer). It executes the query in parallel, and supports dynamic query re-optimization, i.e. changing the query execution plan during the execution of a query.

For a Conquest execution environment, we assume a local area network and a cluster of workstations and/or PCs each of which can be a different platform. Therefore, all computer resources in an environment can be used for query execution. Each machine is registered in the Conquest system catalog, and is considered as a potential *executor* of a Conquest query. Physical instances of user-defined operators are executed inside an *evaluator* as shown in Fig. 3. A typical evaluator contains:

1. a user-defined *operator instance* that performs the computation;
2. *input buffers* that temporarily store input data objects from producer evaluators;
3. *output buffers* that temporarily store output data objects to be distributed to consumer evaluators;
4. a *distributor* (either built-in or user-defined) that sends produced data objects to consumer evaluators.

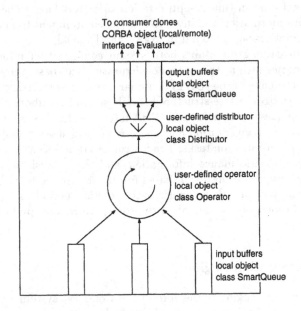

Fig. 3. The Conquest evaluator object.

A logical operator used in a query might be split up into several evaluator instances during execution, each of which processes a portion of the input data (on one machine or on several machines). Evaluators can be distributed over any

number of hosts, and evaluators on different hosts are connected via the Object
Request Brokers (ORB) on each platform (using the IIOP protocol). Evaluators
take care of synchronization issues such that input/output buffers do not get
overflown or underflown; they also batch small data items which are output data
of an operator to larger data blocks since larger data blocks are more efficient
to transmit over the network (as input data to a remote evaluator). Evaluators
provide functionality to assist dynamic re-configuration of a query execution plan
(QEP), e.g., check-pointing operators that are suspended, support of saving and
restoring buffers (and other elements of the execution state) before and after
reconfiguration, etc..

As mentioned, an evaluator is created as a thread within an *execution server*.
Evaluators on the same machine can share one execution server process with
other evaluators from the same query, or share it with evaluators from different
queries, or can be executed in a separate process. Executing evaluators from
different queries in the same execution server is not safe because a misbehaved
evaluator can cause the execution server process to crash and abort other queries
sharing the same execution server. Executing evaluators of the same query in separate execution servers, however, is in many cases "over-safe", but has proven to
be necessary for running operators wrapped from legacy C/FORTRAN programs
which use global static variables. All three styles are supported in Conquest.

When a query is executed, the *performance collector* collects various performance statistical information about operators and the environment. The statistical information is used as the basis for run-time query re-optimization.

2.3 Query User Interface Subsystem

The query user interface subsystem provides several ways to access the Conquest
query execution subsystem. A query can be defined by using (a) the graphical user interface (GUI), (b) the text interface, or (c) the query management
CORBA interface.

The GUI allows scientists in an easy-to-use interface to define Conquest
queries in a graphical manner. The GUI extracts operator definitions from the
operator dictionary in the system catalog, and displays them as buttons in the
graphical front-end. The GUI allows the user to compose a data flow diagram by
selecting operators from the operator menu, dragging and dropping them into a
composition area, and connecting them with arrows representing data flow between operators. Furthermore, clicking on an operators starts a menu displaying
an operator's necessary parameters, and allows the user to enter values (e.g. file
system path for a file). The text interface does all this defining the query via a
textual language (e.g., SQL).

The result display can be user-defined and displays the query result (e.g.,
cyclones) either in text format, or (more commonly) in visualized form using
Research Inc.'s IDL. A result can also be stored in a persistent store such as a
file system or a spatial-temporal database.

Another user interface allows for manipulating the system catalog. A graphical user interface is provided for users or administrators to add, remove, or

modify system configuration information, user-defined operators, user-defined operators, and user-defined triggers.

3   Integrating User-Defined Operators in a Parallel Execution Environment

Our goal is to fully support parallelism [Ng99b] and run-time query re-optimization [Ng99a] in an extensible distributed environment, and still accommodate user-defined operators in the Conquest data streaming environment. Implementing an operator in such an environment, however, requires a fair amount of support code to fit into the execution and optimization environment in addition to the core data processing logic within an operator. As a result, programming an operator in such an execution environment can be quite cumbersome.

3.1   Integrating User-Defined Operators

To (partially) alleviate the overhead, an earlier version of Conquest proposed a declarative API called "CODL" (*Conquest Operator Definition Language*) [Da95] that assists scientists in developing user-defined operators. The overall goal of "CODL" is to simplify and minimize the amount of system support code a programmer has to write. A CODL definition is composed of four sections: *input, output, parameter,* and *state.* In the *input* and *output* section, the input and output data schema of an operator are specified. The *parameter* section contains the definitions of read-only execution parameters which are well-known Conquest data types and whose values are specified at run-time by the optimizer. Variables defined in the *state* section are used to accumulate and record execution information (e.g., aggregate read records) internally at run-time. A code generator scans the CODL definition and generates an operator implementation skeleton in the C language. In the skeleton code, the user fills in the core processing logic of an operator.

Although CODL is successful in alleviating some of the tediousness of operator implementation, there are some areas for improvement. First, the source code generated by CODL is not complete yet. It is still cumbersome to change and complete an operator definition. An inexperienced operator implementor might mistakenly delete or alter some support code, since the support code (required for Conquest execution control) generated by CODL is integrated with the user-defined operator code. Also, due to this fact, any changes to the extension of execution services in Conquest (e.g., the new dynamic QEP re-configuration) can require operator implementors to modify and recompile each operator definition manually. Thus, each change to the Conquest environment might result in scientists having to rewrite existing operators. Finally, CODL does not provide an approach for wrapping legacy code for operators which is important requirement since scientists have invested effort in building analysis tools with proven algorithms and analytical processes that are widely used today. A need exists to wrap and integrate this 'legacy' code as operators rather then re-implement the analysis processes from scratch. The tradeoffs, resulting design principles, and implementation issues for the Conquest operator programming interface are discussed next.

3.2   Operator Development Tool *opGen*

We developed the *operator development tool opGen* to alleviate the problems mentioned above that are not solved by CODL. The operator development tool *opGen* accepts C++ code as input and produces C++ and Java code as output. The choice of C++ was motivated by its common use as a programming language in computing systems. Java, on the other hand, is the primary implementation language of the Conquest system. However, the principles presented can also be applied to other object oriented programming languages[4].

In designing the Conquest operator development tool, we had to consider how to integrate a user-defined operator programmed in a native programming language (e.g., C++) with the Conquest execution environment which is programmed in OrbixWeb (a Java-based implementation of the CORBA architecture) [Io97]. We separated the code that is needed to execute programs in a native language other than Java from the operator implementation itself. As a result, developers can focus on implementing operators with their familiar languages without considering the language used for the execution environment. Our approach is illustrated in Figure 4.

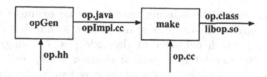

Fig. 4. Implementing Operators

Given a C++ header file in which an operator's attributes and function interfaces, and input and output data schema are defined, the operator development tool **opGen** is used to generate Java and JNI (Java Native Interface) code for an operator under development. The tool generates the necessary C++ wrapper code which is is 'filled in' by the programmer. Now, an operator implementor works as if he/she is programming in a pure C++ environment (or other programming languages) and does not need to be concerned with the idiosyncrasies

---

[4] Fortran, a popular programming language used in scientific computing, is not object oriented. Our current approach to handle the legacy Fortran code is to identify them as library functions called by C++ operator objects. A similar attempt can be found in [Br96]. Since we have de-coupled the execution support code (in Java) from user-defined operation implementation, the update of an operator implementation, e.g., a pure C++ implementation replaces the existing Fortran code, does not cause any change in use of this operator.

of the *real* execution environment. To program a user-defined operator, the implementor completes two required functions: **init()** and **next()**. The *init()* function initializes an operator's object variables with parameters and/or default values. The *next()* function performs an iteration of the computation. The implementor can choose either processing one input data object per iteration (hence there may be no output after an iteration) or out-putting one data object per iteration (hence, one or more input data objects are processed). Both approaches are supported.

Conquest supports run-time query re-optimization as an optional feature [Ng99a]. Therefore, to participate in a run-time re-optimization, an operator has to provide three more functions: **isSuspendable()**, **getContext()** and **setContext()**. The *isSuspendable()* function indicates whether the computation can be suspended at the current point (between two iterations). The *getContext()* function captures the execution state of this operator. This information is used for rebuilding the execution state later on via the *setContext()* function. The details about run-time re-optimization can be found in [Ng98,Ng99a]. Having finished the code for the user-defined operator in C++, an operator implementor uses a makefile generated by **opGen** to produce a Java executable class and a C++ shared library. At run-time, the Conquest environment executes the Java classes which call the actual user-defined functions in the C++ shared libraries.

3.3   Example

In the following, we use the *minima* operator as an example to illustrate the concepts used in implementing an operator. Given a snapshot of extracted sea-level pressure data which contains 44 (latitudes) × 72 (longitudes) sea level pressure values, the user-defined operator *minima* is responsible for extracting the location of local minima in a sea level pressure field with certain constraints. An algorithm chosen here is often based on a user's (typically a scientist) unique definition of the phenomenon. In our example, a local minimum is detected at point (x, y) if the sea-level pressure recorded at that locale is a certain defined amount less than the average value computed using a 5 × 5 neighborhood of grid points centered at (x, y). A threshold was set to 5.5 millibars to permit the detection of large, shallow low pressure areas. If the spatial resolution of the data set is coarse, the *minima* operator may also smooth the grid data with a surface pressure function to better estimate locations of extracted minima.

The C++ header file of the minima operator is defined as shown in Figure 5(a). Given the input data type (i.e., NDimArray) and the output data type (i.e., SetOfPoints), the operator development tool produces, as mentioned above, **minima.java**, *minimaImpl.cc* and a makefile. The **minima.java** is defined as shown in Figure 5(b). The Java operator object and the C++ operator object are "*bridged*" with the *mPeer* specified as an attribute of the Java object class. This means that the access to a method of the Java operator used in the internal Conquest environment is transferred to the respective method of the user-written C++ operator which performs the computation. After the scientist

```
#ifndef MINIMA_HH
#define MINIMA_HH
//////////////////////////////////////////////
#include "Operator.hh"
#include "NDimArray.hh"
#include "SetOfPoints.hh"
//////////////////////////////////////////////
class minima : public Operator {
public:
  minima();    // default constructor
  ~minima();   // destructor
  // required member functions
  void init( PParam *paramSeq );
  PUDT *next( JNIEnv *env, jobject obj );

  // other member functions
private:
  // parameter info
  long  mSmooth;  // fit minima to a spline? 1-Yes; 0-No
  // state information
  int mCount;    // frame count
  int mNumMin;   // External variables used in minutil.cc
  // other methods
  ...
};
// handle to minima
typedef minima* Pminima;
//////////////////////////////////////////////
#endif
```

(a) `minima.hh`

```
// User-defined operator --
//    standard to all operators except the operator name
import edu.ucla.ConquestV2.user.*;
import java.io.*;
public class minima implements Operator
{
  // load shared library of operator in C++
  static { System.loadLibrary( "minima" ); }

  // pointer to C++ class
  protected int      mPeer = 0;
  protected UDTInput mInBufSeq[] = null;

  // constructor
  public minima() {
    // create a C++ operator object
    mPeer = (int)nativeCreate();
  }
  // native methods linked to C++
  public static native int nativeCreate();
  public native void      nativeInit( Param[] params );
  public native UDT[]     nativeNext();
  public native void      nativeClose();
  public native boolean   nativeIsSuspendable();
  public native byte[]    nativeGetContext();
  public native void      nativeSetContext( byte[] );
  // other methods
  ...
}
```

(b) minima.java

Fig. 5. Definition of User-Defined Operator Minima

has implemented the core logic of the minima extraction algorithm, the makefile is used to generate executable code that is used in the Conquest execution environment. Note, that if additional library functions which can be developed in the same native language (i.e., C++) or another language (e.g., FORTRAN) are used, the makefile can be modified to include them in the library path; this allows to implement an operator in different programming languages.

4 User-Defined Raster and Vector Geometry Data Types

Large scale non-traditional databases systems in the geospatial and GIS area often involve the processing and handling of a large variety of data objects such as rasters, vector geometry, etc., which can not be represented conveniently within the relational data model. Therefore, abstract data types have been introduced to model more complex, user-defined data objects for these applications. A large variety of today's database systems such as the *PREDATOR* database system [Se97b] view the world as an integrated collection of data types, each of which supports a declarative, optimizable query language, and optimizes queries in an object-relational database management system with enhanced abstract data types [Se97a].

4.1   User-Defined Spatial Data Types

Conquest provides a set of well-known spatial data types based on the OpenGIS object model. The Conquest data model supports vector data types such as points, polygons, line string, etc. as well as raster data types. Both categories are available in different temporal spatial reference systems such that e.g. vector data can be represented in 2D and 3D Cartesian coordinate systems as well as in 2D and 3D Geographic coordinate systems. Furthermore, Conquest also allows users to define their own spatial data types, and use them in combination or without the predefined set of spatial types. Types are normally chosen based on the operators used.

Data that is used for queries is available via heterogeneous data sources such as databases, GIS, or archive file formats such as netCDF, HDF or even data set-specific formats. Traditional query systems require that data is made available in a uniform format, and normally is ingested into a centralized or distributed DBMS before queries can be executed. On the other hand, heterogeneous DBMS and their query components [Ni97,Pap95,To97,Ha97,Ro97] provide a middleware that makes a uniform (spatial) data model and query language available to the scientists/users, and provides automatic mapping of data types and queries to the data model and query language (if available) of the underlying data stores. Thereby, the middleware takes advantages of the query capabilities of the data stores, and processes parts of a query within the data stores. Such a model, however, does not work well with a data streaming query execution model as the one used in Conquest.

Therefore, Conquest 'wraps' data sources via so-called *data source scan operators*, and 'streams' the data into the Conquest environment for execution. A data source scan operator has, as all operators in Conquest, a predefined input data type, and output data type. E.g. an input data type for a *DBMSScan* operator is the *table name*, the *return attribute names*, and the *where-clause* to subset the table content. The DBMS returns the data via a cursor or the complete data might be buffered in the *DBMSScan* operator. Next, the operator uses the data to instantiate Conquest data objects of the equivalent Conquest data type, and makes the data available in a data streaming fashion to the first consumer operator. Similarly, an *HDFScan* operator that accesses multidimensional arrays in HDF files exports the Conquest data type *n-dimensional array*; the input to the operator are the number of dimensions of the array, the file path, and other data. Parts of these parameters are provided by the user when defining the query (e.g. file path), others are determined by Conquest. All input parameters for data source scan operators are bound at compile time.

A similar scheme is applied to store the results of a query. A query result can either be streamed to a visualization operator implemented using the IDL package, or to an operator that stores the data either to a DBMS, geographic information system, a file, or any defined data store and format.

4.2   Conquest Schema Translator

When using Conquest in the geoscientific area, a strong emphasis on user-defined operators exists. Unlike in traditional database systems, the emphasis on operators is more significant than the one on data types. This is due to the fact that scientists have been investing effort in building analysis tools for over 20 years with proven algorithms and analytical processes that are widely used today. Thus, scientists are more interested in porting analysis code as operators to Conquest, rather than defining a uniform data model and adapting analysis algorithms to this model.

These kinds of data types include various geometric object types of different dimensionality such as points, lines, polygons and volumes. These data objects may further be used to construct more complex data types in particular applications, e.g., set of points, temporal sequences of polygons, etc. To support efficient geoscientific computing, we have proposed the *field model* in the previous version of Conquest [Sh96a], which supports a variety of OpenGIS compliant data types by capturing recurring characteristics of spatial-temporal data.

Though the *field* model has been proven to be simple but powerful to describe geoscientific data, scientists rather expect the data types commonly used in their current analysis tools to be recognized in the Conquest system so that experiments or parts of experiments can be ported directly. This leads to the problem that Conquest might support a variety of operators that originate from different sources each one expecting slightly different input parameter data types[5]. Thus, structural conflicts may occur as a result of schema conformation. Therefore, data records from a 'producer operator' (of data items) have to be translated to conform to the target schema of the 'consumer operator' according to the data streaming paradigm. This leads to different issues.

First, it is obvious that the schema translation will introduce additional overhead. For example, assume that a producer operator and a consumer operator use different data representations. If a structural conflict occurs, data records need to be re-structured to conform to the input schema of the consumer operator before they can be processed by the operator. This cost has to be reasonably low; otherwise, it would not be worthwhile to integrate these two data models.

Second, the schema translation has to be available in both directions. For example, a schema represented in well-known data types should be translatable to an equivalent schema represented with equivalent, but slightly different data types, and vice versa. With both translations available, the choice of operators during query optimization will not be limited to the data model issue. However, if there are n data types and all of them can be translated directly, the number of required translation functions will be $n(n - 1)$! On the other hand, such an approach is not flexible since new translation functions must be added to all existing types when a new type is introduced. Therefore, the best option is to choose one neutral data model as the media. All other data types are equipped with translation functions to and from the chosen model. Whenever a

---

[5] Note, that our intend is to simplify the task of wrapping 'legacy' analysis code.

new data type is introduced, translation functions from/to the chosen model can be supplies so that it can be translated from/to other types via the media model. Since the Conquest field model has been proven to be powerful in representing geoscientific spatial-temporal data objects, we chose it as the media.

Third, the schema translation should "fit" in the *stream processing* paradigm that is used in the Conquest execution environment. In other words, operators in a QEP can continuously consume portions of input streams and produce portions of output streams using the schema translation in between as another operator. Fourth, the translation structure should be extensible. A well-known data type can be added into the Conquest query execution environment whenever the corresponding translation rules are defined. With this feature, scientists can start with a small subset of the well-known data types and then define more data types that are suitable for the geo-science studies later.

Finally, the schema translation should be transparent to geo-scientific operator implementors, thus, programmers can focus on the core data processing logic. Once a well-known data type is registered in the system catalog, scientists should not get involved to resolve the differences of underlying data models when programming an operator.

As a consequence of these decisions, we introduce an operator that does not correspond to any operator in the logical algebra. The purpose of this operator is not to perform any logical data manipulation but to complete the data and schema translation. This operator is called the *translator* operator which is comparable to the "glue" operators in Starburst [Lo88] and "enforcer" operators in Volcano [Gr94] if we consider the schema as a "property" of data records. However, while the "glue" and "enforcer" operators change properties of the data stream such as the order of elements the *translator* operator in Conquest changes the properties (schema) of the data items, i.e. the elements of the data stream.

The *translator* operator is inserted into a QEP by the optimizer if schema translation is necessary which is transparent to the operator implementor. Also due to the data streaming paradigm used in Conquest, the operator is only inserted in-between two actual data processing operators. The additional cost introduced by schema translation is available to the optimizer via the cost function of the *translator* operator. As a result, the optimizer can decide on schema translation in a QEP optimally.

In designing the *translator* operator, we de-couple the schema translation functions of well-known data types from execution support code required in the Conquest execution environment by adopting the *Bridge pattern design* [Ga95] as shown in Figure 6. This separation allows that a new well-known data type can be introduced any time since the appropriate schema translation function is dynamically linked at QEP execution time. Two major schema translation functions should be defined for each well-known data type: *fromField()*, which translates the schema from the Conquest field model to the well-known data type, and *toField()*, which translates the schema from the well-known data type to the Conquest field model. We note that *fromField()* and *toField()* methods are optional to data type developers. If these two object functions are not defined,

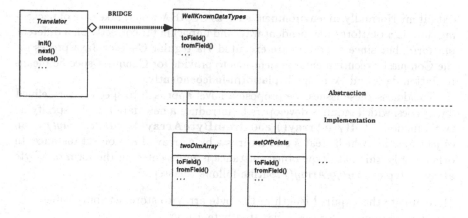

Fig. 6. Schema Translator Operator

it allows less optimization options but does not affect the validity for the query processing.

4.3   Marshalling and Un-marshalling

User-defined types typically refer to other (user-defined) types. For instance, if a *setOfPoints* is modeled as a set of point locations and associated values, a *trajectory* of *setOfPoints* is complex because it is represented as an ordered list of references to setOfPoints objects. In a workstation farm environment, which is typically used for executing a parallelized query in Conquest, complex data objects have to be passed among processes, and machines; the machines might additionally be different platforms. Therefore, operations to "flatten" data objects, i.e. to represent a complex data object via a simple structure, and operations to rebuild those complex data objects are required. Also, efficient exchange of data streams is achieved by grouping and packing several data items into a larger package. However, without knowing the semantics of a data type, data objects that are grouped may be misinterpreted during the communication process. For example, data objects each of which contains a list of points may not be equal in size. To properly identify the single items, the system has to know how many points each data object contains. Therefore, a semantic-oriented means to support data marshalling is necessary. Furthermore, the process of data passing should be transparent to geo-scientific operator implementors, and scientists/programmers should not need to get involved in resolving any data communication problems during operator programming. Finally, a uniform interface should be provided such that a user-defined type developed in programming language A can be automatically 'imported' into an equivalent data type implemented in a different language. Also, as we already described, schema translator operators might be inserted by the Conquest system during compilation and optimization which also need to rely on a uniform interface to read and translate data item. Normally, an environment such as CORBA would take care of packaging data in a platform-independent way, and unpacking it correctly on a different platform, but since operators are executed via regular C++ or Java processes, the Conquest execution environment has to provide for Conquest-specific means to flatten data and exchange it platform-independently.

To address these issues, we propose a novel approach to specify user-defined data types, which requires developers to introduce a new data type by specifying two functions: **toByteArray()** and **fromByteArray()**. *toByteArray()* is an object function which creates and returns a byte array of *this* object instance. In other words, this data type object instance is represented in the form of a byte array. A typical *toByteArray()* routine follows the steps:

1. compute the required length of the byte array to store attribute values;
2. allocate memory for the designated byte array;
3. copy attribute values to the byte array;
4. return the byte array as the result.

In case, attributes that are references (pointers to other object instances) exist, those referenced object instances must be duplicated into the byte array so that they can be re-created in another memory space.

In contrast to *toByteArray()* which is an object *instance* function (object method), *fromByteArray()* is a *static* function of a user-defined type class (class method) which creates and initializes an object instance with a given byte array. A typical *toByteArray()* routine follows these steps:

1. create a new object instance of the user-defined data type class;
2. allocate memory for (referencing) attributes if necessary;
3. set attribute values with data in the byte array;
4. return the reference of the newly created user-defined data type object as the result.

Additionally, to allow the definition of data types in different languages, Conquest provides a uniform interface for each language so that an user-defined data type (UDT) can be defined in one programming language, but still automatically can be represented in other languages by Conquest. For example, to define a type **SetOfPoints** (a set of points), a developer can specify the definition in C++ as shown in Figure 7(a). The two required functions together with other functions associated with type SetOfPoints are defined. We note, that the UDT.hh file defines the C++ interfaces for the two mandatory functions, and hence they are inherited by each C++ user-defined type. To apply such a user-defined type in Conquest, an associated Java "wrapper" class has to be specified (due to the fact that Conquest is implemented with Java-based OrbixWeb), which is shown in Figure 7(b). In the Java "wrapper" class, an attribute "mPeer" references the "actual" user-defined data type object (i.e., a C++ object) to *bridge* the data objects implemented in different programming languages. Access to a Conquest Java data type object will be transferred to the actual C++ object instance, hence performing the desired manipulation.

```
#ifndef SETOFPOINTS_HH
#define SETOFPOINTS_HH
#include "UDT.hh"

// user-defined type definitions -- SetOfPoints
class SetOfPoints : public UDT {
public:
  // constructor
  SetOfPoints( long year, long timeframe, long numpoints );

  // two required member functions
  static SetOfPoints *fromByteArray( char * );
  char *toByteArray();

  // other member functions
  long getYear()       const;   // return the year
  long getTimeFrame()  const;   // return the time frame
  long getNumPoints()  const;   // return the number of points
  ...

private:
  long mNumPoints; // number of data items
  long mYear;      // year
  long mTimeFrame; // time frame
  float *mX;       // x-axis
  float *mY;       // y-axis
  float *mValue;   // value
};

// handle for SetOfPoints
typedef SetOfPoints* PSetOfPoints;
#endif
```

(a) SetOfPoints.hh

```
// User-defined type
import edu.ucla.ConquestV2.user.*;
public class SetOfPoints extends UDT
{
  static { System.loadLibrary( "SetOfPoints" ); }
  // pointer to C++ class
  protected int mPeer = 0;
  // constructor - with C++ object reference specification
  public SetOfPoints( int peer ) {
    mPeer = peer;
  }
  // A required method for C++ interface
  public int getCPeer() {
    return( mPeer );
  }
  // required native methods
  public static native int nativeFromByteArray( byte[] data );
  public native byte[]    nativeToByteArray();
  // two methods required by the execution environment
  public static UDT fromByteArray( byte[] data ) {
    return( new SetOfPoints( nativeFromByteArray( data ) ) );
  }
  public byte[] toByteArray() {
    return( nativeToByteArray() );
  }

  // methods from C++ definition
  public static native int createNew( int year, int timeframe, int numpoints );
  public native long getYear();      // return the year
  public native long getTimeFrame(); // return the time frame
  public native long getNumPoints(); // return the number of points
  ...
}
```

(b) SetOfPoints.java

Fig. 7. Definition of UDT SetOfPoints

To ease developers programming burdens, the tool **UDTGen** provided with the Conquest system automatically generates all Java and JNI (Java Native Interface) code with the header file of C++. As a consequence, Conquest developers are relieved of as much as possible of the Conquest coding.

5   Related Work

In the last two decades, scientists have developed a large variety of specialized science tools that allow them to perform their scientific tasks either on workstations or on large supercomputers. These tools range from general-purpose image visualization and animation tools that import common image formats, to scientific visualization tools with an extensible library of data processing and analysis functions that can import diverse archive file formats commonly used to represent scientific data sets. On the other end of the spectrum, scientists use programs that have specifically been implemented to accomplish a single analysis or visualization task. Due to performance reasons, scientists are often restricted to perform an analysis on a small subset of the original data set. Conquest, on the other hand, provides the capabilities of tools in the later two categories, and allows to combine different analysis tasks to a larger experiment, and also supports the efficient query execution on complete data sets.

Since long-running queries in database systems are common for non-traditional application domains such as geoscientific computing, a high degree of parallelism within a query execution (intra-query parallelism) is desired. Due to the nature of the application domain, user-defined data types have to be made available by the database system; therefore, an extensible query optimizer has to be supported by the query system to allow the inclusion of user-defined data types and operators in the optimization process. An early system to support an extensible optimizer was the Volcano system [Gr93,Gr94]. Conquest extends the open-next-close stream processing model proposed in Volcano with more features such as dynamic re-optimization.

Related work has been done in the area of mapping a data model with geoscientific data types to differing geoscientific data types made available by heterogeneous data sources in the *geoPOM* (Geoscientific Persistent Object Manager) system [Ni96] as part of the *OASIS* project. geoPOM provides geoscientific data types and internally supports the optimized mapping to stores such as files in archive file formats and geoscientific DBMS, and generates code so that user-defined geoPOM types are mapped to spatial types of the local spatial data repositories. Often, semantic and syntactic discrepancies between geospatial data types exist, and have to be reconciled during the mapping process. In geoPOM, an approach is presented to ensure that all mappings of one geospatial data type of the geoPOM data model to the equivalent, but differing geospatial are almost identical, so that queries are answered with a similar accuracy. In Conquest, however, we take an unrestricted approach, and allow a user to define rules for mapping the output data type of one operator to the input data type of another operator.

Distributed applications are usually too complicated to be implemented without system support. Therefore, systems have been developed that provide an auxiliary interface definition language (IDL) to assist code development for clients and servers in distributed environments [Su95]. This language, e.g. the Interface Definition Language of OMG [Ob98], allows to define a server interface in a uniform language that can be mapped automatically to different programming languages for the subsequent implementation of the server code. This approach requires programmers be familiar with both the interface language and the host programming language. This requirement may be too severe for scientists. To remedy this disadvantage, [Par95] proposed the approach to generate system support stub code by processing already existing C++ header files, thus, allowing users to work with a single programming language, and generating the system support code automatically. Developing Conquest's tools for user-defined data types and operators, we adopted a similar idea which is, however, more specific to generating Java object code and native interface code.

There are several approaches to build wrapper architectures for legacy data resources (e.g., [Pap95,To97,Ro97,Ni97]). Usually, a middleware is built to mediate between different data resources and query managers in these systems. However, to have such a middleware not only complicates the execution environment but also potentially violates the stream processing paradigm. Therefore, we "wrap" an existing data source in the form of an operator object function (data source scan operator), stream the data into the Conquest environment, and execute the query within the Conquest environment. During query optimization, functions to subset data that is retrieved from a data store could be 'pushed' to the data store for execution; this work however, is not supported in the actual Conquest environment.

6   Conclusions

High performance query processing in non-traditional database application domains such as geoscientific computing is desired due to vastly growing data sets and complex analysis algorithms. In this paper, we have presented the Conquest system — an extensible and distributed query processing system that supports both data and operator support for query evaluation. Our contributions can be summarized as follows.

- We have designed and implemented a distributed query processing system that delivers high computation performance with advanced distributed system architecture, i.e. CORBA and IIOP protocol. Query operations and data access can be executed across heterogeneous platforms over the internet.
- Both pipelined and bushy parallelism is supported in Conquest. In addition, operators may be cloned for multiple instances each of which processes a portion of input data streams hence implementing data parallelism.
- Scientists can arbitrarily introduce their particular algorithms for specific application queries. With the provided operator development tool, operator implementors can focus on programming the core logic of complex algorithms instead of paying attention to interfacing to the execution environment.
- Well-known raster and vector geometry data types can be specified in the Conquest system so that scientists can use their familiar data structures to present individual phenomena and experiments. In addition, our schema translation approach allows heterogeneous data types working together for collaborative scientific experiments.
- The analysis computation against massive data sets with complex algorithms often result in long running queries. During the execution, system configuration and characteristics may change hence resulting in sub-optimal query evaluation. Conquest provides triggered run-time re-optimization as an option so that query plan may dynamically reconfigured to adapt to the changing environment and data characteristics.

There are several issues with respect to high performance query processing that require further investigation. First, we currently use mean-based methods to forecast the trend of system parameter changes and data characteristics during execution. More sophisticated algorithms are under study and development for more accurate estimation hence performing query evaluation optimally. In addition, we have designed and implemented a triggered run-time re-optimization technique for guaranteeing high performance by taking advantages of up-to-date system parameters and data characteristics. Nonetheless, the mechanisms are not enough to handle the situation when an unpredictable accident happens, e.g., network partition due to a broken physical cable. In such cases, query evaluation must be re-started from scratch. The cost to re-start evaluation could be expensive for long running queries. Therefore, how to apply the techniques we developed for query plan reconfiguration for providing a fault tolerance query processing environment is an interesting future research topic.

Acknowledgements

The authors would like to thank Eddie C. Shek who started the Conquest project and has given us insightful comments. Thanks are due to Zhenghao Wang, Siddhartha Mathur, Suhas Joshi, Murali Mani and all other members of Data Mining Laboratory in Computer Science Department at UCLA. Randy Blohm and Howard Lee at JPL helped to build experimental applications and provided us with useful feedback.

The source code of Conquest and some examples can be downloaded from `http://dml.cs.ucla.edu/projects/oasis/Conquest/conquest.html`.

References

[Br96] R.E. Bruccoleri. WRAPGEN - A Tool for the Use of Fortran and C Together in Portable Programs. *ACM SIGPLAN*, vol.31, number 4, April 1996.

[Co89] P.T. Cox, F.R. Giles, T. Pietrzykowski. Prograph, a step towards liberating programming from textual conditioning, *IEEE Workshop on Visual Languages*, pp. 150-6, Rome, October 1989.

[Da95] Data Mining Laboratory. The Conquest Execution Server 1.0 Programming Manual. Department of Computer Science, UCLA, June 1995.

[ESP98] ESP2Net Project. http://dml.cs.ucla.edu/projects/dml_esip/index.html. Data Mining Lab, Department of Computer Science, UCLA, April 1998.

[Ga95] E. Gamma, R. Helm, R. Johnson and J. Vlissides. BRIDGE. *Design Patterns: Elements of Reusable Object-Oriented Software*, Addison-Wesley, 1995.

[Gr93] G. Graefe and W.J. McKenna. The Volcano Optimizer Generator: Extensibility and Efficient Search, *Proceedings of the Ninth International Conference on Data Engineering*, April 1993.

[Gr94] G. Graefe, R.L. Cole, D.L. Davison, W.J. McKenna and R.H. Wolniewicz. Extensible Query Optimization and Parallel Execution in Volcano, *Query Processing for Advanced Database Systems*, 1994.

[To97] Tork Roth, M. and Schwarz, P., "Don't Scrap It, Wrap it! A Wrapper Architecture for Legacy Data Sources *Proc. of the 23rd Conference on Very Large Databases*, Athens, Greece, 1997.

[Ha97] L.M. Haas, and D. Kossmann, and E.L. Wimmers, and J. Yang. Optimizing Queries across Diverse Data Sources, *Proc. of the 23rd Conference on Very Large Databases*, Athens, Greece, 1997.

[Io97] IONA Technologies PLC. OrbixWeb Programmer's Reference, November 1997.

[Lo88] G.M. Lohman. Grammar-Like Functional Rules for Representing Query Optimization Alternatives, *Proc. of ACM SIGMOD*, June 1988.

[Me96] E. Mesrobian, R.R. Muntz, E.C. Shek, S. Nittel, M. Kriguer, M. La Rouche and F. Fabbrocino. OASIS: An EOSDIS Science Computing Facility, *International Symposium on Optical Science, Engineering, and Instrumentation, Conference on Earth Observing System*, August 1996.

[Ni96] S. Nittel, J. Yang and R.R. Muntz. Mapping a Common Geoscientific Object Model to Heterogeneous Spatial Data Repositories, Proc. of the 4th ACM International Workshop on Advances in Geographic Information Systems, Rockville, Maryland, November 1996.

[Ni97] S. Nittel, R.R. Muntz and E. Mesrobian. geoPOM: A Heterogeneous Geoscientific Persistent Object System, Proc. of the 9th International Conference on Scientific and Statistical Database Management, Olympia, Washington, August 1997.

[Ng98] K. Ng, Z. Wang, R. R. Muntz and E. Shek. On reconfiguring query execution plans in distributed object-relational DBMS, in Proceedings of *the International Conference on Parallel and Distributed Systems*, Tainan, Taiwan, December 1998.

[Ng99a] K. Ng, Z. Wang, R. R. Muntz and S. Nittel. Dynamic Query Re-Optimization. *The 11th International Conference on Scientific and Statistical Database Management*, Cleveland, Ohio, July 1999.

[Ng99b] K. Ng and R. R. Muntz. Parallelizing User-Defined Functions in Distributed Object-Relational DBMS. *International Database Engineering and Applications Symposium*, Montreal, Canada, August 1999.

[Ob98] Object Management Group. *The Common Object Request Broker: Architecture and Specification*, http://www.omg.org/library/c2indx.html, February 1998.

[Pap95] Y. Papakonstantinou, A. Gupta, H. Garcia-Molina and J. Ullman. A Query Translation Schema for Rapid Implementation of Wrappers, *Proc. of the 4th International Conference on Deductive and Object-Oriented Databases, DOOD'95, Singapore*, December 1995.

[Par95] G.D. Parrington. A Stub Generation System For C++, *Department of Computing Science, The University of Newcastle upon Tyne*, Technical Report number 510, 1995.

[Pi95] E. Pitoura, O. Bukhres and A. Elmagarmid. Object Orientation in Multidatabase Systems, *ACM Computing Survey*, vol.27, number 2, June 1995.

[Ro97] M.T. Roth and P. Schwarz. Don't Scrap It, Wrap It! A Wrapper Architecture for Legacy Data Sources. *Proc. of the 23rd VLDB Conference*, August 1997.

[St95] P. Stolorz et al. Fast Spatio-Temporal Data Mining of Large Geophysical Datasets. *The First International Conference on Knowledge Discovery and Data Mining*, Montreal, Quebec, Canada, August 1995.

[Sh96a] E.C. Shek, E. Mesrobian and R.R. Muntz. On Heterogeneous Distributed Geoscientific Query Processing. *The Sixth International Workshop on Research Issues in Data Engineering: Interoperability of Nontraditional Database Systems*, New Orleans, Louisiana, February 1996.

[Sh96b] E.C. Shek, R.R. Muntz, E. Mesrobian and K. Ng. Scalable Exploratory Data Mining of Distributed Geoscientific Data. *The Second International Conference on Knowledge Discovery and Data Mining*, Portland, Oregon, August 1996.

[Se97a] P. Seshadri, M.Livny and R. Ramakrishnan. The Case for Enhanced Abstract Data Types. *Proceedings of VLDB conference*, 1997.

[Se97b] P. Seshadri and M. Paskin. Predator: An OR-DBMS with Enhanced Data Types. *Proceedings of ACM SIGMOD*, 1997.

[Su95] SunSoft. NEO Programming Interfaces Reference. *Sun Microsystems, Inc.*, 1995.

[Wo97] R. Wolski. Dynamically Forecasting Network Performance to Support Dynamic Scheduling Using the Network Weather Service. *Proceedings of the 6th High-Performance Distributed Computing Conference*, August, 1997.

CHOROCHRONOS - Research on Spatio-temporal Database Systems

Timos Sellis

National Technical University of Athens, Dept. of Electrical and Comp. Engineering, Zografou 15773, Athens, Greece
timos@dbnet.ece.ntua.gr

Abstract. Spatio-temporal database management systems can become an enabling technology for important applications such as Geographic Information Systems (GIS), environmental information systems, and multimedia. In this paper we address research issues in spatio-temporal databases, by providing an analysis of the challenges set, the problems encountered, as well as the proposed solutions and the envisioned research areas open to investigation in the European Commission funded project CHOROCHRONOS.

1   Introduction

Temporal databases and spatial databases have long been separate, important areas of database research, and researchers in both areas have felt that there are important connections in the problems addressed by each area, and the techniques and tools utilized for their solution. Many papers in temporal databases conclude with phrases such as "the ideas in this paper may be extended to spatial databases." Similarly, many papers in spatial databases suggest that techniques developed for spatial databases apply to temporal databases, by restricting attention to one dimension only. But so far relatively little systematic interaction and synergy among these two areas have occurred. CHOROCHRONOS aims to achieve exactly this kind of interaction and synergy, and aims also to address the many real-life problems that require *spatio-temporal concepts* that go beyond traditional research in spatial and temporal databases (support moving objects is a good example of the latter [8, 21, 22]).

Spatio-temporal database management systems (STDBMSs) can become an enabling technology for important applications such as Geographic Information Systems (GIS), environmental information systems, and multimedia. As a step towards the realization of this technology, CHOROCHRONOS was established as a *Training and Mobility Research Network* with the objective of studying the design, implementation, and application of STDBMSs. The participants of the network are the Institute of Computer and Communication

P.Agouris and A.Stefanidis (Eds.): ISD'99, LNCS1737, pp. 308-316, 1999

Systems of the National Technical University of Athens, Aalborg University, FernUniversität Hagen, Universita Degli Studi di L'Aquila, UMIST, Politecnico di Milano, INRIA, Aristotle University of Thessaloniki, Agricultural University of Athens, Technical University of Vienna, and ETH. All these are established research groups in spatial and temporal database systems, most of which have so far been working exclusively on spatial or temporal databases. CHOROCHRONOS enables them to collaborate closely and to integrate their findings in their respective areas. The network has the following main objectives.

- To stimulate research in the areas of spatial and temporal databases.
- To allow researchers working on spatial and temporal databases to improve their understanding of each other's work, to integrate their results, and to avoid duplication of work. The design and partial implementation of an STDBMS architecture will result.
- To allow researchers working on temporal and spatial databases to cooperate with researchers from *other disciplines* that are faced with spatial and temporal information and that would benefit from spatio-temporal database technology.

To achieve these objectives, CHOROCHRONOS pursues an extensive research program, covering issues related to the ontology, structure, and representation of space and time; data models and query languages for STDBMS; graphical user interfaces for spatio-temporal information; query processing algorithms, storage structures and indexing techniques STDBMSs; and architectures for STDBMSs. The participants also organize workshops with the participation of researchers from other disciplines faced with temporal and spatial information.

The network is coordinated by Timos Sellis (National Technical University of Athens); more information about the network and its activities can be found at http://www.dbnet.ece.ntua.gr/~choros.

2   Overview of Research in CHOROCHRONOS

Put briefly, a spatio-temporal database is a database that embodies spatial, temporal, and spatio-temporal database concepts, and captures simultaneously spatial and temporal aspects of data. All the individual spatial and temporal concepts (e.g., rectangle or time interval) must be considered. However, attention focuses on the area of the intersection between the two classes of concepts, which is challenging, as it represents inherently *spatio-temporal concepts* (e.g., velocity and acceleration). In spatio-temporal data management, the simple aggregation of space and time is inadequate. Simply connecting a spatial data model to a temporal data model will result in a temporal data model that may capture spatial data, or in a spatial data model that may capture time-referenced sequences of spatial data.

The main technical goal of CHOROCHRONOS is to study the issues involved in the design and implementation of an STDBMS. To achieve this goal, we carry out research covered by the following six tasks:

- *Ontology, Structure, and Representation of Space and Time.* This involves the study of temporal and spatial ontologies, including their interrelations and their utility in STDBMSs. In addition, structural and representational issues as they have been articulated in spatial and temporal database research should be considered in order to obtain a common framework for spatio-temporal analysis.
- *Models and Languages for STDBMSs.* The focus here is on three topics: (i) the study of languages for spatio-temporal relations, (ii) the development of models and query languages for spatio-temporal databases, and (iii) the provision of design techniques for spatio-temporal databases. This work builds on previous proposals and covers relational and object-oriented databases.
- *Graphical User Interfaces for Spatio-temporal Information.* Research in this area has two goals: (i) the extension of graphical interfaces for temporal and spatial databases, and (ii) the development of better visual interfaces for specific applications (e.g. VRML for time-evolving spaces).
- *Query Processing in Spatio-temporal Databases.* Techniques for the efficient evaluation of queries are the focus of this area. These studies cover a variety of optimization techniques, ranging from algebraic transformations to efficient page/object management.
- *Storage Structures and Indexing Techniques for Spatio-temporal Databases.* Research in this area involves the integration or mixing of previously proposed storage and access structures for spatial and/or temporal data.
- *The Architecture of an STDBMS.* Finally, care must be taken in developing real systems, and therefore the architecture of a STDBMS is of high interest.

After this brief outline of the research areas, we proceed to give more detailed descriptions of some of these areas. The emphasis of the material to follow is on ontological and modeling issues

3   Spatio-temporal Data Modeling

In this section we address some issues involved in the ontology of spatial entities as well as the ontology of space itself, and issues corresponding to the development of conceptual and logical models, along with respective languages, for spatio-temporal data.

3.1. Ontological Issues

Regarding the *ontology of spatial entities*, in order to model change in geographic space, a distinction is made between *life* (the appearance and disappearance, and merging and splitting of objects) and *motion* (the change of location over time) of objects. At its outset, this research identified and investigated prototypical situations in the life and movement of objects in geographic space. Particular focus has been on the life and movement of socioeconomic spatial units.

A formal model of object lifestyles has been developed, in which the notion of *lifestyle* is applied to cover a variety of changes that an object or a group of objects can undergo through time [15]. The possible temporal constructs are formalized using the Haskell programming language. These constructs, when combined, have enough expressive power to represent very complicated worlds of change.

Regarding the *ontology of space*, a region-based ontology of geographic space was proposed. Spatial objects are located at regions in space. The concept of *exact location* is a relation between an object and the region of space it occupies. Spatial objects and spatial regions have a composite structure, i.e., are made up of parts. The ways in which parts of objects are located at parts of regions of space are captured by the notion of *part location*. Since there are multiple ways for parts of spatial objects to be located at parts of regions of space, multiple part location relations are identified, and a classification of part location relations is provided.

The work on ontology is coordinated by the group at the Technical University of Vienna. Additional work on spatio-temporal ontology is also carried out in Task 2 of CHOROCHRONOS where specifications of spatio-temporal objects (e.g., moving points and regions) and operations on these are defined.

3.2. Models and Languages

Models and languages for spatio-temporal database systems are a central activity in CHOROCHRONOS, as it serves as the basis for several other tasks (for example query processing and indexing). In this area, several aspects of spatio-temporal data modeling are covered: logical data models, conceptual data models, and ECA rules. Special emphasis has also been put into issues relating to the representation of uncertain information.

New Data Models for Spatio-temporal Information. This research may be divided into two categories: a) research initiated in the project that focuses on tightly integrated spatio-temporal support, and b) previously initiated efforts that have dealt mainly with temporal aspects, but are being extended to also cover spatial aspects. We consider in turn research in each category.

An important effort led mainly by the group at FernUniversität Hagen, focused on identifying the main requirements for a spatio-temporal data model and a spatio-temporal DBMS. Based on a *data type approach* to data modeling, the concept of *moving objects* has been studied [5, 6]. This has led to a research plan consisting of several steps leading from data model specifications (at two different, abstract levels) to implementation aspects. We have also investigated the basic properties of spatial, temporal, and spatio-temporal data types. Having specified mappings between different data type models and their relational DBMS embeddings, a precise landscape of the models' relative expressive powers has been drawn in [7]. Finally, a concrete spatio-temporal data model for moving objects has been provided. Here the focus is on a systematic classification of operations on relevant data types that facilitates a highly generic specification and explanation of all types and, in particular, of the operations on them. A detailed description of this model, including formal specifications of the types and operations is presented in [8] along with examples demonstrating the data model in action.

A significant effort in the area of models and languages deals with the use of constraint database models. These models constitute a separate direction that CHOROCHRONOS researchers are exploring in modeling spatio-temporal information. The Verso database group at INRIA has been working on DEDALE, a prototype of a constraint database system for spatio-temporal information [9, 12]. DEDALE is implemented on top of the O2 DBMS and features graphical querying. DEDALE offers a linear-constraint abstraction of geometric data, allowing the development of high-level, extensible query languages with a potential for optimization, while allowing the use of optimal computation techniques for spatial queries. It was also shown in [11] that the complexity of manipulating data of higher dimension depends not so much upon the global dimension, which as it is well known constitutes an exponential factor, but upon the orthographic dimension. In particular, in the context of spatio-temporal data (dimension 3) [10] developed techniques to represent it with an orthographic dimension 2, thus leading to an efficient evaluation of queries.

Other research teams pursue research in the second category of models and languages, i.e. extending the relational ones. The team at Aalborg has continued previous research on temporal query languages. First, a framework consisting of temporal relations and algebraic operations on these has been provided, within which query language properties, e.g., the notion of snapshot equivalence, the reducibility of algebraic operators, and the notions of point-based and interval-based semantics have been studied formally [1]. This framework may be generalized to cover also spatial aspects. Second, the core of an SQL-based language, STSQL, has been proposed [18]. This language generalizes previous proposals by permitting relations to include multiple temporal as well as spatial attributes, and it generalizes temporal query language constructs, most notably statement modifiers, to apply to both the spatial and temporal attributes of relations. Because space and time are captured by separate attributes, the STSQL is intended for applications that do not involve storing the movement of continuously moving objects [3].

Another approach is pursued by UMIST. This group has developed the TAU system, which offers a formal, integrated framework for developing temporal object databases [13]. TAU is being extended to support also spatio-temporal data. TAU is fully upward compatible with the ODMG de-facto standard. It provides a rich set of temporal modeling constructs; temporal querying facilities; and a temporal modeling, analysis, and design methodology. TAU offers a set of tools that can extend any ODMG-compliant ODBMS with support for the concepts defined in TAU and provide temporal object query services in the syntax of TOQL. The main components of the TAU system are: the TAU Library that provides a set of built-in temporal literal types, the TODL compiler for specifying temporal database schemas in the syntax of TODL, and the TOQL compiler for supporting TOQL queries. TAU ensures design and source code portability across multiple platforms.

Conceptual Modeling. The work on spatial and temporal conceptual modeling extends the participants' previous work on temporal and spatial data modeling.. Spatial modeling aspects, e.g., the representation of objects' "position" in space, as well as temporal modeling aspects, e.g., the capture of the valid time of objects' properties, have been studied; and resulting new modeling constructs have been applied to existing conceptual models such as the ER model. Furthermore, the structure and behavior of so-called spatio-temporal phenomena (e.g., a "storm") have been investigated, and a formal framework with a small set of new modeling constructs for capturing these during conceptual design, has been defined [17, 19].

ECA Rules. Research has been initiated aiming at the modeling of *interactive spatio-temporal configurations* using ECA (Event-Condition-Action) rules [4, 16, 20]. The ECA rule model can represent efficiently all the features of novel application domains (VRML data, video data, etc.) such as interaction, constraints/conditions, and spatio-temporal actions to be taken [14]. The Event part of a rule represents a piece of interaction in terms of event(s) (simple or composite) that will trigger the actions included in the Action part of the rule, given that the constraints in the Condition part of the rule hold.

Imprecision and Uncertainty in Spatio-temporal Information. Work in this area has focused on the problem of representing *indefinite* (or *imprecise*) *temporal information*. In previous research, researchers from Politecnico di Milano have proposed the TSOS model for representing imprecise temporal information, emphasizing in particular temporal constraints on data, defined at schema level; applications have been proposed in the area of office information systems and traffic control. Subsequently, in cooperation with the University of Turin, the LaTeR approach has been proposed to specify imprecise temporal data (both quantitative and qualitative) and to reason about such data by using the STP constraint reasoning approach [2]. In recent work, the LaTeR temporal reasoner has been integrated with a commercial relational database, in which imprecise times are stored, and extensions of relational algebra operations are defined to formulate queries on the temporal relational database. The semantics and properties of the extended relational algebra with temporal operators have been studied [2]. The approaches of TSOS and LaTeR are being extended and applied in CHOROCHRONOS to the design of interactive multimedia scenarios [16].

Finally, modeling issues related to uncertain spatio-temporal data have been examined at the National Technical University of Athens. By adopting fuzzy set methodologies, a general spatial data model has been extended to incorporate the temporal dimension of geographic entities and their uncertainty. In addition, the basic data interpretation operations for handling the spatial dimension of geographic data have been extended to also support spatio-temporal reasoning and fuzzy reasoning.

4   Other CHOROCHRONOS Work

Substantial efforts within the project have also been devoted to the study of *storage structures and indexing*. In particular, (a) efficient extensions of spatial storage structures to support motion have been proposed, and (b) benchmarking issues have been studied.

In order to efficiently support the retrieval of data based on the spatio-temporal extents of the data, existing multidimensional access methods need to be extended. Work has already initiated in this area. For example, approaches that extend R-trees and quadtrees have been devised, along with extensive experiments on a variety of synthetic data sets.

Work on benchmarking issues for spatio-temporal data first introduced basic specifications that a spatio-temporal index structure should satisfy, then evaluated existing proposals with respect to the specifications, and illustrated issues of interest involving object representation, query processing, and index maintenance. As a second step, a benchmarking environment that integrates access methods, data generation, query processing, and result analysis should be developed. The objective is to obtain a common platform for evaluating spatio-temporal data structures and operations that are connected to a data repository and a synthetic data set generator. Work on this is already under way as well as work on generating spatio-temporal data in a controlled way so that benchmarks can be run.

Work on *query processing and optimization* has focused thus far on (a) the development of efficient strategies for processing spatial, temporal, and inherently spatio-temporal operations, (b) the development of efficient cost models for query optimization purposes, and (c) the study of temporal and spatial constraint databases.

5   Conclusions

In this paper we presented briefly some of the research going on within CHOROCHRONOS, a European Commission funded research project in spatio-temporal databases. Throughout the three years that have passed since the beginning of the project, significant progress has been achieved in several areas. These include the understanding of the requirements of spatio-temporal applications, data models, indexing structures, query evaluation, and architectures for STDBMSs.

Although CHOROCHRONOS has made significant progress, much work remains to be done before an STDBMS may become a reality. Open areas include

- devising data models and operators with clean and complete semantics,
- efficient implementations of these models and operators,
- work on indexing and query optimization,
- experimentation with alternative architectures for building STDBMSs (e.g. layered, extensible, etc).

We welcome other database researchers to join us in these exciting efforts!

Acknowledgement

The research presented has been influenced by the work done in the European Commission funded Training and Mobility of Researchers project, "CHOROCHRONOS: A Research Network for Spatio-temporal Database Systems", contract number ERBFMRX-CT96-0056 (http://www.dbnet.ece.ntua.gr/~choros/). The input from all participating institutions and the partial sponsoring of this work by that program is gratefully acknowledged.

References

1.   Böhlen M. H., R. Busatto, and C. S. Jensen, Point-Versus Interval-Based Temporal Data Models, Proc. 14th Int'l. Conf. on Data Engineering, Orlando, Florida, 1998.
2.   Brusoni V., L. Console, B. Pernici, and P. Terenziani, LaTeR: An efficient, General Purpose Manager of Temporal Information, IEEE Expert (12) 4, 1997.
3.   Böhlen M. H., C. S. Jensen, and B. Skjellaug, Spatio-Temporal Database Support for Legacy Applications, Proc. 1998 ACM Symposium on Applied Computing, Atlanta, Georgia, 1998.
4.   Brisaboa, N. R., I. Mirbel, and B. Pernici, Constraints in Spatio-Temporal Databases: A Proposal of Classification, Proc. 3rd Int'l. Workshop on Evaluation of Modeling Methods in Systems Analysis and Design. Pisa, Italy, 1998.
5.   Erwig, M., R.H. Güting, M. Schneider, and M. Vazirgiannis, Spatio-Temporal Data Types: An Approach to Modeling and Querying Moving Objects in Databases. FernUniversität Hagen, Informatik-Report 224, 1997, to appear in GeoInformatica. Also Chorochronos TR. CH-97-08.
6.   Erwig, M., R.H. Güting, M. Schneider, and M. Vazirgiannis, Abstract and Discrete Modeling of Spatio-Temporal Data Types. 6th ACM Symp. on Geographic Information Systems, 1998.

7. Erwig, M., M. Schneider, and R.H. Güting, Temporal Objects for Spatio-Temporal Data Models and a Comparison of Their Representations. Intl. Workshop on New Database Technologies for Collaborative Work Support and Spatio-Temporal Data Management (NewDB), 1998.
8. Güting, R.H., M.H. Boehlen, M. Erwig, C.S. Jensen, N.A. Lorentzos, M. Schneider, and M. Vazirgiannis, A Foundation for Representing and Querying Moving Objects. FernUniversität Hagen, Informatik-Report 238, 1998, submitted for publication. Also Chorochronos TR. CH-98-03.
9. Grumbach, S., P. Rigaux, and L. Segoufin, The DEDALE System for Complex Spatial Queries, Proc. of the Fifteenth ACM SIGACT-SIGMOD Symp. on Principles of Database Systems, Seattle, Washington, 1998.
10. Grumbach, S., P. Rigaux, and L. Segoufin, Spatio-Temporal Data Handling with Constraints, Proc. ACM Symp. on Geographic Information Systems, Washington, DC, 1998.
11. Grumbach, S., P. Rigaux, and L. Segoufin, On the Orthographic Dimension of Constraint Databases, Proc. Intern. Conf. on Database Theory (ICDT 99), Jerusalem, Israel, 1999.
12. Grumbach, S., P. Rigaux, M. Scholl, and L. Segoufin, Dedale: A spatial constraint database, Proc. of the Workshop on Database Programming Languages, Boulder, 1997 (Also in Proc. 13e Journées de Bases de Données Avancées)
13. Kakoudakis, I., and B. Theodoulidis, The TAU System Architecture and Design, TR-96-9, TimeLab, Dept. of Computation, UMIST, United Kingdom, 1996.
14. Kostalas I., M. Vazirgiannis, and T. Sellis, Spatiotemporal Specification and Verification for Multimedia Scenarios, First Chorochronos Intensive Workshop on Spatio-Temporal Database Systems, Austria, 1997.
15. Medak, D. Lifestyles - A new Paradigm in Spatio-Temporal Databases. TR, Department of Geoinformation, Technical University of Vienna, 1999.
16. Mirbel I, B. Pernici, T. Sellis, and M. Vazirgiannis, Integrity Constraints on Interactive Multimedia Scenarios. Submitted for publication, 1998.
17. Tryfona, N. and C. S. Jensen, Conceptual Data Modeling for Spatiotemporal Applications, Chorochronos TR CH-98-08.
18. Tsotras, V., C. S. Jensen, and R. T. Snodgrass, An Extensible Notation for Spatiotemporal Index Queries, ACM SIGMOD Record, 27(1), 1998.
19. Tryfona, N., Modeling Phenomena in Spatiotemporal Applications: Desiderata and Solutions, Proc. 9th Int. Conf. on Database and Expert Systems Applications, LNCS, 1998.
20. Vazirgiannis M., Y. Theodoridis, and T. Sellis, Spatio-Temporal Composition and Indexing for Large Multimedia Applications, ACM Multimedia Systems, 6(5), 1998.
21. O. Wolfson, Modeling and Querying Moving Objects, Proc. 13th Int. Conf. on Data Engineering, Birmingham, UK, 1997.
22. O. Wolfson, Moving Objects Databases: Issues and Solutions. Proc. of the 10th Int. Conf. on Scientific and Statistical Database Management, Capri, Italy, 1998.

Author Index

Lecture Notes in Computer Science

For information about Vols. 1–1676
please contact your bookseller or Springer-Verlag